CIVIL WARS AND RECONSTRUCTIONS IN THE AMERICAS

CONFLICTING WORLDS:
NEW DIMENSIONS OF THE AMERICAN CIVIL WAR

T. Michael Parrish, Series Editor

CIVIL WARS AND RECONSTRUCTIONS IN THE AMERICAS

THE UNITED STATES, MEXICO,
& ARGENTINA, 1860–1880

Evan C. Rothera

LOUISIANA STATE UNIVERSITY PRESS

BATON ROUGE

Published by Louisiana State University Press
lsupress.org

DESIGNER: Michelle A. Neustrom
TYPEFACE: Arno Pro

JACKET ILLUSTRATION: Map of the Western Hemisphere, 1877, courtesy Library of Congress.

Portions of chapters 1 and 2 appeared in "'The Men Are Understood to Have Been Generally Americans, in the Employ of the Liberal Government': Civil War Veterans and Mexico, 1865–1867," in *The
War Went On: Reconsidering the Lives of Civil War Veterans,* eds. Brian Matthew Jordan and Evan C.
Rothera (Baton Rouge: Louisiana State University Press, 2020) and are reprinted with the permission of Louisiana State University Press. Portions of chapter 4 appeared in "Our South American
Cousin: Domingo F. Sarmiento and Education in Argentina and the United States", in *Reconstruction
in a Globalizing World,* ed. David Prior (New York: Fordham University Press, 2018) and are reprinted with the permission of Fordham University Press.

LIBRARY OF CONGRESS CATALOGING-IN-PUBLICATION DATA

Names: Rothera, Evan C., author.
Title: Civil wars and reconstructions in the Americas : the United States, Mexico, and
    Argentina, 1860–1880 / Evan C. Rothera.
Other titles: United States, Mexico, and Argentina, 1860–1880
Description: Baton Rouge : Louisiana State University Press, [2022] | Series: Conflicting
    worlds: new dimensions of the American Civil War | Includes bibliographical references
    and index.
Identifiers: LCCN 2022023275 (print) | LCCN 2022023276 (ebook) | ISBN 978-0-8071-7147-9
    (cloth) | ISBN 978-0-8071-7843-0 (pdf) | ISBN 978-0-8071-7842-3 (epub)
Subjects: LCSH: Civil war—America—History—19th century. | Postwar reconstruction—
    America—International cooperation. | United States—History—Civil War, 1861–1865—
    Influence. | Mexico—History—European intervention, 1861–1867. | Argentina—
    History—1860–1910. | America—Politics and government—19th century |
    Pan-Americanism—History—19th century.
Classification: LCC E18.83 .R68 2022 (print) | LCC E18.83 (ebook) | DDC
    973.7—dc23/eng/20220628
LC record available at https://lccn.loc.gov/2022023275
LC ebook record available at https://lccn.loc.gov/2022023276

for Mom and Dad

CONTENTS

Illustrations follow page 124

ACKNOWLEDGMENTS

The debts I accumulated while researching and writing this book are legion. If I have forgotten to thank anyone, you have my deepest apologies and my gratitude nonetheless.

As an undergraduate at Gettysburg College, I had the good fortune to work with Magdalena Sofia Sánchez, Michael J. Birkner, Allen C. Guelzo, and Matthew D. Norman. All four of these generous and talented historians had a profound impact on my development as a scholar, and I am immensely grateful for their guidance and support. Matt deserves additional thanks. During my sophomore year, I took his "Reconstruction and the Legacy of the Civil War" seminar. It proved an excellent decision, and I went on to take another five classes with him. Matt helped me develop my writing, offered advice as I researched and wrote this book, and helped me navigate the academic job market. He has been a source of support and encouragement and a very good friend.

From the beginning of my time at Penn State, Amy Greenberg, Bill Blair, and Mark Neely gave unsparingly of their time, wrote countless letters of recommendation, and helped me refine my ideas. Mark always pushed me to think boldly. His mastery of the historiography is second to none. Amy can find the weakness in any argument and always has ideas about how to fix it. At a critical moment, Bill suggested I expand my comparative study of Argentina and the United States to include Mexico. Russell Lohse, Zachary Morgan, and Nicolás Fernández-Medina have my thanks for their thoughtful comments and suggestions about early drafts of this book.

Other members of the Penn State faculty deserve my thanks. Carol Reardon provided sound advice during a period when writing seemed overwhelming and generously supported my research. The late Tony Kaye offered guidance during my first semester at Penn State. Nan Woodruff, Bill Blair, Mike Milligan, Dan Letwin, Gary Cross, Sophie de Schaepdrijver, Carol Reardon, and Wilson Moses taught me a great deal about how to be an effective teacher. I came to know Annie Rose toward the end of my time at Penn State, largely through our shared interest in legal and constitutional history, and she has become both friend and mentor. Annie read the first draft of my manuscript and offered a detailed and insightful critique. This book is much stronger due to her advice, and I look forward to many more conversations with her about new book projects and the oddities of academia.

I would also like to thank Penn State's Department of History, College of the Liberal Arts, and the George and Ann Richards Civil War Era Center for awarding me a McCourtney Family Distinguished Graduate Fellowship in American History, a Mark and Lucy Stitzer Seed Grant, a McCourtney Pre-Dissertation Grant, an RGSO Dissertation Support Grant, and an Edwin Erle Sparks Fellowship in the Humanities. The librarians at Penn State were absolutely terrific about tracking down books and microfilm. Barby Singer and Matt Isham are second to none in running the day-to-day operations of the Richards Center and helping students and faculty navigate academic bureaucracy. I would also be remiss if I did not extend special thanks to the many donors who support the Richards Center. Their generosity with their financial resources enables us to pursue cutting-edge scholarship, and I hope they know how much we appreciate them. Will Bryan, Alfred Wallace, Paul Matzko, J. Adam Rogers, Antwain Hunter, Bill Cossen, Mallory Huard, and Cecily Zander greatly enriched my time at Penn State. I also benefited from conversations with Scott Cave, Courtney Rong Fu, Chris Hayashida-Knight, Carolyn Levy, Rebekah Martin, Megan McDonie, ShaVonte' Mills, Emily Seitz, Sean Trainor, Tyler Sperrazza, Kwok-leong Tang, and Peter van Lidth de Jeude. It has been my good fortune to be able to coordinate some of my research trips with visits to friends. I greatly enjoyed seeing Will and Mary in Atlanta and Columbia, and I look forward to meeting Teddy in person! Spending time with Antwain in Indianapolis was a blast! Visiting friends makes even the most tiring research trips more than worthwhile.

After leaving Penn State, I spent a year at Sam Houston State University. I would like to thank Steve Rapp for inviting me to present a chapter of my manuscript at the Department of History's Brown Bag Seminar and Ty Cashion and Jadwiga Biskupska for their feedback and suggestions.

Ever since August 2019, my academic home has been the University of Arkansas—Fort Smith. Steve Kite, Eric Baker, Svetla Dimitrova, Billy Higgins,

Dan Maher, Matt McCoy, Josh Packwood, Todd Timmons, Tom Wing, and Williams Yamkam welcomed me to the department and made me feel at home. I cannot emphasize enough how lucky I am to have such wonderful colleagues. Debbie Hepler and Roxy Wylie deserve considerable credit for helping the department run smoothly. Associate Dean Paulette Meikle, Dean Paul Hankins, Provost Georgia Hale, and Chancellor Terisa Riley have my thanks for their inspiring leadership, particularly during an unprecedented pandemic.

I thank the following institutions for financial support: the Institute for Political History (Thomas Critchlow Award); the Thomas J. Dodd Research Center at the University of Connecticut (Rose and Sigmund Strochlitz Travel Grant); the Virginia Historical Society (Andrew W. Mellon Research Fellowship); the North Caroliniana Society (Archie K. Davis Fellowship); the Filson Historical Society (Filson Fellowship); the Frances S. Summersell Center for the Study of the South at the University of Alabama (Short-Term Fellowship); the Dolph Briscoe Center for American History at the University of Texas (William and Madeline Welder Smith Research Travel Award); the Texas State Historical Association (Lawrence T. Jones III Research Fellowship in Civil War Texas History); Baylor University (Burney Parker Research Stipend); the University of North Texas (Portal to Texas History Research Fellowship); the New Orleans Center for the Gulf South at Tulane University (Research Fellowship for the Study of the Global South); the Association of Centers for the Study of Congress (Richard A. Baker Graduate Student Travel Grant); the Louisiana Historical Association (Amos E. Simpson Travel Award); the Maryland Historical Society (Lord Baltimore Research Fellowship); and the Society for Historians of American Foreign Relations (Lawrence Gelfand—Armin Rappaport—Walter LaFeber Dissertation Fellowship). I also thank the generous librarians who processed my requests for materials and offered suggestions about useful items in their collections.

Some of the ideas in this manuscript appeared in different form in David Prior's *Reconstruction in a Globalizing World*. I thank Dave for his helpful comments as well as for his continued friendship and Fordham University Press for allowing me to reprint some of that material. Greg Downs deserves my thanks for reading an early draft of this book and for writing letters of recommendation on my behalf. The members of my writing group—Megan Bever, Angela Esco Elder, Laura Mammina, Laura June Davis, Lindsay Privette, and Jonathan Lande—offered incisive comments about the introduction and chapter 1.

Rand Dotson, Mike Parrish, and Neal Novak have been superb editors at Louisiana State University Press. They answered all of my questions with dispatch and patiently guided me through the publication process. Susan Murray is a remarkable copyeditor, and her careful eye made this a better book. Don Doyle wrote a lengthy reader report, and I deeply appreciate his engagement with the manuscript because his feedback helped make this a stronger book. Don is a very generous scholar and, from the first time I met him at a conference in Germany in 2011, he has taken a lively interest in my work. Finally, I look forward to the resumption of in-person conferences so I can catch up with John Quist, Frank Towers, Don Frazier, Andy Lang, and Pat Kelly.

In addition to the many people mentioned throughout these acknowledgments, five friends deserve particular recognition. In an age of instantaneous electronic communication, Emily Flyntz and I sought refuge in an older model: correspondence by letters. Her advice has always proven welcome, and I treasure our correspondence. I have been friends with Brian Jordan since our days at Gettysburg. For the past fifteen years, he has offered sensible advice and served as a sounding board for my ideas. I look forward to new collaborative projects with him. I have known Claire Wolnisty for more than a decade and have enjoyed our friendship immensely. Claire graciously read the first draft of the manuscript, and her feedback helped me strengthen the book. Casey Nitsch is a brilliant scholar and a true friend who helped me though an incredibly painful ordeal. For that she will always have my gratitude. Finally, I met Shae Smith Cox at the 2018 Society of Civil War Historians Biennial Meeting. When the pandemic turned the world on its head, we passed many pleasant moments talking via Skype about our respective book projects, the job market, and life. I cannot wait to see Shae's innovative work about material culture and memory published. I sometimes wonder what I did to deserve such wonderful friends.

Throughout this process, many people asked me about the status of the book, listened to my ideas, and offered encouragement. I cannot thank everyone by name, but I would like to mention Alison and Paul Neu, Ron and Mary Klein, David H. Green, Brenda and Roy Campbell, Susan Reisinger, Evelyn Rugg, Rich Palmer, Harlan and Janet Greenman, Conrad Cone, and Jean Woodman.

I extend my deepest thanks to my family. After all, they supported me throughout a difficult process, listened when I spoke about my project, and offered sympathetic ears when I complained about academic life. Candy and John Poklembo, Kelsey and Ian Day, Heather, Jim, Tyler, and Christopher Correll, Allison and Bill Sterner, Marti Ratcliffe, Anne Davis, Mark and Kathy Davis, Margo and Larry Gassman and my many cousins all deserve my most effusive thanks. I am overjoyed about the arrival of the newest member of our family, my niece Lilly, and look forward to getting to know her better.

I have always considered myself fortunate to have such strong relationships with my family. Every year Allison and Bill hosted Thanksgiving. As I grew older, I saw how much thought and coordination went into this, but their efforts allowed us to share a great deal of laughter and create many happy memories. I would be remiss if I did not mention Anne's sweet potato muffins—always the highlight of the Thanksgiving dinner—and my conversations about history and politics with Marti. Everyone should have an aunt and an uncle like Candy and John Poklembo. I spent at least a week with them, and often longer, each summer. We went on many fun trips, including to Gettysburg, where a much younger me took pictures of the battlefield and the monuments with a camera that held actual film. In addition, Candy and John have hosted innumerable holiday celebrations, birthday parties, and family gatherings. They have never hesitated to open their home to us and have always modeled the best kind of generosity.

After I graduated from Gettysburg and began working at Penn State, it was my good fortune to live within easy driving distance of most of my family. Driving on the weekend to see Tyler and Chris play soccer, vacationing in the summer with Candy, Heather, Tyler, and Chris or with my parents, Kelsey, and Ian, as well as our semiannual trips to Ocean City, Maryland in the spring and fall are also moments I will always cherish. Particularly so since Tyler and Chris are now in college and are embarking on the first stages of their own journeys. One of my great regrets is that Steve Ratcliffe, Laura Beadle, Dorothy Rugg, Lois Ivins, John and Donna Davis, Marjorie and Donald Rothera, and Patsy and John Poklembo did not see the completion of this book.

My parents, Robin and Andrea Rothera, have lived with this project for as long as I have. Their unconditional love has meant the world to me. They believed in me even when I was uncertain. Quite simply, I could not have done it without them. For this reason, and for many others, I dedicate this book to them.

CIVIL WARS AND RECONSTRUCTIONS IN THE AMERICAS

Introduction

NORTH & SOUTH (AMERICA)

The progress of efforts by the United States to subdue the so-called Confederacy did not provide Abraham Lincoln with much comfort in February 1863. Military affairs proved particularly vexing. Time and again US forces made bold advances against the rebels. These advances, especially those in the Eastern Theater of the war, often resulted in humiliating defeats such as the failure of the Peninsula Campaign in 1862 and the Battles of Second Bull Run and Fredericksburg. To be sure, US armies won victories in late 1862. The Army of the Potomac narrowly defeated the Army of Northern Virginia at Antietam. The Army of the Cumberland emerged victorious over the Army of Tennessee at Stones River.[1] The narrow victory at Antietam provided cover for Lincoln to issue the Emancipation Proclamation, which, in turn, produced an important change to US war aims by transforming a conflict initially fought over union into one that focused on union and emancipation.[2] Unfortunately for Lincoln, the reaction against the Emancipation Proclamation, coupled with military failures and panic over the rebel invasions of Kentucky and Maryland, worked against Republicans in the midterm elections of 1862. Republicans lost seats in the House of Representatives. They lost the governorships of New York and New Jersey. They lost the legislatures of Indiana, Illinois, and New Jersey. The growing antiwar faction of Peace Democrats, whom Republicans labeled Copperheads, promised trouble.[3] Lincoln's palpable sense of relief that the Battle of Stones River resulted in a victory, especially after the bloodletting at Fredericksburg, was evident in a communication to General William S. Rosecrans, in which he exclaimed, "God bless you, and all with you! Please tender to all, and accept for yourself, the Nation's gratitude for yours, and their, skill, endurance, and dantless [sic] courage."[4] Another defeat, Lincoln later wrote to Rosecrans, might have doomed the United States.[5]

Despite the sliver of hope provided by Stones River, Lincoln faced additional headaches over the Army of the Potomac's command structure. Shortly after Lincoln replaced Ambrose Burnside with Joseph Hooker as the commander of the Army of the Potomac, word reached Lincoln that Hooker engaged in dangerous talk about authoritarian rule. This called forth one of the more remarkable letters Lincoln sent while president, in which he rebuked Hooker for these sentiments. "I have heard, in such way as to believe it, of your recently saying that both the Army and the Government needed a Dictator," Lincoln noted. "Of course it was not *for* this, but in spite of it, that I have given you the command. Only those generals who gain successes, can set up dictators. What I now ask of you is military success, and I will risk the dictatorship."[6] That the new commander of one of the principal US armies felt this was the best way to save the Union, and said so publicly, is an excellent illustration of how low US morale had fallen in early 1863 and how Lincoln lacked the confidence of many civilians and some military officials.

As he penned those extraordinary words to Hooker, Lincoln could not have helped noticing that authoritarianism was on the rise throughout the hemisphere. Most obviously, the so-called Confederacy tried to frame its form of government as republican, but Lincoln and many people correctly saw that this particular political organization was created by, for, and to benefit the slave oligarchy. When the slave aristocrats lost the presidential election in 1860 and faced the prospect of not controlling the federal government, they appealed from ballots to bullets. Furthermore, some rebels flirted with monarchy and, in the later stages of the war, looked to illiberal European powers and potentates like Pope Pius IX for assistance. In addition, the rise of the so-called Confederacy was hardly the only form of authoritarianism in the world. In 1861, Spain took advantage of the turmoil in the United States and annexed the Dominican Republic, a flagrant violation of the Monroe Doctrine. Despite outrage in the United States, Spain correctly gambled that the impending war would preclude US intervention. Consequently, Dominicans waged a fierce struggle that eventually ended in Spanish defeat, without US help.[7]

President Benito Juárez of Mexico also knew, from painful experience, that authoritarianism threatened the republics of the New World. Emperor Napoleon III of France determined to take advantage of a distracted United States to further his imperial schemes in the New World. Originally, Great Britain, France, and Spain intervened in Mexico in 1861—the Tripartite Intervention—

when Juárez suspended debt payments after the War of the Reform. Quickly, however, France made it obvious that they were there to oust Juárez, install a puppet ruler in Mexico, and make Mexico the nucleus of a French New World empire. Liberal forces humiliated the French on May 5, 1862, when they defeated them at Puebla, but Napoleon sent more troops and vowed to conquer Juárez. Several months after Lincoln wrote to Hooker, Juárez retreated north from Mexico City. Contemporaries hammered the point that the United States and Mexico fought interconnected wars against the forces of reaction. Juárez, like many Mexicans, desperately wanted to see Lincoln and the United States succeed and would have been disgusted with Hooker's sentiments, particularly given Juárez's fervent opposition to Mexico's most infamous dictator, Antonio López de Santa Anna. Lincoln did not explicitly make this point, but Hooker's comments were doubly dangerous because of the growth of authoritarianism in the Americas.

Lincoln and Juárez were mired in the doldrums, and who could blame them? Lincoln's armies had suffered too many defeats. The voters punished his party at the polls in 1862. Hooker wagged his tongue about a dictatorship as the answer to the country's problems. The Spanish were recolonizing the Caribbean. France was doing its level best to overthrow a democratically elected government in Mexico. The United States could do little about these violations of the Monroe Doctrine. Juárez knew Napoleon would spend the lives of French soldiers profligately in an attempt to re-create a French empire in the Americas. The bright spots for the two men were exceedingly rare. Great Britain and France had come extremely close to intervening in the US Civil War in late 1862 but backed off at the last moment. That decision came as a relief to Lincoln and Secretary of State William H. Seward, although talk of intervention did not die.[8] Liberal General Ignacio Zaragoza defeated the French at Puebla on May 5, 1862, although Juárez knew the French would soon regroup. In sum, Lincoln and Juárez both faced a difficult autumn, a hard winter, and a bitter spring. Consequently, they had to content themselves with any bright spots they could find, all the while watching as rebels won victories and Europeans moved into the Americas in an attempt to destroy republics and build monarchies on their ruins.

Despite the terrible situation, an unanticipated bright spot occurred in an unexpected place: Argentina. On February 6, Lincoln dispatched, via Secretary of State Seward, a note in response to a letter he had received from Bartolomé

Mitre, who had recently been elected president of the Argentine Republic. "This event," Lincoln commented, "has inspired me with the liveliest gratification. After so many years of discord and strife the Provinces of the Argentine Confederation have buried their jealousies and again present themselves to the world as a united nation having a common interest and a common destiny." Furthermore, Lincoln continued, "I congratulate the nation and Your Excellency upon this result, and upon the elevation of Your Excellency to the Chief Magistracy of the reunited Republic. And I do not doubt that the earnest patriotism and enlightened statesmanship of Your Excellency will speedily obliterate all painful remembrances of the past and inspire the people of the nation to give you a hearty and unanimous support in the development of their best interests."[9] In the midst of a brutal civil war, with morale at a dangerously low ebb, Lincoln saw something comforting in a nation emerging from a protracted period of internal strife that had endured far longer than the conflict in the United States. Had he also written to Mitre, Juárez would no doubt have shared Lincoln's sentiments. Lincoln's letter to Mitre, which is not usually included in histories of the US Civil War, demonstrates that nations throughout the Americas faced similar concerns and travails as they endured bitter violent conflicts.

An Era of Civil Wars and Reconstructions

Civil Wars and Reconstructions in the Americas analyzes three violent conflicts—the latter stage of the Wars of Unification in Argentina, the War of the Reform and French Intervention in Mexico, and the US Civil War—and the reconstructions that followed each war. It employs transnational and comparative methodologies to highlight similarities and differences between each civil war and reconstruction and to analyze flows of goods, people, and ideas across borders during a fascinating era marked by significant cooperation among people from all the three countries. It insists that this period (1860–80) was a moment of intense Pan-American cooperation and that some people saw these conflicts as interwoven or at least parallel. Furthermore, people in all three nations, as they moved from civil war into reconstruction, engaged in similar discussions about and struggles over the contours of government and the political systems of their nations. In sum, the experiences of all three nations fit into a larger struggle, both hemispheric and worldwide, that pit republicanism and democracy against forces of reaction such as aristocracy, monarchy, oligarchy, and conservatism.

Why these three conflicts and these three nations? For one, because some people in each of the three nations saw their wars as interconnected and part of a much broader struggle. Also, because each nation shared similar challenges during their reconstruction, specifically implementing programs of internal improvement and suppressing insurgencies that wanted to re-create worlds and hierarchies that had been destroyed by war. Finally, because the Americas during this period contained, by far, the largest number of republics in the world. Many people, both contemporaries and scholars, have long dismissed the Latin American republics that arose during and after the Wars of Independence as disordered, anarchical, backward, unstable, and perhaps even contemptible. East-west links (between the United States and Europe) tend to receive primary billing, and the north-south axis (between the United States and Latin America) generally receives less attention.[10] Recent scholarship has begun to emphasize the relationship between the United States and the other nations of the Americas. Moreover, several historians of Latin America have undermined dismissive analysis of backward republics in Latin America by arguing, with considerable justification, that the Americas (not just the United States but also the Spanish American republics) were the true locus of republicanism and modernity during this period.[11] Placing the United States, Mexico, and Argentina alongside each other and analyzing the fierce struggle within each nation together rather than separately produces a broader history of the Americas revealing common hemispheric patterns about republics and republicanism in the nineteenth-century world.

What happened in the Americas during 1860–80 was neither inconsequential nor ephemeral. The United States, Mexico, and Argentina underwent similar violent conflicts. Some people at the time understood them as interconnected or as moving along the same general path. In retrospect, it becomes crystal clear, just as it was to some people at the time, that each of the three conflicts and the reconstruction that followed fit into a much broader struggle, one that began long before 1860 and endured long after 1880. Lincoln himself expressed one understanding of this struggle in his debate with Senator Stephen A. Douglas at Alton, Illinois, in 1858. The great issue, Lincoln explained to the audience, was nothing less than "the eternal struggle between these two principles—right and wrong—throughout the world," or, expressed another way, "the one is the common right of humanity and the other the divine right of kings."[12] Although Lincoln focused specifically on the United States, he noted that the country faced the same issues people all over the world confronted. Relatedly, each of the three violent conflicts discussed in this book was part of a much broader struggle setting democracy and republicanism against aristocracy, monarchy, oligarchy, conservatism, and the assembled hosts of reaction. It can be easy to fall into the trap of assuming people in the nineteenth century had little understanding of life beyond the narrow bounds of their own communities, let alone what happened in the rest of the world. However, as newspapers and correspondence demonstrate, people in each of the three nations employed hemispheric and global lenses to help them make sense of cataclysmic conflicts. Some explicitly saw the struggles as interlinked where some saw them as part of a larger conflict. Others did not, but these conflicts were nonetheless part and parcel of a wider struggle.

The victors in each conflict faced similar issues and concerns despite different contexts. For instance, emancipation in the United States occurred much later than emancipation in Mexico (1837) and Argentina (1853). In 1865, the Thirteenth Amendment freed millions of enslaved people, far more than when Mexico and Argentina abolished slavery. Despite this difference, the victors in each struggle confronted similar questions about leniency, state power, and what to do with rebels. Consequently, as they sought to bind their nations back together, all three groups of victors discovered that this process was beset with a host of challenges. The vanquished in each of the conflicts, and, as time passed, some of the discontented victors, turned to similar methods; principally, although not exclusively, paramilitary violence. For the insurgents, violence became the best strategy to contest the programs of the victors and promote their own worldviews and preferences about the specific shape of each nation. Each of the three countries, due to these bitter struggles, eventually ended up by 1880 on similar trajectories to a type of order and stability that emphasized discipline and proved costly for large sectors of the population in all three nations. Millions of people, Black people in the US South, Indigenous people in Mexico and Argentina, and members of the lower classes in all three nations, found themselves largely disfranchised and locked out of the corridors of power.

The links between the United States and Mexico are reasonably apparent. From the beginning, the destinies of the two countries have been connected, largely, although not exclusively, due to border issues. Consequently, it makes sense to analyze the War of the Reform and the French Intervention and the US Civil War alongside each other. The people who understood these conflicts as linked and the struggles of each nation as inextricably caught up with each other were not shy about trumpeting this point. Likewise, Liberals in Mexico and Republicans in the US often saw themselves as kindred spirits (sometimes for strategic reasons but also due to genuine ideological kinship). Matías Romero, the indefatigable Mexican minister to the United States, who appears throughout part 1, did more than anyone to emphasize the linked nature of the two violent conflicts. So, too, did Secretary of State Seward and General Ulysses S. Grant, although both men preferred somewhat different strategies to throw the French out of Mexico. That these conflicts occurred almost simultaneously also recommends analyzing them alongside each other. Mexico's War of the Reform began several years before the US Civil War (1857) and ended about the time the US Civil War began (1861). After a short pause, the Tripartite Intervention, which eventually morphed into the French Intervention, began in Mexico (1861–62). The US Civil War ended in 1865, two years before the end of the French Intervention (1867). Thus, these events were both simultaneous and, in the eyes of some contemporaries, connected struggles.

If the links between the violent conflicts in the United States and Mexico are obvious, Argentina may seem like an odd choice for the third case study. After all, Argentina did not share a border with either nation. Rather, it was located thousands of miles away from the United States and Mexico in the Southern Cone of South America. Moreover, the timetable of Argentina's Wars of Unification differed greatly from that of the other violent conflicts in this study. Like Mexico, Argentina engaged in a lengthy war of independence from Spain in the 1810s. Argentina won independence earlier than Mexico, but, after independence, the Wars of Unification began. This conflict pitted the interior provinces against Buenos Aires and Unitarios (Unitarians) against Federales (Federalists) for decades. An important milestone in this conflict occurred in 1853 with the writing of the Constitution of 1853 and the formation of the Argentine Confederation. Eight years later, Buenos Aires, which had refused to join the confederation of the interior provinces, triumphed at the Battle of Pavón, which sparked the formation of the Argentine Republic.

Rather than analyzing the entirety of the wars of unification, this volume focuses on the post-1861 portion of Argentina's long struggle to create a liberal state, the period that featured the consolidation of the national state under Presidents Bartolomé Mitre, Domingo F. Sarmiento, and Nicolás Avellaneda. Sarmiento wrote, in 1865, that the growth of the United States and its institutions provided a model for Argentina given the similarity of the colonial origins of the two countries. While Argentina was closer to the beginning of the journey, Sarmiento nevertheless placed the two countries on the same path.[13] Adding Argentina to the story, in other words, demonstrates that the arguments advanced in this book were not just part of the particular history between the United States and Mexico but, rather, part of an American story that resonated through the Western Hemisphere—from Washington, DC, to Mexico City, to Buenos Aires. These three case studies illustrate that some people saw each of the three violent conflicts and reconstructions as linked or connected as well as what other people saw at the time but what becomes even more obvious in retrospect: that they were all part of a much larger global struggle.

The three major arguments that appear in this book hold considerable implications for understandings of the US Civil War, the Americas, and the global history of republicanism more broadly. First, this period, 1860–80, featured many different instances of cooperation among the people of the United States, Mexico, and Argentina. To be sure, anti–Latin American sentiment existed during this period in the United States and anti-US sentiment occurred in Mexico and, to a lesser extent, in Argentina.[14] That said, anti–Latin Americanism and anti-US sentiment were only one side of the coin. The other side was a rich world of cooperation that took a staggering array of different forms.[15] People in all three countries corresponded with each other, traveled to different nations, and worked to create stronger economic, political, and cultural ties. The victors took cues from each other about creating new worlds and making sure conflicts such as these never occurred again.

To put it bluntly, this was a Pan-American moment of cooperation. Historians have highlighted three such distinct moments of cooperation between the United States and Latin America in the nineteenth century. The first occurred in the 1810s and 1820s during the Spanish American Revolutions. Although many people in the United States—from James Monroe, John Quincy Adams, and Henry Clay, to many others—thrilled in the disintegration of the Spanish Empire and the formation of a new group of "sister republics" in the New World, this moment, one historian argued, came to a screeching halt in the debate over whether the United States should send delegates to the 1827 Panama Congress.[16] Even had this debate not occurred, it seems unlikely that this moment would have survived the US War with Mexico (1846–48), when Polk the Mendacious manufactured a war against a sister republic to gain territory for the United States. The second moment occurred in the 1860s.[17] The third moment occurred in the late 1880s and 1890s, when Secretary of State James G. Blaine worked to create the Pan-American conferences.[18] The period 1860–80 was an important Pan-American moment but in broader ways than scholars have understood. The inclusion of the Argentine case study demonstrates that this was a much broader moment than one focused simply on the Lima Congress of 1864 or the Monroe Doctrine. Indeed, the three case studies illustrate a hemispheric Pan-Americanism showcasing close links among the three nations. People revived elements of the 1810–27 period such as the language of sister republics, but cooperation also occurred in new and exciting forms. One important manifestation of this Pan-Americanism was cooperation between the United States and Mexico during the final years of the French Intervention, and one unexpected consequence was how Mexico and Argentina came to embrace celebrations of the Fourth of July, something that would not have appeared likely in 1860, when anger about the US War with Mexico burned bright in Mexico. Some of the connections between the United States, Mexico, and Argentina may appear asymmetrical, but it is imperative to note the significant amount of sentiment in each country for creating cooperative and mutually beneficial relations throughout the Americas.

Second, and related to the first point, 1860–80, the time period of this study, represented an important moment in the Americas because some people understood their world in hemispheric terms and privileged cooperation among the nations of the New World over conflict. To be sure, as violent conflicts wracked the United States, Mexico, and Argentina, some people naturally turned inward to focus on their particular conflict with laser-beam intensity, but others turned outward to consider how their specific violent conflict was related to other such conflicts or part of a much broader struggle. It is tempting to understand this period as one of discrete civil wars and reconstructions, in which each country focused exclusively on their own struggle with little understanding of other nations. However, this tendency is incorrect because this was a period in which some people saw individual conflicts—the Wars of Unification in Argentina, the US Civil War, and the War of the Reform and French Intervention in Mexico—as part of a larger struggle raging throughout the world. Their understanding of this larger struggle varied depending on their specific circumstances. In the United States, for example, Lincoln and Republicans cast the rebels as the enemy of republican ideals, emphasized the power of slave oligarchs and slave aristocrats, placed the responsibility for the war on an elite aristocratic minority, and correctly argued that some rebels favored monarchy.[19] Rebels, in turn, claimed they were the true republicans fighting against an oppressive power analogous to Great Britain in the 1770s (in their eyes King Abraham I became the new King George III).[20] In Mexico, the Liberals did not have to exert much effort to demonstrate that theirs was a conflict pitting republicanism against monarchy, especially once Mexican Conservatives invited Austrian Archduke Ferdinand Maximilian to become the emperor of the Second Mexican Empire. Argentina's conflict was not so much about monarchy; Spanish American countries clung to republicanism tenaciously and generally did not revert to monarchy after independence despite the potential temptation posed by Brazil's political trajectory. Thus, Argentina's was more a conflict among liberals and republicans who fought against conservative caudillos. That did not stop both sides from denouncing oligarchy and aristocrats at various points throughout the conflict.

Despite these differences, the three violent conflicts were nevertheless part and parcel of a much larger struggle that pitted democracy and republicanism against monarchy, aristocracy, oligarchy, conservatism, and other forms of reaction. Romero, Grant, and Seward, among others, made a powerful case for the linked nature of their wars. Sarmiento spoke of nations moving along the same path and subject to the same struggles. In addition to elite voices, many people embraced an understanding of these conflicts as linked through their actions. This explains why people circulated from one country to another and fought in many different wars; why policymakers ignored or even encouraged violations of neutrality laws and why many people eagerly ignored them; why Mexicans and Argentines celebrated the Fourth of July; and why the victors worked from similar ideas about how to remake their countries with aggressive programs of modernization and internal improvement. In sum, during a period of tremendous conflict, new understandings emerged, and many people favored cooperation because they understood that they were not going it alone; their wars were part of a much broader struggle. While some people at the time clearly did not embrace or accept this understanding, it is clear, particularly in retrospect, that these conflicts all embraced the same themes.

Third, analyzing these conflicts together illustrates the existence of a common search for order in the three countries. Specifically, this order referred to the government and the political system (primarily, although not exclusively) of each nation. It is absolutely crucial to remember that, as Romero and others illustrated, the violent conflicts in the United States and Mexico threw the two nations into an existential struggle for the survival of republicanism and democratic government. Mitre and Sarmiento said the same of Argentina's War of Unification. In other words, Liberals in Mexico, Republicans in the United States, and Unitarios in Argentina believed, with considerable justification, that they fought for the survival of republicanism and democracy against whatever force(s) opposed them. Their opponents also searched for (admittedly very different) types of order. Mexican Conservatives and Imperialists desperately craved the order held out by Napoleon III and Maximilian. Confederates wanted order and, to secure it, left the United States and the apocalyptic threat they knew Republican antislavery ideology posed to their world.[21] Federales in Argentina also wanted order and did not want an oppressive central government dictating to them. Republicans and Liberals opposed these groups and fought for republicanism and democracy against the threats posed by various groups. Order and stability risk sounding clinical, antiseptic, apolitical, detached, or nonideological, so here is the point in its most basic form: each of the three conflicts involved showdowns between very different visions of the ways that societies and governments should be organized. Consequently, they were all historically important and not just to the Americas! Each of the three conflicts, in other words, pitted the liberal state against premodern conservative forces that wanted specific hierarchies based on race and class.

Finally, each of the three countries faced a similar problem of violence and disorder. It can be easy to forget, as one historian of Argentina recently noted, that the US Civil War did not really have an equivalent in the Spanish American republics in the nineteenth century.[22] Consequently, the timetable of political disorder was longer in both Mexico and Argentina, but disorder was part and parcel of republicanism. The United States certainly faced episodes of instability in the pre-1861 period and a larger-scale war than anything that occurred in Spanish America. Moreover, each of the three countries faced a significant amount of violence and instability following the three conflicts, when the vanquished again turned to extralegal means to contest the victors. Some people in the United States pointed to Mexico as the classic example of a disordered and chaotic country and employed the word "Mexicanized" to make this point crystal clear.[23] While Mexico certainly suffered from these problems, so too did the United States and Argentina.

After 1861 in Argentina (the Battle of Pavón), 1865 in the United States (the end of the US Civil War), and 1867 in Mexico (the withdrawal of the French and execution of Maximilian), all three countries faced very similar situations. In each of the three nations, the victors confronted the enormous challenges of pacifying countries containing numerous people who did not agree with their worldviews. In imposing order, the victors followed similar patterns and sometimes made similar decisions about how they treated vanquished populations. The vanquished, in turn, adopted similar language and similar violent strategies as they waged war against the victors during their reconstructions. How the victors sought to impose order, and how the vanquished and discontented victors resisted, also reveals a common hemispheric history of attempts to knit the sinews of nations back together. Finally, the three countries followed similar paths and, by the 1880s, had embarked on comparable programs of stability. These conflicts involved intense showdowns between worldviews and demonstrated how the victors adopted both similar and different strategies to stitch their nations back together, as well as how all three countries came to embrace a particular type of stability by the 1880s, the dawn of new eras in each nation.

Reconstruction and the Transnational Turn

In recent decades, the transnational turn in US historiography has produced a veritable explosion of work about the international dimensions of the US Civil War Era.[24] For instance, one study of whether the US Civil War was a total war included a chapter on Maximilian's Black Decree and guerrilla violence during the French Intervention.[25] Some scholars have explored links between liberals in the United States and a broader community of reformers.[26] Others have analyzed similarities between the US Civil War and the French Intervention.[27] The transnational dimensions of abolition and nationalism continue to fascinate historians.[28] Numerous volumes discuss the diplomatic history of the conflict.[29] Several recent edited volumes have considered the conflict in a transnational or a global context.[30]

In contrast to the ever-growing number of books about the international dimensions of the US Civil War, Reconstruction history, with a few exceptions, has been written as though the rest of the world did not exist.[31] Indeed, three distinct schools of Reconstruction historiography largely limited their analysis to internal elements of the period and process.[32] The Dunning school condemned vindictive Radical Republicans, venal scalawags, vicious carpet-baggers, and "Negro misrule."[33] This analysis stood until the 1950s, when Revisionists made Radical Republicans and African Americans the heroes of the story.[34] Post-Revisionists then challenged Revisionists by demonstrating the conservatism of Republican policymakers and how the Constitution restrained Republicans.[35] For thirty years, Eric Foner's justifiably impressive synthesis has dominated the field.[36] Foner, like his predecessors, covered domestic but not international elements of Reconstruction.[37] The focus on the domestic elements, given the vast degree of change that occurred in the United States, should not surprise. However, concentrating on the international elements of Reconstruction reveals the hemispheric perspectives, cooperation, Pan-Americanism, and the fights over different visions of society that took place throughout the Americas during this period.

The current, or fourth, school of Reconstruction historiography encompasses a broad range of topics.[38] Scholars continue to produce many fine books about the eleven states of the so-called Confederacy.[39] However, some have shifted their focus beyond the confines of the US South. If a name exists for this school, and none currently does, perhaps it should be "Greater Reconstructionists," after Elliott West's iconic phrase. In other words, some look to the US West and the Pacific Coast.[40] Others consider the Northern and Midwestern United States.[41] In sum, the post-Foner generation of historians has found a great deal to admire in the idea of the Greater Reconstruction as they expand the boundaries of the period and process in time and space. *Civil Wars and Reconstructions in the Americas* takes this idea one step further by adopting a hemispheric approach to this period to argue that the three violent conflicts occurred during a period of Pan-American cooperation. Moreover, they were part of a broader struggle between republicanism and democracy against various forms of reaction that played out throughout the hemisphere, reinforcing the fact that the Americas were the true locus of debates about modernity and republicanism and the critical arena in which these battles occurred.

Methodologies

Civil Wars and Reconstructions in the Americas contains two parts. Each part uses a different methodology that merits some attention.[42] Part 1, "Transnational Histories of Pan-American Cooperation," contains four chapters that employ a transnational methodology to analyze flows of goods, people, and ideas across national borders.[43] Collectively, these chapters explore connections, illustrate how people's "imagined communities" often overlapped the boundaries of their nations, and demonstrate how the impulse to cooperate took many different forms throughout the Americas.[44] In sum, the chapters in part 1 explore connections and cooperation. They analyze the transnational warriors who circulated around the Americas in order to fight in different conflicts. They discuss efforts to raise arms and funds for Mexico and how Mexicans and people in the United States reinterpreted the Monroe Doctrine. They establish the development of a closer US relationship with Mexico and Argentina and illustrate elements of a new world—Fourth of July celebrations in Mexico, for example—that would have been unimaginable before 1860. They describe how the victors enacted similar programs of internal improvement and held similar ideas about the importance of education. They illustrate, in sum, Pan-American cooperation.

Part 2, "Comparative Paths to Order," utilizes a comparative methodology to analyze how the vanquished and, as time passed, some of the discontented victors, contested the direction of affairs in each of the three countries. As George Fredrickson explained, US historians frequently engage in comparative analysis because they hope "they can learn something new about American history by comparing some aspect of it with an analogous phenomenon in another society."[45] This book compares reconstructions to determine what they reveal about all three countries, not just the United States. Cross-national comparisons tend to dominate comparative history, but recent studies have illustrated how this methodology permits other types of comparisons, such as comparisons of regions within nations or comparisons of more than two countries.[46] Consequently, the chapters in part 2 make comparisons among the United States, Mexico, and Argentina, as well as within each of the three countries.[47]

Historians have employed comparative history to shed light on comparative slavery, comparative emancipation, and comparative postemancipation societies.[48] Comparative history can also reveal a great deal about comparative reconstructions in the United States, Mexico, and Argentina.[49] Despite an important difference—the United States had a much larger population of freed slaves than Argentina and Mexico—similarities in how reconstructions unfolded merit close attention. Chapters 5, 6, and 7 highlight similarities, particularly in terms of the violence that occurred as rebels and pronunciados challenged the visions of the victors, although they also note differences. These chapters illustrate how all three countries suffered from similar problems of disorder and, ultimately, all sought a particular type of stability by the 1880s.

A Note about Names

Civil Wars and Reconstructions in the Americas uses "US Civil War" whenever possible to refer to the conflict that took place in the United States from 1861 to 1865. This conflict has long been called the "American Civil War," or "the Civil War," but these names could lead to the conclusion that one important civil war took place during "the Civil War Era" and that it occurred from 1861 to 1865 in the United States.[50] The problem with casting the US Civil War as "the Civil War" or "the American Civil War" is that it implies that civil wars in Mexico and Argentina, not to mention civil wars in other Latin American countries, are less important than the "American" (US) Civil War. Scholars have illustrated how people in the United States have appropriated the term "American" to refer to themselves. Many Latin Americans argue, quite correctly, that they have an equal claim to this term.[51] Consequently, this book urges linguistic precision by using "US Civil War" whenever possible and avoids using the term "American" to mean "United States" except in quotes from people at the time.

Setting the Stage: The Americas in 1860

Because this book analyzes three countries and because readers may not be familiar with the history of all three, brief background about the history of each country since their independence will provide context for the rest of the volume.

MEXICO

Napoleon's invasion of Spain in 1808 sparked a protracted guerrilla insurgency in Spain and revolutions throughout the Americas. On September 16, 1810, Father Miguel Hidalgo y Costilla ordered the bells of his church in Dolores, near Guanajuato, rung. Hidalgo addressed the crowd that gathered and encouraged them to revolt. Hidalgo's pronunciamiento, el Grito de Dolores (the Cry of Dolores) marked the beginning of the War for Independence.[52] Hidalgo's followers quickly swelled into the tens of thousands and defeated royalists in several engagements. For a time, it looked like Hidalgo would take Mexico City, but he retreated. Royalists defeated revolutionaries at the Battle of Calderón Bridge and captured Hidalgo at the Wells of Baján. Royalists executed Hidalgo and, subsequently, other revolutionary leaders. As the years passed, the conflict became a seemingly endless cycle of insurgency and counterinsurgency.[53] In 1820, a coup in Spain forced King Fernando VII to reinstate the liberal Constitution of Cádiz. Royalist Colonel Agustín de Iturbide formed an alliance with Vicente Guerrero and issued the Plan de Iguala. Commanding the Army of the Three Guarantees, Iturbide attracted support from royalists and revolutionists alike. In August 1821, royalist officials recognized Mexican independence. In September, the Army of the Three Guarantees entered Mexico City. By May 1822, Colonel Iturbide had become Emperor Agustín I.[54]

Agustín I reigned for less than a year before he abdicated. Shortly thereafter, a constituent Congress drafted the Constitution of 1824. In a few short years, Mexico went from being part of the Spanish Empire to an empire to a republic.[55] Unfortunately, the transition from empire to republic did not solve Mexico's problems. Guadalupe Victoria served as the first president of Mexico, but he was the only president to complete a full term for decades. Vicious fighting between federalists and centralists defined politics in Mexico during this period. In 1835, the centralist Siete Leyes replaced the Federalist Constitution of 1824. In 1846, the Constitution of 1824 was restored. The Constitution of 1824 remained the law of the land until the Liberal Constitution of 1857.[56]

Antonio López de Santa Anna played an important role in Mexican politics.[57] Sometimes a federalist and sometimes a centralist, Santa Anna was, first and foremost, a Santanista. Reviled by many Mexicans as the incompetent traitor who lost Texas and the Mexican Cession, Santa Anna had a talent for supply and logistics, although he preferred to lead armies. Santa Anna went into exile many times but usually managed to return. He repeated this cycle until the 1850s, the time of his most vicious dictatorship. A group of Liberals declared their opposition to Santa Anna in the 1854 Plan de Ayutla. Juan Álvarez, Ignacio Comonfort, and Santiago Vidaurri led armies throughout Mexico and defeated Santa Anna's soldiers. Santa Anna again fled the country. Although he returned to Mexico near the end of his life, he never regained power.[58]

Santa Anna's departure did not end Mexico's troubles. Liberals were determined to attack the privileges accorded to two powerful segments of Mexican society: the army and the clergy.[59] This they did in the Constitution of 1857.

Conservatives, disgusted by the Liberal triumph, struck back.[60] President Co-monfort, after alienating both friends and opponents, resigned the presidency. President of the Supreme Court Benito Juárez became interim president, and Conservatives fraudulently claimed the presidency. Thus began the destructive War of the Reform. Although Conservatives drove the Liberals from Mexico City, the Liberals eventually gained the upper hand. The cost of their triumph, however, proved dear. Mexico's treasury was nearly empty, and Conservative ire still burned fiercely. In an effort to save money, Juárez suspended foreign debt payments. This led to the Tripartite Intervention by Spain, England, and France in 1861 and, ultimately, to the French Intervention.

THE UNITED STATES

The story of the imperial crisis in the British Empire and the US War of Independence has been told many times.[61] With considerable assistance from France, not to mention Spain and the Netherlands, the Thirteen Colonies won their freedom from Britain. With that freedom, however, came new questions. What sort of government should be put in place? What about the balance of power between the federal and state governments? In 1787, a Constitutional Convention produced the US Constitution.[62] This Constitution, as well as the Declaration of Independence, became important models, although not the only ones, for other countries yearning to emulate the United States.[63]

Slavery soon became one of the most contentious issues roiling the politics of the antebellum United States.[64] In 1819, for instance, a crisis between free and slave states threatened to rip the young country apart.[65] When Missouri, which was carved out of the Louisiana Purchase Territory, applied for admission to the Union as a slave state, US Representative James Tallmadge of New York offered an amendment prohibiting slavery in Missouri and mandating gradual emancipation. Southerners refused to vote for the admission of Missouri with the Tallmadge Amendment. Many northerners refused to admit Missouri as a slave state. Speaker of the House of Representatives Henry Clay negotiated a compromise. Missouri would be admitted as a slave state, with Maine admitted as a free state to maintain the sectional balance in the US Senate. Congress also divided the Louisiana Purchase Territory along the 36°30' parallel. Any states carved from territory south of this line could enter the Union as slave states. Congress barred slavery north of this line.[66]

Sectional tensions continued to increase during the following decades.

Proslavery ideologues such as John C. Calhoun crafted a belligerent proslavery defense. They stopped referring to slavery a "necessary evil" and instead labeled it a "positive good." In addition, a small, but vocal, group of abolitionists began to agitate for immediate emancipation.[67] Most northerners did not sympathize with abolitionists. Indeed, abolitionists were often attacked, and sometimes killed, by mobs. Abolitionists deeply frightened white southerners, who considered their way of life under siege.[68]

In 1845, the United States annexed Texas and then fought a war with Mexico (1846–48) that many people considered unjust, immoral, and illegal. Mexicans resented the fact that a sister republic made war against them at a time when many opponents of republicanism desperately desired to see the republics of the New World fail.[69] The Compromise of 1850 postponed the storm of civil war for a decade, but it created new problems.[70] The most controversial component of the Compromise of 1850 was the new Fugitive Slave Law. This law angered northerners not inclined to sympathize with abolitionists because it made them tools of the slave power.[71] It also caused thousands of Black people, some fugitives and some free, to flee to Canada in an attempt to avoid being kidnapped and transported to the South.

The 1850s, the Decade of Crisis, saw one conflict after another.[72] Northerners, both white and African American, began to resist the Fugitive Slave Law. In some cases, abolitionists succeeded in rescuing fugitive slaves and helping them escape to Canada. In other cases, the government returned them to slavery.[73] The portrayal of slavery in Harriet Beecher Stowe's Uncle Tom's Cabin captivated a worldwide audience and enraged white southerners. Senator Stephen A. Douglas's Kansas-Nebraska Act declared the Missouri Compromise superseded by the legislation of 1850 and opened the Kansas and Nebraska Territories to slavery. Northerners erupted in fury, and Democrats paid a high price in the 1854 midterm elections.[74]

The Republican Party, an explicitly sectional party, formed during the period 1854–56.[75] When Charles Sumner, an abolitionist and Republican senator from Massachusetts delivered a bitterly antislavery oration insulting Senator Andrew Butler of South Carolina, Preston Brooks beat Sumner with a cane on the Senate floor. Northerners growled that slaveocrats assaulted white liberties and controlled the government.[76] Warfare in Kansas pitted abolitionists against border ruffians.[77] Abraham Lincoln portrayed the Supreme Court's Dred Scott decision as additional evidence of a slaveholder plot to nationalize slavery.[78] President James Buchanan tried to ram a proslavery constitution for Kansas through Congress, and the result further divided Democrats.[79] John Brown's raid on Harpers Ferry in 1859 made white southerners believe Brown represented all northerners.[80] Abraham Lincoln's election in 1860 became the final straw for many white southerners, and they seceded from the Union.[81] Thus came the US Civil War (1861–65).

ARGENTINA

Argentina's path to independence, like that of Mexico, began with Napoleon's invasion of Spain.[82] Creole revolutionaries determined to break away from Spain. Argentina's War of Independence began in 1810 and continued through 1816.[83] General José de San Martín played an important role in Argentina's struggle for independence as well as in other independence movements in South America.[84] When Napoleon invaded Spain, San Martín fought fiercely for Fernando VII against the French invaders. However, in 1811, he left Spain for Buenos Aires and joined the revolution. Perhaps because he himself was a Creole, San Martín sympathized with the Creole elite leading the revolution.

    Although Buenos Aires proved fertile ground for revolutionaries, the interior regions of the Viceroyalty of Río de la Plata demonstrated significantly less enthusiasm about war with Spain. Indeed, victory in the interior provinces proved, for a time, elusive. San Martín initially organized grenadiers to defend Buenos Aires. After achieving several victories, he went to Tucumán, a northern Argentine province, to assume command of General Manuel Belgrano's Army of the North. San Martín realized Argentina would not be free until he drove royalists out of Peru. Rather than marching his army through Bolivia, he developed an innovative strategy. San Martín determined to cross the Andes, unite with Bernardo O'Higgins and his army of Chilean patriots, and then attack Peru by sea. San Martin staged his army in Mendoza and began the difficult crossing in January 1817. San Martín's skillful handling of his troops through the treacherous mountain passes produced favorable comparisons to Hannibal and Napoleon. San Martín defeated the Chilean royalists at Chacabuco and retook Santiago, Chile. These victories did not mean the immediate end of royalist control of Chile, and it took San Martín another year to destroy the last pockets of resistance, a process concluded in the decisive Battle of Maipú on April 5, 1818.

    In 1816, representatives at the Congress of Tucumán declared the independence of the United Provinces of South America. It is important to note that Argentina achieved independence earlier and in a different fashion than Mexico. Still, as in Mexico, independence did not mean peace. Heated tensions between Unitarios and Federales dominated Argentine political life. Unitarios favored a stronger central government, whereas Federales preferred a weaker central government and stronger provincial governments. San Martín, the hero of the revolution, attempted to remain neutral during the brutal factional struggles, but he eventually left Argentina for Europe in 1823. Federales detested Unitario President Bernardino Rivadavia and engaged in open rebellion. After Rivadavia's resignation in 1827, Unitario/Federale tensions worsened. Caudillos, or strongmen, controlled many of the interior provinces and formed a loose alliance with Governor Juan Manuel de Rosas of Buenos Aires, the most powerful Argentine caudillo, to rule the country.[85] Unitarios fiercely opposed this arrangement but could not, for many years, dislodge Rosas from power.[86] Many people fled Argentina to avoid Rosas's tyranny.[87]

Although Rosas, through his alliance with other caudillos, ruled the country for many years, his power did not last indefinitely. In 1852, a caudillo from the province of Entre Ríos, Justo José de Urquiza, raised an army and defeated Rosas at the Battle of Caseros. Unitarios like Domingo F. Sarmiento and Bartolomé Mitre grew distrustful of Urquiza and preferred to see Buenos Aires exist autonomously rather than be part of the Argentine Confederation.[88] The Confederation and Buenos Aires sparred with each other for several years.[89] In 1859, Urquiza defeated an army led by Mitre at the Battle of Cepeda. Urquiza and the Porteños (residents of Buenos Aires) entered into the Pacto de San José de Flores, which promised concessions to mollify Buenos Aires and opened a path for the province to join the Argentine Confederation and accept the Constitution of 1853. Mitre ultimately abrogated this pact. In 1861, he led the armies of Buenos Aires to victory at the Battle of Pavón against Urquiza. This victory propelled him to the presidency of the Argentine Republic, news of which he communicated to Lincoln in October 1862, and which brought Lincoln some measure of comfort in February 1863.

By analyzing three violent conflicts—the latter stage of the Wars of Unification in Argentina, the War of the Reform and French Intervention in Mexico, and the US Civil War—and the reconstructions that followed each war, *Civil Wars and Reconstructions in the Americas* illuminates a fascinating era of intense Pan-American cooperation. These three conflicts were certainly different in some respects. Argentina's war was essentially internal and pitted liberals against proponents of caudillo government. Mexico's War of the Reform, a civil war, broadened into an international conflict when the French and Austrians intervened in favor of the Mexican Conservatives. During the US Civil War, the rebels sought foreign intervention from European powers, and their failure to secure foreign assistance helped doom the so-called Confederacy. Nevertheless, some people at the time saw these conflicts as interwoven or at least as parallel. Furthermore, people in all three nations, as they moved from civil war into reconstruction, engaged in similar discussions and struggles about the contours of government and the political systems of their nations. The experiences of all three nations fit into a larger struggle, both hemispheric and worldwide, that pit republicanism and democracy against forces of reaction such as aristocracy, monarchy, oligarchy, and conservatism. By placing the three countries alongside each other, this book draws the United States into a closer conversation with some of the other nations of the New World and offers new information about republicanism and democracy in the Americas. The arguments advanced in this book offer not only a different understanding of the past but also speak to the present and future.

PART I

TRANSNATIONAL HISTORIES
OF PAN-AMERICAN COOPERATION

1

Transnational Warriors

SOLDIERS OF FREEDOM (NOT FORTUNE)

In 1873, after more than a dozen years of fighting in wars throughout the Americas, Edelmiro Mayer, an Argentine soldier (and later statesman and writer), returned to Argentina. Some Argentines claimed that Mayer, due to his participation in foreign wars and service in foreign armies, had forfeited his citizenship. They cited Argentina's Law of Citizenship, passed by the Argentine Congress on October 1, 1869, which stated, in Article 8, that "political rights will not be exercised in the Republic . . . by those who have accepted employment or honors from foreign Governments without the permission of Congress."[1] Because he had not sought permission from Congress before serving in the US and Mexican armies, his opponents argued, Mayer was no longer an Argentine citizen. Mayer fervently disagreed and petitioned Congress to declare that he had the use and enjoyment of his rights as a citizen.[2] He did not fight in Mexico and the United States as a mere mercenary adventurer, lured by the seduction of battle or by the prospect of easy gold in his pockets. Rather, he fought in the US Civil War and the French Intervention for the same reasons that he did in Argentina's Wars of Unification: in defense of liberty and republicanism against the forces of reaction.

In the Chamber of Deputies, Aristóbulo del Valle, a brilliant orator, supported Mayer.[3] Del Valle's stirring address buttressed the claim that Mayer fought for noble causes for honorable reasons. Del Valle began by posing a series of rhetorical questions linking Mayer with other transnational warriors. What would the civilized world have said, he thundered, if France had negated Lafayette's citizenship because he fought for US independence? Or if Britain denied Byron's citizenship because he died defending liberty in Greece? Or if anyone in Italy disputed Garibaldi's citizenship because he fought on Argentine beaches? For del Valle, the answer was clear: the civilized world would have condemned such actions and would also condemn Argentina's denying Mayer's citizenship.[4] Furthermore, just as Lafayette, Byron, and Garibaldi fought for principles, not money, so too did Mayer.

Del Valle also dissected the nature of Mayer's military service. Mayer served under Bartolomé Mitre and Wenceslao Paunero in the Army of Buenos Aires in Argentina's Wars of Unification. After leaving Argentina, Mayer traveled to the United States, where some of his family lived, to fight for a great principle: liberty. To vindicate that principle, he fought for the United States until the end of the war in 1865. Rather than resting on these laurels, he then went to Mexico and fought with the Liberals against the French and their Mexican collaborators. Thus, Mayer fought for an American cause—for liberty in Argentina; in the US Civil War, "one of the largest wars in modern times"; and in the French Intervention, "which undoubtedly is also the holiest war in modern times."[5] Mayer, del Valle thundered, "is the representative of that immense limitless love toward all things republican, toward all that is free among the Americans, from Patagonia to the Mississippi."[6] In other words, when Mayer fought for Lincoln and Juárez, he was not an adventurer hopping from country to country in pursuit of glory or a soldier of fortune offering his services to the highest bidder.[7] Rather, in each conflict, he fought for republicanism and democracy against the assembled forces of monarchy, aristocracy, oligarchy, and reaction. For that reason, del Valle argued, Mayer deserved to have his citizenship restored. Both chambers of the Argentine Congress concurred and passed a resolution declaring that Mayer was "in full enjoyment of his political rights."[8]

Immigrant soldiers and transnational warriors played an extremely important role during many nineteenth-century conflicts.[9] For the US Civil War, specifically, the stories of the Irish and Germans who swelled the Union ranks have received some attention.[10] The stories of Mayer and his fellow Latin Americans, not to mention the transnational group of warriors who circulated throughout the Atlantic World, are often overlooked, perhaps because they do not neatly fit into the narratives scholars have developed about the middle years of the nineteenth century, namely, that civil wars are usually internal conflicts.[11] After all, what was an Argentine doing fighting in the US Civil War and the French Intervention in Mexico? Why did people from the United States fight in Mexico after the US Civil War? Why did Garibaldi spend years in Montevideo fighting in an Uruguayan war? In sum, why did people circulate throughout the Atlantic World fighting in conflicts in which they seemingly had no stake?

The answer is that some people did not see the Wars of Unification in Argentina, the US Civil War, and the War of the Reform and the French Intervention in Mexico in isolation. Rather, they saw them as individual parts of a much larger struggle that the forces of reaction waged against republicanism and democracy.[12] Each conflict thus became a critical arena in which the tree of liberty had to be protected from the people who wanted to uproot it and chop it up into firewood. Kings, princes, aristocrats, and oligarchs sneered that the republics of the New World were disordered, anarchical, unstable aberrations. They did their best to undermine them with an eye toward undermining the republican dreams of the downtrodden European masses who looked to the New World for inspiration as well. As many people understood at the time, liberty, freedom, republicanism, and democracy were fragile forces that were constantly under siege. Safeguarding republican experiments required constant vigilance. It also required people to travel throughout the Americas and fight in conflicts in nations where they did not claim citizenship.

Each war was part of a larger struggle in which proponents of democracy, freedom, liberty, and republicanism squared off against champions of autocracy, aristocracy, oligarchy, and reaction. Some people at the time understood this point and said so, but it also becomes very clear in retrospect. This larger conflict was not limited to the United States. As scholars have recently demonstrated, although many people saw the United States as the banner example of a successful republic, due to its stability, the Americas featured many different republican experiments. People thus looked at Latin American republics like Mexico and Argentina, among others, with equal interest.[13] This chapter adopts a broader chronology by analyzing two additional conflicts—the Uruguayan Civil War and the Revolutions of 1848 in Europe—in addition to the Argentine Wars of Unification, the US Civil War, and the War of the Reform and French Intervention in Mexico, in order to drill down into the experiences and motivations of different groups of transnational warriors, and examines those who fought for liberal as well as illiberal causes.[14]

The conflicts mentioned above pitted liberty, democracy, and republicanism, all fragile forces that could at any moment collapse, against the concerted opposition of monarchists, imperialists, oligarchs, and aristocrats. For many years, a constant flow of people occurred throughout the Atlantic World, as people circulated from one conflict to the next. These transnational warriors showcased the cooperation that sprung up among people of different nationalities as well as the interconnected nature of this world. Through their actions, they also illustrated the contested nature of freedom during this period. Most of the men analyzed in this chapter fought for liberal causes and ideas. However, a smaller subset fought for decidedly illiberal causes while nonetheless claiming that they fought for freedom. Transnational warriors illustrate the complex nature of ideas about freedom in the nineteenth-century Americas and offer an important reminder that people fought in diverse conflicts in pursuit of goals and causes that transcended the borders of any one nation.[15]

Understanding these conflicts as components of a much larger struggle reveals the fragility of democracy, republicanism, and liberty. During this period, the forces of autocracy and reaction constantly threatened them. Nineteenth-century republicanism consisted of two principal strands, both concerning fears.[16] The first strand featured persistent fears of corruption.[17] The second, and probably more important, strand worried that liberty was fragile and must be safeguarded. These fears often created paranoias. As Mark E. Neely Jr. helpfully explained, promoters of the "republican thesis" argued that "American political parties operated most effectively by arousing the electorate to crusades against imaginary conspiracies with sinister designs to destroy the republic." Thus, "politicians conventionally relied on creating irrational monsters against which to rally the people into mortal political battles to save the republic."[18] In even more colorful language, republicanism created the tendency to attempt to slay imaginary dragons or tilt at windmills.

In one sense, this analysis is indisputably correct. Nativists and xenophobes throughout the Americas, for instance, fashioned irrational monsters. In the United States, lurid Know-Nothing stories of papal plots to catechize Protestant children and subvert democracy were indeed figments of an overheated political imagination. Nativism and xenophobia existed throughout the hemisphere; from anti-Spanish sentiment during and after the Wars of Independence in Mexico and Argentina to fears of immigrants in all three nations.[19] That said, employing an international lens illustrates that the paranoia republicanism generated was often neither unreasonable nor irrational. In each of the conflicts, a powerful antimodern, aristocratic, imperialistic, oligarchic, or authoritarian force (or one that combined some of each element) stood waiting in the wings to destroy fragile republican experiments. Republicanism and liberty were, quite often, under siege. Thomas Jefferson's assertion that "the tree of liberty must be refreshed from time to time with the blood of patriots & tyrants. It is it's [sic] natural manure," should not be taken lightly.[20] Many people agreed and believed that only constant vigilance and battle, when necessary, could stave off the forces determined to destroy republicanism.

The struggle Mayer waged in the Argentine Congress demonstrated that he prized maintaining his Argentine citizenship. He refused to surrender, at least without a fight, his membership in a particular imagined community. However, his participation in the US Civil War and the French Intervention suggested he did not see being a citizen of Argentina as precluding him from fighting in foreign wars on behalf of noble causes. Mayer was a proud Argentine, but this did not limit him to caring only about Argentina. When the call came, Mayer willingly journeyed to new lands and fought, as del Valle contended, for all things republican. Many of his contemporaries agreed that they did not lose their citizenship by fighting in other wars. Proud nationalists, in other words, could also be internationalists.[21]

Garibaldi and Garibaldinos

Although most famously associated with the Italian Risorgimento, Giuseppe Garibaldi's globe-spanning career took him to places far beyond the Italian Peninsula. Like Lafayette, Garibaldi won the title "hero of two worlds" and became "the preeminent symbol of the nineteenth-century Atlantic world's struggle for liberty against the old regime," or *the* transnational warrior of his day.[22] Garibaldi's participation in the Uruguayan Civil War was one example of his transnational career. The Uruguayan Civil War pitted the liberal Colorados led by Fructuoso Riviera against the conservative Blancos commanded by Manuel Oribe. Because of the complicated geopolitics of the period, the war became international in scope. The French, in the midst of blockading Buenos Aires, supported Riviera and the Colorados when they overthrew Oribe, then president of Uruguay. Juan Manuel de Rosas, the Argentine dictator, then aided Oribe. Consequently, Argentine Unitarios, many of whom were in exile because of their opposition to Rosas, cast their lot with the Colorados, as did Garibaldi. As he assessed the situation, Garibaldi concluded that "a fresh opportunity had come to 'serve the cause of nations,'" and he formed the Italian Legion "from amongst the ever increasing number of Italians in Montevideo, some of them genuine political exiles."[23] Garibaldi did not fight for money or sell his services to the highest bidder. Rather, he fought for the "cause of nations" by joining the Colorados.

Garibaldi and the Italian Legion provided considerable assistance to the

Colorados.[24] After the Colorados were defeated in the Battle of Arroyo Grande (1842), Oribe and the Blancos invested Montevideo. The city remained under siege for nine years, but it never fell under Blanco control. Montevideo survived "thanks to its command of river navigation, the aid of the foreign legion, the efforts of Garibaldi whom the *Gaceta Mercantil* called the 'jackal of the Anglo-French tigers,' the alliance of the Argentine exiles, and the efforts of the Uruguayans themselves."[25] Indeed, "by the early 1840s, newspaper reports had already begun to speak of Garibaldi as a romantic 'bandit leader' and to tell of (and often condemn) his adventures in Brazil and of his formation of an 'Italian League of Montevideo' to defend liberal Uruguay against the aggression of Buenos Aires."[26]

Garibaldi's assistance reinforced Montevideo's defiance of Oribe's siege and ensured that the conflict festered. Eventually, Governor Justo José de Urquiza of Entre Ríos, Argentina, helped the Colorados defeat the Blancos, thus beginning a chain of events leading to the defeat and exile of Juan Manuel de Rosas. Argentine Unitario Domingo F. Sarmiento, among others, believed Garibaldi deserved considerable glory for his actions in South America. Sarmiento later wrote that Garibaldi's name "was inseparable from those of Paz, Alsina, Velez, Mitre and many others" and that the Italian hero deserved praise and honor for helping Uruguay elude the grasp of Rosas and Oribe.[27] Rosas certainly disagreed with this assessment, but Garibaldi, alternately labeled "Col. Garibaldi, the commander of the Republican troops" and "Italian buccaneer Garibaldi," fascinated people throughout the Atlantic World, not least because of his service as a transnational warrior but also because of people who readily embraced his mantle and image and sought to cast themselves as transnational warriors as well.[28] James E. Sanders observed that Garibaldi's time in Uruguay should not be understated: "After all, it was in Uruguay, not the Old World, where Garibaldi and the Garibaldinos first began to wear the famous red shirts by which they became known. Like the raiment, ideas and inspirations spread east across the Atlantic."[29] Far from being an unimportant moment for Garibaldi, his time in the Americas, particularly Uruguay, proved formative for him and, consequently, for many other transnational warriors.

After years of fighting in Uruguay, Garibaldi decided, in 1848, to return to Italy.[30] Revolutions erupted in Europe throughout 1848. The tumultuous year began with turmoil in France, which led to King Louis-Philippe's abdication and the creation of the French Second Republic.[31] Uprisings and violence also occurred in the German states, Austria, Denmark, Hungary, Sweden, Switzerland, Belgium, Ireland, and the Italian States. The crowned heads of Europe and old-fogy aristocrats shuddered when confronted with this eruption of popular sentiment. Many people throughout the world, however, rejoiced over the seemingly forward march of liberty and progress. A writer in the *Methodist Quarterly Review* labeled 1848 an "annus mirabilis," or a miraculous year.[32] William Lloyd Garrison, as well as other editors, politicians, and commentators, lent rhetorical and moral support.[33] People from the Western Hemisphere journeyed to the Old World and proved ready to follow Jefferson's advice about watering the tree of liberty with the blood of patriots and tyrants.

The Revolutions of 1848 failed and led to a subsequent wave of reaction in 1849. The suppression of the revolutions drove a significant number of revolutionists into exile. Colonel Silvino Olivieri, for instance, went to Argentina. Other revolutionists, such as Hugo Hillebrandt of Hungary, ended up in the United States. Many Germans settled in the US Midwest and became an important constituency in the fledgling Republican Party in the post-1854 period.[34] Some revolutionaries, like Alexander Asbóth of Hungary, later became officers during the US Civil War.[35] German and Irish immigrants also enrolled in large numbers in the US armed forces during 1861–65 and in much smaller numbers in the rebel armed forces. Although the Revolutions of 1848 failed, transnational warriors did not simply collapse and lick their wounds. Rather, they, not to mention many sympathizers who did not take up arms, continued to dream and scheme and sought out new opportunities and new conflicts in the Americas and elsewhere. Hugo Hillebrandt of Hungary and John T. Pickett of the United States represented two divergent, but nonetheless illuminating, post-1848 revolutionary trajectories.

Hillebrandt and Pickett: Transnational Warriors, Revolutionary Counterpoints

The currents from the Revolutions of 1848 flowed in many directions. Hungarian Hugo Hillebrandt was a "true revolutionary" whose "experiences with governments from monarchies to republics, were as broad as anyone's."[36] Hillebrandt began his globe-spanning career fighting in Hungary. When Lajos Kossuth sparked a revolution, Hillebrandt left the military academy he attended to become a lieutenant in Kossuth's army. He served "with much distinction during the whole of that ill-starred revolution, showing even in his early youth that military genius and cool courage for which he was later conspicuous both in the Revolutionary Army of Garibaldi in Italy and in the Volunteer Army of the United States during the Civil War."[37] After the revolution failed, authorities interned many Hungarians in Turkey. Despite offers to enter the sultan's army, "Hillebrandt was too much of a lover of liberty to accept the tempting offers of the Sublime Porte to enter its service, and he came to the United States with Kossuth."[38] Once in the United States, Hillebrandt chafed at his forced inactivity. When he received information about Garibaldi's Italian uprising, Hillebrandt left the United States to join Garibaldi and served under him "in both of the famous descents into Sicily."[39] Hillebrandt then left Italy and returned to the United States just in time to enlist in the Thirty-Ninth New York and fight his way through the US Civil War.[40] The Thirty-Ninth New York, known as the Garibaldi Guards, contained eleven companies of German, Hungarian, Swiss, Italian, French, Spanish, and Portuguese immigrant soldiers.[41]

Hugo Hillebrandt should not be dismissed as a restless adventurer or a hot-blooded youth. He was not an indiscriminate joiner of armies; he picked his wars very carefully. Hillebrandt preferred fighting for liberty, or what he saw as the forces of liberty—Kossuth in Hungary, Garibaldi in Italy, and Lincoln in the United States—against despotism and reaction. For that reason, he did not join the sultan's army. Neither did he participate in the Crimean War nor in filibustering expeditions. Hillebrandt's choices emphasize the ideological motivations of the transnational warriors. Like Edelmiro Mayer, Hillebrandt was not inspired by a concern for the coins jingling in his pockets or by a desire for the next adventure. Rather, both men, as well as many of their fellow transnational warriors, fought to preserve and defend republicanism and democracy against the forces of reaction.

Garibaldi's decision to move from Uruguay to Italy or Hillebrandt's journey from Hungary to Italy to the United States made sense in light of their ardent desire to fight for freedom. Other transnational warriors followed very different trajectories that did not look at all like fighting for freedom. Nowhere was this more evident than the case of John T. Pickett of the United States. Like Hillebrandt, Pickett fought alongside Kossuth in Hungary.[42] After the failure of the revolution, Pickett's career took a very different turn. In an article reporting a meeting with Theodore O'Hara, the *Mississippi Free Trader* praised "this distinguished gentleman, distinguished no less for his spirit and ability as a political writer than for his prowess as a *Liberator*. Col. O'Hara has retired from the Louisville *Times*, a flourishing Democratic paper, of which he was an original founder in connection with Col. John T. Pickett, also well known as one of the Liberators."[43] The newspaper's use of "Liberator" referred to O'Hara and Pickett's participation in the Narciso López filibustering expedition. López intended to wrench Cuba from Spain, and Pickett, O'Hara, and Thomas T. Hawkins "breathed fresh life into the filibuster" by offering to raise a regiment of Kentuckians to fight in Cuba.[44] The expedition ended badly for many of the "liberators," who barely escaped Cuba with their lives.[45]

Once he returned to the United States, Pickett's ardor did not cool, and he continued plotting. Although the evidence is unclear, Pickett may have concocted a scheme wherein he would raise men to conquer Haiti. Kossuth, with assistance from the Dominican Republic, would organize the expedition. After the conquest of Haiti, the soldiers would liberate Hungary.[46] Pickett's plan would have served several objectives. For one, it would have eliminated Haiti, a Black republic and an object of fear and loathing by many white southerners in the United States In addition, it would have led to a free and republican Hungary under Kossuth's guidance, a man Young Americans like Pickett admired very much.[47] Ultimately, Pickett's plans came to naught. In a letter to C. F. Henningson, Pickett griped about an unproductive meeting with "His Mulatto Excellency Buenaventura Baez," president of the Dominican Republic, and took gleeful pleasure reporting that the archbishop called Baez "an ass (*tonto* was, I think, the expression)."[48] Although Pickett's idea seems far-fetched, one scholar noted that "militarily experienced Hungarians were all too ready to support filibusters" and that Louis Schlesinger, an exiled Forty-Eighter joined Narciso López's "army of liberation to bring freedom to the Cubans, something reminiscent of their own uprising two years earlier."[49] Like Latin Americans who fought for the rebels during the US Civil War, Pickett and a small group of Hungarian exiles also claimed to fight for freedom while either owning slaves or attempting to win Cuba or Haiti for the United States.

Should Pickett be called a "liberator," at least with a straight face, for attempting to bring Cuba into the orbit of a slaveholding republic? Modern observers would likely vociferously disagree, but Pickett and many of his contemporaries would have answered the question in the affirmative. For one, Pickett wanted to rescue Cuba from the (as he saw it) decadent Spanish Empire. In addition, Pickett was a Democrat and a proud Young American. "Your Enthusiasm in favor of Douglas + Young America," O'Hara wrote to Pickett after the failed López Expedition, "accords entirely with my own views."[50] The Revolutions of 1848 captivated Young Americans. After the failure of the revolutions, they "bided their time and waited for new opportunities."[51] To a Young American, prying Cuba away from Spain and helping spur republicanism abroad would have served the cause of freedom, as they saw it, very well. In sum, Pickett demonstrated the multilayered nature of ideas about freedom during this period. Specifically, he began by fighting for a republican Hungary in 1848; then he attempted to wrench Cuba away from Spain; and then he schemed to destroy one New World republic (Haiti) and midwife an Old World republic into being (Hungary under Kossuth). Pickett's proposed actions in the Americas would have dealt a grievous blow to the cause of republicanism and strengthened slavery by eradicating the hemisphere's only Black republic and by pulling Cuba into the US orbit.[52] Nevertheless, Pickett believed he would serve the cause of freedom abroad. Pickett's actions are a good reminder that while many transnational warriors fought for both liberal causes, others fought for decidedly illiberal causes.[53]

Pickett and Hillebrandt both claimed to fight for liberty and freedom, but their definitions of these concepts differed greatly. Their careers as transnational warriors began together—fighting with Kossuth in Hungary—but then dramatically diverged. Pickett became involved with filibustering expeditions to expand slavery where Hillebrandt fought alongside Garibaldi in Italy. During the US Civil War, Hillebrandt fought for Lincoln and Pickett sided with the rebels. Indeed, Pickett served as a rebel envoy to Mexico, and his outrageous behavior damaged the already tenuous rebel cause.[54] Hillebrandt, on the other hand, commanded the Thirty-Ninth New York, also known as the Garibaldi Guards, at the Battle of Gettysburg. Pickett and Hillebrandt clearly had different definitions of liberty and freedom. Hillebrandt never evinced a shred of interest in fighting for the rebels during the US Civil War and later served as an agent of the Freedmen's Bureau during Reconstruction. Pickett, on the other hand, wholeheartedly embraced white supremacy and proslavery arguments, although he did not consider his support of slavery as incompatible with a certain set of ideas about liberty and republicanism. Hillebrandt and Pickett should not be seen as analogous. Both had a similar initial revolutionary trajectory in Hungary that diverged because of the considerable differences in their ideas about freedom. Transnational warriors were not a monolithic group.

People could, and did, embrace wildly different causes all the while arguing their actions served a broader cause. Both liberals and reactionaries, in other words, laid claim to a language of freedom and liberty, albeit for very different reasons, as they circulated throughout the Americas and the Atlantic World.

Italians in the Argentine Wars of Unification

As Pickett contemplated filibustering for his conception of freedom and as Hillebrandt moved among Hungary, Italy, and the United States, other struggles occurred simultaneously in the Western Hemisphere. One of them, the Argentine Wars of Unification, drew in exiled revolutionists from Europe.[55] After Justo José de Urquiza helped defeat the Blancos and ensured a Colorado triumph in Uruguay, he turned his attention to Juan Manuel de Rosas. Urquiza's army contained a diverse array of soldiers: Argentines from Entre Ríos, the province he governed; Unitarios like Domingo F. Sarmiento; Brazilians; and Uruguayan Colorados. Sarmiento served as an officer in the army and a traveling newspaper correspondent. He did not think much of Urquiza, "a poor peasant without education," or of his army, "nothing more than a *levee en masse* of country dwellers."[56] However, he decided Urquiza was preferable, at least in the short term, to Rosas. After defeating Rosas at the Battle of Caseros (1852), Urquiza entered Buenos Aires. When his Brazilian soldiers departed the city to return home, Urquiza issued a proclamation complimenting them for "their valiant deeds in the cause of liberty."[57] Never a modest man, Urquiza framed his victory as a triumph of liberty against the tyranny of Rosas.

Some Porteños, as residents of Buenos Aires were known, disagreed with this framing. Urquiza, they complained, aspired to replace Rosas and subvert their liberties. Initially an unwilling member of the Argentine Confederation, the province quickly seceded, preferring an autonomous existence. The period between 1852, the defeat of Rosas at Caseros, and 1861, the defeat of Urquiza at the Battle of Pavón, did not involve constant war, but Buenos Aires and the Confederation often engaged in hostilities. In late 1852, for instance, Colonel Hilario Lagos placed Buenos Aires under siege.[58] Urquiza sustained Lagos and sent a fleet to blockade the port, a smart decision because Buenos Aires relied heavily on customs revenue.[59]

In the emergency, many people tendered their services to Buenos Aires. Jose Llames, a Spaniard who fought alongside Garibaldi's Italian Legion during the siege of Montevideo as a captain of artillery, offered to form an artillery reserve.[60] Logically, one would think the minister of war would gladly accept his service, but José Jareguí, commander of the Spanish Volunteers, wrote to Llames that the governor did not consider additional artillery necessary.[61] The governor of Buenos Aires did not see fit to employ Captain Llames, but the government did, following the example of Garibaldi, create an Italian Legion of their own.[62]

Colonel Silvino Olivieri commanded the Italian Legion.[63] An admirer of Giuseppe Mazzini, Olivieri fought with revolutionists in Italy in 1848 and, during the reaction, fled to Argentina.[64] The provincial government, as well as military officials, responded well to Olivieri's Italian soldiers. In a letter to José María Paz, the minister of war, the colonel commanding the Valiant Legion asked Paz to send him exclusively Italian soldiers. As he explained it, undisciplined German and French soldiers in his command demoralized the rest of the unit. The minister of war permitted him to swap problematic soldiers for Italians.[65]

In a letter to Paz, Olivieri reported the death of Second Lieutenant Cayetano Sachi and asked Paz to authorize him to "render [to Sachi] the same honors that have been made to many officials of the line killed in defense of the fatherland."[66] Olivieri's use of "patria" is important because it means fatherland, native land, or, in some cases, adopted land. Since Olivieri and his men were Italians by birth, his word choice demonstrates that their motivations in fighting for Buenos Aires ran deeper than money and adventure. Olivieri and his fellow Italians had a genuine commitment to the health of the state. They had begun to see Buenos Aires not just as a place to wait out their time before returning to Italy, but as a new home.[67] Indeed, Olivieri and some of his compatriots later founded New Rome, a "quasi-military agricultural colony," and began to build a life for themselves on the Argentine pampas.[68] Similarly, many refugees from the Revolutions of 1848 built new lives for themselves in the United States and, when the call came, fought for their new homes with equal intensity as did Olivieri's Italians.

The same language cropped up in a letter from the commander of the Valiant Legion to the minister of war. The commander argued that since the "fatherland was no longer in danger and the laws had triumphed, and that liberty was a reality," there was no need for the Valiant Legion. Most of the men, the commander wrote, "only left their jobs to defend the institutions of the country."⁶⁹ In this case, the commander used both "patria" and "país," which also means country. Like Olivieri, he saw Buenos Aires as something more than an autonomous state, something closer to a nation or a country.

Olivieri and others considered Buenos Aires a nation and a beacon of liberty. José Jauregui observed that he was "animated by the good desire to be useful to this fatherland that I have adopted as my own, and to cooperate by whatever means may be possible in favor of the sacred cause of civilization and liberty."⁷⁰ Like Olivieri, Jauregui used "patria" to refer to Buenos Aires, which, at this point, had barely begun an autonomous existence! Like the Italian Olivieri, the Spaniard Jauregui conceptualized Buenos Aires as his country. In addition, Jauregui also spoke of a sacred cause of civilization and liberty, words often employed to describe these conflicts. Olivieri, as well, asserted that his soldiers were "dedicated to defending the most Sacro-Sanct principles" and, several weeks later, that his soldiers were "more than compensated with the glory of having cooperated in the salvation of the liberty of this their second fatherland."⁷¹ At one point Olivieri complained to Paz about mistreatment of Italians in Buenos Aires. "The efforts that the Italians make and have previously made under the orders of your servant, to be useful in some way to the good cause in the Rio de la Plata," Olivieri noted, should protect them from discrimination.⁷² His Italian Legion might be composed of immigrant soldiers, but they were no less committed, and perhaps even more so, to the success of the good cause than many Porteños. The efforts of Buenos Aires to resist the Argentine Confederation, whether enunciated by Olivieri, Jauregui, or Sarmiento, fit neatly into the narrative of interconnected struggles to preserve liberty and republicanism.⁷³ Indeed, as with many other transnational warriors, the Italians who fought for Buenos Aires were no mere mercenaries or adventurers, but people who were genuinely committed to fighting for republicanism and the defense of their new home.

Recruiting Garibaldi

As the war between Buenos Aires and the Argentine Confederation moved toward a conclusion, Garibaldi continued to fascinate many people in the United States. In a campaign speech in 1860, Republican US Senator Henry Wilson of Massachusetts observed that the "long down trodden people of Italy were following the brave Garibaldi" to "recover their rights," and his audience responded with cheers.[74] During the months leading up to the US Civil War, Lincoln's correspondents invoked Garibaldi in numerous ways. David Chambers, for example, commented that "the praise of the modest soldier Garibaldi the Liberator of enslaved Italy, is in the mouths of the lovers of Liberty in every land"[75] Joseph Blanchard, on the other hand, warned Lincoln that "the People of the North & West are losing confidence in the stamini [sic] of our government and they are begining [sic] to look around for a Garibaldi or a John Brown to organize the hosts of freedom and lead them on to victory or death."[76] The notion that a Garibaldi would take the fortunes of the Union in hand and save the day also appeared in modified form in the Southern states of the United States. Many white southerners assumed, given the battles Garibaldi had waged throughout his long career as a transnational warrior, that he would naturally side with them. His decision to support the United States angered many of his former admirers in the Southern states and caused them to reevaluate his image.[77]

Given the intense interest in Garibaldi, not to mention the power of his fame and accomplishments, US diplomats made a concerted effort to recruit Garibaldi, the preeminent transnational warrior, to lead a US army. As Don H. Doyle noted, "to have Garibaldi take command of a Union army would have been a brilliant public diplomacy coup."[78] Despite the fact that Garibaldi himself played a role in floating these rumors, he never commanded a Union army, although he was on the US payroll and many Garibaldinos served in the US armed forces. In addition, Garibaldi's support of Lincoln proved important, particularly when he lavished praise on Lincoln after the Preliminary Emancipation Proclamation. Garibaldi lauded Lincoln as "heir of the thought of Christ and of Brown" and assured Lincoln he would "pass down to posterity under the name of *the Emancipator,*! more enviable than any crown and any human treasure."[79] When British abolitionist Edward Yates wrote Lincoln "we have very many more Republicans this side the water than you have any idea of," he cited the reception accorded Garibaldi. "No Emperor in the World would have been received with a millionth part the enthusiasm," Yates enthused, and "what is Garibaldi except the Symbol of Republicanism."[80] These examples illustrate Garibaldi's geographic mobility and cosmopolitanism and how, for many people, he had become a living embodiment of republicanism.[81] The rhetorical support of the world's preeminent transnational warrior proved a boon to the United States.[82]

Transnational Warriors and the US Civil War

Garibaldi admired the Union's cause, but he never took up arms to vindicate it. Edelmiro Mayer, however, did.[83] In January 1863, Reverend William Goodfellow of Buenos Aires wrote Lincoln that "Major E. Mayer goes from the Argentine National Army to offer himself to the cause of the Union."[84] Mayer, Goodfellow observed, "has the most flattering testimonials from some of the best men and ablest officers of this country testifying to his many public, private and professional virtues. He speaks fluently English and German and he has won distinction on the bloodiest fields of South America. No son of the forest is more at home on horseback than he and he has the endurance of an Arab." Goodfellow urged Lincoln to assign Mayer a place "on the staff of one of our Generals" as it would "fill his ambition . . . and such an honor would not only be worthily bestowed, but it would be gratefully appreciated by this Republic."[85] Mayer received a commission as a major in the Forty-Fifth Regiment of United States Colored Troops (USCT). Interestingly, Mayer was not the only foreign soldier to gain a commission as a USCT officer.[86] The US government may have assumed that foreigners had more liberal attitudes toward USCT soldiers or, especially for individuals of color from abroad, government officials may have wished to avoid angering white soldiers by placing them under the command of foreign officers.

By all accounts, Mayer acquitted himself well in battle and was popular with his soldiers. Oscar W. Norton wrote to his sister that "the greatest excitement here is caused by the advent of new regimental commander, Major Edelmiro Mayer. He is a South American and has been ten years in the army in foreign countries. He speaks several languages . . . and with his inexhaustible fund of anecdotes and his quaint remarks keeps everybody in the best possible humor." Mayer, Norton concluded, "got right down to the bottom of things and our regiment is going to improve under his direction."[87] After Lee's surrender, General Ulysses S. Grant sent General Philip Sheridan to the US-Mexico border with fifty thousand soldiers, many of them USCT regiments, to intimidate the French and aid the Mexican Liberals. As the following chapter illustrates, Sheridan and his soldiers aided the Liberals by depositing arms across the border and volunteering to fight alongside them. Mayer crossed the border on several occasions and, taking advantage of his ability to speak German, harangued Maximilian's Austrian soldiers and encouraged them to desert.[88]

In his 1866 biography of Abraham Lincoln, Sarmiento asserted that Mayer's letter to Lincoln about the efficacy of Black soldiers in South America had a profound influence on Lincoln.[89] This was an overstatement. However, Mayer indisputably authored two letters about Black troops, written in English, and published in *Harper's Weekly*. After comparing those who denied the ability of African Americans to be good soldiers to the Spaniards who doubted the humanity of the Amerindians, Mayer stated, quite bluntly, that Black soldiers do "not lack any of the qualities of a soldier; and this opinion of mine is founded upon severe tests of their worth, seen and known by me in a long experience with them in the wars of the Argentine Republic."[90] Not only did Mayer serve the cause of liberty with the sword, by leading men into battle, he also served it with his pen.

Mayer argued for African American soldiers because he firmly believed Black soldiers had proven their valor during the South American Wars of Independence. "The army of the Argentine Republic," Mayer asserted, "aided in giving liberty to five other republics (Peru, Bolivia, Chili, Paraguay, and Uruguay), and in that army were many battalions of negroes. The Spanish armies, which had just come from combating the legions of Napoleon the Great, know very well of what metal those negroes are made, for the Spaniards were defeated by them in many battles."[91] Finally, Black soldiers always fought for the side of liberty. "In the long and cruel civil war of the Argentine Republic, in which two opposite elements wrestled—civilization and barbarity—the negroes were always on the side of the civilized party, and they have always been sublimely faithful to it. Never were the leaders of the barbarian party able to persuade these negroes to serve them."[92] It is difficult to measure the influence of Mayer's article, but it offered additional firepower to opponents of slavery. Mayer crafted a striking argument for the use of Black troops by drawing on Argentine experiences and by insisting on the similarities between the two countries. An immigrant soldier himself, Mayer fought throughout the Americas for the same great principle and offered Argentina's experiences as a guide for the United States.

Mayer kept himself busy, first fighting for Argentina, then the United States, and then Mexico.[93] This led one newspaper to comment that his disposition and military capacity "enabled him to find employment in the cause of republicanism here and in Mexico."[94] Other Latin Americans also wore the blue and fought for republicanism. Colonel Federico Fernández Cavada and his brother Captain Adolfo Fernández Cavada, both of Cuba, joined the Twenty-Third Pennsylvania Infantry Regiment.[95] Adolfo served with distinction and kept a vivid diary of his experiences.[96] Federico also served with distinction, became an officer in the 114th Pennsylvania Infantry Regiment, and authored a narrative of his experience in Libby Prison.[97] Spaniard Carlos Alvarez de la Mesa immigrated to the United States specifically to fight with the US Army. On July 20, 1861, de la Mesa wrote his wife that "I really enjoy being a part of my regiment. Because I am European, I am happy to be a member of a regiment that bears the name of Garibaldi, the hero of liberty in Italy."[98] De la Mesa joined the Thirty-Ninth New York, the Garibaldi Guard, and gloried in fighting for a cause similar to the one the hero of liberty fought for in Uruguay and Italy.

White Southern rebels delighted in deriding immigrant soldiers and transnational warriors. The Garibaldi Guard, one newspaper sneered, were nothing but "desperate adventurers."[99] Phrases like "scum of Europe" and "dregs of Europe" occurred frequently among the rebels. They also charged immigrant soldiers and transnational warriors with being mercenaries, especially in the case of Germans, and compared them to the Hessian soldiers who fought for the British during the US War of Independence. Furthermore, they wondered, how could European separatists fight for the United States rather than the rebels? Were they not colossal hypocrites?

The words of the immigrant soldiers and transnational warriors refute these calumnies. Many of them, although certainly not all, freighted the conflict in the United States with tremendous significance. Alexander Asbóth, a Hungarian who fought in the Revolutions of 1848 and then immigrated to the United States, published an appeal to his fellow Hungarians in the *New York Times* on May 3, 1861, to enlist in the US Army. We see, Asbóth told his fellow Hungarians, "the glorious Republic of the United States, our adopted Country, upon the verge of dissolution, the realization of which would be a triumph for all despots and the doom of self-government."[100] He fervently urged his fellow Hungarians to volunteer their military services to the United States as he had. One of Asbóth's fellow Hungarians, Charles Zagonyi, infuriated by charges that he fought as a mercenary, tartly replied, "I took service in the United States army only for the reason that I wanted to see this great country united again and put down the rebellion, and not to divide it more and more. I am not a fortune hunter."[101] Indeed, transnational warriors like Asbóth and Zagonyi were not fortune hunters, mercenaries, or adventurers but people who, like Mayer and others, fought for ideological reasons.

Other soldiers echoed this language. The Irish, one scholar commented, "saw their struggle as part of a larger international conflict."[102] Peter Welsh, an Irish immigrant, said as much when he asserted that "America is Irlands refuge Irlands last hope"[103] Germans also subscribed to this language. Adolph Frick commented, "I haven't been able to send anything recently because since the beginning of this perfidious revolution against the best government in the world, business has been very bad."[104] A month later, Captain August Horstmann informed his parents that "even if I should die in the fight for freedom & the preservation of the Union of this, my adopted homeland, then you should not be too concerned." Like Germany, Horstmann contended, "the free and industrious people of the North are fighting against the lazy and haughty Junker spirit of the South. But down with the aristocracy who are lacking only in titles."[105] These men were not soldiers of fortune at all; they were soldiers of freedom who clearly understood how the US Civil War fit into a larger struggle and sought to do their part to protect the tree of liberty. This is a small sample of such language from "soldiers of conviction."[106] Furthermore, many Forty-Eighters understood that they had a chance to refight a revolution they had lost and, this time, win.

Just as Pickett did during the 1850s, some transnational warriors fought for a decidedly illiberal cause—in support of the rebels during the US Civil War. Why would transnational warriors fight for a cause that was, in the words of Ulysses S. Grant, "one of the worst for which a people ever fought, and one for which there was the least excuse"?[107] The answers varied from person to person. Polish Democratic societies in Europe, for example, "questioned how [Kacper] Tochman could be in such gross violation of their constitutional principles and support the Confederacy." Tochman, in turn, "claimed that, as a citizen of Virginia, he had not violated any laws. He embraced the states' rights identity so dear to many southerners."[108] Cubans Ambrosio José Gonzales and Enrique B. D'Hamel both fought for the rebels likely due to personal circumstances. Gonzales married into a prominent Southern family and thus belonged to the Southern elite. In addition, he was an old filibuster who possibly recruited Pickett, O'Hara, and Hawkins to the Narciso López expedition.[109] D'Hamel, on the other hand, seemed mesmerized by powerful expressions of white Southern nationalism.[110] Tejano Santos Benavides supported the Confederacy because, like Tochman, he sympathized with the states' rights language utilized by fire-eaters.[111] Confederate rhetoric about resisting a powerful federal government helmed by Republican radicals and about fighting for one version of freedom, the freedom to hold other people in bondage, resonated with Benavides and others. Both sides again claimed to fight for freedom, although it is quite obvious that they had radically different definitions of this important concept.

Francis P. Blair, Garibaldi, and Mexico

In January 1865, Francis Preston Blair Sr., an old Jacksonian, secured permission from Lincoln to travel to Richmond to speak with Jefferson Davis about peace. Blair fretted about the French presence in Mexico and raised the topic, among other points, in his conversation with Davis. Blair argued Davis could drive Maximilian from the Cactus Throne and, by so doing, restore the position of the Southern states in the Union. Transfer portions of your army to Texas, Blair advised, equip them, send them to Mexico, and Juárez and the Liberals will give you aid and assistance. Blair believed he and his son Montgomery could persuade Matías Romero to "induce Juarez to devote all the power he can command on President Davis—a dictatorship if necessary—to restore the rights of Mexico & her people and provide for the stability of its government."[112]

In his mind, Blair's proposal to Jefferson Davis accomplished several ends. For one, it took care of the Confederacy. Davis and his fellow secessionists could be welcomed back into the loving embrace of the Union. Then the reunited United States could vindicate the Monroe Doctrine by driving the French and Austrians out of Mexico. As an added bonus, Liberal sanction of this plan would avoid a repeat of the US War with Mexico. Finally, the icing on the cake, Davis could become both the savior and the dictator of Mexico and could make Mexico a haven for southerners irritated about living cheek to jowl with Yankees. Indeed, Mexico under Davis might become a safety valve to bleed off unhappy fire-eaters. Gather your armies in Texas, Blair whispered into Davis's ear, strike a blow deep into the vitals of the Austrian pretender, humiliate the French, and reap your reward. It is utterly inconceivable to envision Juárez approving this idea.[113] That Blair entertained it demonstrates the bizarre schemes people concocted about ways to end the war.[114] Blair clearly thought this an excellent idea and wrote to Lincoln, "Davis I am convinced desires to make common cause with us for Republicanism on this continent."[115] Davis did not concur with this assessment.

Blair's efforts led to the Hampton Road Conference, where rebel commissioners met with Lincoln and Seward.[116] One of the commissioners, rebel Vice President Alexander H. Stephens, expressed a great deal of interest in Blair's plan about an invasion of Mexico and "began waxing patriotic about the 'sacred' principles of the Monroe Doctrine."[117] Stephens wanted to see a joint invasion of Mexico, by both United States and rebel forces, to expel the French, after which both sides could come to a settlement. Lincoln quashed the idea, and the conference did not result in peace. Nevertheless, it is interesting that Stephens seized on the idea of a Mexican expedition at the same time that, as we will see in the following chapter, many people were beginning to raise recruits to fight in Mexico alongside the Liberals to expel the French and Austrians.

Several weeks later, Blair performed an amazing about-face. Writing to Lincoln about nominees for secretary of the Treasury, his letter took an odd turn. One of his relatives acted as a US agent for Garibaldi. This relative suggested that "if France made any movements against us in our present conflict justifying a war against the usurpation of the Emperor in Mexico, it should be judicious in you to contenance [sic] Garibaldi as a General in Mexico to assist in restoring its Republic." Because of Garibaldi's association "with all the Liberals of Europe, if he triumphed on our continent, like the French Generals of our revolution, he might put the Ball in motion again in France."[118] Blair's idea about Davis and a Confederate army cleaning out the French vanished. Now he believed Garibaldi could be the man of the hour. Juárez would certainly have fiercely opposed thousands of rebels moving across the border or giving Jefferson Davis dictatorial powers (as Blair first recommended). He might, however, have approved tendering Garibaldi command of the Mexican armies. As a friend of liberty and a foe of the Catholic Church, Garibaldi looked very much like a Mexican Liberal.[119] Although this idea came to naught, it spoke to Garibaldi's stature and prestige and the interconnected nature of these conflicts. Blair also hoped a Garibaldi victory in Mexico would topple France's Second Empire.[120] Garibaldi did not fight in Mexico, just as he did not fight in the US Civil War, but his importance as a transnational warrior made the idea of him as a recruit resonate nonetheless.

Confederates and Mexico

As the US Civil War drew closer and closer to an end, some rebels began to make noise about leaving the United States and heading to Mexico.[121] Some professed a desire to fight for Maximilian and the Imperialists against Benito Juárez and the Liberals. Mary Elizabeth Mitchell, for instance, wrote in her journal that her cousin, Jeff Bradford, "with my brother and several other of our relatives who are in his battalion of Scouts expect to cross the Mississippi when this Department is given up and join the Trans Mississippi department. If that also is surrendered, he will go into Mexico and offer his services to Maximilien [*sic*]." Mitchell hoped "it will not be necessary for him to leave the Confederacy, for I feel sure this is not the end of the war."[122] Sterling Price, Jo Shelby, Matthew Fontaine Maury, to name a few, all fled to Mexico and sought shelter with Emperor Maximilian, first securing land for a colony and later attempting to enlist under his banner.[123] Maximilian's decision to allow rebels who emigrated to Mexico to bring their slaves with them horrified many observers. Mexico abolished slavery in 1837, and Maximilian's decision to permit slavery's return appeared even starker once the United States ratified the Thirteenth Amendment.[124]

Other Confederates claimed to sympathize with the Liberals, not Maximilian. In a letter to US General Gordon Granger, written several months after Lee's surrender at Appomattox, rebel General J. E. Harrison assured Granger that the disbanding of the rebel forces in Texas was not "for the purpose of going into Mexico to join Maximilian." Discussions about leaving the United States for Mexico were a product, not a cause, of rebel disbandment. Some officers, he conceded, "believing they would be harshly dealt with by the US Government and that their only personal security was refuge in a foreign country, were disposed to go to Mexico and take commands of troops with them. But to my best knowledge and belief the subject never assumed any definite shape." Given how many rebels joined Maximilian, Harrison asserted, preposterously, "not only was there no general purpose to join Maximilian, but the more common feeling was in behalf of the Liberal cause." Harrison even noted that had the US authorities given it their blessing, "the movement might have been a serious one, and its entire direction given in favor of the Liberal party in Mexico." "No Texas organization," he concluded, "has crossed or is expected to cross the Rio Grande; and so far as my information extends, the few adventurous individuals who do cross the river and had any previous connection with our army are likely to be found sympathizing with the Liberals."[125]

Harrison overlooked, either accidentally or deliberately, the hundreds of former Confederates under Jo Shelby who crossed the Rio Grande to join Maximilian.[126] He also overlooked high-profile rebels like Isham Harris of Tennessee and Henry Watkins Allen of Louisiana, and Generals Edmund Kirby Smith and John B. Magruder, who did the same. More importantly, his denial that Confederates wanted anything to do with Maximilian flew in the face of what former rebels actually did in Mexico. It also minimized the tendency among rebels to sympathize with and aid Conservatives and Imperialists, especially when Maximilian revealed that he did not oppose rebels bringing slaves with them to Mexico. Thomas Alexander Hamilton demonstrated this tendency when he informed his friend Hamilton Yancey that the subject of an upcoming public debate was "will the occupation of Mexico by [Maximilian] be beneficial to the world or not." In other words, continued Hamilton, "will it be more beneficial to the human race to have a monarchical or republican form of government in Mexico." Hamilton explained to Yancey that he intended to argue for monarchy.[127] Granted, Hamilton did not make plans to leave the United States for Mexico. Nor did his commitment to monarchy impel him to take up arms for the Austrian pretender. However, his sentiments rebuke Harrison's claim. Here is another case where transnational warriors took up arms in pursuit of an illiberal cause (although, ironically, Maximilian fancied himself a liberal). Lincoln and the liberal transnational warriors were quite correct in their framing about rebels embracing aristocracy and monarchy. The struggle in Mexico involved the same great principles as the war that took place in the United States. However, as we will see in the following chapter, thousands of other transnational warriors flooded the borderlands to help the Liberals, and they more than countered the rebels who fled to Mexico.

Some rebels clearly went to Mexico to fight for monarchy, specifically Emperor Maximilian, and likely agreed with Hamilton. Others may have journeyed there because they agreed with General Ulysses S. Grant's assertion that the US Civil War would not end until the French left Mexico.[128] Because the wars were so intimately linked, many people believed fighting for Maximilian would prolong the US Civil War and continue the fight against Yankees. It might even mean, if Confederate assistance helped the Austrian pretender triumph, they could secure an ally who would help them fight the United States.

Joining with Maximilian, therefore, could destabilize the Liberals and the Yankees and, perhaps, secure victory against a weary Union and roll back Reconstruction.[129] In this vision, rebels could ally with a European monarch and the borrowed soldiers of a French emperor, keep their slaves, and still fight for their particular vision of freedom. In sum, many transnational warriors fought for liberal causes. A smaller group claimed they were fighting for freedom (at least in their eyes) but nonetheless fought for illiberal causes. In other words, freedom fighters put their lives on the line for republicanism and democracy throughout the hemisphere, but other people, who often saw a benefit in arguing that they fought for freedom, preferred to seek out and join reactionary causes. The journeys of rebels to Mexico as well as people who fought for the United States in 1861–65 provided additional evidence that Mexico became another arena to continue the larger struggle that also took place during the US Civil War.

Conclusion: "The Last Best, Hope of Earth"

Abraham Lincoln's 1862 Annual Message to Congress included some of his best prose, particularly his powerful summation of the task facing the Union and the importance of the US Civil War:

> Fellow-citizens, *we* cannot escape history. We of this Congress and this administration, will be remembered in spite of ourselves. No personal significance, or insignificance, can spare one or another of us. The fiery trial through which we pass, will light us down, in honor or dishonor, to the latest generation. We *say* we are for the Union. The world will not forget that we say this. We know how to save the Union. The world knows we do know how to save it. We— even *we here*—hold the power, and bear the responsibility. In *giving* freedom to the *slave,* we *assure* freedom to the *free*—honorable alike in what we give, and what we preserve. We shall nobly save, or meanly lose, the last best, hope of earth.[130]

Lincoln was indisputably correct that millions of people, both in the United States and abroad, including Sarmiento and Mayer, believed a Union victory to be absolutely critical to vindicating republicanism and democracy. Dietrich Gerstein, a German immigrant soldier, also concurred: "If this republic is actually lost, mankind's struggle for freedom will be pointless for years to come, since the moral defeat of the entire liberal party will be so severe that it will be unable to rise again any time soon."[131] In sum, if the United States could not weather such a severe internal crisis, it would provide additional ammunition to every monarch, aristocrat, and oligarch who sneered that republics were, at best, unstable aberrations doomed to failure.

That said, was the US Civil War *the* "last best hope of earth"? Without doubt, it was a tremendously important conflict. However, it is also important to remember that some contemporaries saw the individual conflicts surveyed in this chapter as interlinked or as part of a larger struggle. Even if some people did not make this connection, each war or each revolution nevertheless became another arena in which to vindicate democracy and republicanism against the forces of reaction. People throughout the Atlantic World shared common dreams and similar aspirations. They drew inspiration from the same ideologies. In other words, one can readily agree with Lincoln that the US Civil War involved paramount questions of epic importance but also agree that the other conflicts covered throughout this book involved the same questions. Transnational warriors, in their determination to fight for specific causes in specific places, testify to how people viewed these conflicts and, more importantly, how cooperation and connection could and did present important alternatives to prejudice, isolationism, and coercion.

The struggle of the rebels in the United States had some superficial similarities with that of Buenos Aires against the Argentine Confederation or that of Hungary during the Revolutions of 1848. Edelmiro Mayer and Hugo Hillebrandt could have chosen to support the Confederacy. However, they had no desire to throw in with a gang of slaveholding oligarchs. Both saw in the United States what Hillebrandt saw in Garibaldi's march on Rome and what Mayer saw in the French Intervention: grander and more glorious causes. Mayer and Hillebrandt, not to mention many other transnational warriors, fought for the liberty of African slaves during the US Civil War and, more broadly, in this and other conflicts, for liberty, democracy, and republicanism. Mayer, Hillebrandt, Olivieri, Asbóth, and others made deliberate and considered choices about fighting for freedom for liberal causes and revealed that their true motivations were ideological, not about glory or gold. But even transnational warriors who lent their swords to reactionary and illiberal causes—Shelby, Magruder, Benavides, and Pickett, for example—also claimed to fight for freedom. Their assertions no doubt strike modern observers as risible, but they force us to think about the many different conceptions of freedom and how people ascribed their actions to similar motivations. They also illustrate how people saw individual conflicts as parts of a larger struggle and how each became another arena in which democracy and republicanism faced off against the forces of reaction. Transnational warriors, soldiers of freedom, not fortune, pursued cooperation and circulated throughout the Atlantic World in their efforts to vindicate democracy and republicanism.

As the US Civil War concluded, both US and non-US actors turned their eyes to the French Intervention in Mexico. After the fall of Richmond, Jefferson Davis led the rebel government into exile and aimed for Mexico, a possible safe haven, especially under the auspices of Emperor Maximilian, where he might regroup in order to continue and prolong the US Civil War. Rebels contemplated crossing or actually did cross the US-Mexico border. Many US soldiers longed to go home in the spring and summer of 1865, but others also turned their sights south.[132] US military men and government officials began to work out policies that would guide their actions toward the French Intervention. Transnational warriors moved to a new conflict in a new arena where they saw another chance to fight for republicanism and democracy against Emperor Maximilian—Emperor Napoleon III of France's cat's paw—and Maximilian's Mexican collaborators. Mexican Conservatives and Imperialists continued to fight to suppress the dogged resistance of the Mexican Liberals, who, in turn, doubled down on their opposition to France and Austria and, simultaneously, made overtures to the United States and adeptly invoked the language of sister republics, not to mention the Monroe Doctrine, to encourage the United States to get involved. All these actors and forces converged on Mexico in 1865, the newest arena in a much larger struggle that would again pit republicanism and democracy against monarchy in another epic contest.

2

Sister Republics and the Monroe Doctrine

Our sister republic of Mexico must be relieved from foreign domination.
—JOHN M. SCHOFIELD, *Forty-Six Years in the Army*

President Benito Juárez of Mexico, Minister of Foreign Affairs Melchor Ocampo, and Mexican chargé d'affaires Matías Romero crafted a strategy during the winter of 1860–61 to reorient the US/Mexico relationship. Juárez, Ocampo, and Romero hoped Abraham Lincoln's election as president of the United States would usher in a new era in US-Mexican relations, in contrast to the tensions engendered between the United States and Mexico by the unjust war waged by Democratic President James K. Polk and the aggressive expansionist rhetoric of Democratic Presidents Franklin Pierce and James Buchanan.[1] Ocampo instructed Romero that Juárez wanted him to visit Lincoln in Springfield during the Secession Winter and express Juárez's urgent desire to maintain friendly relations with the United States. Tell Lincoln, Ocampo commanded, that "the policy of the Constitutional Government of Mexico is founded upon de [sic] principles of liberty, progress and justice, which principles the United States have follow [sic] hetherto [sic]," that Mexicans were firmly antislavery, and that "President Juarez will be very glad if this similarity of principles and policy with the principles and policy of Mr. Lincoln may consolidate more and more every day, the friendship of both countries."[2] Romero visited Lincoln and concluded that "my trip to Springfield was, I believe, very opportune, and I expect it was very profitable for Mexican interests."[3] Juárez, Ocampo, and Romero deftly emphasized the similarities between the two countries and between Republicans in the United States and Liberals in Mexico. This language anticipated arguments made during the US Civil War and French Intervention that the "sister republics" fought simultaneous wars that were part of a much larger struggle. By utilizing words like "liberty" and "progress," Mexicans linked themselves to the United States, as well as a larger international struggle.[4]

The seeds planted at the Lincoln/Romero meeting flowered. Case in point, more than five years later, on June 12, 1865, Edward Conner, the US consul at Guaymas, complained to Secretary of State William H. Seward about US citizens crossing the US-Mexico border to fight with the Mexican Liberals. "We have scores of worthless fellows," Conner snarled, "deserters from Whalers, deserters from our Army and fugitives from California, who are noisy and boisterous in their declarations of friendship for the Mexicans and their opposition to the French." Many of these people, Conner complained, "took service with the Mexicans some months since and were most prominent in their denunciations of the French." The "uncalled-for and senseless ajitation [sic] of the Monroe doctrine on the part of a few here, was rapidly creating prejudices and feelings of suspicion in the Minds of the French Officers." Conner also deplored the fact that "the ajitation [sic] of the [Monroe] doctrine became a sort of pastime with some, and a passion with others."[5] At a time when it seemed like the US Civil War had ended and many US veterans sought to return home, other people, both veterans and nonveterans, turned their sights south and saw in Mexico another case of republicanism under siege, in this case by French Emperor Napoleon III and Emperor Maximilian, his Austrian cat's paw. Many determined to do something about it, a sentiment Mexicans heartily encouraged.

Conner's complaints about US citizens agitating the Monroe Doctrine likely resonated with Seward. After all, Seward worked assiduously to keep the United States out of a war with France. The streams of people moving across the border to aid the Liberals threatened to pull the United States into the very war that Seward and others sought to avoid. That said, Conner's lament also testified to the surge of people who went to Mexico. Conner clearly considered many of them worthless trash, but plenty of his contemporaries favored some form of US intervention in Mexico. They saw the conflicts as interwoven, used the same language to make sense of the world, and, despite some disagreement about methods, forged a new anti-imperial interpretation of the Monroe Doctrine and reinvigorated the language of sister republics. Transnational warriors played an important role in Mexico during the French Intervention.

Mexicans adeptly invoked the language of sister republics and the Monroe Doctrine to prod and cajole the United States to act. Officials within the US government, both civilian and military, debated the proper role that the government should take toward the French and, although advocating different methods, arrived at a similar conclusion—the French had to go, and the Monroe Doctrine had to be vindicated. The struggle in Mexico, which pitted citizens from two sister republics against French and Austrian soldiers and Mexican Conservatives, became a moment of profound Pan-American cooperation in which US citizens and Mexican Liberals both redefined and vindicated the Monroe Doctrine. Working together, they taught the world an important lesson: the Mexican republic led by Benito Juárez was far stronger than Napoleon III, Maximilian, and their myrmidons. Monarchy, save in Brazil, was unwelcome in the Americas; republics and democracies were the only forms of government suited to free peoples.

Andrew Johnson's Dilemma

Nobody ever looked at Andrew Johnson and thought about the meek inheriting the earth. In a June 10, 1864, speech in Nashville, in which he accepted the vice-presidential nomination of the Union Party, Johnson blasted the "exclusive aristocracy about Nashville," declared fire-eaters had killed slavery, proclaimed his belief in emancipation even as he urged African Americans to work rather than be idle, and asserted "treason must be made odious and traitors must be punished and impoverished."[6] As military governor of Tennessee, it made perfect sense for Johnson to discuss the death of slavery and punishment for traitors.

Strikingly, Johnson did not confine himself to domestic issues. European nations, he growled, conspired to destroy the United States. While Johnson painted with overly broad strokes—certainly not all Europeans wanted to see the United States ripped apart—he accurately captured Emperor Napoleon III's position.[7] Johnson deplored the French attempt to install Archduke Ferdinand Maximilian of Austria as Emperor Maximilian of Mexico. "The time is not far distant," he vowed, "when the rebellion will be put down, and then we will attend to this Mexican affair, and say to Louis Napoleon, 'You can set up no monarchy on this continent."[8] A US expedition into Mexico "would be a sort of recreation to the brave soldiers who are now fighting the battles of the Union, and the French concern would be quickly wiped out."[9] Johnson's assertion that the United States would clean up the mess in Mexico had more than a tinge of racial superiority, but his gaze, like many of his contemporaries, was hemispheric. He understood the need to vindicate the Monroe Doctrine and drive the French out of Mexico.[10]

Like Andrew Jackson, his political idol, Johnson had little tolerance for European meddling in the New World.[11] However, once a bullet placed him in the presidential chair, he seemingly forgot about Mexico in favor of designing his (lenient) program of reconstruction.[12] Johnson, one biographer asserted, deferred to Secretary of State William Henry Seward on foreign policy: "Willing to yield to Seward's pleas for a patient course of watchful waiting to force the French to withdraw—in the fall of 1865 he had even sent General John M. Schofield on a mission to Paris to defuse the situation—Johnson drew upon himself the ire of more bellicose Republicans who wanted the French intruders expelled at once."[13] "Watchful waiting" is an ambiguous phrase that does not really capture Seward's approach to Mexico. Insofar as it meant the United States wanted to avoid war with France, that was indeed Seward's operating principle, not to mention that of some of his contemporaries. Neither General William S. Rosecrans nor Speaker of the US House of Representatives Schuyler Colfax, for instance, favored war with France in 1865.[14] However, this phrase tends to render Seward overly passive, especially in comparison with men like Ulysses S. Grant and Philip H. Sheridan.

As secretary of state, many contemporaries saw Seward as the evil genius behind US refusal to intervene in Mexico to fight the French (not to mention whatever other policies of the Johnson administration they opposed). Francis Preston Blair Sr., several months after his communication to Jefferson Davis about going to Mexico and his advice to Lincoln to recruit Garibaldi, also sent Johnson unsolicited advice. Blair huffed that Mexican affairs would not change "so long as France & her Puppet have a steadfast friend in the Secretary of State, whose appointee and instrument is still retained in the War Department. So long as they are retained the country may be pardoned for distrusting your disposition to maintain the inviolability of our continent from the invasion of European powers."[15] Contemporaries were often unsure what to make of Johnson's Mexican policy. Horace Maynard, for example, observed to Johnson that "Mr. Blair's late speech at Hagerstown has been published here [Cincinnati], & it is thought by some to be a reflex of your views on the Mexican Question."[16] The Mr. Blair in this case was Francis P. Blair's son Montgomery (Lincoln's former postmaster general), who attacked "American spinelessness" and argued that United States should do more to aid Mexico to expel the French.[17] Matías Romero informed the Mexican minister of foreign affairs that Johnson "has not wanted to precipitate action on the Mexican question, Rather, he has preferred to settle Reconstruction first, leaving the initiative in United States policy regarding Mexican affairs to Congress."[18] Presidents and their cabinets often like to keep their options open to preserve different courses of action. Consequently, perhaps it is not entirely surprising that Johnson's contemporaries did not see a consistent policy toward Mexico.

That said, the picture of an inattentive Johnson and a Seward engaged in "watchful waiting" misses some important elements. For one, Johnson did little to curtail the flow of US arms, munitions, and soldiers into Mexico and thus became complicit in widespread violations of US neutrality favored by men like Grant, Sheridan, and Romero. In addition, Seward's policy was more complex, evolved over time, and featured both hard power and soft power elements. Finally, and perhaps most importantly, although somewhat counterintuitively, Seward was not the only man directing US foreign policy. He faced challenges from the center and the periphery, from elite and nonelite actors, from men as eminent as Ulysses S. Grant to nameless veterans who crossed the US-Mexico border to fight with the Liberals, and from recruiting movements, public rallies, and angry editorials calling for armed intervention in Mexico. Many people (both military and nonmilitary) agitated for a war with France to vindicate the Monroe Doctrine and help a sister republic. Seward had to counter the cries for war—he and Johnson did not want to begin a war with France—without losing sight of the fact that the people crying for war shared his ultimate objective, namely, getting the French out of Mexico.[19] Mexicans, in turn, adeptly played on prevailing sentiments. They urged the United States not to fail to aid a sister republic and to vindicate the Monroe Doctrine. The story of US foreign policy toward Mexico from 1865 through 1867 involved a vast array of people. Grant and Seward disagreed, at times, over methods and appropriate courses of action, but both were committed to the same ends, namely, forcing the French to withdraw and helping the Liberals reclaim Mexico from an Austrian pretender and his Mexican collaborators.[20]

The rapprochement between the United States and Mexico, which began in earnest during the Secession Winter under the careful stewardship of Romero, Ocampo, and Juárez, accelerated and became even more pronounced during this period. Grant, Romero, Philip H. Sheridan, and Edward Lee Plumb, among others, reinvigorated an older way of understanding the two nations when they spoke of the United States and Mexico as "sister republics."[21] For example, Plumb, a friend of Romero, a proponent of US aid to Mexico, a railroad promoter, and a diplomatic officer, lobbied members of Congress to take action.[22] "Is it not now time," he badgered Senator Charles Sumner of Massachusetts, that Congress should "by formal resolution let it be known to the world that the people of the United States have not abandoned the Monroe Doctrine, that they do not and cannot look with favor or with indiference [sic] on the attempt of a European Power to overthrow Republican institutions and to introduce an European form of Government into their neighbor and sister Republic."[23] Just as the transnational warriors surveyed in the previous chapter saw the conflicts they fought in as either connected or part of a larger struggle, so too did Plumb and many others during this period see the US Civil War and the French Intervention as part and parcel of a much larger conflict. This, in turn, fed a powerful argument that both countries should aid the other. Grant, Romero, Sheridan, Plumb, and others truly believed the sister republics fought similar battles—the US Civil War and the French Intervention—and that the fate of one rested on the other. The cooperation that flourished during this period encompassed much more than simply creating economic bonds. Proponents of assistance emphasized the need to vindicate the Monroe Doctrine. In other words, many people, both well-known and forgotten, played a role in determining US foreign policy.

Ulysses S. Grant Looks South

General Ulysses S. Grant made no secret of his desire to expel the French from Mexico. In late May 1865, he drew up orders sending General Philip Sheridan and fifty thousand soldiers to the US-Mexico border. Sheridan's official objective was to restore Texas and Louisiana to the Union as quickly as possible, while compelling the surrender of rebel General Edmund Kirby Smith and his soldiers. However, Grant observed, "I think the Rio Grande should be strongly held, whether the forces in Texas surrender or not, and that no time should be lost in getting troops there."[24] On the off chance that Sheridan missed what the order implied, Grant personally told Sheridan that "he looked upon the invasion of Mexico by Maximilian as a part of the rebellion itself, because of the encouragement that invasion had received from the Confederacy, and that our success in putting down secession would never be complete until the French and Austrian invaders were compelled to quit the territory of our sister republic."[25] Critically, Grant cautioned Sheridan to "act with great circumspection" because Seward "was much opposed to the use of our troops along the border in any active way that would be likely to involve us in a war with European powers."[26] Grant moving Sheridan to the US-Mexico borderlands represented a very strong warning to Maximilian. Sheridan, in turn, relished his chance to menace the French and their Mexican collaborators. Seward fretted about hotheaded generals drawing the United States into a war with France, but he approved sending a strong message to Napoleon III and Maximilian.

In a letter to President Johnson, several weeks after he dispatched Sheridan, Grant echoed the language from his meeting with Sheridan and explained that he regarded "the act of attempting to establish a monarchical government on this continent in Mexico, by foreign bayonets as an act of hostility against the Government of the United States."[27] The French violation of the Monroe Doctrine posed a threat to the United States. Grant hardly needed to remind Johnson that many rebels in the Trans-Mississippi Theater had not surrendered, hence a compelling reason for dispatching Sheridan. Some of the Trans-Mississippi rebels crossed the border into Mexico. Moreover, rebels from the eastern United States also refused to surrender and aimed for Mexico. General John M. Schofield, discussing the surrender of rebel General Joseph E. Johnston's army, observed: "General Johnston thinks about 800 cavalry went south, refusing to accept the terms. He thinks they want to go to Mexico."[28] If these men did indeed go to Mexico, there they joined some of their old compatriots like John Magruder, Sterling Price, Jo Shelby, and Isham Harris in finding new opportunities by working with Maximilian.

Napoleon III's actions lengthened the odds against the North winning a successful peace. They also lent additional evidence to anyone inclined to see the two conflicts as either interlinked or components of a much larger struggle.[29] Grant was not the only person to realize this. In 1864, for example, August Horstmann told his parents that "he who fights for ideals and principles cannot stop halfway! This is the opinion of our government, of the people here, and I share it! Believe me, this war will be fought to the end, the rebellion will be defeated. Slavery abolished, equal rights established in *all America,* and then finally 'your Maximilian, Emperor of Mexico owing to Napoleon's grace, will be sent packing.'—And until this happens, war will not cease."[30] Interestingly, and perhaps not coincidentally, Horstmann wrote from Nashville, about a month after Andrew Johnson's stemwinder.

Grant's language sharpened in a subsequent letter. "Looking upon the

French occupation of Mexico as part and parcel of the late rebellion in the United States," Grant growled, "and a necessary part of it to suppress before entire peace can be assured, I would respectfully recommend that a leave of absence be given to one of our General officers for the purpose of going to Mexico to give direction to such emigration as may go to that country." Grant also recommended selling arms to the Liberals, "the only Government we recognize on Mexican soil."[31] He insisted peace in the United States depended upon peace in Mexico. In less than a month, Grant dramatically accelerated, in his correspondence with Johnson, his ideas for expelling the French. His recommendation about the propriety of sending a general to coordinate the movement of US citizens to Juárez's armies and selling weapons to the Liberals were striking and bellicose. They also violated US neutrality.

Grant's bellicose sentiments heartened Matías Romero.[32] An indefatigable proponent of US aid to Mexico, Romero conducted, during the period 1861–67, an impressive charm offensive.[33] In addition to writing thousands of dispatches to the Mexican minister of foreign affairs, meeting frequently with Grant, Johnson, and high-level policymakers, Romero worked ceaselessly to help the beleaguered Liberals and deftly finessed would-be allies.[34] One scholar noted the magnitude of Romero's task: "In addition to the usual diplomatic duties, Romero was involved with attempts to secure a fifty million dollar loan in the United States, the purchase of several million dollars worth of munitions, propaganda activities on behalf of the Mexican republic, and diplomatic maneuvering to thwart the agents of Napoleon III and his puppet Maximilian."[35] In discharging his many and varied duties, Romero found kindred spirits in Grant and Sheridan, and they collaborated in developing strategies for removing the French from Mexico and restoring Liberal control.

Two months after dispatching Sheridan to the US-Mexico border, Grant determined to act on his recommendation to Johnson about sending a general to direct US citizens to the Liberal forces. Grant, in concert with Romero, chose General John M. Schofield.[36] Grant praised Schofield's "aptitude, character, sound judgment, and military knowledge," and Schofield decided he would "take charge of the matter."[37] When writing his memoirs thirty years later, Schofield remembered "no division of sentiment" among the people of the United States or "among the responsible American statesmen of that time" about driving the French from Mexico.[38] Indeed, "it was their unanimous voice that the French intervention in Mexico must be speedily terminated."[39] Still, widespread agreement on the ends—the expulsion of the French—did not guarantee widespread agreement about the means. Schofield understood the tension between men like Grant, Sheridan, and Romero, who did not mind US neutrality violations, and Seward, who worked toward the same ends, but preferred different means.

Grant's July 25, 1865, communication to Sheridan about Schofield's mission is instructive. Johnson, Grant commented, "agrees in the duty we owe to ourselves to maintain the Monroe doctrine, both as a principle and as a security for our future peace."[40] Moreover, Grant advised Sheridan, "with a knowledge of the fact before you, however, that the greatest desire is felt to see the Liberal Government restored in Mexico,—and no doubt exists of the strict justice of our right to demand this, and enforce the demand with the whole strength of the United States,—your own judgment gives you a basis of action that will aid you."[41] Grant still advised circumspection—the United States preferred to avoid a shooting war with France—but he made it very clear that their ultimate goal was the restoration of the Liberals to power and that both Schofield and Sheridan had key roles to play to achieve this outcome.

Seward disapproved of Schofield getting anywhere near Mexico and worked to neutralize Grant's actions so that they would not draw the United States into a war with France. Seward met with Schofield and "proposed to me to go to France, under authority of the State Department, to see if the French emperor could not be made to understand the necessity of withdrawing his army from Mexico, and thus save us the necessity of expelling it by force."[42] Schofield accepted the assignment, and Seward made his objective very clear: "I want you to get your legs under Napoleon's mahogany, and tell him he must get out of Mexico."[43] Reflecting on his mission after the passage of thirty years, Schofield praised Seward's sagacity: "Too much cannot be said in praise of the able and patriotic statesmanship displayed by Secretary Seward in his treatment of the French violation of the Monroe Doctrine."[44] Again, Seward and Grant differed on means, as many of their contemporaries noted, but they nonetheless worked toward the same end.

Romero detested how Seward interfered with his and Grant's plans. As Robert Ryal Miller observed, Grant and Romero "were so angry with Seward's frustrating their plan for armed intervention in Mexico that they attempted, secretly and unsuccessfully, to force him out of the cabinet."[45] Romero complained to the Mexican minister of foreign affairs that Seward "is indisputably the most influential man in this country" and "while he remains in the cabinet policy will not change."[46] Romero was skeptical of Schofield's assurances that Seward "had a well-matured plan that could not fail and ought to compel the French army to depart from Mexico."[47] He unenthusiastically informed his bosses, in early November 1865, that Schofield sailed to Paris on a confidential mission to talk to the US minister about whether the French were "disposed to retire from Mexico and, in the affirmative case, under what conditions."[48] In this instance, Seward outfoxed Grant and Romero by sending Schofield to France. Seward was unquestionably a powerful voice when it came to foreign policy, but he was not the only voice. As this episode demonstrated, he had to scramble to offset Grant and Romero.

Recruitment: Lew Wallace and Others

In the midst of his conferences with Grant and Schofield, Romero received an agreement between General Lew Wallace and Liberal General José María de Jesús Carvajal.[49] On April 26, 1865, Carvajal offered Wallace "a commission as Major General in the Mexican army."[50] Wallace would command "a corps or division of American troops, organized after the American system, not to exceed ten thousand (10,000) men in number," would not "be placed under command of any American or foreign officers, unless it be by special direction of the proper authority of my Government," and could select his own officers.[51] Wallace assured Carvajal he wanted to "instantly accept" the offer, but worried acceptance would leave his family without provision. However, if Carvajal would "secure them [Wallace's family] beyond the ordinary chances of want or suffering during my absence or in the event of my death," he would accept the terms.[52] If Wallace gathered sufficient US soldiers to fight with the Liberals, Carvajal promised, the Mexican government would pay him one hundred thousand dollars.[53] Wallace accepted these generous terms.[54] The agreement displeased Romero. In addition to being skeptical about Carvajal's authority to recruit Wallace, Romero echoed Grant's dislike of Wallace.[55] Before Seward redirected Schofield to France, Romero planned to have Schofield assume command of any men Wallace recruited once they crossed into Mexico.[56]

Wallace's agreement with Carvajal, which displeased Romero, was not the first time the Indiana general had contemplated fighting in Mexico. In January 1865, Wallace engaged in the same sort of thinking as Francis Preston Blair Sr.

and Alexander H. Stephens, namely, that a joint US-rebel expedition into Mexico was both possible and desirable. As he observed in a letter to Grant, based on information received from one of his Texas friends, "the "rebel soldiery in Western Texas, particularly those at Brownsville, would gladly unite with us and cross the river under the Juarez flag."[57] Wallace successfully convinced Grant to send him on an inspection tour of Western Texas and the Rio Grande. While in Texas, Wallace met with General James E. Slaughter, who seemed to support the idea of a joint expedition and even suggested that "Confederate officers might more honorably get back into the Union if they attacked and annexed some Mexican territory from the French."[58] Nothing came of Wallace's efforts, which was good because it is as hard to imagine Juárez welcoming a wave of ex-rebels who sought to annex portions of Mexico for the United States as it is to imagine him welcoming Jefferson Davis as a potential dictator.

It can be easy to dismiss Wallace's engagement with Mexico as superficial or ill-conceived, but that would be a mistake. Robert Ryal Miller demonstrates that Wallace made serious efforts to recruit a corps of men. Moreover, "by bringing to Washington and New York General José Carvajal, who had broad powers from his government, Wallace served as a catalyst in the important financial and logistic negotiations that led to succor for the Juárez forces." It was Wallace who "conducted a shipload of munitions to Mexico and through his friends in the United States army arranged for some surplus American weapons to be turned over to Mexican officers."[59] Finally, through Wallace's good offices, another Indiana general, Herman Strum, became involved in the Liberal cause. Strum, "purchased over $2,000,000 worth of military supplies in the United States and forwarded them to the Juárez government in Mexico."[60]

While Wallace and Strum negotiated with Carvajal and other Mexicans, other people in the United States engaged in their own recruitment plans. Colonel William Allen of the First and 145th New York Volunteers founded the Mexican Emigration Company in May 1865. Allen placed advertisements in newspapers under the heading "Mexico, Maximilian and Monroe Doctrine." Allen urged all "persons who desire joining a company soon starting 'to make a strike' for fame and fortune in the land of golden ores and luscious fruits, aided and protected by the patriotic President of that republic" to address him via a New York post office box.[61] Just in case anyone was fooled by this advertisement, which dressed up efforts to recruit volunteers to fight in Mexico in the trappings of an emigration company, other newspapers pulled back the veil: "It is now evident that hundreds of men, nearly all discharged officers and soldiers, will before long take their departure from this city for Mexico, ostensibly as emigrants, but really to fight in defense of the Republic, or whatever is left of it, against the troops of Maximilian and Napoleon." Furthermore, "since this so-called 'emigration scheme' has been thoroughly ventilated in the newspapers, and the few leaders concerned in it perceive that the Government authorities do not interfere, they have become bolder."[62]

Surveying the landscape in 1865, one newspaper noted that "the movement under the direction of agents of Juarez, President of Mexico, for the emigration to that country of military colonists, are multiplying themselves rapidly and absorbing a large share of public attention." In addition, "large numbers of our discharged veterans are manifesting their desire to accept the invitation thus extended." Allen's operation was booming, and "he is daily recording numerous names of individual subscribers to his company."[63] In addition to Allen's Mexican Emigration Company, other companies also called for recruits and organizations formed to provide various forms of aid (arms, money, and men) to Mexico. The American Legion of Honor, for example, which fought alongside the Liberals, joined them "at the nadir of their power and at a critical time boosted the morale as well as the fire power of the Republicans."[64] In sum, many people found their way to the Liberal forces and numerous people, from generals and elites to members of the middle and lower classes, strategized about aiding the Liberals.

Sister Republics and the Monroe Doctrine

Grant, Romero, Carvajal, Schofield, Wallace, Strum, and Allen placed a great deal of importance on getting the French out of Mexico, vindicating the Monroe Doctrine, and helping a sister republic. Other people, both military and civilian, made similar arguments. In a letter to Andrew Johnson, written shortly after Johnson's accession to the presidency, General Robert H. Milroy offered strident advice. "I hope you will teach the world that the Munroe [sic] Doctrine is a reality," Milroy snapped, "and that the great insult to our nation by a European power in forcing an emperor on our neighboring Republic in violation of that doctrine, while our hands were tied, will now be speedily avenged by at once giving Mexico all needed assistance in expelling the insolent intruder and tool of a foreign despot."[65] Milroy's sentiments mirrored Grant and Romero's position. Similarly, in 1866, the Mexican Emigration Company "adopted a resolution declaring that the vindication of the Monroe doctrine should be regarded by the American people as paramount in importance to any other question now before the people."[66] Robert Ryal Miller observed that "propaganda stressing the French violation of the Monroe Doctrine was also effective in gaining American recruits for the Mexican front" and noted that the following organization cropped up throughout the United States: the Defenders of the Monroe Doctrine (New Orleans and Brownsville); the Monroe Doctrine Committee of New York; and the Monroe League (San Francisco).[67]

The struggle against the French and Austrians in Mexico became an important moment in the evolution of the Monroe Doctrine. Originally issued in 1823 by President James Monroe as a warning against further European colonization in the Americas, many people, both in the United States and abroad, redefined the Monroe Doctrine into a statement against the imposition of a monarchy on an American republic. Many Mexicans, one scholar asserted, "actively hoped (or even assumed) that the United States would directly intervene in the war as their ally; after all, the Old World threatened them all, and mutual protection was the duty of sister republics and in the spirit of the Monroe Doctrine."[68] While Mexicans called upon people in the United States to vindicate the Monroe Doctrine, many people in the United States contributed in concrete ways toward these efforts. These Pan-American efforts produced an important triumph over the forces of monarchy (Napoleon, Maximilian, and Mexican Conservatives) and reveal again the perceptions of a larger struggle between, in this case specifically, republicanism and monarchy.

Edward Lee Plumb, as we saw earlier, lobbied members of Congress to act and help a sister republic. Plumb suggested to Senator Charles Sumner that the time had arrived to "let it be known to the world that the people of the United States have not abandoned the Monroe Doctrine, that they do not and cannot look with favor or with indiference [sic] on the attempt of a European Power to overthrow Republican institutions and to introduce an European form of Government into their neighbor and sister Republic."[69] After learning about Maximilian's Black Decree, a horrified Plumb mailed a copy to Sumner.[70] The decree, Plumb growled, "condemns by trial by Court Martial and death within twenty four hours all Mexicans who continue to struggle to maintain republican institutions in their country or who continue to resist the imposition upon them of a government established by foreign agents." Plumb unleashed the full measure of his anti-Maximilian fury: "Is it not about time these things shall stop? Can the United States remain much longer an idle spectator of such atrocities?"[71] Several months later Plumb sent a letter to Sumner and Chairman Nathaniel P. Banks of the House Foreign Affairs Committee decrying the "hollocaust [sic] of blood" produced by Maximilian's reign and suggesting the United States had a moral duty to help a suffering sister republic.[72] The United States, in Plumb's eyes, could not stand idly by and fail to help Mexico, a sister republic.

The language of "sister republics" proved popular. Participants in a dinner given in Romero's honor, from Romero himself to George Bancroft and David Dudley Field, utilized it frequently.[73] General John C. Frémont, the darling of Radical Republicans, derided the French desire "to plant an Austrian throne on the ruins of a sister republic" as "an attempt which shocks the public sentiment of this country, and which is eminently hostile to the stability of our institutions."[74] Upon being presented to President Benito Juárez, US Minister to Mexico Thomas Corwin hoped "to be able to confirm our present friendly relations with Mexico by extending still further our commercial exchanges on principles mutually advantageous, thus binding together the sister Republics in bonds of interest, as well as those of sympathy, which grow out of the similarity of their respective political organization."[75] Joseph C. Breckinridge told his father, Robert C. Breckinridge, that "this generation is pledged to interfere and place our finger in the hot fire of Mexico." Although some people "say we are unable to protect our Sister Republic from being ravished by this foreign bully while weak from the fever of the rebellion," he felt the United States should teach the Austrian pretender a sharp lesson.[76]

The language of "sister republics" did not remain confined to dinners, speeches, and correspondence; it also appeared frequently in newspaper articles. At the beginning of the US Civil War, California newspapers commented, "should the triumph of the Constitutional Government result in the restoration of peace to our sister Republic, it is hard to calculate the importance of the Mexican trade to this city [San Francisco]."[77] The *New York Herald* opined that Lincoln's administration would lend "the influence and power of the United States, wherever it may be proper, for the security and welfare of our sister republics of the South."[78] The *Springfield (MA) Republican* growled, in the aftermath of the tripartite French, British, and Spanish intervention, that "the Monroe doctrine is not yet a dead letter." Furthermore, "there is no motive to induce any American to look with favor or toleration upon the designs of the old world dynasties against the liberties of a sister republic."[79] The *Sacramento (CA) Daily Union* predicted that if the French stayed in Mexico, US anger would "burst forth like a great volcano, and before the news could reach France our armies would be on the march to the relief of our sister Republic."[80] Newspapers frequently vented their rage about nefarious French behavior in the Americas.

Lincoln's political opponents quickly learned how to use this language as a cudgel against Republicans. The *World* lamented the "humiliating position" of the US government toward the French Intervention. "When a sister republic to whom we were bound by the ties of interest, neighborhood, and the standing pledge implied in the Monroe doctrine," the paper wailed, Seward did nothing.[81] The *Cleveland (OH) Daily Plain Dealer* charged the "shoddy party" with inviting "Louis Napoleon to destroy a sister Republic."[82] The *Plain Dealer's* argument was patently absurd, but the editor nonetheless considered it an effective attack.[83] The *Sacramento Daily Union* moaned that "a servile European king planted upon the ruins of a sister republic is an ignominious conclusion to the Monroe doctrine proclaimed and maintained in the better days of American nationality."[84] After the conclusion of the US Civil War, many vowed the time had come to do something about the pestilential Austrian and vindicate the Monroe Doctrine.[85] "The people of this country," snapped the *New York Evening Post* "do not wish to sit still and do nothing."[86]

Mexicans adeptly invoked this language as well. The *Janesville (WI) Daily Gazette* printed a letter from Governor Diego Álvarez of Guerrero. Álvarez argued that the Imperialists and the French worked to exterminate democracy in Mexico. He hoped "the United States will hasten to co-operate in favor of a sister republic, for it is not alone Mexico which will be destroyed, but the very source of the democratic element."[87] Mexicans, according to the *Sacramento Daily Union*, wondered if "the United States fear the French and acquiesce in the occupation of a sister republic whose feelings and sympathies are with the Government of the United States."[88] The *Daily True Delta* printed the appeal of Francisco N. de Bordon, a "distinguished gentleman and patriot of our sister Republic, Mexico." Bordon offered a heartfelt plea to his "Republican brothers and sisters, supporters of the Monroe doctrine," asking if they could "behold this awful scene and bloodshed without a shudder?"[89] Finally, *El Nuevo Mundo*, using language similar to that of many of the transnational warriors discussed in the first chapter and proponents of rapprochement treated in other chapters, grandly proclaimed, "the cause of republicanism in Mexico is the cause of America" and offered a lengthy discussion of the Monroe Doctrine, ending with a provocative statement: "if Mexico succumbs and the influence and power of the United States are annulled, everything is lost forever."[90] The papers echoed people throughout the Americas including Lincoln (the last best hope) and Grant and Romero (the safety of each nation depends on that of the other).

When people deliberately and repeatedly linked the United States and Mexico as "sister republics," they reinvigorated an older way of conceptualizing the two nations. In the 1810s and 1820s, during the Spanish American Revolutions, people in the United States displayed fervent enthusiasm about revolutions in the former Spanish colonies. Many considered the new countries sister republics.[91] However, this way of thinking began to fall out of use by the late 1820s in the United States and did not prove very popular during the US War with Mexico in 1846–48.[92] By speaking about sister republics, proponents furthered US-Mexico rapprochement. If the United States and Mexico were sister republics, it would be unacceptable for the United States to do nothing, especially after the Northern triumph. Furthermore, this language helped burn away some of the hostilities of the US War with Mexico and illustrated the profound way people in both countries began to reorder their visions of the world. Less than twenty years earlier, the United States provoked a war with Mexico and took a considerable portion of Mexico's territory. Now people saw themselves as partners in the republican experiment. The widespread usage of this language of sister republics and invocation of the Monroe Doctrine, by people in both nations, revealed how many people promoted cooperation and mutual assistance. They saw these conflicts as interwoven and as part of a larger struggle and, together, they reinterpreted the Monroe Doctrine.

Transnational Warriors in the US–Mexico Borderlands

An important cabal of pro-Mexico men in Washington, such as Ulysses S. Grant and Matías Romero, played a critical role in establishing the lines of argument. People cheered when Grant publicly rebuked French subjugation of Mexico.[93] That said, plenty of people, in the borderlands and throughout Mexico, from General Philip Sheridan to diplomatic officials and anonymous veterans, influenced US-Mexico foreign policy. This is critical to remember because studies of foreign policy sometimes focus on top policymakers, particularly the secretary of state, to the exclusion of everyone else. However, here we see a different and much wider impulse. People embraced these ideas— sister republics and vindicating the Monroe Doctrine—and ran with them, indicating the popular appeal of cooperation and the sheer variety of actors who influenced foreign policy.

"Little Phil" Sheridan, the commander of US forces in Texas, had no patience with French meddling in Mexico and champed at the bit to teach the foreign invaders a lesson. He made no effort to hide his opposition to Maximilian and the French. One newspaper noted that Sheridan "recently declared that 'the United States did not mean to rub elbows with an Austrian-French monarchy.'"[94] Another commented Sheridan and General John A. Logan emphatically claimed that "it should not be the policy of the United States to permit a monarchy supported by foreign arms to exist on the ruins of a sister Republic."[95] Plumb wrote to Sumner that after having "many very full and frank conversations" with Sheridan about political affairs, Plumb discovered "our ideas harmonize so entirely both with reference to the Union cause and upon the subject of Mexican affairs, that doubtless greater frankness has been shown by him to me than would otherwise have been the case."[96] Sheridan tended to overstate the differences between himself, Romero, and Grant on the one hand and Seward on the other, particularly in a letter he sent to Grant, that Grant showed to Romero, where Sheridan argued that "Seward was no friend of our cause."[97] Sheridan's soldiers made demonstrations along the border and demanded the return of munitions given by the rebels to General Mejía. Sheridan believed this alone would have caused Maximilian to evacuate, but the US government weakened, and "a golden opportunity was lost, for we had ample excuse for crossing the boundary, but Mr. Seward being, as I have already stated, unalterably opposed to any act likely to involve us in war, insisted on his course of negotiation with Napoleon."[98] The passage of two decades had not softened Sheridan's insistence that the generals could have managed foreign policy better than the diplomats, although his actions might conceivably have drawn the United States into another war.

Sheridan's opposition took various forms, from rhetoric to concrete action. In a confidential letter to Andrew Johnson, J. E. P. Doyle, a reporter for the *New York Herald,* informed the president that the "'gallant little soldier' Phil.

Sheridan" had permitted Henry R. H. McIvor, a member of Liberal General Mariano Escobedo's staff, to recruit men in the United States to fight with the Liberals.[99] It is hard to verify if Sheridan actually permitted McIvor and Escobedo to recruit in the United States. If true, it was a flagrant violation of the Neutrality Act of 1818. Given some of Sheridan's other actions, Doyle's charge was not implausible. Little Phil sometimes allowed his hatred of the French to lead him into gray areas of the law. For example, R. Clay Crawford and Arthur F. Reed secured commissions in the Liberal army and, "with tacit approval of the Federals, opened a recruiting office where they offered $50 a month in gold and all expenses for anyone who would join in an invasion of Mexico."[100] In addition, perhaps even more egregiously, when the US army occupied Texas in 1865, Juan Cortina "was allowed to set up a recruiting office in Brownsville," and "the Federals were openly courting and sheltering Cortina and his guerrillas."[101] If Little Phil allowed McIvor and Escobedo to recruit, it was hardly his only violation of the Neutrality Act and, given Cortina's status as the bête noire of many Texans, not even his most egregious.[102]

Sheridan not only permitted Mexican recruiting on the United States side of the border but also facilitated arms drops across the border. In late 1865 Sheridan and his soldiers supplied the rebels with "arms and ammunition, which we left at convenient places on our side of the river to fall into their hands."[103] Remarkably, Sheridan revealed in his *Personal Memoirs* that "during the winter and spring of 1866 we continued covertly supplying arms and ammunition to the Liberals—sending as many as 30,000 muskets from the Baton Rouge Arsenal alone."[104] Sheridan had no interest in securing the border and curtailing the passage of people and arms from the United States into Mexico. Andrew Johnson knew full well Sheridan sympathized with Radical Republicans and opposed most of Johnson's policies. Johnson nevertheless appointed Sheridan commander of the Fifth Military District (Texas and Louisiana) created by the Military Reconstruction Acts of 1867. Johnson did not remove Sheridan until several months after Maximilian's execution. He either appreciated having Little Phil watching the French and Imperialists or determined that, for the moment, his strengths outweighed his weaknesses.

Sheridan was the most famous pro-Liberal actor on the periphery but hardly the only one. Many veterans, nameless and known, crossed the border to fight in Mexico.[105] Plenty of people wrote of their desire to fight.[106] Numerous US citizens aided the Liberal cause. J. B. Hart "joined the Mexican troops at El Paso, and was present at the execution of that unfortunate prince [Maximilian]."[107] Samuel Brannan "loaned the struggling Republicans a large sum of money."[108] Dr. Eugene Wakefield "served as a surgeon in the Mexican Republican Army of Sonora during the French intervention; and was known by the name of 'Guarda campo.'"[109] Edelmiro Mayer, the Argentine transnational warrior who fought in the United States and Mexico as well as in Argentina, crossed the border on several occasions and, taking advantage of his ability to speak German, harangued Maximilian's Austrian soldiers and encouraged them to desert.[110]

Several consular dispatches contain tantalizing hints about other transnational warriors. On August 22, 1864, US Consul Lewis S. Ely in Acapulco sent a contrite dispatch to the State Department. He wrote that H. W. Spencer, from San Francisco, called on Ely and "satisfied me of his Citizenship." Spencer told Ely he needed a passport to visit mines near Acapulco. Ely told him to apply to the French commander as "I could not pass him through their lines." The French commander told Spencer that if Ely gave him a pass, he would endorse it. "Without reflection," Ely wrote, "and regarding it as a Compliment I complied so far as to give him a brief paper as a pass for his use with Genl Alvarez." However, when Spencer "reached the Mexican Camp he proposed to join their Army. I am creditably informed that he told the French com^te that he was going in the interests of Maximilian's government." Ely hastened to add that he had "committed no unfriendly act toward the French, And Aim to discharge My duty with fidelity, and deeply regret My connection with this affair."[111] Spencer served as US consul in Paris in the late 1850s.[112] After knocking around San Francisco he decided, for reasons of his own, to go to Mexico and join the Liberals. More interesting is Ely's account of affairs. Ely appeared rather careless in issuing Spencer a pass, but he had a very strained relationship with the French authorities. Was his seeming carelessness accidental or deliberate? Spencer joining the Liberals infuriated the French and illustrated how people employed different ruses to cross borders.

Other US citizens made similar decisions. From Tampico, US Consul Franklin Chase reported a battle between several hundred French soldiers led by Colonel Dupin and a force of Liberals under Carvajal. The French took the field, but the Liberals fought like tigers: "The troops under the Mexican Genl Carbajal [sic] fought so bravely, wounded and killed so many of the French officers and soldiers, that they are declared to be nearly all Americans from our forces on the frontiers, or Texans enlisted under Carbajal [sic] in that section of the Country."[113] The French could not believe, despite their embarrassing loss at Puebla in 1862, and their mixed success dealing with roving Liberal armies, that Mexicans could fight. Carvajal's force, they assured themselves, must have been composed of Texans. The French, as they shaded the truth to protect their own ego, unwittingly demonstrated that recruiting across the borders was a common phenomenon. While Carvajal did recruit in Texas and likely had some Texans in his ranks, Mexicans could, and did, fight just as well as men from the Lone Star State.

From Matamoros, US Vice Commercial Agent Lucius Avery informed the State Department that a Liberal force under the command of General Escobedo, "estimated at from 1800. to 3000. men," was poised to defeat the Imperialist defenders. Among Escobedo's force, noted Avery, "are said to be several companies of negroes, made up of deserters and discharged soldiers from the US army."[114] R. Delevan Mussey, Andrew Johnson's private secretary and colonel of the 100th United States Colored Troops, planned to persuade Secretary of War Edwin M. Stanton to send Black troops to Arizona to quell Indian incursions. Once in Arizona, Mussey would "inform his superiors that all is quiet and there is nothing to fear from the Indians." The government would muster out the troops, who would then "follow their inclination to cross into Mexico and enter our [Liberal] service in Sonora." This plan, Romero noted somewhat wryly, was "obviously subject to many contingencies."[115] Nothing came of Mussey's plan, but Black troops from the United States fought just as well against the Imperialists as they did against the Confederates.

Consul F. B. Elmer of La Paz sent fascinating descriptions of US citizens' involvement with Liberals. On April 9, 1866, he reported that a ship was "boarded and captured by a small force of armed men under the command of one F. F. Dana." Dana carried orders from General Corona, the commander of the Liberal forces in Sinaloa. Dana's men, "with one exception, were natives of the United States, who had been sworn into the service of the Juarez Government."[116] Imperialists were so angry that they attempted to sever all communication between La Paz and the outside world.[117] Several months later, a squad of armed men seized a US sloop and took it to Cabo San Lucas. Shortly thereafter, the same squad of men "some ten or twelve in number who presented themselves as holding commissions under, and being in the employ of General Corona of the Liberal Army," boarded the steamer *Sierra Nevada*. No one knows, Elmer observed, "whether the steamer passed under the control of these men or not." Elmer concluded by noting the general impression that "the men are understood to have been generally Americans, in the employ of the Liberal Government." His final comment, "the proceedings detailed above, partake more of the nature of piracy, than of legitimate warfare" is fascinating.[118] It was not a particularly vehement statement. Elmer sent information to the State Department but did little to attempt to stop this "piracy," if, indeed, he even considered it a problem.

Many of the warriors left minimal traces on the historical record. They might have left no trace at all save for their involvement in the French Intervention and the fact that US diplomats noticed them in their dispatches to the State Department or that newspaper articles mentioned them. Their motivations are harder to discern, but they nonetheless risked their lives alongside the Liberals.

Consular Neutrality(?)

US consuls and other diplomatic officials greatly exceeded their instructions and displayed, through their actions, that even members of the diplomatic service who should have maintained a strict neutrality and avoided politics, did not. The most telling example of this trend is Vice Commercial Agent John A. Sutter Jr., son of John A. Sutter of California gold rush fame. Sutter Jr. was appointed to this position by the commercial agent Gilbert Cole (who replaced Lewis Ely). Sutter's "open sympathy for the Liberal cause was well-known."[119] According to one story, during the French bombardment in 1863, some of the French shells hit the town. Sutter "leaped into a small boat, flung out the American flag, and, defying the danger of falling shot, headed out into the harbor. Boarding the French flagship, he sought out the admiral and, threatening him with the consequences of an international incident, demanded that he instantly cease firing on unarmed civilians."[120] Although this story has the ring of embellishment, Sutter detested the French and Imperialists and did what he could to help the Liberals.[121]

Cole departed Acapulco July 7, 1866, on a leave of absence and left Sutter in charge. Sutter's voice soon fell silent. George F. Bowman, a US citizen resident in Acapulco, transmitted proceedings from a meeting of US citizens. They noted Sutter "has withdrawn from Acapulco" and George M. Hedges took charge of the consulate.[122] Hedges offered additional clarification several days later. The captain of the port, the chief of police, and a military officer seized a mailbag directed to the US consul and compelled him to open it. Their object, Hedges commented, "was to seize any correspondence directed to Mr John A. Sutter. I opened the bag but found nothing." Not satisfied with violating a consular mailbag, the same men took from the Express mailbag of the Wells Fargo Co. and the private mailbag of the Pacific Mail S. S. Company "letters and papers directed to Mr Sutter." Hedges remarked that "three letters and a package of papers were returned to me open, they were private letters for Mr Sutter."[123]

The authorities did not target Sutter's mail as a form of harassment. The chief of police informed Hedges that General Montenegro, the commander of the Imperial forces, had "detained a number of letters that came under care to Mr Sutter for General Deigo [sic] Alvarez and other officers of the Liberal Government, that in them was found a full account of a shipment of Arms from San Francisco on the Schooner A. J. [illegible word], to be delivered to General Alvarez at the mouth of the revir [sic]." Sutter, in other words, like Sheridan, facilitated arms shipments to the Liberals. Sensibly, Hedges asked Montenegro for information, but the Imperialist replied "the case was in the hands of the Fiscal, who was making out a charge against Mr Sutter, that as soon as it was ready he would furnish me with a copy."[124] Writing several days later from Syracuse, New York, where he spent a leave of absence recuperating from illness, Cole enclosed a snippet from the *New York Herald* reporting Sutter's arrest for "forwarding correspondence to Gen. Juarez [sic]" and that he anticipated finding "an unpleasant state of affairs" when he returned to Acapulco.[125]

Two weeks later, Cole returned to Acapulco. Sutter, he explained, had been compelled to "flee for safety from this town which is still in possession of the Imperial garrison." Despite "loosing [sic] his hat and spectacles," Sutter "succeeded in getting safely within the lines of the Liberalists who occupy all of the country outside of this town." Imperialists and their French allies were livid and charged Sutter with passing letters to Liberal General Diego Álvarez. "It was their intention," Cole gasped, "to have shot him if they had caught him."[126] The image of Sutter ditching his hat and glasses as he ran away might have seemed amusing, but it was no laughing matter. Sutter barely escaped a firing squad. Seward asked Cole for a report about the seizure of the mailbag, and Cole duly sent the results of his investigation and several documents.[127] Fascinatingly, Cole maintained Sutter did a good job directing commercial affairs in Acapulco, even as he served as a spy for the Liberals. Moreover, and very tellingly, the State Department took no action against Sutter. Considering that this was one arena where Seward held unchallenged power, lack of action against Sutter was noteworthy and spoke to the evolving nature of Seward's Mexican policies.

This exciting story of Sutter's espionage and escape ended anticlimactically. On February 23, 1867, Cole noted that "the so called Imperial Mexican Garrison who had occupied and distressed the town for more than Eighteen months past" evacuated Acapulco. "There is no other place on this coast that is not strongly Liberal," Cole commented, so Sutter's actions fit with the mood of the region.[128] In May 1867, Sutter returned to Acapulco, and Cole maintained that "political matters here are quiet, and a good state of feeling existing toward our Government."[129] Residents of such a strongly Liberal region could not have failed to appreciate Sutter's actions.

Other consular actions were more ambiguous. Consul Edward Conner, for example, highlighted one example of his pragmatism toward the French paying dividends. An unnamed old man who "claims to be an American" ran into problems because he "fearfully compromised himself by secreting, or allowing to be secreted in one of his houses 80,000 rounds of Cartridges a large quantity of powder and other Ammunition" for Governor Igancio Pesqueira's Liberal forces. "When called upon by the French Officers to permit them to enter the house, during a skirmish, he stubbornly refused, denying that there was anything in his house and threatening Vengeance upon the French." French officers subsequently searched his home and found the munitions. Conner claimed the old man "had no interesting in saving the articles as they belonged to the State Government and were Merely put in his house for safe-keeping— nor had he any particular bias for the Mexican Authorities." Regardless, he was sentenced to death by firing squad. Because he claimed US citizenship, the French commander offered to pardon him if Conner promised to vouch for his future good behavior. "Knowing him to be an inoffensive honest fellow," Conner commented, "I Cheerfully agreed and he was set at liberty."[130]

Conner's dispatch contained important ambiguities. Although he twice observed the old man claimed US citizenship, Conner did not actually state whether this was true, simply that the man was inoffensive and honest. If the old man was not a US citizen, Conner became complicit in protecting a Liberal collaborator. If he was a US citizen, Conner's conciliatory relationship with the

French likely saved him from a hail of bullets.[131] Conner did not seem inclined to make a lengthy investigation to resolve the question of the man's citizenship. For that matter, it is worth asking what sort of "inoffensive honest fellow" would store eighty thousand cartridges for the Liberals when the French were a mile away? The old man's rationale, that he was asked to store the supplies but had no sympathy or affinity for the Liberals, makes no sense. Why do something that could easily result in death without having anything to gain? The likelihood the man was paid to do so was slim, given Pesqueira's cash-strapped situation. In sum, the old man had Conner's pragmatism to thank for the fact that he did not meet a grim end before the muzzles of French rifles.

Consular neutrality often failed to obscure bitter hatred of the French and unvarnished admiration of the Liberals. Most diplomatic officials did not take their resistance as far as Sutter. However, the messages they sent the State Department generally emphasized the negative elements of the French occupation, praised the Liberals, and argued for a more bellicose policy. Critically, the State Department rarely rebuked pro-Liberal diplomats, although it occasionally happened.[132] Even when Sutter entered into open resistance, the State Department did not remove him from office. Consular officials furthered US-Mexico rapprochement by helping the Liberals and by demonstrating that people in the United States were fully as invested in Liberal success as the Liberals had been in US success during the US Civil War. They provided an additional demonstration, along with the actions of the transnational warriors, recruiting companies, and efforts to raise money, arms, and ammunition, that many people viewed the conflicts as interlinked and saw the French Intervention as they saw the US Civil War—as a conflict in which republicanism was again under siege by the forces of reaction, specifically monarchy.

To say that the US-Mexico border was porous would be an understatement. Consuls did not overexert themselves to control the inflow of people. Sheridan and other military officers facilitated recruiting and arms shipments. For that matter, Andrew Johnson allowed Sheridan, borderlanders, diplomatic officials, and many other people to get away with a lot, including routinely defying the Neutrality Act of 1818.[133] People violated the Neutrality Act of 1818 with relative impunity along the Southern border, but also elsewhere, by recruiting US citizens to fight in Mexico, shipping arms to the Liberals, and crossing the US-Mexico border to fight with the Liberals. Johnson's choice not to prosecute neutrality violations and to turn a blind eye to these actions suggests that he either appreciated what people were doing or preferred to maintain flexibility when it came to foreign policy. Seward, of course, as secretary of state, did not have the luxury of winking at clandestine arms shipments and neutrality violations, but it is telling that he did not take a firmer hand with some of the extreme pro-Liberal diplomatic officials like Sutter. Flexibility, in other words, became an asset in many eyes.

The years featuring overlap between the US Civil War and the French Intervention, 1861–67, saw particularly intense Pan-American cooperation. The United States and Mexico began an important period of rapprochement, fueled by the language of sister republics and a shared desire to vindicate the Monroe Doctrine. Many people cooperated in pursuit of a shared goal, ousting the French, and that cooperation took many different forms. Mexicans did the lion's share of the fighting in Mexico, but assistance from the United States proved critical. Combine all the US activities outlined in this chapter with the fervent and dogged Mexican resistance to the French and Imperialists, and the inescapable conclusion is that many actors, both at the center and the periphery, convinced the French of the futility of their errand. They also provided a concrete demonstration of the widespread anger in the United States about the French and Austrian assault on a sister republic and the violation of the Monroe Doctrine. Even more critically, both sides cooperated in modifying the meaning of the Monroe Doctrine. What began in 1823 as a unilateral assertion by the United States, via President James Monroe, against further European colonization in the Americas became, in the 1860s, in the hands of both the United States and Mexico, a Pan-American cause that said monarchy could not and would not be imposed on American republics. These concerted efforts helped create a Pan-American alliance.[134]

Conclusion: Plumb and Juárez

On August 15, 1867, roughly a month after Maximilian's execution, Edward Lee Plumb wrote a letter to President Benito Juárez. Plumb thanked Juárez for sending him a description of "the proud and happy events of your reentry into the ancient Capital of the Republic after the long and valiant and patriotic struggle which under your faithful and determined lead, has been so gallantly sustained by the loyal sons of Mexico + has now resulted in the complete triumph of the national arms in the cause of republican Constitutional Gov^t, over foreign foes and domestic faction." No one, Plumb proclaimed, "among all the friends of republican institutions rejoices with a more sincere or a warmer pleasure in this event and in the bright prospects of peace and prosperity that now open before Mexico," than he did.[135]

Indeed, in August 1867, a happy glow suffused the Western Hemisphere. Plumb, Juárez, Sarmiento, Grant, and millions of people had many reasons to celebrate. Argentina had passed through decades of civil war and charted a new course as a republic. In the United States, the Northern victory vindicated democracy and ushered in emancipation. In Mexico, dogged resistance by the Liberals, with US assistance, destroyed Napoleon III's schemes and sent Maximilian to the firing squad. Nevertheless, as the victors looked to the future, they confronted one immediate question. Namely, would the rapprochement among the three nations continue or would it fade away now that their respective wars had concluded?

The language cited again and again in this chapter about sister republics and vindicating the Monroe Doctrine could have been purely pragmatic. After all, as numerous examples reveal, when countries that do not like each other or have never cooperated with each other are forced by circumstances into an uneasy alliance, they sometimes create superficial veneers of positivity. Case in point, in World War II, the United States had to cooperate with "Uncle Joe" Stalin. When that conflict ended, so did the alliance between the United States and the USSR because it was the ultimate marriage of convenience. In contrast, the language of sister republics did not fade away but remained strong and vibrant. Multiple factors contributed to this phenomenon. Most prominently, the experience of passing through extremely similar violent conflicts made many people think internationally in more substantive ways. Fourth of July celebrations in Mexico and Argentina provide one demonstration of the continuation of the idea of sister republics engaged in similar struggles and testify to the strength of cooperation and Pan-American sentiment. Thus, as to the question of whether rapprochement continued when the guns stopped firing, the answer was an emphatic yes.

3

What to the Mexican and the Argentine Is the Fourth of July?

On July 4, 1865, Governor Gregorio Méndez sent a heartfelt letter to US Consular Agent B. W. Sanders. Méndez tendered his condolences on the assassination of President Abraham Lincoln and deplored "the death of the illustrious champion of liberty in the city of Washington." He offered his congratulations, both as a private citizen and as governor, on "the anniversary of that auspicious day when your ancestors proclaimed their independence in the city of Philadelphia." Méndez assured Sanders that Mexico, and "Tabasco in particular, will be worthy members of the great democratic family that people the world of Columbus." Méndez also hoped that the newly conquered peace in the United States "may last long, for the good of humanity."[1] Méndez's remarkable letter, part of a larger Fourth of July celebration that took place in Tabasco, reveals that the Fourth of July mattered a great deal in Mexico and Argentina. Mexican, Argentine, and US officials, proved adept at using Fourth of July celebrations to proclaim Pan-American kinship and ideological sympathy and reinforce the power of the idea of sister republics.

Historians have rarely considered US nationalist festivals in non-US areas.[2] Fourth of July celebrations in Mexico and Argentina took many forms. They ran the gamut from relatively simple affairs to ornate commemorations. During the pre-1867 period in Mexico, before the end of the French Intervention, Mexican authorities generally had less involvement in most July Fourth celebrations. When Mexicans participated, their involvement was often the result of a concrete action on the part of the United States. After 1867, Mexican authorities began celebrating the Fourth more consistently. These celebrations reinforced the idea of the United States and Mexico as sister republics and furthered the Pan-American cooperation and rapprochement that developed as the two countries fought simultaneous civil wars. Fourth of July celebrations took place in Argentina as well. In 1865, a major celebration occurred in Buenos Aires involving both US and Argentine citizens.

Fourth of July celebrations, whether in Mexico or Argentina, proclaimed and demonstrated the links and cooperation among the sister republics of the New World. July Fourth celebrations illustrated that the strong positive feelings that had developed among many people in the United States and Latin America because of their ideas about being sister republics engaged in similar struggles, not to mention the Pan-American cooperation produced by vindicating the newly redefined Monroe Doctrine, continued long after the wars in each of the three nations ceased. Furthermore, embrace of these celebrations, particularly in Mexico, went hand in hand with efforts to tamp down xenophobia. Nationalism, nativism, and xenophobia were not exclusively US, Mexican, or Argentine issues. Rather, they were hemispheric issues best understood from a transnational perspective.

Celebrating the Fourth in Mexico, 1860–1864

In March 1860, at the Battle of Antón Lizardo, a US fleet, including the USS *Saratoga,* captured the Mexican Conservative steamers *General Miramon* and *Marquis of Havana.*[3] In a letter to the State Department, US Consul Franklin Chase reported that the capture of these vessels "caused much excitement and all feeling on the part of the Spaniards and other foreigners, against our National character, whilst the authorities celebrated the event, with their usual exultation on the receipt of the news of a good and important victory."[4] Military action taken by the United States deprived Conservative General Miguel Miramón of the additional ships and armaments he needed to capture Veracruz.

US intervention at Antón Lizardo likely explained the decision of Governor Juan José de la Garza of Tamaulipas to celebrate July 4, 1860. "The good and friendly intercourse which bind the United States of America to the Mexican Republic," Garza proclaimed, "as also the sympathy which exists between both Nations is the cause that makes all the great events which have taken place in the former Nation, to be considered in the same manner as if occurred in this Republic." Garza informed the delighted consul that "I have ordered that with the object of commemorating the anniversary of the ever glorious independence of the United States of America, the 4th of July Instant, be saluted in the morning, at noon, and at the close of the afternoon and the National flag hoisted on all the public edifices."[5] Garza, Chase wrote to Secretary of State Lewis Cass, "has been pleased to cause the day of our National Anniversary to be celebrated with the highest military honors" and three twenty-one-gun salutes. Furthermore, Garza "caused a full military band to serenade this Consulate on the night of the 3[d] Instant, and on the following day the same courteous attentions were repeated."[6] "I indulge the hope," Chase concluded, "that you will be pleased to make such acknowledgments to General Garza or to his Government as your feelings may dictate, to the end that the perfect harmony and good understanding which now so happily exist between the two nations may be uninterruptedly prolonged."[7]

Garza and Chase offered overly optimistic assessments of the state of the US-Mexico relationship. Few people, in either country, would have described relations between the two countries, in July 1860, as marked by "good and friendly intercourse," "sympathy," "perfect harmony," and "good understanding." However, within a few years, this language became reality as the swelling Pan-American sentiments indicate. This Mexican celebration of the "natural birth day" of the United States proved exceptional because, in the period between 1848 and 1860, the bitterness engendered by the US War with Mexico, filibustering attempts, and US attempts to wrest additional territory away from Mexico, did not make Mexicans inclined to celebrate the Fourth. Chase and Garza adroitly used the occasion to argue for friendship and amity between their respective nations in the face of powerful countervailing trends, as did other proponents of cooperation in different contexts.[8]

During the US Civil War and French Intervention, 1861–67, US citizens residing in Mexico celebrated the Fourth of July. Mexican officials sometimes participated. For instance, on July 4, 1861, sailors on the USS *Lancaster*, stationed at Acapulco, engaged in a unique ceremony while firing a twenty-one-gun salute: "As the first gun was discharged an effigy of Jeff Davis was run up the fore peak, and after the firing ceased the effigy was lowered and beheaded."[9] A response from Mexican authorities, either a reciprocal cannon salute or running up the US flag to mark the day, did not prove forthcoming. "Verdad," a correspondent of the *Sacramento (CA) Daily Union*, spent the Fourth of July of 1861 in Manzanillo. "I cannot say that I have spent quite so happy a Fourth of July as perhaps I might have done in my own Golden State," he wrote. However, "the glorious day was not suffered to pass by unnoticed." Consul A. Morrell's decision to fly the US flag "gladdened the hearts of the few Americans who had congregated together in this barbarous country to celebrate the only day in the calendar worth keeping." Morrell invited US citizens residing in Manzanillo "to partake with him at his house a glass of the best punch that ever was made, and certainly the finest champagne."[10] "Verdad" did not use the holiday to further US-Mexico relations, and his letter displayed contempt for Mexico. This particular July Fourth celebration in Mexico did not feature any Mexican participation, just that of the US citizens resident in Manzanillo.

US citizens did not celebrate the Fourth of July in Monterrey in 1863. However, Vice Consul M. M. Kimmey complained to Secretary of State William H. Seward that "the Confederate flag was flying here all day on the 4th of July. I wrote Governor Vidaurri a few lines calling his attention to the fact. As the Governor obliges me to ask his permission to put up the U.S. Flag the Rebel Flag was of course flying without consent."[11] Kimmey seethed with fury that rebels desecrated the Fourth with their treasonous banner. Kimmey did not note any response from Vidaurri. However, one newspaper observed *"Vidaurri took no notice of the note except to say that the impertinent author might wake up some warm morning and find himself in the hands of the Texans."*[12] Given Vidaurri's open sympathy for the rebels during the US Civil War, this language was a very clear death threat.

In contrast to 1861, Juarista authorities in Manzanillo celebrated the Fourth of July with great gusto in 1863. "The Mexican federal + state authorities, military as well as civil, and headed by the venerable Governor of the State," narrated Consul John Xantus, "came in solemn procession and escorted by the whole military to the Consulate at noon, and the Governor and Comandante Militar delivered each an oration highly congratulatory + complimentary to the U.S." In addition, "they fired a salute of 34 cannons on the plaza, the Mexican flags were unfurled the whole day on all public buildings; in the morning, noon, & evening all the church bells rang, closing the orations with a general & spontaneous illumination of the whole city."[13] This celebration impressed the US State Department. One official wrote on the back of the dispatch, "reports the extraordinary celebration of the 4th of July by the Mexican Authorities at Colima." Since the Department let most reports pass by without comment, this suggests they noticed and appreciated the celebration. Mexicans invoked the anniversary of the birth of the United States, and, by extension, the revolution the United States waged against British tyranny. In so doing, they linked their struggle against the French to that of the United States in a powerful demonstration of sister republics fighting similar struggles. They also high-lighted friendship and Pan-American cooperation between the United States and Mexico.

In addition to describing the actions of the Mexican authorities, Xantus attempted, rather ham-fistedly, to use a Fourth of July party he held at the con-sulate to achieve a certain effect. "Thinking the opportunity to [sic] good, to establish friendly relations between all Americans here," Xantus explained, "I invited to me all our southern citizens also, who formerly annoyed me always good deal, and were always vehement enemies of the US Government. They accepted all my invitation, and drank all the health of the President, the Gov-ernment, the Army + navy, and the success and prosperity of the Union; so as far as appearances go, they left my house without exception, as good Union citizens."[14] One can only imagine how Lincoln and Seward reacted to the news that one Fourth of July celebration converted the rebels into good Unionists—this, incidentally, was a figment of Xantus's imagination—and the consul's er-ratic behavior.[15]

1865: Dual Celebrations in San Juan Bautista and Buenos Aires

The triumph of the North in the US Civil War led to two extraordinary cele-brations in 1865. The first occurred in San Juan Bautista, the capital of Tabasco, and the second in Buenos Aires.[16] The French took control of San Juan Bautista in 1862, but concerted Liberal resistance, led by Gregorio Méndez, resulted in several French defeats. The Liberals recaptured the state capital in 1864 and continued fighting until they fully expelled the invaders from the state in 1866. The celebration in 1865 thus came at an important moment; Liberals under Méndez had won a major victory, but they still faced additional fighting to fully remove the French from Tabasco.

"The day was celebrated here," Consular Agent Sanders informed the US State Department, "as it had never been before in Mexico—the different forti-fications that surround the City were decorated with flags and the occasion as observed by their garrisons in a manner, alike becoming and flattering, to our national pride—In the morning, I received from the Governor of the State a letter of Congratulation."[17] Sanders also received a printed address from the civil authorities. To top things off, "at eight o'clock at night the military and civil authorities and a large concourse of citizens, preceded by a band of music, called upon me at my residence on the Plaza de las Armas—I addressed them in a brief speech, thanking them for the honor conferred upon my flag and inviting them to partake of a collation which had been prepared in anticipation of their visit."[18] The celebration marked the anniversary of US independence and the end of the US Civil War and, implicitly, urged the United States to help the Liberals defeat the French. A sister republic should not stand idly by while French and Austrian invaders ripped another one apart; the United States and Mexico had to stand together.

In addition to describing the celebration, Sanders offered Seward unsolicited advice about Mexican affairs. "This unusual demonstration on the part of the Mexican authorities and people," he observed, "has a signification which may not appear on the surface—It is now evident to all those who reflect for a moment, that their cause is irretrieveably [sic] lost, unless their difficulties are adjusted by the armed interference of the United States."[19] Sanders's dispatch mixed a contemptuous attitude toward Mexicans—"though indolent and in Many instances superstitious [they] are essentially democratic in action and in thought"—with advocacy of a protectorate. He urged Seward to "claim and secure privileges, guarantee by treaty stipulations between the two Nations, such as would give us the control of the commerce of the Gulf of Mexico." "Under our administration of affairs," he observed, "this fair land, so magnificently favored by nature, would bloom and blossom as garden."[20] If Sanders had ended his report here, the Fourth of July celebration at Tabasco would have been noteworthy, but not necessarily earth-shattering.

This celebration became even more fascinating because Sanders adopted very different attitudes and ideas in his responses to a committee of Mexican citizens and Governor Méndez than in his communications with Seward. The Mexicans citizens, led by Felipe J. Serra, praised the United States and hoped that "soon the united banners of our respective nationalities shall proclaim that Americans must rule America, that each of the republican governments of which this continent is composed shall be free from all European intervention, and that the fleets of the Old World shall not sail upon our seas without first saluting the flags of Washington and of Hidalgo."[21] Serra explicitly linked the United States to Mexico and promoted cooperation and friendship. He also argued that the United States should vindicate the Monroe Doctrine by expelling the Austrian pretender, his myrmidons, and his deplorable French puppeteers. Serra offered another example of a Mexican citizen using the Monroe Doctrine

and similarities between the United States and Mexico to argue for cooperation in expelling the French.

Sanders, in his reply, praised the Fourth of July as "a day replete with reminiscences that must always thrill with joy the hearts of the friends of liberty
in every clime." Tabasqueños, he asserted, were "famous for their devotion to
freedom as well as for their valor in defending their homes and firesides when
invaded." Sanders contended that "the great heart of our people anxiously turns
toward Mexico." The United States did not want Mexican territory and "the
policy of my government has been, in behalf of the best interests of the American Republics, to prevent Europe from intervening in the political affairs of
this Continent." Europeans respected this policy, Sanders asserted, until they
thought domestic discord would destroy the United States and permit New
World adventures. This costly miscalculation demanded a strong response by
the United States.[22]

We mean, thundered Sanders, "to reassert and reinforce one of the violated
principles of our political faith, formerly known as the 'Monroe doctrine'—No
Republic shall disappear from this continent for any reason whatever." He concluded with a stirring peroration. Americans, in the broadest sense of the term,
would not accept the ablest European statesman. "Here, Providence raises of
neither Ceasars [sic], Charlemagnes, nor Napoleons to accomplish in a few
years the work of centuries—Here, the people inspire their agents and not
the agents the people—Here, we overthrow bad and ambitious men without
believing for a moment that we are like the Jews who crucified their Messiah—
Here, the voice of no one can dictate laws to his fellow men—Here, all believe that the voice of God is the voice of the people—vox Dei vox populi."[23]
Sanders's stirring promise that the United States would vindicate the Monroe Doctrine must have thrilled his audience. Admittedly, he tended at times
toward jingoism, and his reflexive anti-Semitism would have displeased Jews
throughout the Americas.[24] Still, Sanders offered an important example of a
US diplomatic official who all but promised that the United States, with its
army and navy, would teach the French to respect the Monroe Doctrine. In effect, Sanders guaranteed the integrity of the Mexican Republic at a time when
there were no ironclad guarantees that the Liberals would triumph against the
French and the Imperialists.

Incredibly, Sanders went even further! He thanked Méndez for his letter,
discussed at the beginning of this chapter, and found it appropriate "that the

Sister Republic of the New World should rejoice over the happy termination of our gigantic internal struggle—We must all admit, that had the integrity and unity of our Republic been destroyed, ten years could not have elapsed, before the entire Western Hemisphere would have again passed under the domination of the Old World."[25] Sanders deftly mobilized ideas of hemispheric solidarity and the language of sister republics to argue for cooperation between the United States and Mexico. Furthermore, his language invoked similar ideas to those of many other people during this period, Namely, that the conflicts were critical arenas in which democracy and republicanism were challenged by the forces of reaction, specifically, monarchy and slavery, and that people should cooperate to defeat these forces. Finally, his frequent use of the language of sister republics provides another demonstration of how people throughout the Americas made an argument for interconnected struggles and, more broadly, an interconnected world. Sanders, like Matías Romero, Robert Milroy, Edward Lee Plumb, and many others, demonstrated how people paired invocation of the language of sister republics with the desire to vindicate the Monroe Doctrine.

The documents Sanders sent to the State Department open important windows into the meaning of the Fourth of July celebrations, the impact they had on both countries, and the particular nature, in this case, of the US response. Someone, possibly Seward, scrawled a note on one of the pages of the report. It read "he is therefore recalled—The President reserves all political questions for his own decision."[26] The State Department revoked Sanders's commission on September 11, 1865.[27] In his reply, Sanders claimed, loftily, "I attempted, in all that I said and did on that occasion, to confine myself to a legitimate expression of patriotic devotion to the cause of republican institutions and constitutional liberty on this continent."[28] Johnson may have determined on his own to recall Sanders. Such a decision would have resembled Lincoln overruling John C. Frémont's (1861) and David Hunter's (1862) decisions about emancipation, on the basis that the president, not subordinate officials, should make policy. However, Seward probably asked Johnson to recall Sanders. The bellicose sentiments Sanders proclaimed publicly threatened to lead the United States into war with France, something Seward sought to avoid. Furthermore, consuls were not supposed to engage in diplomacy on their own. Moreover, Sanders's veiled private references to a protectorate likely worried Seward. All these points explain why Sanders was recalled. Still, it is important to note that

Sanders was one of the few diplomatic officials recalled during this period. John A. Sutter Jr., who did everything he could to aid the Liberals and sought shelter with them when the Imperialists discovered the extent of his actions, was never recalled.

In Buenos Aires, US citizens residing in Argentina and Argentines celebrated the Fourth in 1865. The day, one newspaper proclaimed, "will long be remembered by both Americans and Argentines. It may be said to have been the first 4th July that was ever properly kept up in the city of Buenos Ayres."[29] As the article explained, "the Provincial Government took the initiative by declaring it a national holiday, private parties followed the example by keeping open house that day; and the Americans themselves determined that the day should pass off with the greatest 'éclat,' gave one of the most magnificent banquets ever given in this city."[30] The banquet included US diplomatic officials and citizens and powerful Argentines such as Vice President Marcos Paz, Governor Mariano Saavedra of Buenos Aires, Minister of the Interior Guillermo Rawson, and Minister of Foreign Affairs Rufino de Elizalde. Organizers decorated the room with US and Argentine flags and portraits of George Washington and Bartolomé Mitre.[31]

After a sumptuous meal, participants offered toasts, orations, and renditions of US and Argentine patriotic songs. Argentines used their toasts and orations strategically. Vice President Paz, for instance, observed "the United States is a phenomenon for the world" and hoped the "new era of peace which is ushered in be the harbinger of a bright and happy future for the American people."[32] Governor Saavedra proclaimed he never lost faith in the United States during the Civil War and that the "true soldiers of democracy" fought "for the liberty of their fellow man." Rawson praised the abolition of slavery in the United States, glad that the country had joined Argentina, among others, in stamping out the foul practice. Elizalde lauded the US triumph and considered the US victory one for republicans throughout the hemisphere.[33] The banquet broke up at 11:00 p.m., after nearly five hours of celebration.[34]

Celebrating the Fourth in Argentina and Mexico, 1866–1880

Fourth of July celebrations occurred in Argentina throughout the rest of the period of this study.[35] In 1867, for instance, the US cutter *Kate Sergent* hoisted the flag and fired a salute. "In an instant the Port Capt. of B, Ayres lowered the Argentine flag and hoisted the Stars and Stripes." The captain of the *Kate Sergent* entertained guests, and members of the party offered toasts to Andrew Johnson, Bartolomé Mitre, and US Minister Alexander Asbóth.[36] At the same time, in another part of the city, US citizens and Argentines gathered to celebrate the Fourth. In addition to the usual toasts, a Señor Varela "drank success to the U. States, and hoped that the Argentine Republic on the Southern Continent would ere long assume the same role as the United States in the North." The attendees responded with "great cheering."[37]

Unlike their counterparts in Mexico, Argentine authorities had a more ambiguous role; sometimes they were involved, other times, not. In 1868, the *Standard* reported that "the glorious 'Fourth' was handsomely celebrated in these parts." Some people went to a celebration held at Major Hall's estancia. Others remained in the city of Rosario and attended a banquet in a room "completely draped with the flags of different nations."[38] Argentines officials were not really involved in either celebration.[39] However, at other celebrations, Argentines explored the meaning of the Fourth of July. For example, on July 9, 1869, at the first celebration of Argentina's Independence Day in Asunción, Paraguay, Dr. Luis Alvez "characterized the month of July as the American month of liberty; he spoke on the Fourth of July, and its glorious associations for Americans; he then touched on the liberties of Europe, and the great French revolution."[40] In 1876, ex-president Domingo F. Sarmiento, seizing the opportunity offered by the US Centennial, celebrated the Fourth with a group of Argentines and US officials in US Minister Thomas O. Osborn's house.[41] Sarmiento delivered a speech on the meaning of the Fourth of July. Invoking religious imagery, he proclaimed that, just as "the trumpets of Jericho broke down walls," the first Fourth of July "crumbled the structure of the old social order."[42] Sarmiento deftly linked the United States and Argentina as partners in the future and concluded with a toast to Abraham Lincoln and Horace Mann, whom he labeled his household gods.

In 1865, Argentines put a great deal of effort into commemorating the Fourth. The provincial and national authorities marked the importance of the day, and some of the most powerful Argentines attended the banquet and gave speeches linking the destinies of the two nations. However, in other years, the efforts of Argentine authorities to celebrate the anniversary of US independence proved inconsistent. The state of the US-Argentine relationship explained why. Unlike Mexico, Argentina's relationship with the United States was nowhere near as strained. Thus, while the language of some of these celebrations suggests a conscious desire, on the part of citizens of both nations, to maintain good relations, Argentines did not feel the need to celebrate every year.[43] In a sense, the United States and Argentina were already on the sister republic path. The great transformation in this period was the recalibration, by both US citizens and Mexican citizens, of their feelings toward each other. Sarmiento and other Argentines employed similar techniques as Mexicans to reinforce the ties between their respective nations, although they did not feel the need to hammer this point every year.

As the French Intervention ended, Mexican authorities became more and more involved with Fourth of July celebrations. Writing just weeks after Maximilian's execution, Consul E. H. Saulnier of Veracruz informed Seward of two important developments. On June 28, 1867, the USS *Tacony* gave the Mexican flag a twenty-one-gun salute, and Fort Santiago replied in kind.[44] The salute commemorated Liberal General Rafael Benavides's entry into Veracruz. Several days later, on the Fourth of July, "at Noon a Salute of 21 guns was given simultaneously to the American flag from the fortress of San Juan de Ulloa and the U.S.S. Tacony."[45] It is uncertain if the simultaneous salute was coordinated or spontaneous. Nevertheless, this salute to US independence represented an amazing development. Barely two decades earlier, General Winfield Scott bombarded Veracruz into submission during the US War with Mexico. Now the city celebrated the Fourth of July.

On July 5, Franklin Chase of Tampico informed Frederick Seward that Governor Desiderio Pavón of Tamaulipas "ordered this Consulate to be serenaded, and during its performance he attended in person and accompanied with his staff. At early dawn on the 4th, he caused all the public edifices to be decorated with the flag of his country, with other demonstrations of joy, and at Meridian he saluted our flag with 21 guns." Chase gloried in these developments. "The authorities here" he enthused, "have manifested the most grateful marks of respect towards this Consulate, and our country men have been treated with special Kindness."[46] Although the United States did not replicate their role at the Battle of Antón Lizardo and capture or destroy Imperialist vessels stationed at Tampico, the United States had provided various forms of assistance to the Liberals over the past two years. Pavón, thinking hemispherically, may have reasoned that celebrating the Fourth of July could mark the "new birth of freedom" in Mexico. Given the recent end of the French Intervention and execution of Maximilian, not to mention the end of the US Civil War two years earlier, both the United States and Mexico had much to celebrate, particularly the Pan-American cooperation that helped ensure these outcomes.

Several July Fourth celebrations occurred throughout Mexico in 1868. In Mexico City, "the Government of the Republic ordered a display of the national flags on the Fourth of July: and in a letter to a breakfast party of Americans on that day, Minister Mariscal proposed a hearty cheer for the great sister Republic of the North."[47] La Paz, in Baja California Sur, featured a "magnificent" celebration. "The military paraded and the first salute of thirty-seven guns was given at noon and twenty guns at sunset. The Declaration of Independence was read, followed by speeches. The day closed with a grand supper at the United States Consulate rooms."[48] In Vera Cruz, in a repeat of the events of 1867, the USS *Marblehead* "fired a salute of thirty-seven guns," and San Juan de Ulloa replied.[49] Similarly, in Mazatlán, "the Saranac fired the national salute, which was answered from the Fort. The Mexican ensign floated from every public building in honor of the occasion. The American Consul received congratulations from his friends during the day and evening. Gen. Corona and thirty or so forty friends presented their compliments."[50] Finally, "in Tehuantepec city, as a compliment to the American people, the Fourth of July was celebrated with a serenade, fireworks and a procession. Thomas H. Woolrich gave a ball and supper in commemoration of the occasion, which was attended by the *elite* of the place," in the same way that the Argentine elite turned out for the 1865 celebration.[51] This wave of fetes illustrated the staying power of the rapprochement between the two nations. People continually discovered and embraced new ways to understand their world; no longer bitter antagonists, but cooperative and understanding friends.

In Chihuahua, Consul Charles Moye wrote excitedly to Secretary of State Hamilton Fish in 1869 about July Fourth developments. On the evening of July 3, "I verbally apprised the Governor of this State, that the next day would be the 94th anniversary of the Independence of the United States of America." The purpose of this conversation was to ask "at the same time his permission of hoist the U. S. flag over this Consulate, in commemoration of that great event." Moye delightedly reported that "he readily acceded to my application, assuring me, that also the Mexican colors should be displayed from all the public edifices for the same purpose. This is the first time that the fourth July has been celebrated by the State Government of Chihuahua."[52] Importantly, the governor not only acceded to Moye's request but also ordered a reciprocal gesture. Also in 1869, in Mazatlán "Governor Rubi, being unwell, sent his Secretary to make the usual congratulatory visit to the American Consul."[53] Additionally, "the Fourth of July was duly observed here [Mexico City] by the flying of the Stars and Stripes from the United States Legation and Consulate, and similar customary observances at the national palace and other public buildings."[54] More and more places and people, throughout Mexico, celebrated the Fourth of July as the years passed.

In 1872, the city of San Luis Potosí, in the State of San Luis Potosí, suffered from a rebellion. The rebels made life ferociously difficult for government troops and foreigners in general. US Commercial Agent Julius Noureau discussed the running conflict between rebels and government soldiers and noted an important difference in the two groups. Whereas "the General Government behaved uncommonly well, not having exacted any forced loans or extra Contributions as it is the custom of the country," the rebels "imposed very heavy taxes in all the places they got to, and in fact are living entirely on the country they have occupied."[55] Several months later, he observed that the rebels received the worst in a fight with the government forces and "the [state] government is expecting a lot of arms from the capital with which they will be able, to put up a force, strong enough to finish with the revolution in our part of the country." In the same despatch, Noureau informed the State Department, "on the 4th of July the flags were hoisted on all the public buildings, and on the Consulate of the German Empire, in honor to our flag exhibited at this Consulate"[56] Even when the state government had far more important concerns— such as the suppression of rebellion and the restoration of order—they still took the time to celebrate the anniversary of US independence.

An 1880 exchange between Mexican General M. de la Peña and US Consul Warner P. Sutton of Matamoros raised vexing questions about the frequency of July Fourth celebrations in Matamoros. On July 3, de la Peña wrote to Sutton, "by the order of Genl in Chief Servando Canales, that on Monday there will be a salute of 21 guns fired on the bank of the Rio Bravo, at sunrise and sunset in honor of the Anniversary of the Independence of the United States. The national colors will be displayed on all public buildings."[57] In reply, Sutton acknowledged de la Peña's letter and expressed "the hope that the present cordial relations between the two Republics may be lasting and mutually beneficial."[58] In his letter to the State Department, Sutton noted: "on the 3ᵈ a letter was received from General M. de la Peña, the Mexican Chief of Staff, notifying me that the usual salute and display of flags would be made on the 5th, the 4th coming on Sunday. The flag of this consulate, as also those of the Mexican authorities, was displayed on the 4th, and the 5th."[59] Sutton's reference to the "usual salute" was frustratingly vague. Did he mean a "usual salute" in the sense that this is what the authorities of Matamoros always did on the Fourth of July? Since this was the first mention of a Fourth of July celebration in Matamoros, it is possible Sutton spoke in a more general sense. However, by the same token, he may have underreported Fourth of July celebrations. Sutton and de la Peña wrote in 1880, several years after the United States recognized Porfirio Díaz as president of Mexico. Since this action pleased many Mexicans, it is unsurprising that Mexican officials friendly to Díaz marked the date of US independence with a celebration, but it would have been odd for them to wait until 1880 to do so.

The city of Guaymas celebrated the Fourth of July every year beginning in 1869. The consistent celebrations stimulated goodwill and helped reinforce the friendship between the two countries and Pan-American cooperation. In 1869, Consul A. Willard wrote to the assistant secretary of state that "the 4th of July passed off quietly and pleasantly in this place. The General, commanding the Department of Sonora, together with the Federal & State officials of this port, called at the Consulate to offer congratulations, and the Mexican Flag was displayed over all the Federal & state buildings & offices in honor of the day."[60] This celebration became the first of many.

The 1870 celebration looked very similar to the 1869 celebration. "The 4th of July passed off quietly and pleasantly in this port," reported Consul Willard, "the Mexican flag was displayed during the day over all the public offices and buildings of the city." Willard received visits from a steady stream of officials including "the 'Association del Pueblo,' with their band of music; the President and members of the Common Council (ayuntamiento): the Judges of the Federal and District Courts; the Collector and other officers of the Custom House; and the Prefect of the District—(The Genl of this Dept being absent)." Critically, Willard also observed "the most friendly feelings were expressed towards the United States, and particular mention was made, in endorsing the action of the Commander of the U.S.S. 'Mohican,' in burning the [illegible word] 'Forward' [illegible word] San Blas on the 18th."[61] The burning of the

Forward, a Mexican pirate ship in rebellion against President Juárez, by the *Mohican* delighted many Mexicans who fervently approved of this type of US intervention, which differed greatly from intervention of the James K. Polk expansionist stripe.

An article in a Mexican newspaper described a dinner for United States and Mexican officials and how they emphasized the friendship between the two nations. Mexicans "manifested in eloquent phrases of sincere friendship their sympathies for the gigantic country that stands at the head of civilization." Consul Willard "expressed his ardent desire to see an enlarged and happy Mexico."[62] Mexican officials toasted the presidents of the two nations and the prosperity of the two republics. Willard responded by toasting the federal and state authorities and the prosperity of Mexico. All told, "during the dinner there were a thousand demonstrations" given by the attendees "of mutual sympathy and sincere friendship, demonstrating with this once more the perfect harmony that exists between the citizens of both republics."[63] Mexican officials certainly welcomed the US destruction of a dangerous pirate vessel. That said, the celebration was not due to this fact alone but, rather, to highlight the friendship and cooperation between the two countries.

From 1871 to 1875, Fourth of July celebrations in Guaymas followed the same basic script. Consul Willard generally wrote the State Department that "the anniversary of our National Independence (the 4 of July) was duly observed in this Port.—The General Comdg the Dept: the officers of the Federal garrison: the Prefect and other civil authorities, called at the Consulate and offered their congratulations, and the courts throughout the city were not opened till 4 o'clock P.M.—The Mexican flag was displayed on all of the Public buildings in honor of the day."[64] Sometimes a military band accompanied the officers and serenaded the consulate.[65] July Fourth celebrations, in other words, followed a set pattern in Guaymas. It is unclear if Sonoran officials were more conscientious about observing July Fourth or if the consul was more conscientious about sending reports.

In 1876, the Centennial of the United States, the celebration was much more extravagant. "The 4th July, went off here, brilliantly," Vice Consul A. F. Garrison explained. "At sunrise Gen[l] Mercial [*sic*], had a salute of Guns fired, and all the *flags*, in the City and harbour, unfurled;—In morning Gen[l] Mercial [*sic*] & Officers & some 600 citizens with band of 20 musicians visited the US Consulate where hospitality in abundance prevailed.—Very complimentary toasts exchanged, and warm fraternity, and cordiality, marked the day. In the Evening, fire works [sic], and musick [sic] on public Palaza [sic]."⁶⁶ But for the fact that the majority of people spoke Spanish, Garrison could have been in any US city celebrating the Centennial. After the Centennial celebration, the celebrations for the rest of the 1870s and early 1880s returned to the pre-1876 formula. In 1880, for instance, Willard explained that federal and state officials, as well as US and Mexican citizens, called on the consulate and, in the evening, "appropriate toasts were drank to the Presidents of the United States and of Mexico, and to the friendship between the two countries—a friendly spirit was manifested by all and the day passed off pleasantly."⁶⁷ From start to finish, the ready conclusion inspired by the celebrations of July Fourth in Guaymas is that they reinforced friendship and amity between the United States and Mexico and showcased the continuation and strength of Pan-American cooperation.

Celebrating Washington's Birthday

Interestingly, in 1872, Guaymas also began celebrating George Washington's birthday. These celebrations were neither as elaborate nor as consistent as the celebrations of the Fourth of July. Nevertheless, celebrations of this nature also reinforced the friendship and cooperation between the United States and Mexico. In 1872, for example, Consul Willard wrote that "the anniversary of the birth day of 'Washington' was duly observed at this port: the Mexican flag being unfurled over all of the public offices and buildings of the City in honor of the day"⁶⁸ Vice Consul A. F. Garrison reported in 1873 that "The Anniversary of Washingtons birth day, was appropriately celebrated here, and at US Consulate—all the Flags in the city and harbor—Public and Private— Mexican, German, French and English were displayed, upon invitation by Circular from this office—and wave fraternally with the 'Stars and Stripes'—and the Lavee [sic] of the U. S. Vice Consul numerously attended where great unity and cordiality prevailed and the correspondence published."⁶⁹ Washington's Birthday celebrations also occurred in 1875, 1876, and 1877.⁷⁰

The 1877 celebration took place several months after the Sonoran authorities proclaimed the Plan de Tuxtepec. This Plan, issued by a group of Porfirista officers determined to make Díaz president of Mexico, produced bloody fighting between supporters of Díaz, Sebastián Lerdo de Tejada, and José María Iglesias.⁷¹ Thus, in the midst of a fierce struggle, the authorities took the time to commemorate Washington's birthday. This decision might have been strategic; not necessarily an appeal for arms but looking to the future and realizing US recognition of Díaz would be vital. However, it might just as easily have been another attempt to cement the friendship between the two countries. In sum, Washington's Birthday celebrations, while neither as elaborate nor as consistent as July Fourth celebrations, clearly occurred for a reason.

Fourth of July Celebrations, Nationalism, and Xenophobia

Fourth of July celebrations, quintessential nationalist festivals, became something more during this period—festivals of friendship and cooperation. To be sure, Argentines and Mexicans sometimes celebrated the Fourth of July for strategic reasons, and some of their more effusive language should be handled carefully. All that said, people skillfully employed these celebrations to highlight cooperation and friendship and the greatly improved relations among the nations of the New World. In a discussion of US nationalism, one scholar observed that celebrating the Fourth of July after the US Civil War ended allowed US missionaries abroad to express new feelings of national identity.[72] Non-US actors, such as Mexicans and Argentines, also played a role in reforging US nationalism by invoking their own understandings of national identities. Orators tied the United States, Mexico, and Argentina together by invoking the language of sister republics and insisted that both countries traveled a similar path and pursued democracy and freedom with vigor. By so doing, they reminded people that while the United States might define itself as a providential nation—a city on the hill and the light to the world—Mexico and Argentina were equal partners in the republican experiment. All three nations had passed through their own new birth of freedom.

Strong responses to Fourth of July celebrations revealed how people continued to see the United States, Mexico, and Argentina as "sister republics" and the benefits of Pan-American cooperation. Plenty of people appreciated how Mexicans and Argentines used nationalist festivals to broaden US nationalism by linking the countries together. Nationalism, therefore, was made as much abroad as it was at home.[73] To be fair, many people never subscribed to these ideas and continued to spout racist ideas about Latin Americans in general and Mexicans in particular. However, when people embraced the sister republic idea, they promoted a vision of cooperation among the nations of the New World.

Some of these celebrations, to modern eyes, might not seem particularly noteworthy. Was it really that difficult to raise a flag and fire a gun? Did it signify anything? However, in Mexico's case, the context made these celebrations much more significant. Less than twenty years earlier, in 1846–48, the United States waged a war against Mexico that the vast majority of Mexicans, as well as many in the United States, regarded as an appallingly unjust land grab. Consequently, in the period between the US War with Mexico and the US Civil War, anti-US sentiment ran particularly strong in Mexico. That Mexicans would hoist the colors and salute the US flag, not to mention put on far more elaborate ceremonies and celebrations, illustrates the remarkable rapprochement between the two countries—an extraordinary departure from the preceding years—and the continuation of that rapprochement after the end of the French Intervention. The continued celebrations also illuminate how anti-US sentiment decreased, often strikingly, in some Mexican states.[74]

The cities of Chihuahua and Guaymas provide a striking illustration of how xenophobia could and did decline in parts of Mexico. In Chihuahua, ten years before Charles Moye reported the first celebration of the Fourth of July, Consul George L. McManus snarled to Secretary of State Lewis Cass that "these people are so prejudiced against Foreigners that they will visit the sins of the Nation upon the individual."[75] Several months later, McManus growled, "we have just passed through a revolution here which had the conservative or Church party been successful, would have cost the foreign residents of this place their property and perhaps their lives." José Maria Zuloaga, the brother of the "would-be President," marched on the city, intending to sack the foreign merchants who allegedly sympathized with the Liberals. McManus warned Cass that "it is a well known fact that that rabble readily join any such enterprize, and it is also well known if they are once let loose in these Cities they immediately bellow 'death to the 'Gringos' and we are not sufficiently numerous here to resist an organized mob." Fortunately, Governor Antonio Ochoa of Chihuahua suppressed the rebellion.[76]

The relationship between Mexico and US citizens improved once McManus left.[77] His successor, Reuben W. Creel, had a good working relationship with Liberal officials. As part of his retreat from Mexico City to the northern Mexican states, Benito Juárez made Chihuahua a seat of the government for a period of time. Creel admired Juárez and got along well with Mexican ministers.[78] Although Creel had been replaced by 1869, when the first celebration of the Fourth of July occurred in Chihuahua, the seeds planted during his tenure bore fruit. The celebration offered another manifestation of the rapprochement between the United States and Mexico. Mexican officials promoted a stronger relationship with the United States by means of July Fourth celebrations.[79] Xenophobia and nativism were not destroyed in Chihuahua by any means, but, in ten years, Chihuahuenses stopped screaming "death to the Gringos" and started celebrating July Fourth.

In Guaymas, the presence of a US Surveying Commission in 1858–59 caused no end of trouble. On January 8, 1859, the Commission "gave a ball which was attended by all the principal people of the town, where the best possible feeling seemed to prevail: but the Judge of [illegible word] instance, not being in the best circle of society was not invited." Therefore, the judge "presented himself, drunk and armed with a revolver, at the windows, and shouted 'death to the Yankees!' and called on the populace to take advantage of the opportunity and kill them all—After a little disturbance he was taken away by the guard and carried home, no notice being taken of the occurrence by the Americans."[80] This episode might seem a farce, but it hinted at ugly feelings simmering beneath the city's placid surface.

Less than a year later, Vice Consul Farrelly Alden wrote a harrowing letter to Captain William Porter of the US Navy: "On the 20th inst when you furnished this Consulate with a flag staff, the 'Stars and Stripes' were raised in Guaymas for the first time since the close of the Mexican War. The flag should command respect and afford protection, but the coat of arms over the entrance was spat upon and wantonly defaced." In addition, the US flag, Alden shrieked, "has been shot at repeatedly from the surrounding eminences, the balls whizzing into the Consulate enclosure to the imminent danger of the inmates, whilst night is made hideous with cries of ('muerto a los Americanos') death to the Americans." Alden also told Porter that "defenceless Americans have been stoned in the public Streets of Guaymas at mid-day." "The distracted condition of this unhappy country, the threats of the Mexicans to exterminate all foreigners, and their hostile acts," Alden concluded apocalyptically, "compel me to urge upon you the necessity of remaining in this Port for our protection till relieved, if withdrawn it will doubtless be the death knell of all American citizens in Sonora."[81]

A month later, Alden wrote again to Porter, noting "to day at one o'clock my consulate was invaded by some Mexican Soldiers, who mounted my office, cut down the consular flag, dragged the same through the streets and stamped upon it, in the presence of scores of soldiers, shouting 'muerto a los Americanos' last night the consular coat of arms was torn down at the point of the bayonet and carried off by the Mexican soldiers." Alden begged Porter to protect him.[82] In addition, as if this was not enough, "this noon whilst walking to the house of his Excellency Governor Pesqueira on urgent official business, through one of the most public streets in Guaymas which extends from the wharf with the prison, Court House, + Police Office on one side and the Fort on the other to the Plaza, I was without cause thrust aside and received a stunning blow with a musket by a soldier who was aided and abeted [sic] by forty or fifty others thirsting for my blood, who seized and doubtless would have massacred me but for an officer high in rank who quickly came to my rescue."[83]

Despite the sympathy of a few officials, for their own reasons, nativism and anti-US sentiment in Sonora ran deep. In 1861 Consul William L. Baker wrote to Seward that "the life + property of our American Citizens imperitively [sic] demand a National Vessel to be stationed here immediately and I desire you will take the necessary steps at once to have one placed here."[84] The relationship between the consulate and the authorities, at least in Guaymas, improved after the expulsion of the French and the execution of the Austrian pretender. July Fourth celebrations in Guaymas served as a way to cement US-Mexico friendship. In a decade, in another striking transformation, the people of Guaymas went from firing on the consulate, dragging the US flag through the streets, and assaulting the consul, to marking the anniversary of the independence of the United States and of Washington's birth. Like Chihuahua, nativism and xenophobia did not lose their hold, but July Fourth celebrations help explain their partial loss of power. When analyzing the Americas during this period, it is important to remember that no country avoided these forces. Nativism and xenophobia never disappeared in the United States, Argentina, or Mexico, but accounts of this period sometimes overemphasize these forces while ignoring rapprochement and cooperation.

If authorities had some success in taming nativism and xenophobia in Guaymas and Chihuahua, they raged out of control in other Mexican states. Consul Rollin C. M. Hoyt, stationed at Minatitlán, enclosed to Secretary of State Hamilton Fish "a warning to foreigners on this Isthmus, which was first posted up on public places in Tehuantepec, afterwards here and other places on the Isthmus. One of them was posted on the door of the US Consular

Agency in Tehuantepec."[85] Several months later, Deputy Consul John Wolf hurriedly advised the State Department that "some alarm was felt by much of the foreigners here, upon the approximation of the Celebration of Mexican Independence, on account of the bad feeling expressed by many Mexicans against foreigners here of late, but everything passed off in harmony and Cordiality, and no offence was given to foreigners, neither in the public Speeches nor otherwise."[86] Wolf made it clear the citizens of Minatitlán were fortunate this nationalist festival did not degenerate into violence.

State and national authorities in the United States and Mexico often could not control these powerful forces, nor did they always want to. Affairs in Nuevo León, for example, worried diplomatic officials.[87] Consul Joseph Ulrich of Monterrey fretted that several US citizens had been murdered and argued there was a "growing insecurity for the lives of foreigners in this portion of Mexico."[88] Consul John Weber derided Governor Genaro Garza García as a "notorious Knownothing [sic]." According to Weber, Garza not only approved of the bitterly anti-US editorials published in the *Periodico Oficial* but actually ordered them published. In addition, Weber wrote, García was a former rebel who, as a self-proclaimed governor during a pronunciamiento "comitted [sic] so many outrages on foreigners generally, and on Americans particularly."[89] Weber also noted that the editorials in the paper displeased General Treviño. As much as he detested García, Weber admired Treviño, who, he claimed, worked to secure Mexican prosperity and friendship with the United States, "notwithstanding the many difficulties thrown in his way by hotheaded 'Knownothings' calling themselves mexican patriots."[90]

The difference of opinion between García and Treviño on the issues of Mexico's relations with the United States and antiforeign sentiment more generally revealed that nativism and xenophobia oscillated in Mexico, as they did throughout the Americas. A series of hostile officials in Monterrey made life dangerous for US citizens living in Nuevo León. The situation differed greatly in La Paz. US relations with territorial officials were not particularly friendly in the 1850s. Consul Thomas Sprague wrote to William L. Marcy that the Mexican government had made Baja California a penal colony, that the governor had "instructions to keep out of the country all foreigners, and to sustain and protect all such persons as would commit depredations in the persons or property of American citizens," and that "the local authorities of this Territory have *paid* Mexican [?] to murder American citizens." Sprague also labeled the authorities of Baja California "robbers and thieves without exception."[91] Local authorities reciprocated Sprague's sentiments and regarded him as an evil-intentioned filibusterer.[92]

The problems Sprague claimed US citizens faced in La Paz seemed to disappear once his replacement arrived and Liberals took possession of the city. The new consul, F. B. Elmer, asserted, in 1863, that the Territorial Administration is "remarkably liberal in their ideas and favorable to progress + evince unmistakably the greatest goodwill towards the American Government. I find among them no perceptible sympathy with the southern rebellion." Furthermore, "the Territorial and local authorities evince a disposition favorable to the immigration of foreigners, especially Americans and Germans, and seem inclined, as a general thing, to avoid unjust discrimination, when the interests of strangers, and those of their own people come into conflict."[93] Territorial officials did their best to protect US citizens.[94] However, during the final months of the reign of the Austrian pretender, Elmer informed Seward that "hardly a month passes without an attempt at revolution, and the present government maintains itself by sheer force. The general government is too busy, or is disinclined, to give any attention to the matter, and the people have fallen, as a consequence, into the hands of a lot of demagogues, who lead what is known here as the 'Exclusive' (which means here just now anti-American) anti-progressive party."[95] This party represented one-quarter of the people of the territory, but they were an extremely vocal minority, and Elmer fretted about the problems this group might cause in the future.

Pro- and anti-US sentiment continually alternated in La Paz. "I have known more than one American Citizen to be brutally murdered by the Authorities, or by men acting under their orders," Consul David Turner complained, and "others have been imprisoned and abused without law or reason; American vessels have been detained, annoyed and robbed, the American Flag has been insulted."[96] On the other hand, Turner reported, four years later, that the killing of a Mexican by an Englishman produced unfortunate results: "The Mexicans generally exhibited great animosity toward foreigners, marching through the streets crying, 'Mueran los gringos,' (death to the foreigners) and fears were ascertained that an attack would be made by them upon the foreigners in the place." Fortunately, government troops "displayed great prudence and firmness, and soon reduced the people to quiet."[97] All evidence, Turner concluded, pointed to a "far better state of feeling towards Americans than that which

existed five years ago."[98] Nativism and xenophobia lessened significantly in
Guaymas and Chihuahua, ran strong in Minatitlán and Monterrey, and oscillated in La Paz. These forces became important issues in Mexico during this
time, as in the United States and Argentina. July Fourth celebrations demonstrated how officials worked to reduce these virulent sentiments while promoting friendship and cooperation.

There are several important points to take away from this discussion. One,
if nationalist festivals helped to unify countries, they could also help tear them
apart. Witness some of the comments in this chapter from consuls who feared
celebrations of Mexican nationalist festivals would result in violence, from consuls who were careful to note that celebrations of the Fourth of July passed off
well, thus breathing an implicit sigh of relief, and from consuls who feared celebrations of US nationalist festivals could lead to anger and violence by sectors
of the population and derail US-Mexico rapprochement. Two, nativism and
xenophobia were not just issues in the United States, Mexico, or Argentina,
they were hemispheric problem. Thus, rather than thinking about sporadic and
discrete episodes in each country, historians should look at the long, conjoined
history of nativism and xenophobia in the Western Hemisphere.[99]

Ultimately, nationalist festivals could, and did, produce both positive and
negative results. While they drew the three countries closer together, they
could also pose a threat to US citizens in Mexico or to foreigners in the United
States.[100] Nationalism cannot and indeed should not be analyzed in a void or
with a lens that considers only internal factors. To understand nationalism in
the United States, Argentina, and Mexico, we have to look abroad and employ an international lens to think about a national problem. Many Mexicans
and Argentines saw their destiny as inextricably linked with that of the United
States and said so through Fourth of July celebrations. In the words of Felipe J.
Serra, "soon the united banners of our respective nationalities shall proclaim
that Americans must rule America, that each of the republican governments of
which this continent is composed shall be free from all European intervention,
and that the fleets of the Old World shall not sail upon our seas without first
saluting the flags of Washington and of Hidalgo." Responses to such sentiments
illustrated that many people agreed with this type of language and understood
the virtues of cooperation among the sister republics of the New World in an
important Pan-American moment.[101]

Conclusion: Progress and Sarmiento's Fourth of July

July 4, 1873, the ninety-seventh anniversary of US independence, also became an important moment in Argentine infrastructural development. As one newspaper noted, "direct instantaneous communication was obtained between Buenos Ayres and Valparaiso by means of the Provincial telegraph line to Rosario, and thence the Central Argentine wires to Villa Maria." Mr. Sarratea, the chairman of the company constructing the wires, sent messages from Valparaiso to a company representative in Buenos Aires standing in for President Sarmiento, who was attending a celebration of the Fourth of July.[102] Much as John C. Calhoun did decades earlier in the United States, Sarmiento dreamed about conquering space. Thus, as he celebrated July Fourth with US citizens residing in Argentina and gloried that the United States and Argentina had a strong, productive relationship, he also directed the internal improvement of his own nation.

The victors in each civil war—Republicans in the United States, Unitarios in Argentina, and Liberals in Mexico—shared Sarmiento's vision. The following chapter explores how the victors designed new worlds in order to achieve their visions of order, modernization, and progress. It also briefly considers how the vanquished in each country responded to the monumental changes in their worlds. Even as Pan-American cooperation continued among the sister republics of the Americas, particularly in the realm of educational policy and reform, each nation remained riven by severe internal conflicts. In their attempts to secure the fruits of their victories, the victors planted seeds that ultimately bore bitter fruit.

4

Visions of the Victors

EDUCATION & INTERNAL IMPROVEMENT

In the early 1850s, Domingo F. Sarmiento grandly asserted that his purpose in life was to "educate the mass of the South American population" and that he had devoted his entire existence to this purpose.[1] Sarmiento wore many hats during his lifetime. At one point or another, he was a teacher, soldier, statesman, author, and diplomat. Still, of all those different jobs, Sarmiento considered teaching and education his primary purpose. When Justo José de Urquiza defeated Juan Manuel de Rosas at the Battle of Caseros in 1852, Sarmiento celebrated the overthrow of Rosas, because he had fought the tyrant for decades. However, after the province of Buenos Aires subsequently refused to be part of the Argentine Confederation, Sarmiento cast his lot with Buenos Aires. He quickly became an important voice calling for the development of the Buenos Aires school system and, later, Argentina's educational system.[2]

Sarmiento, like many of his contemporaries in the United States, Mexico, and Argentina, understood the transnational nature of the world, one marked by flows of people, goods, and ideas.[3] In this world, it was perfectly logical for transnational warriors to circulate from country to country fighting in different wars, for people in the United States and Mexico to invoke both the language of "sister republics" and the Monroe Doctrine to argue for US intervention to expel the French, and for people in Mexico and Argentina to celebrate the Fourth of July. It was also natural and logical for reformers from the United States, Mexico, and Argentina, not to mention Great Britain and other European nations, to consider themselves part of a broader community with shared values and ideas.[4] Sarmiento and many Argentine Unitarios; US reformers and Republicans like Mary Mann and Edward Lee Plumb; and Mexican Liberals like Matías Romero collaborated with each other, responded to common intellectual movements and traditions, and considered themselves part of what *Harper's Weekly* called "the great liberal party of the world."[5]

A central tenet of republicanism, and one that Sarmiento and his fellow liberals fervently embraced, is the need for a virtuous and informed citizenry. Consequently, reformers believed that their educational efforts, which were about making good citizens as much as education, could strengthen republics beset by reactionary forces. This chapter analyzes educational efforts in the United States, Mexico, and Argentina, with particular emphasis on Sarmiento's decades-long struggle to develop Argentina's educational system and how his ideas evolved over time. People in each of the three countries embraced similar ideas about education and citizenship, observed educational practices in other countries, imported and modified ideas, and cooperated across borders. In sum, Pan-American cooperation drove educational reform and efforts. Sarmiento, like many other people in the United States, Mexico, and Argentina, saw an important connection between education and citizenship and believed that educated citizens were not only good citizens but also a bulwark against tyranny.[6] Finally, the victors in each of the three civil wars imposed their ideas about civilization, modernity, and progress on the vanquished and some discontented victors. This, in turn, generated backlash that helps explain the ferocity of the challenges by the vanquished and discontented victors analyzed in part 2 of this book.

Education in the Americas

Nothing in Sarmiento's background suggested he would become, as one newspaper put it, the "Father of Education in South America."[7] Sarmiento was born in 1811, in the province of San Juan, to a poor family. Nevertheless, from these humble beginnings, he rose to the zenith of Argentine politics.[8] He came of age during the bitter war between two political parties—the Unitarios and the Federales. Unitarios believed in a strong centralized government whereas the Federales favored a weaker central government and more powerful provincial governments.[9] Fighting between the two parties lasted nearly fifty years and engendered hatred on both sides.[10] Federales banded together under the leadership of regional caudillos (strongmen), like Juan Manuel de Rosas, the governor of Buenos Aires and the caudillo of the Río de la Plata, and Juan Facundo

Quiroga. Quiroga, a fierce and impetuous man nicknamed "El Tigre de los Llanos" (the Tiger of the Plains), controlled the province of La Rioja for several
years, until political opponents assassinated him. Rosas, a wealthy landholder,
initially won election as governor of the province of Buenos Aires but quickly
assumed dictatorial powers and ruled the province from 1828 to 1835 and from
1832 until his defeat in 1852 at the Battle of Caseros.[11] Federales and caudillos
fiercely resisted the centralizing tendencies of Sarmiento and the Unitarios.[12]

As a teacher in San Juan, Sarmiento came to understand education as the
key to destroying the power of dictators like Rosas, a man who, in Sarmiento's eyes, was the "the most barbarous representative of barbarism."[13] People
throughout the Americas believed that oligarchs and aristocrats deliberately
withheld education to keep large masses of people subservient. Furthermore,
numerous people in the United States, particularly in the northern states, as
well as Atlantic reformers, shared Sarmiento's belief that education was a bulwark against tyranny and that republics, in order to survive and thrive, needed
informed citizens. Sarmiento likely developed his views through his own experiences and from what he read.[14] Sarmiento read many of the same books
and newspapers as his reform-minded contemporaries and shared a common
intellectual background with them that allowed people throughout the hemisphere to arrive independently at similar ideas. Specifically, that in the never-
ending struggle between democracy and republicanism on the one hand and
the forces of reaction on the other, education was crucial.

Sarmiento's anti-Rosas ideas fed his anti-Rosas activism. In other words,
he took up arms with his fellow Unitarios in San Juan against the Federales.
The failure of this appeal to bullets led to multiple exiles in Chile. Sarmiento
returned to Argentina in 1835, after Quiroga's assassination, founded a school
for women in 1839 (the Colegio de Santa Rosa de América), and established
and edited a newspaper—*El Zonda.* Sarmiento's blend of democratic ideals
and biting satire irritated Nazario Benavídez, the Federale governor of San
Juan, who exiled Sarmiento to Chile in 1840.[15] This return to Chile proved
extraordinarily consequential for him and for the rest of the world. He edited
El Mercurio and founded *El Nacional,* two important newspapers, but, more
importantly, continued writing anti-Rosas tirades. This included perhaps the
most important book published in Latin America in the nineteenth century,
Facundo: O civilización y barbarie (1845).[16]

Although *Facundo* appeared to be a biography of Quiroga, it offered far more than just a biography of a caudillo. Sarmiento presented lengthy and damning analysis of the conditions in Argentina that produced a man like Quiroga and a scathing denunciation of the Federales. Rosas, Sarmiento proclaimed, would not remain in power forever, and education would play a critical role in his downfall: "Hundreds of Argentine students are sheltered in the schools of France, Chile, Brazil, North America, England, and even Spain. They will return later to realize in this country the institutions that gleam brightly in these free States; and will put their might behind overthrowing this semi-barbarous tyrant."[17] Sarmiento, who spent large portions of his life in exile, not only understood how the exile experience could shelter and protect enemies of Rosas, but also the connections between Argentina and the rest of the world. Even Spain, a country Sarmiento despised because it was monarchical and aristocratic, could aid in overthrowing tyranny and assist the cause of democracy.

Sarmiento saw in the rise of Rosas the culmination of a vicious cycle. "An ignorant people will always elect a Rosas,"[18] he thundered. Therefore, "the Dictator had arisen to power through the barbarism of the people; and the poverty and ignorance of the provinces secured him from all dangerous opposition."[19] Rosas exploited the ignorance of the people, but Sarmiento realized other dictators could just as easily seize and maintain power. Education, therefore, became the answer to ending the reign of dictators. "Primary education," Sarmiento declared, "is the measure of the civilization of a village. Where it is incomplete or abandoned . . . there is a semi-barbarous unenlightened village without customs, industry, or progress."[20] Sarmiento saw in education a panacea; increasing education and decreasing barbarism would facilitate the overthrow of Rosas and prevent other dictators from gaining power by populating republics with an educated citizenry.

Sarmiento's invocation of civilization and barbarism throughout *Facundo* found echoes throughout the Atlantic World. Indeed, the civilization and barbarism rhetoric pervaded Sarmiento's writings, as well as Hinton Rowan Helper's famous book *The Impending Crisis;*[21] the writings of abolitionists;[22] the correspondence, speeches, and presidential proclamations of Abraham Lincoln;[23] and newspapers.[24] When he spoke of a fundamental conflict between a barbarous countryside and civilized cities, Sarmiento engaged with transnational discussions about civilization and modernity.[25] Furthermore, when he used "civilization," he meant the civilization and progress he claimed European immigrants brought to Argentina.

Facundo succeeded on many levels. Sarmiento's strident condemnation of everything wrong in Argentina infuriated Rosas, cheered Sarmiento's fellow Unitarios, and proved Sarmiento's commitment to education.[26] Still, as an exile in Chile, Sarmiento had no impact on Argentine schools in the 1840s, although he gained practical experience in Chile.[27] Manuel Montt, the Chilean minister of justice and public instruction, appointed Sarmiento director of the Escuela Normal de Perceptores in 1842, the first teacher training school established in Chile. In addition, Sarmiento, at Montt's request, undertook a mission of observation for the Chilean government and spent the period 1845–47 studying schools in Europe and the US. *Facundo,* not to mention Sarmiento's other writings and intellectual achievements, won him a chance to play an important role in Chile's educational system. In turn, Montt's favor gave the Argentine exile an opportunity to take an extended trip to observe schools, where he accumulated knowledge about education that could benefit Chile and, perhaps, Argentina.

As he traveled through Europe, Sarmiento's experiences challenged some of his long-cherished notions. Although he admired European monuments and scientific achievements, and although he had long been an admirer of European civilization, Sarmiento found troubling the condition of "millions of farmers, proletarians, and workingmen, who are degraded and unworthy of being counted among men."[28] His findings disheartened Sarmiento, especially since he had long argued, particularly in *Facundo,* that "the genius of European civilization" offered many benefits for Argentina.[29]

Europe proved a disappointment, but a subsequent visit to the United States fascinated Sarmiento.[30] While in Europe, Sarmiento read one of Horace Mann's reports on primary education, which fired his ardor to speak with the influential Massachusetts educational reformer. Thus, the principal objective of his trip to the United States became conversing with Mann, whom Sarmiento lauded as "the great primary education reformer, a traveler, like myself, to Europe in search of methods and systems."[31] During his time in Massachusetts, Sarmiento spent long hours conversing with Horace and his wife, Mary Mann.[32] This fruitful meeting introduced Sarmiento to a prominent US educational reformer and provided Sarmiento with a host of new ideas, including the employment of women as teachers.[33] Prior to this, Sarmiento had clearly been interested in female education, but he thought more about educating women—hence the formation of the Colegio de Santa Rosa de América— than hiring women as teachers.

Sarmiento proved receptive to the Manns' ideas because they produced results. Mann established a teacher training school for women, Sarmiento wrote, and Massachusetts now had, in addition to 2,589 male teachers, 5,000 female teachers. The number of teachers in Massachusetts, Sarmiento marveled, was greater than the total size of Chile's permanent army![34] Sarmiento also viewed Horace and Mary Mann as kindred spirits, a sentiment they reciprocated, and stayed in contact with them. When he returned to the United States in 1865, Sarmiento spent time in New England with the now-widowed Mary Mann.[35] Furthermore, Mary Mann translated *Facundo* into English in 1868, and Sarmiento translated her biography of Horace Mann into Spanish as *Vida de Horacio Mann*.[36] Sarmiento's admiration of Horace Mann ran so deep that in the oration he delivered at an 1876 Fourth of July celebration he asserted that Abraham Lincoln and Horace Mann "completed the Independence proclaimed in 1776, by the freedom of the slave and the education of the people."[37] Sarmiento's kinship with the Manns occurred because of the similarity of their beliefs, a shared interest in educational reform, and their membership in a transnational liberal community.

After his first visit with the Manns, Sarmiento returned to Chile and published an account of his trips. He remained in Chile until 1851, at which point he returned to Argentina and joined Justo José de Urquiza's army as an officer and traveling newspaper correspondent. Sarmiento supported Urquiza against Rosas but feared Urquiza would topple Rosas and then supplant him. These fears, among others, led numerous residents of Buenos Aires to prefer an autonomous existence rather than joining the Argentine Confederation after Urquiza defeated Rosas at the Battle of Caseros in 1852. Sarmiento cast his lot with Buenos Aires. He served in the Buenos Aires Legislature, edited a newspaper, and worked to improve schools in Buenos Aires. "It is time," he thundered in an 1858 speech to the state legislature, "that one of the concerns of the public should be the betterment of the schools."[38] Sarmiento identified Buenos Aires's lack of buildings, lack of funds, and superannuated teachers as obstacles to progress. In addition, many parents did not want their children, particularly girls, to attend school.

Sarmiento, in his desire to develop schools in Buenos Aires, continued the work begun during President Bernardino Rivadavia's short-lived government in the 1820s. Rivadavia "left a blueprint for social institutions, cultural aspirations, and governing style" and made important strides in education.[39]

Indeed, Rivadavia founded the University of Buenos Aires, designed principally for the province of Buenos Aires as well as the *Colegio de Ciencias Morales,* designed for students from the interior provinces. Rivadavia also "sent bright porteño youths to teach in the interior in an outreach program"[40] In the eyes of Sarmiento and his fellow Unitarios, Juan Manuel de Rosas represented a truly pernicious disaster because he slammed the door closed on Rivadavia's promising efforts and attempted to bring schools to heel. Tómas de Anchorena, minister of government under Rosas, instructed teachers and students to wear the red emblem—the symbol of the Federales—and Rosas and his officials strove to "exorcise partisan politics from the schools."[41] Following Rosas's defeat at Caseros, Sarmiento and others quickly grasped the opportunity to enact their ideas about education, first in Buenos Aires and then, after the Battle of Pavón, in the country more generally.

Sarmiento's speeches and writings from this period demonstrated that he frequently argued for the employment of women teachers in Buenos Aires schools. He based this argument on a pragmatic reason—lower salaries. In 1856, for instance, Sarmiento approved of the tendency in school reform movements to employ women as teachers "because they cost less and are more adept than men at managing small children."[42] At this point, only a few Argentine women taught, and exclusively in schools for girls. Sarmiento thus suggested that women, who drew smaller salaries than men, could be employed in greater numbers in the Buenos Aires educational system. In 1857, he contended that women could help realize a project of "good and cheap education for the people," and "can be used in creating a method of educating all children."[43] Perhaps getting caught up in the moment, Sarmiento claimed that "a day will arrive in which a school of men and women are taught exclusively by women."[44] Critically, Sarmiento promoted employing Argentine women as teachers rather than recruiting women from other countries to teach in Argentina.

In advocating for female teachers, Sarmiento drew on discourses about the naturalness of gender roles and utilized the language of gender inequality. In so doing, he echoed some of the ideas of US reformers like Catharine Beecher and Horace Mann. Like Beecher, Sarmiento argued for the use of female teachers based on the very fact of their unequal pay.[45] Also like Beecher, Sarmiento placed female teachers in a public sphere and declared that women would teach in mixed classrooms and would, one day, be responsible for all of the teaching. In addition, like Horace Mann, Sarmiento argued women were

by nature better teachers than men and that female teachers would inculcate
the rising generation with appropriate values.[46] That Sarmiento, Beecher, and
Mann embraced similar ideas was hardly coincidental. These reformers shared
a common intellectual background and drew on the same ideas and concepts,
including about gender. Furthermore, reformers corresponded with each other
and visited each other to observe new strategies and tactics.

Sarmiento faced tremendous obstacles as he attempted to strengthen the
educational system in Buenos Aires. Not all Argentines agreed with his idea
of employing women as teachers. Some parents did not want their children to
attend schools, and others worried about the state taking too active a role in
education or about the secularization of education. Nevertheless, despite opposition, Sarmiento furthered education in Buenos Aires. In 1859, for example,
he wrote to US Minister Benjamin C. Yancey that "we are making all possible
efforts to introduce and generalize among us that system of common school
education, which [makes?] the power and glory of the United States, to the end
that our Republic may be based upon the principles of equality and a public
enlightened sense of reason" and invited him to visit a Buenos Aires school.[47]
Yancey cordially replied that he could not attend due to a prior commitment,
but added, "I have only time now to invoke the highest prosperity + success
upon yr noble effort in the system of 'common school education.' For the only
true basis of Republican institutions is virtue and Education."[48] Educational
efforts, under Sarmiento's watchful eye, continued in Buenos Aires.

Education and Citizenship

People in the United States and Mexico agreed wholeheartedly with Sarmiento
that a lack of education produced bad citizens.[49] Governor John B. Weller of
California, in his Annual Message in 1859, reminded people that "if education is regarded so essential in despotic or monarchical Governments, how
much more important is it in a Government like ours founded upon the will
of the People."[50] The State Gazette of Austin, Texas, offered similar analysis,
commenting, "education and the exercise of American citizenship, should be
regarded as necessarily dependent, one upon the other."[51] These sentiments
hearkened back to the ideas of many of the US Founding Fathers about the
necessity of informed citizens in a republic. War in Argentina complicated
Sarmiento's efforts, and war in Mexico confounded Liberal efforts, but the

United States did not face the same type of internal conflict until 1861. People in the United States patted themselves on the back for avoiding the civil wars that plagued many Latin American nations. Moreover, the Catholic Church played an outsized role in life in Latin America, including education, from the conquest through the nineteenth century, until Liberals began serious efforts to secularize schools and clip the Church's wings.[52] Although the Catholic Church did not wield such power in the British North American colonies or in the antebellum United States, religion quickly became a major fault line in education in all three countries.

Of the three countries, the United States had the most developed educational system and the highest literacy rates. In the 1850 US Census, for example, the literacy rate for the entire nation was an impressive 89.31 percent.[53] However, the quality of schools and people's access to education varied tremendously. Northern schools prospered, thanks to the efforts of reformers like Horace and Mary Mann and like-minded politicians.[54] Southern schools offered a different story. For one, despite the comments in the State Gazette, many Southern politicians did not see any need to extend educational opportunities to poor white people.[55] One resident of Alabama told Alexis de Tocqueville, in 1832, that "there is no regular system of schools, a third of our population cannot read."[56] Twenty years later, the 1850 census revealed tremendous regional variance in literacy rates. In 1850, the literacy rate for the free states was 93.25 percent and 81.10 percent for the slave states. However, the slave state rate was really 59.12 percent because laws and planter opposition meant roughly 90 percent of enslaved people were illiterate.[57] In sum, education and literacy rates lagged considerably in the US South. Some northerners and southerners believed this was deliberate; after all, lack of education could be an effective tool for aristocrats and oligarchs to keep the masses subservient. People like Sarmiento and Unitarios in Argentina, the Manns and other education reformers and politicians in the United States, and Valentín Gómez Farías, José María Luis Mora, Benito Juárez, and Mexican Liberals consistently argued for better schools and more funding in education. Critically, they faced deep-seated obstacles as they made education part of their internal improvement programs in order to make good citizens and strengthen republics.

In attempting to increase the literacy rate and strengthen the educational system in Buenos Aires, Sarmiento shared a common vision with numerous people, both Black and white, before, during, and after the US Civil War. Before the US Civil War began, abolitionists and reformers derided the US South for a host of reasons. US Senator Charles Sumner's scathing indictment of the barbarism of slavery represented one of the most prominent denunciations, but other people argued that slavery produced both a lack of education among poor white southerners and a concerted effort to deny education and literacy to enslaved people.[58] Some enslaved people learned how to read and write. Frederick Douglass, for example, narrated his struggle to obtain education in *My Bondage and My Freedom*.[59] Slaves fully understood the importance of literacy and, despite numerous obstacles, sought out education wherever and whenever possible. Abolitionist fulminations and the powerful writing and oratory of Frederick Douglass did not lead to increased educational opportunities for enslaved people. If anything, they reinforced for masters the danger of educating enslaved people.

Education and War

The initial months of the US Civil War did not suggest major changes loomed on the horizon. In July 1861, during the special session of the 37th Congress, Representative John J. Crittenden of Kentucky offered a resolution which read, in part, "this war is not waged upon our part in any spirit of oppression, nor for any purpose of conquest or subjugation, nor purpose of overthrowing or interfering with the rights or established institutions of those States; but to defend and maintain the supremacy of the Constitution and to preserve the Union."[60] In other words, the war occurred for one reason—preserving the Union. It was not to be an abolition war that would result in citizenship and civil rights for African Americans. Of course, US war aims never remained static; they evolved during the conflict. Despite the narrow framing of the Crittenden-Johnson Resolution, Black and white people, from the beginning, understood the possibilities war offered and challenged the notion that the war was a white man's fight. The actions of enslaved people had an enormous impact on the conflict.[61] Scholars estimate that hundreds of thousands of African American refugees fled to Union lines during the US Civil War.[62] When enslaved people relocated to places controlled by the US army, they forced US policymakers to confront questions about refugee status, the government's duty toward refugees, and Black soldiers. Enslaved people helped transform a war for Union into a war for Union and for emancipation.

Many officials, both civilian and military, distrusted African Americans, but other commanders quickly realized they could play a role in US victory. General Benjamin F. Butler, for example, reassured Governor Thomas H. Hicks of Maryland on April 21, 1861, that he and his soldiers would help suppress a rumored African American insurrection.[63] Less than six weeks later, now in command of Fortress Monroe in Virginia, Butler proclaimed that any slaves that entered his lines were "contraband of war" and could not be claimed by their owners under the Fugitive Slave Act.[64] Frederick Douglass forcefully urged the government to employ Black men as soldiers.[65] When the United States began enrolling Black soldiers, Douglass rejoiced to see the government unchaining "against her foes, her powerful black hand."[66] Black soldiers, through their valor in combat, demonstrated they could fight and die as well as white soldiers.[67]

No linear path from "contraband of war" to the Emancipation Proclamation and the Thirteenth Amendment to the US Constitution occurred. US policy toward enslaved people moved in fits and starts, often subject to local conditions and the prejudices of a particular commander or set of soldiers. The US government's response to the influx of Black refugees proved decidedly inconsistent. On one basic question—should the government support Black refugees with rations—answers varied. Some officials believed men who labored for the United States deserved rations and wages, but numerous accounts abound of formerly enslaved people cheated out of wages or treated badly. Furthermore, Sergeant John Smith of the Second US Artillery did not believe women and children deserved rations. He "cut off the issuance of food rations to anyone except those employed directly by the government," a decision that caused one observer to note that "the poor & infirm find little or no mercy."[68] The strain of thought that Smith embodied never disappeared, but such policies often generated protest by African American refugees and their white allies.

Given the federal government's mixed response to refugees, northerners, both as individuals and as members of religious groups or benevolent associations, sprang into action. Northern civilian, as well as soldiers, went south during the US Civil War.[69] Free-labor advocates quickly understood that the US Civil War represented an incredible chance to remake the US South in the free labor image of the North. Northerners rented plantations in order to grow cotton.[70] The US government welcomed these experiments in free labor due to the potential revenue to be made from cotton, the fact that most Republicans agreed with free labor ideology and saw in it a panacea for the problems of the Southern states, and that these experiments would help Black people transition from slavery to freedom. Many white people believed slavery created dependency and that Black people needed to be prepared for freedom. The new masters and freedpeople quickly disagreed about work/life patterns and labor rhythms. Freedpeople generally preferred to practice subsistence agriculture instead of staple crop cultivation and hoped to acquire land instead of laboring on other people's land. The military sometimes served as an arbiter between new masters and laborers and sometimes as a coercive force compelling freedpeople to sign labor contracts and work on plantations.[71] Some military officers allowed their racial prejudices to dictate their attitudes toward freedpeople, but others did their best to help freedpeople navigate the fraught transition from slavery to freedom.[72]

White and Black abolitionists also desired to help formerly enslaved people transition from slavery to freedom.[73] Some subscribed to the same ideas about needing to teach Black people how to work, but most showed less concern about the profit motive and much more interest in the spiritual, moral, and educational aspects of the transition.[74] Consequently, abolitionists and other northerners traveled south to work in various capacities in refugee camps and in places like Port Royal, South Carolina, and Roanoke, North Carolina.[75] Northerners often focused on educational endeavors and, in so doing, helped African Americans gain the education many desperately wanted. Edward L. Pierce observed, about freedpeople at Fortress Monroe, that "the first generation might be unfitted for the active duties and responsibilities of citizenship; but this difficulty, under generous provisions for education, would not pass to the next."[76] Pierce's patronizing view of the freedpeople aside, he understood that education could help people escape some of slavery's legacies.

One scholar has argued that many Liberals in Latin America looked at education in the United States and saw a "great disciplinary tool" that would "make the pueblo rational and restrained citizens, both aware of their rights and duties."[77] Problematically, this analysis makes education an elite/middle-class project. Many people desperately desired to leave illiteracy behind. They seized any and all opportunities to secure education. The story of education in the US South during and after the US Civil War was not one of imposition. White people did not force, at the point of the bayonet, education on unwilling African Americans. Rather, the efforts of Black and white teachers addressed an issue the freedpeople considered particularly pressing.[78] As Jacqueline Jones noted, "teachers responded to—though they sometimes believed they inspired—a great eagerness for schooling among the freed people," and "black people joined together to establish schools and hire teachers for old and young alike."[79] At times, abolitionists could barely keep pace with African American educational efforts, and they marveled at the thirst for knowledge among the freedpeople. For example, several days after the fall of Richmond in April 1865, "black Richmonders quickly established schools in churches that still stood amid the ruins of the Confederate capital."[80] The desire for education among African Americans and their efforts to obtain it intensified as the US Civil War ended. Opposition to Black educational endeavors also continued.[81] Sarmiento encountered a bustling world of educational efforts when he returned to the United States in 1865–68, which had an important impact on his thinking about education and teachers.

Education and Cooperation

In 1865, as the US Civil War drew to a close, President Bartolomé Mitre appointed Sarmiento Argentine minister plenipotentiary and envoy extraordinary to the United States. This gave Sarmiento an opportunity to observe life in the United States during Reconstruction and visit Mary Mann. Although Horace Mann had died, Mary Mann introduced Sarmiento to the New England literary elite, educational reformers, and politicians.[82] While Mary Mann did not publish an English-language translation of *Facundo* until 1868, many New Englanders knew the book.[83] Sarmiento described his heady experiences in a letter to his friend Aurelia Velez Sarsfield: "The next day I ate with Waldo Emerson, whom I had sent *Facundo*. This book serves as a method of introduction. If being Minister does not matter to everyone, being an educator is here a great title in this town of teachers; but I always have *Facundo* in reserve, it is my Parrott gun. No one can resist it."[84] Emerson thanked Sarmiento for the copy of *Facundo* and "encouraged Mary Mann to continue with her translation of the book."[85] Sarmiento's pleasure about his favorable reception undoubtedly influenced his opinion of New England, and he was not shy about endorsing the idea that Boston was "the American Athens."[86]

Sarmiento's arrival in the United States, shortly after the surrender of Lee's army at Appomattox and Lincoln's assassination, proved particularly fortuitous because he observed the state of education in the US South during the early years of Reconstruction.[87] The fervent efforts of African American to obtain education intensified during Reconstruction and, as one scholar noted, "perhaps the greatest achievement of Reconstruction, and one of the most pressing grassroots demands, was the creation of free public schools. In the span of a few years, dozens of school buildings were constructed across a largely rural landscape, hundreds of teachers were hired, and thousands of children began attending classes."[88] Sarmiento did not pay equal attention to all aspects of this new world, however, and focused on one particular subset of teachers. His correspondence overflowed with laudatory comments about the actions of white men and women. Northerners, Sarmiento observed to Juana Manso, an Argentine educator and longtime collaborator, "have appointed superintendents of the aid societies in the South, and calculated that they need immediately fifteen thousand schools and fifteen thousand teachers, and all the societies have moved to obtain them . . . they contracted eight hundred teachers, one hundred fifty paid for and contracted by New York alone."[89] Sarmiento greatly admired "a girl" who "moved to South Carolina" and who "was placed alone at the head of a cotton plantation of three hundred negroes, whom she not only educated, but taught the exercise of arms, all without losing the prestige of womanhood."[90] Sarmiento argued that these teachers would effect a beneficial and startling transformation of the South: "Fifteen thousand schools that on Sundays will be schools for adults, will, in few years, erase the original sin of absolute ignorance in the South, and the freedmen will be more advanced than us whites."[91] Sarmiento's prejudices dictated his analysis: what would happen to Argentina when African Americans in the South surpassed the Argentine elite? He saw a potential solution: recruit white female teachers from the United States to teach in Argentina.

Sarmiento drew on what he saw in the United States to reformulate his ideas about class, race, gender, and the employment of female teachers. He was hardly in the United States a few weeks before he sent a letter to Juana Manso avidly promoting the recruitment of teachers from the United States. His language merits careful examination. "One hundred Boston girls," Sarmiento wrote excitedly, "at the head of the schools in Buenos Aires, or in the Provinces, would replicate the system of education in Massachusetts, with its efficiency, its extension, and its reality."[92] Enthused about the potential for this project, Sarmiento continued, "would it not be a beautiful sight . . . to see arriving at

Buenos Aires . . . forty blond girls, modest without affectation of modesty, virtuous, of that practical virtue, useful, social, that prepares a mother for a future
family, school teachers, Bostonians, colonizers of education and of republicanism."[93] His language mirrored similar language throughout the Atlantic World
about the cult of domesticity and republican motherhood, another indication
that Sarmiento was in dialogue with transnational concepts. He no longer
advocated women teachers based on lower salaries. Sarmiento now spoke of
blond girls, not women, and the positive impact these blond girls would have
on Argentina. Clearly, Sarmiento clearly had specific people in mind when he
spoke about teachers. A cursory glance at the US South would have revealed
numerous African American teachers, both men and women. Nevertheless,
Sarmiento did not appear interested in Charlotte Forten or Susie King Taylor.[94] He wanted blond, elite or middle-class, white New Englanders to teach
in Argentina and to bring with them particular educational practices and ideas
about republicanism.

Sarmiento, like many of his contemporaries, held certain prejudices. In
Facundo, for example, he argued that one of the causes of Argentina's failure
was the fusion of Spanish, Amerindian, and African "races." He denigrated the
"savage" and "barbarous" descendants of Indigenous peoples, especially in
comparison to "civilized" Europeans, throughout his writings. "Although not
anti-Indian," one scholar argued, "Sarmiento's ideas contributed in an important way to a public discourse that equated civilization with the conquest of
the Indians."[95] In other words, his writing may have helped policymakers justify a campaign of extermination, "la conquista del desierto" (1878–85), waged
against the Indigenous people of Argentina. Sarmiento also held views similar
to moderate and conservative Republicans in that he detested slavery but did
not support Black equality. The similarity of Sarmiento's writings and ideas
to those of Europeans such as Joseph Arthur Gobineau led one historian to
suggest that Sarmiento may have belonged to an international group of racial
thinkers and theorists that included Gobineau and Confederate propagandist
Henry Hotze.[96]

Sarmiento's attitudes toward African Americans and his dismissal of Black
teachers in favor of white New Englanders matched the opinions of many of
his contemporaries. US abolitionists reported, time and again, their surprise
about Black abilities and capabilities. For example, one American Missionary
Association agent in Virginia believed he was there to liberate African Ameri-

cans trapped "in the ignorance of heathenism" and to "give them the blessings of a christian education."[97] Thus, even the people most likely to sympathize with African Americans suffered from racial prejudices, to say nothing of the attitudes of more lukewarm supporters of antislavery measures or outright opponents. Sarmiento, in that sense, was not so different from many of his contemporaries throughout the Americas. Furthermore, just as people from the United States often see what they want to see in the rest of the world, it is worthwhile to remember that people from the rest of the world often do the same thing in regard to the United States. For Sarmiento, the New England women captured his attention in a way that African American teachers did not.

Sarmiento's prejudices limited his vision, as prejudices always do, as well as his understanding of the best lessons to draw from the US experience. His lack of attention to African American teachers meant that he missed certain lessons about how to build an educational system. Furthermore, by focusing on a small group of white teachers, Sarmiento may have missed the fervent support for education among people at the grassroots. African Americans did not always appreciate patronizing and paternalistic white teachers, but they worked with all the allies they could find to develop, maintain, and protect schools.[98] Argentines, on the other hand, seemed more lukewarm about Sarmiento's educational efforts. Sarmiento and reformers echoed each other's prejudices. Consequently, he missed additional elements of the US experience that might have benefited Argentina in his quest to make better citizens and strengthen the Argentine republic.

Education and Internal Improvement

Sarmiento's assertion to a Chilean correspondent that "seven hundred North American teachers in the Argentine Republic, or in Chile, would repair in ten years the stagnation of three centuries," is an excellent window into one aspect of the program he hoped to enact as president.[99] In four years, from 1870 to 1874, he built nearly eight hundred new schools in Argentina; increased the number of teachers from 1,778 to 2,868; and oversaw an expansion in the number of children attending school by 233 percent (from approximately 30,000 students to approximately 100,000).[100] Sarmiento's recruitment of teachers from the United States became an important part of his educational program. Alice Houston Luiggi wrote that sixty-five teachers "went to Argentina from

1869 to 1898 to establish, reorganize, or head eighteen normal schools."[101] These sixty-five teachers did not arrive all at once, but in fits and starts over a period of several years. Although Sarmiento could not personally interview and select the candidates, he relied on friends in New England, particularly Mary Mann, to help him select qualified women and promote his educational project by word of mouth as well as through newspaper publications. Sarmiento's links to reformers and politicians paid dividends and highlighted another important example of cooperation.

When the teachers arrived, Sarmiento modified his ideas in another way: he did not, as he suggested in the 1850s, put women in charge of teaching children. Rather, he placed the women in charge of teacher training schools in the provinces, perhaps remembering the success of Horace Mann's teacher training school in Massachusetts. When set against the impressive increases in pupils, schools, and teachers during Sarmiento's presidency, the number of women who traveled to Argentina might seem a pittance. Nevertheless, they had an important impact through their work training teachers. Teachers from the United States and Argentine teachers helped dramatically increase the literacy rate in Argentina. In 1869, the literacy rate for people ages 6+ in Argentina was 23.8 percent. By 1925, the literacy rate for people ages 10+ in Argentina was 73.0 percent. Sarmiento's methods, and the continued commitment of the government after his presidency to education, yielded impressive results.[102]

The victors in all three countries—Liberals in Mexico, Republicans in the United States, Sarmiento and the Unitarios in Argentina—eventually confronted a thorny set of intertwined issues: religion, education, and the state. On the surface, the three countries look different. Argentina and Mexico were Catholic countries, where many people in the Protestant United States embraced a fervent anti-Catholicism. The reality was not so cut-and-dried. In Mexico, educational reforms composed part of a larger 1833–34 reform program under Valentín Gómez Farías that targeted the power of the clergy and the army. Liberals like José María Luis Mora initially focused on primary education but then placed more importance on secularizing higher education and removing it from the control of the Catholic Church.[103] Opponents of the Gómez Farías reforms drove him from power and sent Mora into exile, but the reforms inspired a later generation of Liberal statesmen and policymakers.

When the 1854 Plan de Ayutla overthrew Antonio López de Santa Anna, victorious Liberals like Benito Juárez, Ignacio Comonfort, and Juan Álvarez enacted Liberal reforms, again targeting the power of the Church and the army, as well as the communal landholdings of Indigenous people. The Mexican Constitution of 1857 mandated free primary education, and Liberals worked to create free, compulsory, and secular primary education. They also "resented the Church's monopoly over Indian education and favored bilingual (preferably Spanish) education controlled by the municipalities."[104] In other words, Liberals strove to seize control of education in order to create, in their eyes, a better-educated populace.[105] Reaction against the reforms produced ten years of nearly continuous warfare—the War of the Reform (1857–61) and the French Intervention (1861–67). Once the Liberals defeated the Conservatives, the French, and the Imperialists, they consolidated their victory by using their control of the educational system, and textbooks in particular, to impose their ideas on the populace.[106] Debates about education continued during the Porfiriato as well as during and after the Mexican Revolution.[107] Moreover, the Church question certainly did not end with the French Intervention, and religious rebellions occurred in the nineteenth and twentieth centuries.[108]

Although no "Church question" existed in the United States comparable to that in Mexico, anti-Catholicism in the United States ran strong in the nineteenth century.[109] Thomas Nast's cartoon "The American River Ganges" offered the classic expression of this sentiment.[110] Catholic priests, whom Nast depicted as crocodiles, menaced a group of children huddled on the bank of a river. Nast tapped into a potent sentiment; during this period, many Protestants feared Catholics intended to subvert democracy, infiltrate the public schools, catechize young Protestant children, and enslave the United States to the pope in Rome. In the period after the Panic of 1873, when it became apparent that Republicans could not win elections running only on Reconstruction issues, they began to emphasize temperance and keeping Catholicism out of public schools. Indeed, Republicans deftly employed anti-Catholicism and the fear of Catholics taking over public schools during the 1875 Ohio gubernatorial election and the election of 1876.[111] The Catholic Church did not have the same power in the nineteenth-century United States as it did in nineteenth-century Mexico, but both Liberals and Republicans nevertheless fought against the Church.[112]

Mónica Szurmuk's observation that "Sarmiento could have saved himself many problems if he had selected Catholic teachers instead of Protestant ones" illuminated a different political context in Sarmiento's Argentina.[113] Sarmiento, however, wanted Protestant New Englanders to teach in Argentina, not Catholics from the United States. Sarmiento, like numerous people in the United States, Mexico, and elsewhere, saw the Catholic Church as backward, antimodern, and a bulwark of reaction. Given that Sarmiento and many of his contemporaries embraced republicanism and a liberal state, both of which the Catholic Church during this period opposed, it is not surprising that they were fervently anti-Catholic. Furthermore, anti-Catholicism echoed throughout the world. In Germany, Otto von Bismarck attacked the Catholic Church during the Kulturkampf.[114] The decision to pick Protestants did not make Sarmiento popular with some of his fellow Argentines. One newspaper commented that the work of the teachers "was for a time very discouraging, and they needed the enthusiastic support of President Sarmiento and his friends to overcome the conservative opposition of the priests to the attendance of the children."[115] Priests objected to the recruitment of Protestant teachers, and the Vatican complicated matters by sending "large numbers of European priests to the spiritual war fronts in Brazil and Argentina."[116] Thus, Sarmiento faced attacks from both internal and external foes.

Sarmiento's religious attitudes likely guided his preference for US Protestants. Although nominally a Catholic, by this point in his life Sarmiento espoused separation of church and state, at least in reference to Catholicism. He did not, like Juárez and the Mexican Liberals or Republicans in the United States, want priests in charge of schools.[117] Despite these attitudes, Sarmiento admired the Puritans because, he claimed, they introduced universal education to the United States.[118] Like many people in the United States, Sarmiento did not want Catholics in the classroom, but he had no trouble with Protestants in the public schools. Importantly, Sarmiento saw Protestants as a homogeneous group, He overlooked how white Protestant teachers and reformers often clashed with African American Protestants throughout the United States.[119] In sum, just as he was interested in one type of teacher, Sarmiento was interested in one type of Protestant—as he saw it, the descendants of the Puritans. The victors in all three nations, as they worked to enact their educational programs, faced similar problems, issues, and types of opposition. They understood the Catholic Church's opposition as of a piece with other reactionary forces attempting to subvert democracy and republicanism.

Education in each of the three countries received significant attention from the victors during this period. However, education was just one type of internal improvement among many. Historians have written a staggering amount about internal improvements, particularly the transportation revolution—the rush to build canals, roads, railroads—and the communications revolution.[120] The subject of internal improvement is so broad that it would be impossible to be comprehensive in one chapter, or even in one book. The purpose of the following discussion of internal improvement is twofold: First, to highlight additional forms of cooperation and to briefly explain how victors enacted similar programs in their respective nations. Second, to note that these programs raised the ire of the vanquished and helped explain the rebellions that are discussed in part 2 of this book.[121]

Like his fellow liberals, Sarmiento advocated a robust program of internal improvement to promote state-building and nation-making. His recruitment of teachers from the United States and his expansion of Argentina's educational system represented one of his many plans to improve Argentina. One scholar labeled Sarmiento's presidency a "crescendo of works initiated and pursued," a characterization that makes Sarmiento sound very much like a Republican or a Mexican Liberal.[122] As president, Sarmiento presided over the development of Argentina's schools; founded a Military College; built libraries; established national academies; erected a national observatory with the help of Benjamin Apthorp Gould; and funded the construction of hundreds of miles of roads and railroad lines and three thousand miles of telegraph wires.[123] Historians have long understood Sarmiento, along with Bartolomé Mitre and Nicolás Avellaneda, presidents of the Argentine Republic from 1862 to 1880, as the consolidators of the Argentine nation-state.[124]

Sarmiento designed his invigorated educational system to create better citizens and destroy the conditions that facilitated the rise of caudillos. Other forms of internal improvement, such as railroads, also helped reduce the caudillo threat. For instance, the Central Argentine Railway, designed to connect Córdoba and Rosario, was intended to "attract support for the political settlement of 1862." The railroad would "enhance communication with the center" and help curtail future rebellions. However, "its major contribution lay in opening up the prairies of southern Santa Fe and eastern Córdoba to agriculture."[125] Thus, the railroad helped ensure domestic tranquility and promote economic growth, like Sarmiento's schools. US Commercial Agent William Wheelwright wrote that Sarmiento, "in his ardent desire to promote the great interests of the Argentine Republic has announced a Public Exhibition to take place in the month of April 1870 in the central city of Cordova and invites the people of all countries to display on the occasion the products of their industry." Wheelwright also noted "it was a happy thought of President Sarmiento to combine the Inauguration of the Central Argentine railway with that of the Exhibition both events of transcendent importance in these provinces."[126]

As Sarmiento built up Argentina's infrastructure, similar developments occurred throughout the Americas as victorious liberals quickly enacted similar programs of infrastructural development. In the United States, the secession of the Southern states gave Republicans strong majorities in both houses of Congress. Republicans lost no time seizing the opportunity to enact their economic program. The Thirty-Seventh Congress passed a flurry of legislation including the Revenue Act (August 5, 1861); the Legal Tender Act (February 25, 1862); the Homestead Act (May 20, 1862); the Morrill Anti-Bigamy Act (July 1, 1862); the Revenue Act of 1862 (July 1, 1862); the Pacific Railway Act (July 1, 1862); the Morrill Land Grant College Act (July 2, 1862); the National Banking Act (February 25, 1863); and legislation establishing the National Academy of Sciences.[127] The Thirty-Seventh Congress also raised tariff rates with the Morrill Tariff, passed the First and Second Confiscation Acts, and abolished slavery in Washington, DC, on April 16, 1862.[128] The Thirty-Seventh Congress was one of the most significant in US history. During Reconstruction, Republicans sought to transform the region by building railroads, schools, and other internal improvements.[129] Shortly before Argentina inaugurated the Central Argentine Railroad, Leland Stanford drove the golden spike into the earth at Promontory Summit, Utah Territory, to link the Central Pacific and the Union Pacific and create the First Transcontinental Railroad.[130] The expansion of the US railroad grid led Matías Romero, the Mexican minister to the United States, to remark, rather matter-of-factly, to the Mexican secretary of exterior relations in 1882, about the proliferation of railroads in the United States.[131]

A similar process of internal improvement occurred in Mexico. After the Liberals expelled the French and defeated the Imperialists, railroad promoters swarmed to Mexico City and beseeched Benito Juárez for land grants and concessions. The governments of Juárez, Sebastián Lerdo de Tejada, and, later, Porfirio Díaz, like that of Sarmiento, built roads and other internal improvements in order to knit the country together.[132] A. Willard wrote from Guaymas in 1873 that the Mexican government appropriated fifty thousand dollars for eight hundred miles of telegraph wires to connect Mazatlán with Ures, Sonora. In addition, "*Rail-Road franchise,* granted by the state of *Sonora,* for a R.R. from this Port to *Arizona territory, U.S.* to connect with the Texas pacific R.R. (mentioned in former reports) subject to the approval of the National Congress of Mexico."[133] In all three countries, the victors avidly pursued internal improvement and modernization. The desire for development, however, reinforced the fears of the vanquished, as well as some discontented victors, that their world was spinning out of control before their very eyes.

One of the most interesting, although unrealized, examples of inter-American cooperation during this period concerned the construction of the Three Americas Railway. The promoters of this project aspired to create a hemispheric railroad beginning in Canada and ending in Argentina, that would knit the nations of the New World closer together. One of the promoters was none other than Hinton Rowan Helper, the North Carolinian who famously denounced slavery in his polemic book *The Impending Crisis of the South.*[134] Helper, who had served as US consul in Buenos Aires, returned to the United States and became a railroad promoter, working hand-in-hand with Hiram Barney of New York and others. One newspaper, in a review of a volume of essays about the proposed project, commented: "The last few years has witnessed a marvelous reaching out in the direction suggested, and things have been accomplished which were before regarded as impracticable, if not impossible. What will be accomplished in the future no man can foretell."[135] Helper sent Romero a copy of his book about the railroad, and Romero, in turn, asked how to obtain one that he could send to the Mexican government.[136] The Three Americas Railway never came to fruition—the logistical challenges of building a railroad from Canada to Tierra del Fuego likely contributed to the failure to launch—but the project symbolized the spirit of the age in its desire to conquer space and promote cooperation.

That political parties argued for government sponsorship of internal improvements suggests a great deal of common ground between Whigs and Republicans in the United States, Unitarios and Liberals in Argentina, and Liberals in Mexico. These parties, and the people who composed them, shared an ideology of state-sponsored economic development explainable because they lived through a global transportation revolution.[137] It suggests how profoundly transformative the mid-nineteenth century was for peoples' expectations about the possibilities of their world. The United States, Mexico, and Argentina, among other countries, followed very similar paths, interacted with each other, and attempted to create common destinies.

Many similarities existed among the internal improvement programs designed by the victors in each of the three countries. For one, the victors understood education as a way to create better, more informed citizens and enacted their programs to achieve their goal. The victors believed the policies they enacted—such as secularization and increased state control of schools—best served their visions of what their nations should become and played a part in the ongoing struggle between democracy and republicanism against the forces of reaction. The victors also invested in the same types of internal improvements—roads, railroads, and telegraph wires—in order to conquer space and tie hinterlands and peripheries closer to centers. These improvements cost money, and, especially during economic depressions, government subsidies to railroad corporations and other entities angered people. Variation among the three nations existed, of course—the United States had a more developed railroad grid than Mexico and Argentina—but people nevertheless operated from a similar set of ideas about the importance of internal improvement.

On a more troubling note, in their quests to impose modernity and progress, the victors sometimes went to extreme lengths, especially in their dealings with Indigenous people. In Mexico and the United States, Liberals and Republicans sought to break up Indigenous communal landholdings. Liberals began this process during the mid-1850s, after they wrested power from Santa Anna, which, in turn, pushed some Indigenous people into the arms of the Conservatives. After 1867, the process accelerated. Liberals sold communal land and ecclesiastical real estate in order to build up the middle class.[138] During and after the US Civil War, the United States waged war against Native Americans.[139] In 1887, the Dawes Act subdivided communal landholdings into individual allotments.[140] The United States, Mexico, and Argentina all waged campaigns against Indigenous people in the periods following their respective civil wars. Argentina's "Conquista del desierto" continued the pattern of previous campaigns against Indigenous people earlier in the century. The "winning of the West" in the United States involved sustained campaigns against Indigenous people. Finally, US and Mexican soldiers cooperated, in the US-Mexico borderlands, to halt raiding by Indigenous people and confine Indigenous groups to reservations. Although Judge James Bell of Texas could write confidently to Benjamin Epperson that "a people cannot, in the Nineteenth Century, be Exterminated," the corpses of Indigenous people killed at Wounded Knee, Sand Creek, the deserts of northern Mexico, and the pampas of Buenos Aires rebuked this misguided assertion.[141]

Visions of the Vanquished

The vanquished in each of the three nations—Federales in Argentina, Conservatives and Imperialists in Mexico, and former white rebels in the Southern states—not to mention increasingly discontented elements of the victors, nursed tremendous resentment against Republican, Liberal, and Unitario policies. The vanquished had to process defeat, which proved difficult in worlds so heavily influenced by honor culture and sharply defined ideas about manliness and masculinity. Moreover, many of them felt like powerless spectators as they watched the victors shape the postwar trajectories of the three countries in ways they found profoundly alienating. These resentments and tensions exploded when the vanquished took up arms and contested, through bullets and other forms of violence, the contours of the new postwar worlds and attempted to re-create or reinstitute old hierarchies based on race and class. Their challenges to the victors are discussed throughout part 2 of this book.

Conclusion: Rejecting and Imagining Common Destinies and Histories

In *Democracy in America*, Alexis de Tocqueville had little good to say about Spanish America: "We see in astonishment the new nations of South America being torn asunder for a quarter of a century by an endless succession of revolutions.... The people dwelling in the beautiful half of the Western hemisphere appear stubbornly determined to tear out each other's entrails.... I am tempted to think that despotism would be a blessing for them." For Tocqueville, the two worlds—the United States and the nations of Spanish America—"will never be linked in my mind."[142] During the nineteenth century, many US citizens echoed Tocqueville's denunciations of Latin America. People worried about being "Mexicanized" and fretted that the problems of order in Mexico would spread to the United States.[143] Hispanophiles certainly existed in the United States, but anti-Latin Americanism proved pervasive.

Focusing on anti–Latin American rhetoric, however, reveals only part of the story of the US–Latin American relationship. Roughly thirty years after Tocqueville, Edward Lee Plumb advised Senator Charles Sumner that "with reference to our relations to Mexico, there is no one good of either the United States or of Mexico, it seems to me, that will not be promoted by the Cultivation of relations of cordial friendship, sympathy and entire mutual confidence between the great republican parties of the two countries."[144] Plumb sought to strengthen this confidence, friendship, and sympathy and, although he tended to focus on Mexico, people in all three countries embraced this sentiment.

By the 1860s, Plumb's vision offered a better statement, in some people's minds, about US–Latin American relations than Tocqueville's. The victors in the United States, Mexico, and Argentina promoted Pan-American cooperation, as the four chapters in part 1 of this book have demonstrated. People in each of the three countries conceived of their struggles as intertwined, worked together during their respective civil wars, and employed nationalist festivals to create closer links with one another. Then, as they sought to rebuild shattered nations, they adopted common strategies and worked across national borders. Indeed, the victors in the United States, Argentina, and Mexico looked to each other as they strove to figure out how to reassemble their countries after violent conflicts, how to consolidate nation-states, how to spur modernization and internal improvement, and how to foment literacy and create educated publics. Long before Herbert Eugene Bolton enunciated the idea, Sarmiento and his like-minded contemporaries attempted to write their own epics of Greater America and promoted cooperation and friendship among the nations of the New World.[145] In many respects they succeeded. However, as the following chapters in part 2 illustrate, each of the three countries faced significant internal dissent generated, in part, by anger among the vanquished about the vision of the victors. The resulting struggles unfolded differently in each nation, but they concluded, by the 1880s, with each country on the same path to a type of stability that disfranchised wide sectors of the population.

FIG. 1. General Ulysses S. Grant believed the US Civil War would not end until the French were forced out of Mexico. Courtesy of the Library of Congress, LC-DIG-cwpb-06941.

FIG. 2. General Philip H. Sheridan aided the Liberal war effort by permitting recruiting in the United States and facilitating arms drops. Courtesy of the Library of Congress, LC-DIG-ppmsca-71309.

FIG. 3. Benito Juárez served as president of Mexico from 1857 until his death in 1872. He led the Liberals during the War of the Reform and the French Intervention. Courtesy of the Library of Congress, LC-USZ62-7875.

FIG. 4. Matías Romero, the indefatigable Mexican minister to the United States, worked with Grant, Sheridan, and many other people to defeat the French and Imperialists. Courtesy of the National Archives, 111-B-1228.

FIG. 5. French Emperor Napoleon III longed to surpass his far more famous and accomplished uncle by re-creating a French empire in the Americas. Courtesy of the Library of Congress, LC-USZ62-131393.

FIG. 6. General Ignacio Zaragoza stunned the French by leading the
Liberals to victory at the Battle of Puebla on May 5, 1862. Courtesy of
the Library of Congress, LC-USZ62–131327.

FIG. 7. Austrian Archduke Ferdinand Maximilian, in accepting the throne of the Second Mexican Empire, became Napoleon III's cat's-paw. Courtesy of the Library of Congress, LC-DIG-ppmsca-54194.

FIG. 8. Maximilian, Miguel Miramón, and Tomás Mejía were executed by firing squad at the Cerro de las Campanas in Querétaro on June 19, 1867. Cerro de las Campanas, Courtesy of the Library of Congress, LC-USZ62-19760.

FIG. 9. Bartolomé Mitre served as the first president of the Argentine Republic and launched a revolution when he lost the presidential election of 1874. Bust of Bartolomé Mitre, Casa de Gobierno. Photo by author.

FIG. 10. Domingo F. Sarmiento, a man of many talents, served as the second president of the Argentina Republic. Bust of Domingo F. Sarmiento, Casa de Gobierno. Photo by author.

PART II

COMPARATIVE PATHS TO ORDER

5

The Problem of Order (Not Mexicanization)

VIOLENCE & POLITICS, 1861–1867

On October 16, 1874, the *Chicago Tribune* ran a brief article entitled "The South American Louisiana." "There is an insurrection in the Argentine Confederation," the *Tribune* reported, "the main features of which bear a strong resemblance to the late trouble in Louisiana."[1] The article compared the events of 1872–74 in Louisiana with the Revolution of 1874 in Argentina. In 1872, Louisiana endured a bitter gubernatorial election featuring fraud, intimidation, and violence. Democrats refused to accept a Republican victory and appealed from ballots to bullets. For nearly two years, Louisiana had two governors and two legislatures. After several violent episodes, events came to a head in 1874 during the Battle of Liberty Place. Thousands of miles south, Argentines faced their own chaos. In the presidential election of 1874, former president Bartolomé Mitre sought reelection to a nonconsecutive term. Current President Domingo F. Sarmiento preferred Minister of Justice and Public Instruction Nicolás Avellaneda. When Avellaneda won the election, an angry Mitre got up a revolution. Like the rebellion in Louisiana, Mitre's revolution failed.[2]

The *Tribune's* comparison of electoral violence in the United States and Argentina focused on the mid-1870s, but, as all three chapters in part 2 argue, taking a comparative approach to the relationship between violence, disorder, and politics in the period 1861–80 sheds light not only on the United States but also on Mexico and Argentina and, more broadly, on reconstructions throughout the Americas.[3] Consequently, chapters 5, 6, and 7 cover the period 1861–80 and analyze individual violent episodes, paramilitary violence by small or large groups, and disorder produced by contested elections at the local, state, and federal levels in all three countries.[4] The elections studied include the presidential elections of 1867 in Mexico; 1868 in the United States and Argentina; 1871 and 1872 in Mexico; 1872 in the United States; 1874 in Argentina; 1876 in the

United States and Mexico; and 1880 in all three countries as well as numerous state and provincial elections. By including violence at the state and local levels as well as the national level, and by employing a comparative methodology, these chapters reveal a very different and more complex story about reconstructions in the Americas.[5]

All governments seek to establish order, and the three in this study were no exception to this rule. Indeed, securing order proved especially critical for each of the war-torn nations as they emerged from their respective violent conflicts (the Wars of Unification in Argentina, the US Civil War, and the War of the Reform and the French Intervention in Mexico). Taming the vanquished and securing the fruits of their victory naturally concerned the Liberals in each nation. In the aftermath of the French Intervention, for example, Francisco Zarco "urged Mexico to show the world that the nation could now follow 'the path of order and progress.'"[6] Similar language about order occurred in the United States and Argentina. Problematically, many members of the vanquished groups had no desire to accept the results of the wars and the Liberal visions of the future. They employed the different types of violence outlined above— specifically paramilitary violence and rebellions—to turn back the clock and re-create worlds and hierarchies either destroyed or overturned in the maelstrom of war. As resistance to the programs of reconstruction put forth by each group of victorious Liberals intensified, national states lost the will, especially in the aftermath of the Panic of 1873—a crushing economic depression—to suppress violent uprisings. A vision of modernity that fetishized order came to dominate, especially as order became "crucial to instigating the economic development that was becoming modernity's hallmark."[7] The type of order that ruled the day by the 1880s had a heavy price because it left large sectors of the population in each nation disfranchised.

Chapter 5 begins in 1861, with the end of Argentina's Wars of Unification, and ends in 1867, with the end of Mexico's French Intervention. Republicans in the United States, Unitarios in Argentina, and Liberals in Mexico won wars against their internal foes. However, although the guns fell silent and the vanquished stacked their arms, that is to say, the shooting wars ended, divisions plagued each nation. No victory was universally accepted, and large pockets of resistance remained. Furthermore, people were all too willing to resort to violence to achieve their ends. This included caudillos like El Chacho in Argentina, angry white Southern ex-rebels in the United States, and disaffected

Liberals in Mexico. The victors also resorted to violence and to constitutionally questionable methods to pacify regions that either rebelled or entered into rebellion after the close of the wars. It quickly became apparent how difficult it would be to tamp down resistance and enact Liberal programs of reconstruction in each nation. The victors won the war, but there was no guarantee at all that they would win the peace.

Mexicanization

People throughout the period covered by this book fretted that the United States was becoming "Mexicanized."[8] One Republican believed "the flight of southern states would balkanize North America and 'Mexicanize' our government."[9] Jonathan Worth, several years later, fretted about becoming "Mexicanized" and losing "sight of civilization."[10] During the furor over the contested election of 1876, one Republican newspaper growled, "the Democrats in the House, under the direction of Mr. Hewitt, have determined to elect Mr. Tilden at all hazards if the Senate elect Mr. Hayes, and thus Mexicanize the country with a dual government."[11] The *Nation* observed, "we hear every day strong expressions of a desire and also of a determination, that this Government shall not be 'Mexicanized.'"[12] The magazine noted, "as well as we can make out, what most of those who use it mean by it is the use of armed force to decide political contests or legal disputes, or to set aside the results of elections, or settle conflicting claims to power or authority."[13] "The South is Mexicanized," the magazine concluded, and they worried that by nursing and manipulating the South, we [the North] have ourselves caught the contagion."[14]

"Mexicanization" involved an obsessive concern about disorder and a fear that the United States had caught the contagion that paralyzed Latin American republics (at least in the eyes of some people in the United States).[15] The assumption that Mexico was the most disordered and chaotic country in the hemisphere cropped up frequently. As evidence, proponents of the idea pointed to the fact that, in the period between Mexico's Constitution of 1824 and the beginning of the Tripartite Intervention in 1861, dozens of men served as president of Mexico, governments constantly changed by nonelectoral means, and dictatorships occurred rather frequently. Furthermore, the divergent responses to presidential elections in the United States and Mexico in 1876 also seemed to support the idea of "Mexicanization." Porfirio Díaz overthrew a democratically elected president in 1876–77. Despite calls by hotheads like Henry Watterson in 1876–77 for Democrats to march on Washington and inaugurate Samuel J. Tilden by force, Democrats rejected Watterson's siren song and did not resort to violence. The election of 1876 produced a revolution in Mexico and a constitutional crisis in the United States that was solved by compromise. Thus, the United States avoided being "Mexicanized" at the national level.[16]

That said, disorder, violence, and instability occurred in the US South as well as in Mexican states and Argentine provinces. It is critically important to remember that all three countries suffered from these phenomena. "Redeemers" in the US South used violence, intimidation, and fraud to overthrow democratically elected state governments. Díaz men in Mexico attempted to, and in some cases did, defeat government troops and depose officials appointed by Presidents Benito Juárez and Sebastián Lerdo de Tejada. In Argentina, Federalist caudillos rebelled against the national government headed by Mitre and Sarmiento. In other words, similar types of disorder, instability, and chaos plagued each of the three countries, often involving central government versus state or provincial forces, but sometimes internecine battles among state/provincial or local forces. The search for order, not to mention violence, disorder, and instability, were issues that all three countries confronted as the victors tried to impose order and protect the fruits of their victory. The United States was hardly the only country in the Western Hemisphere fretting about order and disorder.

Pronunciamientos

Studying nineteenth-century Mexican politics requires some knowledge of the "pronunciamiento."[17] US Commercial Agent Julius Noureau considered pronunciamientos "a thing hardly describable in our language." Nevertheless, he offered the following definition: "Anyone who can raise and arm a small number of men, bids open defiance to law and order, keeps plundering a while, and upon being prosecuted by the troops, disbands his crowd, and disappears for a while only to return shortly afterwards without being held to account for his former misdeeds."[18] For Noureau, pronunciamientos allowed dissatisfied people to express outrage and make some quick cash through plunder. He also identified an important point that bedeviled all three countries: should people who rebelled be amnestied?

Pronunciamientos, written protests or petitions generally drafted as a list of grievances, occurred throughout Latin America. Mexico, however, was a unique case. In the period 1821–76, more than 1,500 pronunciamientos, ranging widely in effect and importance, occurred. Pronunciamientos, one scholar asserted, were *"the* way of doing politics."[19] However, they were not merely coups d'état dressed in fancier clothing. In fact, they were more like lobbying, although they certainly could and did "degenerate into sanguinary revolts."[20] Assuming all pronunciamientos were analogous to Díaz's 1876 Plan de Tuxtepec—designed to overthrow the federal government—is incorrect. Pronunciamientos were often limited in scope. The soldiers of a garrison might pronounce to protest mistreatment. If the government, or the commander, addressed the problem, the garrison would cease pronouncing and resume their duties. On the other hand, when demands went unmet, or when people appropriated someone else's pronunciamiento, bloodshed could and did ensue. At the end of the day, however, violence was not the primary goal of a pronunciamiento. One could even see them as expressions of liberty rather than expressions of violence, due to the importance of the right to petition.

Pronunciamientos did not belong exclusively to one social class; people from the elite, middle class, and lower class all engaged in pronunciamientos. Eventually, pronunciamientos trailed off. As one scholar asserted, during the French Intervention, the Constitution of 1857 was "transformed from a controversial, often unpopular document into the flag of Liberalism and patriotic resistance"[21] Far from being the document that ignited the War of the Reform, the Constitution became beloved to the point that, when Díaz pronounced in 1876, he wrapped himself in the mantle of the Constitution. Liberals had different interpretations of the Constitution of 1857. Such was also the case in the United States and Argentina. But the main point here is that while pronunciamientos could produce violence, they did not always. Moreover, the strategies of some pronunciados in Mexico found analogues in the United States and Argentina.

Argentina's "Conquered Provinces": 1861–1867

The 1861 triumph of General Bartolomé Mitre and the forces of Buenos Aires over General Justo José de Urquiza and the armies of the Argentine Confederation at the Battle of Pavón ushered in a new era in Argentina.[22] One scholar asserted, somewhat grandiloquently, that "a phoenix seemed to be reborn from the ashes of civil war."[23] However, as Mitre and others quickly discovered, the phoenix was not flight-ready. Presidents Mitre, Domingo F. Sarmiento, and Nicolás Avellaneda faced numerous challenges consolidating the nation-state, including the pacification of the interior provinces. Liberals like Mitre and Sarmiento governed from Buenos Aires. The interior provinces, on the other hand, like the states of the so-called Confederacy in the United States, contained many Federales who refused to surrender. They fought Sarmiento and Mitre through traditional political means and guerrilla resistance, just as white Southern ex-rebels did in the US South.

The roots of Unitario/Federale hatred ran deep. For decades, both parties denigrated the other as savage and barbarous. Argentina and Mexico did not have the same racial situation as in the United States because the Argentine Wars of Unification and the War of the Reform and French Intervention did not result in the abolition and subsequent enfranchisement of millions of African slaves. Nevertheless, Unitario/Federale hatred in Argentina and Liberal/Conservative hatred in Mexico was often fully as intense as the animus many white people bore for African Americans. Framing enemies as savage and barbarous occurred in the United States, Mexico, and Argentina because the rules of war do not apply to a savage and barbarous enemy, and people put all tactics on the table in dealing with them.

In order to root out opposition, Mitre sent armies into some of the interior provinces. One of their principal objectives was to remove Federalist governors, install Unitario governors, and liberate the provinces from Federalist tyranny. To Sarmiento and Mitre, these goals seemed laudable. For Federales, the armies advancing into the interior looked like a wake of vultures preparing to strip the bones of a corpse. As one scholar observed, "the military occupation of the interior by the national government's troops after the battle of Pavón, and the Federalist resistance they encountered up until 1868, entailed both one of the worst wars and harshest crackdowns that the provinces suffered in the nineteenth century."[24]

Correspondence to and from Colonel Ignacio Rivas provides a window into the occupation by Buenos Aires of the Cuyo region—the provinces of Mendoza, San Juan, La Rioja, and San Luis. Rivas commanded the division sent to occupy this region. He frequently corresponded with his superior, General Wenceslao Paunero, the commander of the army occupying the province

of Córdoba. Federales watched the approach of Rivas and Paunero with apprehension. On January 3, 1862, Paunero instructed Rivas to make sure the provincial treasuries covered the expenses of his division. After all, "they should
contribute something to the expenses of a war to aid them and to free them
from the despotisms that oppress them."[25] Federales, who did not feel oppressed, recoiled because Paunero, in their eyes, required them to fund their
subjugation to the Unitarios. In a second letter, written the same day, Paunero
congratulated Rivas for arriving at San Luis, despite the difficulty of the march.
He also discussed the seizure of power in Mendoza by Juan de Dios Videla
from Federalist Governor Laureano Nazar. "It is necessary," Paunero growled,
"to not accept, for any reason, the continuation of Videla as the governor of
the Province."[26] Paunero and Rivas exercised the same power the Military Reconstruction Acts of 1867 granted the commanders of the military districts in
the US South, although their occupation occurred five years before the US
Congress passed this legislation. In both the United States and Argentina, the
army often faced the unpalatable role of playing mediator between different
factions and removing people from power, thus becoming ever-more unpopular with the vanquished.

Unitarios gloried in the progress made by Rivas and Paunero. Sarmiento,
who briefly set aside his educational reform efforts after being appointed governor of San Juan, praised Rivas.[27] Santiago Cortínez, a lawyer and politician,
chortled that Federalist power had been broken in San Juan and that "the authorities overthrown by the barbarian Saa were immediately reestablished."[28]
Cortínez's use of "barbarian" was hardly accidental. Governor Domingo A.
Villafañe of La Rioja assured Rivas that his government "has never offered resistance to the consolidation of the liberty and institutions created by the reformed Constitution."[29] Nonelite Unitarios also welcomed the armies. When
Rivas entered San Juan, the people received him with "enthusiastic manifesta-
tions of profound respect and gratitude." "This generous and patriotic conduct
does not surprise me," Paunero asserted, because it is typical of the "heroic
town of San Juan, a martyr, so many times, to despotism and their fanatic love
for liberty."[30]

Unitarios in Buenos Aires and the interior supported armies of occupation,
just as some white southerners supported US forces during Reconstruction.
They approved Paunero's sentiments that government troops liberated provinces from Federalist despotism. However, many of the residents of the inte-

rior provinces did not consider themselves victims of Federalist despotism. In fact, under the new regimes, dissenters complained about Unitario despotism. This situation tracks closely with Mexico and the United States. Many Mexican Conservatives wanted no parts of Liberal "saviors." Plenty of Confederates in the US South considered US occupation forces low, mean men, worthier of a bullet than a handshake. Such attitudes did not augur well for successful reconstructions and threatened liberal visions of internal improvement.

A determined foe rose to oppose Sarmiento, Rivas, Mitre, and Paunero. Ángel Vicente Peñaloza, "El Chacho," a La Riojan caudillo, attempted to derail the Unitario occupation of the interior. El Chacho represented a severe threat to the order and stability of La Rioja, Mendoza, San Juan, San Luis, Córdoba, and Tucumán. In addition, he was not the only caudillo in the field. In early February, Paunero informed Rivas that "Salteños [caudillos from Salta], those vandals of the Republic," allied themselves with "the caudillos of Catamarca and el Chacho" and menaced Tucumán.[31] Despite dire warnings about the "brutal influence of Peñaloza," Paunero remained optimistic because "today all the free Provinces adhere to the thought initiated by Buenos Aires, to organize a Republic on the basis of the reformed constitution."[32] Paunero fit the conflicts against the caudillos of the interior provinces into the same struggle— republicanism versus reaction—that drove transnational warriors to circulate from country and country and people to see their conflicts as interwoven. Republicanism was again under siege in Argentina.

In February 1862, Governor José María del Campo of Tucumán defeated Peñaloza at the Battle of Río Colorado. However, Peñaloza continued to terrorize Unitarios.[33] El Chacho took La Rioja on March 4, although Colonel Ambrosio Sandes defeated him at Salinas de Moreno several days later.[34] These frequent defeats risk underestimating the threat many felt El Chacho posed. A guerrilla band, after all, need not triumph in every engagement, because their goal is to wear down the occupying force and show the government the futility of occupation.[35] In his correspondence with Mitre, Sarmiento frequently discussed the state of "the war of La Rioja."[36] Unitario authorities, acting under Sarmiento's orders, sentenced a gaucho to four hundred lashes for saying, likely while drunk, "shit on the savages [Unitarians], I am a son of Peñaloza and I die for him."[37] Sarmiento's punishment of the gaucho did not win hearts and minds, but it certainly testified to Unitario fear of Peñaloza.

Throughout the spring of 1862, rumors circulated about El Chacho.[38]

Sarmiento complained to Rivas that Peñaloza occupied San Luis.[39] He fretted that El Chacho planned to strike at Mendoza or San Juan "to revive the remains of the Federales who have maintained themselves in their territories in the shadow of our tolerant politics."[40] The Federales who had been run out of town would have disagreed with Sarmiento's phrasing. However, Sarmiento himself, from his wording, perhaps exacerbated by his nervousness about what Peñaloza could do, would have appreciated General Thomas Ewing Jr.'s method for solving the guerrilla problem in Missouri during the US Civil War: wholesale depopulation of contested regions.[41]

In May 1862, affairs took a different turn. Peñaloza easily took San Luis but abandoned the city when Rivas arrived. However, Peñaloza also "sent an ultimatum to our Governor demanding an amnesty for self and fellows; a largess of 1000 patacons, permission to reside in Rioja and an allowance of a cow each day." The *Standard* drew two conclusions. First, "it is absolutely necessary to make terms with him." Second, "it would be rash to permit him to remain in his own province, where the *prestige* of his person would prove a serious obstacle to the influence of B. Ayres."[42] The same day, Paunero informed Rivas the national government would not place a garrison in every town. Succumbing to bitterness, Paunero lamented the government's inability to "maintain order in each province, when Rosas did it all his life."[43] Of course, the order Rosas maintained stifled freedom and liberty.

Paunero's complaint identified an important problem. How could Unitarios maintain order, during a guerrilla insurgency, without resorting to measures people deplored? In another letter Paunero noted that Villafañe was the legal governor of La Rioja and could not be removed. Military men should not become entangled in the internal order of each province and were not to remove or appoint governors. Our mission, he concluded, "is purely military and the only thing we should do is sustain and help the legal Governors."[44] Rivas may have raised an eyebrow at Paunero's words. Porteño armies had already done plenty to interfere in the internal politics of the provinces. Rivas, Paunero, and other Argentines, not to mention Mexicans and US citizens, found a purely military mission difficult to follow. Meddling often seemed the best way to fix the problem, even if it became ever harder to justify to the people.[45]

In June, Peñaloza agreed to an armistice.[46] Peace proved illusory because the caudillo initiated another rebellion in 1863.[47] When he invaded San Luis, "the forces in the town marched out to meet him, but were instantly cut to pieces." In San Juan, "the greatest commotion prevailed," and "Sarmiento held a council of war." In La Rioja, "robberies, confiscations, throat cuttings are the order of the day: all law and the Government have ceased to be respected."[48]

Delighting in the terror he unleashed, Peñaloza continued his rebellion and, despite defeats, remained a threat. "It is not pretty clear whether he be in San Luis, Cordoba, Rioja, San Juan or Santa Fe," complained one newspaper, "but it is certain that he assembles 400 or 1000 men as if by magic."[49] In October, Peñaloza reportedly discussed terms with Paunero including "a general amnesty, the recognition of Chacho's officers in their several grades, garantees [sic] of safety to all who lay down their arms, and permission for the filibuster chief to remain in Rioja."[50] Perhaps El Chacho grew tired of rebellion, because rumors flew that he "wishes to come to terms with the National Government, and will not resume the offensive, pending a final reply to his proposals."[51]

Peñaloza's second rebellion ended not in amnesty but in his death. The *Standard* hoped "all Argentine differences will be buried in the Chacho's grave."[52] Interestingly, Mitre first chose the method of treaty and amnesty to subdue the caudillo. This method did not work well in Argentina, Mexico, or the United States. Rather, it allowed Peñaloza a reprieve to recover his strength. Since he was not punished for his first rebellion, this decision allowed him another chance to dismember the nation. In each of the three countries, the victors often resorted to amnesty, only to find it did not work, or at least did not work in the long term.

The *New York World* discussed Peñaloza's death in several articles. "No local event," one article observed, "has for a long time stirred this community as the death of 'El Chacho.'" The paper also asserted that, for several years "all the upper provinces have been kept by him in a state of anarchy and revolution."[53] Peñaloza inspired such fierce loyalty in his men that they would die for him. A month later, the *World* commented, "the provinces of the confederation are at present enjoying a profound peace. 'El Chacho,' the great disturber, was treacherously killed."[54] Sarmiento and many other Argentines had no use for the vaguely heroic aura the paper painted around El Chacho. For most Unitarios, a savage Federale boogeyman had been destroyed. For Federales, by contrast, the savage Unitarios assassinated a good man who sought to do right by his friends.

Despite the defeat of El Chacho, this episode became an embarrassment for Sarmiento and Mitre. During El Chacho's second rebellion, Sarmiento, as governor of San Juan, declared the province in "estado de sitio," or state of siege.[55] Since he directed the pursuit of Peñaloza, some of Sarmiento's contemporaries, including Juan B. Alberdi, accused him of murdering El Chacho and becoming barbaric.[56] This charge should not be viewed lightly. Federalists such as Ricardo López Jordán hated Sarmiento, and their anger caused him no end of grief. Sarmiento's declaration of estado de sitio was just as damning in many Argentine eyes. One scholar commented that Sarmiento "reacted to the rebellion by declaring a legally irregular state of siege."[57] "Legally irregular" is too mild; Sarmiento's actions were illegal.[58] As governor, Sarmiento could not declare estado de sitio; that power belonged to the federal government.[59] Sarmiento and Minister of the Interior Guillermo Rawson exchanged polemic letters about the subject.[60] Sarmiento claimed the right to declare estado de sitio existed in the government in whatever form, provincial or national, whereas Rawson asserted that such power belonged exclusively to the national government.[61] Rawson needled Sarmiento, asking if he did not "fear that the National Government cements despotism with estado de sitio?" Sarmiento responded, tellingly, "I fear the contrary, that anarchy due to lack of power . . . brings despotism, by the subversion of illustrious and well-intentioned governments, who are nonetheless destitute of the means of guaranteeing social order."[62] Sarmiento placed the maintenance of peace and order, and the security of the government against rebellion, above constitutional niceties. Like Paunero's musings to Rivas about the problem of keeping order, the actions of the victors did not always meet constitutional muster. This raised the hackles of the vanquished as well as some of the victors, which had important consequences.

The controversy over "estado de sitio" was more than a minor debate about interpreting the Argentine Constitution. Sarmiento's actions fed charges that Unitarios ran roughshod over constitutional guarantees. Mitre and others justified, in part, their interference in the interior on the basis of helping the provinces realize the benefits of the Constitution.[63] Federales resisted this interference and claimed, among other points, that Unitarios made a mockery of the Constitution. Sarmiento might have countered, as Benjamin F. Butler did in 1861, that people attempting to subvert or destroy the government do not have the moral high ground to complain about constitutional scruples. Indeed, in his biography of Abraham Lincoln, published in 1866, Sarmiento included the full text of Lincoln's letter to Erastus Corning, which defended the arrest and banishment of Congressman Clement L. Vallandigham.[64] Sarmiento praised the letter and argued that it "will be of much consequence in the South American Republics, where the opinion of enlightened men vacillates, in regard to the faculties of the Executive to conserve the tranquility in times of commotion or invasion."[65] In other words, he used Lincoln's Corning letter to justify executive suppression of traditional liberties. Sarmiento and his fellow Unitarios had the best of intentions as they attempted to pacify the disordered interior, but their methods sometimes proved troubling. The same could also be said of the victors in Mexico and the United States, and this tendency helped inspire resistance by the vanquished and some discontented victors.[66]

The United States: 1865–1867

Robert E. Lee's surrender to Ulysses S. Grant on April 9, 1865, caused an explosion of joy in the North.[67] Serenaders called at the White House and implored Abraham Lincoln to deliver a speech. Lincoln asked for time to prepare something fitting. On April 11, 1865, he surprised the crowd with a speech defending the reconstructed government of Louisiana.[68] Lincoln observed: "It is also unsatisfactory to some that the elective franchise is not given to the colored man. I would myself prefer that it were now conferred on the very intelligent, and on those who serve our cause as soldiers."[69] When John Wilkes Booth, a member of the audience and a fanatical supporter of the Confederacy heard these words, he growled "that means nigger citizenship. Now by God I'll put him through!"[70]

Booth's decision to kill Lincoln stemmed from his rage concerning Lincoln's opinions about Black suffrage. He reasoned that the limited Black suffrage Lincoln proposed would lead to universal manhood suffrage. Like many of his white contemporaries, he foresaw an apocalyptic future wherein the "white race" would be destroyed through amalgamation.[71] This episode is an important reminder of the role race and racism played in driving violence in the United States during Reconstruction. That said, racism was not the only factor motivating white Southern ex-rebels to violence. They were also frightened, as were Federales in Argentina and Conservatives in Mexico, of the new worlds the victors were creating and concerned about the seemingly overarching power of the federal government. Hatred drove violence, and all three countries had plenty to go around.[72] The actions of African Americans during the US Civil War and the Thirteenth Amendment to the US Constitution created a different situation in the United States than in Mexico or Argentina, although, it should be noted, despite this important difference, the vanquished had some similar concerns, adopted similar tactics, and followed similar paths in the United States as elsewhere.

Because there was no Congress in session, President Andrew Johnson held the reins for much of 1865. In May, Johnson issued two proclamations outlining his program of Reconstruction that tended toward leniency rather than remaking the South. His Proclamation of Amnesty and Reconstruction pardoned most rebels, provided they swore a loyalty oath. Johnson exempted certain groups, including government officials who left their posts to serve the rebellion, officers of the so-called Confederacy, and anyone who owned more than twenty thousand dollars' worth of property. These people could make "special application" to Johnson for pardon, and "such clemency will be liberally extended as may be consistent with the facts of the case and the peace and dignity of the United States."[73] This was better than most rebels dared dream. A blanket pardon linked to a proviso that they swear a loyalty oath coupled with liberal clemency meant, given a few months, former rebels could again direct the destiny of their states. This, incidentally, was a far better deal than what Mitre offered the Federales in Argentina's interior provinces.

In another proclamation, Johnson outlined the mechanics for reconstructing North Carolina and, presumably, other states. His program was not particularly stringent. Johnson would appoint a provisional governor. That official would set elections for a constitutional convention, which would amend the state constitution. Once that was done, elections would be held for state officials. Conceivably, all states could be reconstructed by the opening of the Thirty-Ninth Congress in December 1865. Unlike Lincoln, Johnson did not embrace limited African American suffrage.[74] In sum, the people who spent four long years trying to rip the Union apart, once they took their loyalty oaths, would be allowed to vote and determine North Carolina's destiny.[75] Johnson quickly issued similar proclamations for the other states. He pardoned so many people the government had to hire additional clerks to process the paperwork.[76]

Johnson did not make many demands of his reconstructed governments other than accepting the Thirteenth Amendment abolishing slavery and repudiating war debts. Angry northerners, African Americans, and white Southern Unionists quickly realized rebels had no qualms about re-creating the status quo antebellum. As one former rebel general famously stated, freed slaves would have "nothing but freedom."[77] Former rebels, some of whom had the effrontery to wear their old gray uniforms, dominated the constitutional conventions and newly elected state legislatures and designed Black Codes to recreate slavery.

When comparing this early period in the United States with the corresponding period in Argentina, the inescapable conclusion is that the rebels in the US South received a much better deal than the Federales. When rebels took loyalty oaths, they received pardons and quickly became involved in the political process. Furthermore, many felt they had an ally in Johnson. In Argentina, Mitre and Sarmiento prioritized pacification over reintegrating caudillos and their followers into the political system. Despite occasional instances of mercy—Peñaloza's first amnesty for example—Mitre was no ally of the vanquished. Argentina's different response, during the critical years, helps explain their divergent trajectory with the United States in terms of consistent suppression of violence and rebellions.

The records of the Bureau of Refugees, Freedmen, and Abandoned Lands revealed the harsh realities of life in Johnson's "reconstructed" South.[78] In Mobile, Alabama, a group of African Americans sent a petition noting "our people are cruelly maltreated in the interior of this state of Alabama." Numerous tales, the writers asserted, "of untold horror have reached us in Mobile which eye witnesses can prove, tales of terrible and heart rending atrocities which are related not to a civilized and Christian community but to the beasts of the forest, to the rocks & trees and stone, that at the recital of such wrongs those mute and inanimate things would be thrown into confusion."[79] Such language was not hyperbolic. A report from Alabama's assistant commissioner offered, in very laconic language, information about crimes—assaults, torture, and murder—committed against freedpeople. "Alfred killed in Sumter County" on January 2, was a typical entry.[80] Nor was the violence confined to African Americans. From Washington County, Texas, M. E. Davis, a Bureau subassistant commissioner reported the murder of African Americans and one Thomas Alya, a Union man assaulted by rebels.[81] From Sherman, Texas, another subassistant commissioner snarled that "President Johnson's policy is hell on Union men and death to the nigger," and noted the murder of African Americans and white Unionists by rebels.[82]

A deplorable condition of affairs existed throughout much of the Southern United States. In Tennessee, the birthplace of the Ku Klux Klan, reports of violence flew thick and fast.[83] James Scott Havron noted, for instance, that "Tom Nelson in a speech at Greeneville calls upon the concervative [sic] men of *Tenn* to arm themselves to resist unlawful encroachments upon life liberty & property. That there is a Union league formed, that banks of these are driving men from there [sic] homes; robing [sic] & murdering. Mr Turner I fear there is an awful state of things over hanging you in Tenn, more so than any portion of the land."[84]

At first glance, the examples cited above suggest different types of violence. In Argentina, men like Peñaloza led bands of men, ranging from under a hundred to over a thousand, plundered provinces, and sparred with armies. In the United States, on the other hand, once the rebel armies disbanded, violence seemed more individualized. Small groups of men ambushed African Americans and Unionists and assaulted or murdered them. Or, a rebel grabbed his gun and shot someone, sometimes for no discernible reason at all. This seeming difference is misleading. Individualized violence occurred in Argentina as well. Furthermore, in the United States, as the break between Johnson and Congress sharpened, white southerners began to employ tactics closely resembling Peñaloza's violence, in addition to individualized violence. Hence, in 1866, rebels perpetrated the Memphis Massacre and the New Orleans Massacre where large groups attacked and murdered African Americans and white Unionists and Republicans.[85] New Orleans witnessed such foul scenes that General Philip Sheridan, no stranger to carnage and violence, considered the New Orleans Massacre worse than the massacre at Fort Pillow, where Nathan Bedford Forrest's cavalry butchered African American and white soldiers.[86] The Ku Klux Klan, a powerful paramilitary organization, emerged during this period. Unsurprisingly, Forrest became the first Imperial Wizard of the KKK.[87] The Klan was one of the first, but certainly not the last paramilitary group.[88]

The 1866 midterm elections offered voters a chance to assess the success or failure of Johnson's leniency and gave Johnson and Radical Republicans an opportunity to take their respective cases before the people. Many voters became convinced that Johnson's way had failed, and a harder hand was necessary. Consequently, more and more people came to accept the idea that the ballot should be extended to African Americans (at least in the Southern states) as a source of protection. Voters told Johnson they had had enough of his shenanigans, and Republicans won an impressive victory. Still, for anyone in the United States inclined to look at Mexico, or Argentina, and smugly think, "there but for the grace of God," the language people used during the election of 1866 proved chilling. Johnson made a series of intemperate speeches on his "Swing Round the Circle" tour. At Cleveland, Ohio, he responded to audience shouts of "Hang Jeff Davis" by suggesting he would sooner hang Radical Republicans Thaddeus Stevens and Wendell Phillips. To put that into context, the president of the United States suggested hanging his political foes, rather than the man who led a four-year experiment in treason. This, of course, after Johnson had pardoned traitors. Johnson also blamed the victims of the New Orleans Massacre for their own deaths.[89]

Citizens sent Johnson numerous dire letters during this period. Duff Green wrote that former rebel General Thomas L. Clingman planned to raise five hundred thousand men and march on Washington, possibly to overthrow the government.[90] Some correspondents pledged to raise troops to support Johnson. A. R. Johnstone, for instance, noted "if you have need of a regiment of good fighters I can raise men + should be pleased to hear from you."[91] Similarly, Thomas Powell of Ohio pledged himself "to train a thousand men in my Congressional district—the sixth—and I believe within thirty days fifty thousand men will be under arms in the state of Ohio alone—ready to do battle for the Union and the Constitution."[92] These letters may seem like bombast. However, for people during this period, the stakes could not have been higher. Many of Johnson's correspondents considered him locked in a death struggle with a Congress bent on usurping his power and shredding the Constitution. Alarmingly, people seemed fully prepared, even eager, to resort to massive violence and restart the US Civil War. The United States, Mexico, and Argentina faced a similar problem: the shooting wars had supposedly ended, but, in reality, each conflict continued in the form of an insurgency.

One critical difference with Argentina and Mexico, was the fact that in the United States the rebels were quickly reincorporated into the body politic. In Mexico, some Conservatives rejoined the body politic. However, the main lines of division were not, as they had been, Liberal/Conservative, but Liberal/Liberal. In other words, Liberals squabbled among themselves. In Argentina, Unitarios were inclined to stay unified, at least until they dealt with the caudillos, although Sarmiento and Rawson sparred over "estado de sitio." Many did not consider caudillos part of the body politic, but Federales continued to contest elections, particularly in 1868. Mitre dealt in good faith with Peñaloza, but when the caudillo rebelled the second time, Mitre wrote to

Sarmiento that Peñaloza and his ilk were brigands and should not receive the honor of being considered political opponents. Due to leniency by Andrew Johnson and violence, former rebels in the United States played an outsized role in the politics of the US South and, in the late 1860s and 1870s, succeeded in doing what Peñaloza could not: overthrowing and maintaining control of state governments.

Mexico: 1865–1867

Two days after the US presidential election of 1864, Abraham Lincoln discussed the election's meaning. "We can not have free government without elections," he contended "and if the rebellion could force us to forego, or postpone a national election, it might fairly claim to have already conquered and ruined us."[93] Even during the summer of 1864, when Lincoln believed he would lose the election, he did not seriously consider postponing it. In many ways, it was remarkable that the United States held an election during a civil war and did not let an internal rebellion dictate the electoral schedule. President Benito Juárez, Matías Romero, and many other Mexicans had good reason to be pleased about Lincoln's reelection, especially because they spent considerable time and effort hammering the idea that the United States and Mexico were sister republics passing through dual civil wars. It is uncertain if Juárez read Lincoln's postmortem about the election's meaning, but Juárez would likely have disagreed with Lincoln's comment about the ramifications of scuttling elections. The reason for this was because Mexico had to postpone the presidential election of 1865.

When Ignacio Comonfort resigned the presidency in 1857, Juárez, as president of the Supreme Court, became interim president of Mexico. It was not feasible to hold an election during the War of the Reform, so Juárez continued as interim president until 1861, the end of the war. When the conflict ended, Juárez won a four-year term, which was set to expire in 1865. However, it became clear to Juárez and other Mexicans, long before 1865, that holding a presidential election in 1865 would not be possible. Mexico's situation differed profoundly from that of the United States. Where Lincoln and the North retained control of Washington, DC, Juárez and the beleaguered Liberals lost control Mexico City in 1863. Juárez's government evacuated to San Luis Potosí and then continued north, until it ended up in the US-Mexico borderlands. US soldiers in Texas invited Juárez to cross the border for a visit. Juárez refused, not out of antipathy to the United States, but because he did not wish to allow his foes to claim he left Mexican soil.[94]

Juárez refused to concede the legitimacy of his foe and correctly viewed Maximilian as an Austrian usurper intent on overthrowing a democratically elected government. However, Juárez faced a problem: he claimed to be president of Mexico and that Mexico was still a functioning republic, so why not hold an election? Precisely because French and Imperial control of large portions of Mexico precluded holding an election. Before leaving Mexico City, the Mexican Congress granted Juárez extraordinary powers. In late November 1865, Juárez issued a decree extending his term until the French left Mexico. Perhaps not the best solution in the eyes of some of his rivals, but arguably it was the most workable.

Even before Juárez extended his term, Liberals such as General Jesús González Ortega of Zacatecas grumbled about Juárez's conduct.[95] While in Chihuahua, Juárez heard rumors Ortega wanted to be president. In January 1864, US Consul Reuben W. Creel informed Secretary of State William H. Seward that Juárez might be in political danger. As Creel explained, "Generals Ortega and Doblado have formed in Zacatecas, a project which has for its object the ejection of the President from his office." To further their design, they sent letters to the governors of Durango and Chihuahua and invited them to join the call for Juárez's immediate resignation. Both governors refused.[96]

At a time when all Liberals should have remained united against the French, Ortega and Doblado played a dangerous game. A month later, Creel wrote, with evident satisfaction, "the petition, signed by Generals Ortega and Doblado, Chaves of Aguascalientes, and by other public men in Central Mexico, urging upon President Juarez the propriety of his resignation of office, met with an emphatic refusal." When Juárez made his refusal public, Doblado and his men marched to Saltillo, where Doblado "placed himself under the orders" of Juárez. Ortega, on the other hand, "remained in Zacatecas, until the near approach of the intervention forces, when he evacuated that City, which was occupied by 6000 of the French party, without firing a gun."[97] Before abandoning Zacatecas, Ortega published an address "in which he swears fidelity to the Mexican cause, and unrelenting hostility to the intervention." Creel considered doubts about Ortega and Doblado's patriotism wrong, although Juárez may not have shared this assessment.[98]

Ortega believed Juárez's term expired in 1865, which it did, at least until Juárez extended it. As stated above, Mexico was in no condition to hold an election. If Juárez resigned, the president of the Supreme Court would have become interim president, just as Juárez did in 1857. A new election would then have to be held for the full term, but that election would probably have been postponed until after the French left. The president of the Supreme Court at this juncture was none other than Jesús González Ortega. This was neither the first nor the last time that Mexico's succession pattern—president of the Supreme Court taking over if something happened to the president—caused problems.[99]

Juárez was not the only leader in the Americas to face political challenges during wartime. Abraham Lincoln stared down John C. Frémont, the preferred candidate of some radicals in the Republican Party. Lincoln then trounced George B. McClellan, the Democrat candidate, in the election of 1864. Juárez faced something of a no-confidence vote from several of his generals, although Ortega and Doblado did not challenge Juárez in the political arena as McClellan did to Lincoln. To be fair, that was not an option in 1864 or 1865. If an election had taken place, Ortega would likely have run against Juárez. Rather, Ortega and Doblado utilized extrapolitical means to demand Juárez's resignation. Fascinatingly, Ortega's complaint was based on a legitimate constitutional foundation: the president's term expired in 1865 and, if Juárez refused to resign, the office should become vacant and the president of the Supreme Court should fill it. How these machinations would have raised flagging Liberal spirits is uncertain. In addition, the rule or ruin nature of this approach is apparent. Would a Juárez resignation have benefitted Liberals? More specifically, Liberals other than Ortega and his cronies? These episodes illustrated the dangers of mixing politics and brinksmanship during wartime in countries throughout the Americas.

In the period 1865–67, both Juárez and US diplomatic officials, who almost always favored Juárez, realized plenty of people schemed to cause problems for Juárez. In other words, Juárez and his friends had to mind the military might of the French invaders and the "traitor Mexicans" and guard against French political machinations. Marshal Bazaine, among others, stirred up discord among Liberals to help the French.[100] In addition, as Ortega's example proved, the Liberal Party contained many factions, often based on personalities. Juárez worried about men like Ortega and Servando Canales because they did what seemed best for them, not Mexico or Juárez. In sum, Juárez confronted military and political threats from the French and Maximilian and political, and sometimes military, threats from some of his fellow Liberals, who should have been focused on fighting the French and Imperialists rather than coveting his job.

Many threats to Juárez involved General Ortega. From Matamoros, Vice Commercial Agent Lucius Avery sneered that General Servando Canales "continues to act as Governor of Matamoros, or, as he styles himself, Governor of the state of Tamaulipas, although he exercises no authority beyond the city limits." When Juárez sent a duly appointed governor, General Tapia, Canales arrested him. "It is my belief," Avery spat, "that Canales intends to act in concert with the Ortega party, which is now quite strong in this section of Mexico. As the case now stands, we are governed by a man who has no other authority for his acts than the support of a few hundred men with arms in their hands."[101] In the space of two years, Ortega went from issuing manifestos to either organizing or allowing his name to be used to organize an opposition faction within the Liberal Party. Canales, like the Federales in Argentina's interior provinces, did not appreciate the general government naming a governor. His response was eerily similar to Peñaloza's: raise a force and deal with the problem of an unwelcome central government, even a government in exile, imposing authority. But for the fact that he was in the midst of fighting the French and the Imperialists, Juárez would probably have handled Canales with greater dispatch.

US Consul Franklin Chase echoed Avery's complaints that "the notorious Canales" posed a threat. Not only was Canales "en route for this place [Tampico] with a small force of adherents," but he also "pronounced against President Juarez, proclaimed Ortega 'President,' and the recently promoted General Asuncion [sic] Gomez [sic] Governor of the State of Tamaulipas."[102] Chase sent regular reports about Canales. In January, he observed that Canales arrived in Tampico, accompanied by "a few adherents to the cause of Ortega." The rebels made an attempt "to put this Port under a contribution of Three Hundred and Twenty Thousand Dollars." One of Canales's officers, Chase observed, "assures me that Ortega, is now between this Port and San Luis Potosi, and if funds can be raised in this place, a formal 'pronunciamiénto,' will be made here in favor of Ortega, as President of the Republic."[103]

Events worked against Canales. The pronunciamiento he intended to issue "was fortunately frustrated by the majority of the authorities here, who had become convinced that the Government of the United States, would sustain Juarez at all hazards, and that their best policy was to continue under his authority. The recent turn of events in the interior by the arrest of Ortega, and the defeat of Miramon at Zacatecas, serves to convince the inhabitants of this State, that they must also yield for the present, to the rule of Juarez."[104] Ortega's arrest cleared up one problem, but another remained. Gómez disobeyed direct commands by Juárez "to turn over the command of this place to the Prefect Don Ramon Castillo, and to march with the State forces under his command to the scene of action at Queretaro."[105] The arrival of the USS *Tahoma* helped suppress a pronunciamiento. Gómez and his minions feared "the Commander of the 'Tahoma' would have aided the friends of Juarez."[106] In this case, the deepening ties between the United States and Mexico and Pan-American cooperation worked in Juárez's favor by discouraging rebellions.

On May 14, a portion of the soldiers in the garrison rebelled against Gómez. The rebellion "lasted about six hours, when the revolted party were put to flight, some of whom escaped in boats to the United States. Steamer 'Yantic,' from whence they were sent to the opposite shore, and other rushed into the Houses of the foreign Consuls, as places, of refuge, whilst about twenty were shot by their pursuers while in the act of endeavoring to swim to the 'Yantic,' and the merchant vessels in Port."[107] Juárez, fed up with Gómez, instructed General Desiderio Pavón to gather a force and reoccupy the city. Pavón recaptured Tampico and signed accords of surrender with Gómez on June 6, 1867.[108] Unfortunately for Juárez, Gómez and Canales continued to cause problems long after the defeat of the French and Imperialists.

The trouble involving Canales occurred before Maximilian's execution. Therefore, the collapse of the Imperialists, at that point, was by no means assured. Even as the Liberals under General Mariano Escobedo invested Querétaro, Juárez faced backroom intrigues and a significant possibility of violence.[109] These conflicts would have been better saved for after the war ended. However, as the history of the United States and Argentina also demonstrates, brush conflicts, brinksmanship, and petty squabbles characterized most wars. The way these conflicts unfolded supports an argument made in other chapters: the growing US-Mexico rapprochement paid dividends. In this case, it helped by convincing dissenters that the United States would intervene on behalf of Juárez and their revolutions would fail. The United States validated this opinion by sheltering the soldiers who rebelled against the rebels.

As Canales prepared to march on Tampico, Marshal Bazaine meddled in Mexican politics. More so, of course, than he already had by leading an army to sustain an Austrian pretender as the despised emperor of a French client state. In Mexico City, now held by the French and Imperialists, US Consul Marcus Otterbourg explained that Bazaine did not deny rumors which name "him as the chief instigator of a movement industriously fomented in favor of Ortega."[110] A few weeks later, Otterbourg fretted that a proclamation written by Ortega would lead to an alliance between Ortega and the Imperialists, in the event of Maximilian's abdication. The release of this document sowed discord "among the Liberal chiefs around the Capital."[111] In the proclamation, Ortega labeled himself "presidente constitucional interino" (interim constitutional president) and accused Juárez of perpetuating a coup d'état. If Ortega was the patriot he claimed, why not wait until after the French had been expelled and the extraordinary circumstances necessitating the extension of Juárez's term removed?[112] Ortega's actions, apart from being ruthlessly self-aggrandizing, could have been, if successful, a tremendous problem not only for Juárez but for Mexico more generally.

While many Mexican states did not jump on the Ortega bandwagon, regions of Ortega strength existed in Zacatecas, Tamaulipas, and Mexico City. These regions preferred to replace Juárez with Ortega. The French did not attempt to be subtle about interfering in Mexican politics. In fact, the surprising element is not French meddling but that they did not do more to encourage Liberal squabbles. Liberals were not a particularly cohesive party. At a time when all their attention should have been focused, with laser-beam intensity, on defeating the French, fights among factions of Liberals, which had the alarming potential to spark violence, were never far from the forefront. This provides a hint about Mexico's political destiny. The post-1867 period would not be a period of Liberal/Conservative tension but, rather, one marked by battles, both political and military, between factions of Liberals, with the remnants of the Conservatives making trouble when and where they could. Divisions among groups of Liberals bore bitter fruit.[113]

On June 19, 1867, Maximilian, flanked by Generals Miguel Miramón and Tomás Mejía, met his maker on a hill outside Querétaro, several months after the French had evacuated. Juárez returned in triumph to Mexico City, which had been occupied by a newly minted hero of the war, General Porfirio Díaz of Oaxaca. Mexico could now hold a presidential election. Unsurprisingly, Juárez sought reelection. He faced two opponents: his old foe Jesús González Ortega and the relative newcomer Porfirio Díaz. Ortega should have waited for this opportunity to challenge Juárez, not in the midst of a bloody civil war. In the end, Juárez won another term as president. Unlike in 1871 and 1876, there was no national pronunciamiento, no organized uprising designed to topple Juárez or Lerdo. In the happy glow of victory over the French, Ortega and Díaz may have conceded the inevitability of a Juárez victory and consoled themselves that four years is not that long to wait for another chance at the presidency.

The election of 1867, unlike the election of 1868 in the United States the following year, did not produce much violence. Franklin Chase struck a discordant note when he condemned the execution of Maximilian and noted that it generated bad feelings for Juárez.[114] Díaz, Chase wrote, "will now employ every possible means to divest him of the Presidency, and, with the aid of his numerous friends assume the reins of the Government himself. Within the past eight days a certain General of many friends, and great influence, entered this City, incognito, as an emissary from Diaz, [who?] has made arrangements for a pronunciamiento in this place, to take effect on the 12th proximo, for the object of proclaiming Diaz either President or Dictator of the Republic." Chase lamented, "I may be a witness to still more bloody scenes in this place.[115] Fortunately, this did not come to pass, but it spoke to the climate of Tampico, one of the cities with an overt pro-Ortega movement, and the possibility of violence.

On the other hand, in Chihuahua, US Consul Charles Moye noted that the governor "is trying to conciliate and unite the various political parties by not permitting any insult or abuse to his political enemies, and by giving them all the protection against certain measures, adopted by the General Government, especially concerning the confiscation of property as well as the banishing of persons, who had taken an active part in the intervention, a revengeful line of conduct pursued too frequently by the State authorities in this Republic."[116] The governor behaved pragmatically and his conciliatory course and lack of enthusiasm about punishing rebels approximated Andrew Johnson's behavior. Finally, in the state of Veracruz, US Consul E. H. Saulnier noted that the elections took place without any disturbances or violence.[117] Sadly, that did not portend calm in Mexico. In the years to come, violence and rebellions would, like the United States and Argentina, continually plague the victors.

Conclusion: From War to Peace(?)

Argentina, the United States, and Mexico had broadly similar experiences during the transition from war to peace. That said, some important differences merit notice, specifically whether the victors offered the vanquished amnesty and how they dealt with violence, rebellion, and disorder. In the aftermath of his victory at Pavón, Mitre did not offer Urquiza and his men a general amnesty. Rather, he sent armies into the interior to pacify caudillos as well as to spur regime change and nation-building. Still, Mitre had no intention of marching every caudillo before a firing squad, and he left Urquiza alone to rule the province of Entre Ríos. Mitre negotiated an armistice with Peñaloza that amnestied the caudillo and his men. However, less than a year later, El Chacho resumed his old tricks. This time Mitre took off the gloves. He told Sarmiento, and others, to deal with the brigand. Sarmiento did, although his methods crossed a crucial line dividing constitutional and unconstitutional behavior and led some to charge the Unitarios with ordering Peñaloza's assassination. Mitre's actions mixed "shock and awe" with occasional leniency. Mitre's tactics, and Sarmiento's later employment of them, help explain why, in the following chapters, Argentina had a better record dealing with internal discord.

In the United States, Andrew Johnson offered a blanket pardon and amnesty if rebels swore a loyalty oath. Although he exempted eleven classes of people, he freely handed out pardons to them. Johnson justified this decision by pointing to the pardoning power granted the president by the Constitution. His actions meant most rebels were quickly reincorporated into the body politic. Because of the manner in which Johnson formulated his program of reconstruction, rebels played an important role in the initial stages. Even so, angry ex-rebels frequently employed violence and terror. Once Republicans gained control of Southern state governments, rebels resorted even more frequently to these tactics. Their violence was analogous to that of Argentine caudillos, but rebels in the United States received far more lenient treatment.

In Mexico, where the conflict ended last, Juárez confronted opposition from Canales and Gómez and a constitutionally based challenge by Ortega, and he also had to worry about French and Imperialists plots. Every minute he spent putting out brushfires was a minute he lost directing the Liberal war effort. Despite the constitutional foundations of his objection, Ortega played a dangerous game. Still, even though he spent some time in prison, Ortega did not really suffer for his machinations and Canales and Gómez returned to bedevil Juárez another day. Too often, this became the conclusion of violence and rebellions in the Americas: the perpetrators were amnestied or left alone to become serial rebels/serial pronunciados who engaged in the same terrible behavior again and again. However, in an important difference, Juárez executed people. Maximilian, Mejía, Miramón, and Santiago Vidaurri went before firing squads at the end of the French Intervention.[118] Urquiza, on the other hand, retired to and ruled Entre Ríos. Peñaloza, had he not rebelled the second time, could have lived in peace in La Rioja. Jefferson Davis, the leader of the rebellion in the United States, spent less than two years in prison. Victors had much to do and punishing rebels was one task among many.

Another important difference concerned race. Unlike the United States, Argentina and Mexico did not have large populations of freedpeople. However, despite this important difference, the vanquished in each of the three nations invoked many of the same reasons for rebelling, including constitutional justifications; complaints about fraud, illegitimate elections, and an overarching central government; and their anger about the new worlds the victors attempted to create. Hatred, therefore, is an important explanatory factor. People in all three countries framed their enemies as savage, barbarous, and uncivilized. The examples presented suggest the depths of the hatred: from the reports compiled by Freedmen's Bureau officials, to the hatred of the Federalists for the "savage Unitarians" and vice versa, to Canales taking advantage of Juárez's distractions during wartime. The results of the US Civil War, namely African American soldiers and the Thirteenth Amendment, added an additional dimension to the US context, and one should never underestimate the power of racism in driving rebel actions. Still, it is also vital to note how the vanquished offered similar complaints and utilized similar strategies to wrest back control of their worlds.

The conditions of political parties in each country were also an important difference. The Democratic Party survived the Civil War and contested elections long after the end of the conflict. Unitarios in Argentina rallied against Federale caudillos of the interior, and against the remnants of the Federales in the election of 1868. After that, they often fell to squabbling among themselves about other issues, such as the federalization of Buenos Aires and provincial autonomy, that generated new violence. In Mexico, Liberals cooperated while, at the same time, scheming to tear each other down. There were Conservatives left in Mexico, but the principal fault lines soon concerned groups of Liberals. Republicans argued among themselves as well, and these disagreements would grow ever-sharper, but, at least in the 1860s, the main fault line remained Democrat/Republican. Argentina and Mexico, when the Conservatives and Federales eventually died as effective political parties, experienced realignments. These realignments generated violence by pitting groups of Liberals against each other. In the United States, people expected the Democratic Party to die, or for the Republican Party to fade away after the passage of the Fifteenth Amendment. In other words, they expected a realignment. The fact that one did not occur, therefore, was very significant as was the fact that many different types of violence frequently occurred.

Peace in the United States, Mexico, and Argentina, or, more specifically stated, the end of the shooting wars, did not restore harmonious feelings. In fact, it spurred paramilitary violence. Although the election of 1867 was comparatively quiet in Mexico, people wondered what the future would entail. Argentina and the United States faced their own elections the following year. Would the victors ever pacify the vanquished? What would the elections of 1868 bring? Could the victors win the peace and impose their visions? Only time would tell.

6

Suppressing Rebellions and Punishing Rebels, 1867–1872

On February 8, 1869, US Vice Consul Charles W. Brink informed the State Department of a pronunciamiento in Puebla by General Manuel Negrete: "At the head of a Military force of 500 Men—having 'Liberty + death to Juarez' for their war-cry,—he occupied the town, took the government buildings, without resistance; issued a Proclamation to his troops to the People,—declaring the government a Corrupt tyranny."[1] Many people suspected Negrete pronounced on behalf of Porfirio Díaz, but Díaz "is now at his hacienda, + has taken no part in it." Juárez dispatched eight hundred soldiers to deal with Negrete's rebellion.

Brink fretted that the pronunciamiento would radiate out from Puebla to cover a significant portion of Mexico's territory. "Yucatan has 'pronounced,'" he warned, "rumors that the state of Oaxaca + Vera Cruz are rising, are rife— but they require confirmation. Tamaulipas is in a state of chronic insurection [sic]; + the frontier states are unsettled."[2] Consul E. H. Saulnier of Veracruz supported Brink's analysis and observed that Negrete's pronunciamiento was "in favor of the strict observance of the Constitution of 1857."[3] Negrete wrapped his pronunciamiento, as Díaz later did, in the garb of the Constitution of 1857. In that sense, both men mirrored caudillos in Argentina who claimed the constitutional high ground and US rebels who lauded the pre-Reconstruction Amendments Constitution.

Contrary to Brink and Saulnier's fears, the force Juárez sent defeated Negrete. The Mexican government, reported one newspaper, "published an extra, declaring that the forces of Negrete had been completely routed and broken into small squads, and that he was endeavoring to save himself." Negrete's friends contested this interpretation, but "it is generally believed that the efforts of Negrete will prove a failure, and that the government had exhibited its strength in rapidly smothering this rebellion."[4] Faced with rebellion, Juárez responded quickly and decisively to suppress it. In Mexico, Argentina, and the United States, during this period, governments could and often did, defeat revolutions, scatter revolutionaries, and suppress paramilitary organizations. However, they often proved unwilling or unable to punish revolutionists.[5] This attitude did not augur well for the stability and prosperity of the three nations.

The Elections of 1868

During his presidency, Bartolomé Mitre played an important role in shaping Argentina's destiny. He sent armies to pacify the interior provinces, removed Federalist officials, and put down caudillos and rebellions. At the same time, he led Argentine forces during the War of the Triple Alliance, a conflict pitting Argentina, Brazil, and Uruguay against Paraguay. Because the Constitution of 1853 prohibited presidents serving consecutive terms, Mitre, unlike Benito Juárez in Mexico and Andrew Johnson and Ulysses S. Grant in the United States, could not succeed himself. Although Mitre was not a candidate in 1868, Domingo F. Sarmiento was. Still Argentine minister to the United States, Sarmiento was not in Argentina during the election. Nevertheless, his friends looked after his interests and advanced his candidacy. As one scholar noted, this election "was unusual in that the result was not, on the one hand, a foregone conclusion, a mere legitimation of a choice that had already been made, nor, on the other, disputed by force of arms."[6]

Interest in the election ran high in both Argentina and the United States. As one newspaper reported, "the public is greatly interested in the diversity of candidates."[7] Mitre did not support Sarmiento and backed Rufino de Elizalde, his minister of foreign affairs from 1862 to 1867.[8] Although Federales initially remained quiet, "there are not wanting names, and names of great influence, which are kept in the back ground until the last moment."[9] Of all the "names of great influence," General Justo José de Urquiza's, former president of the Argentine Confederation and current caudillo of Entre Ríos, topped the list. Mitre tried to derail Urquiza's candidacy by authoring a letter declaring that "the program of Sarmiento is against the country, Alsina's candidacy is contraband, and Urquiza's is inadmissible."[10] In other words, Mitre denigrated Elizalde's rivals as unfit for command. However, "the old Federal party," one US newspaper reported, "is again showing signs of vigor."[11] Observers saw three possible choices in 1868: "a continuance of *mitrismo*, a return to the rule of Urquiza, or a leap into the unknown with Sarmiento."[12]

The War of the Triple Alliance hovered over Argentina's presidential election.[13] "Hamstrung by the war in Paraguay," Mitre failed "to manipulate the victory of a handpicked successor."[14] Furthermore, where Elizalde supported the war, "Sarmiento is regarded as averse to it, and so is General Urquiza." In such a high-stakes contest, the candidates offered starkly different choices: "Sarmiento—Instruction. Urquiza—Order. Alsina—Reform and peace. Lopez—Legality and peace. Elizalde—Protectorate of Brazil and war."[15] Several newspapers reported that "the peace party in the confederation was in the ascendancy, and the election of Urquiza was considered certain."[16]

After all the votes were tallied, Sarmiento won with 79 out of 131 electoral votes.[17] William Wheelwright, US commercial agent at Rosario, hoped Sarmiento's election "will promote the peace and prosperity of the Argentine Republic." Despite considerable obstacles, Wheelwright observed, including "the absence of Sor Sarmiento, the influence of the present administration which was antagonistic to his Election; the efforts of Genl Urquizas partizans; the powerful influence of military opponents in some of the Provinces of the north," Sarmiento, "the author—and founder of *schools* and *education*," won the presidency. His election, according to Wheelwright, heralded a new age in which Argentines "are beginning to put forth their moral strength in the right direction to vindicate Republican Institutions."[18] Sarmiento returned to Argentina in September 1868, and the predicted tension between Sarmiento and Urquiza did not materialize.[19] Indeed, "letters from Buenos Ayres report that General Urquiza supports the administration of President Sarmiento."[20] Despite the disappointment of Urquiza and his friends at the loss, they accepted Sarmiento's victory. Could the same be said of the losers of the political contest in the United States in 1868?

The election of 1868 was extremely contentious, even for a presidential election in the nineteenth-century United States.[21] Republicans nominated Ulysses S. Grant, one of the heroes of the US Civil War. Democrats selected Horatio Seymour. As governor of New York for a significant portion of the US Civil War (January 1863–December 1864), Seymour's sins, according to Republicans, were legion. As one Republican newspaper growled, "we all remember the terrible New York draft riots of 1863—when he was Governor of the State—which raged for three days, owing to his mingled indifference and inefficiency; and how finally he essayed to put down the rioters by a smooth speech, addressing them from a street corner as 'My friends!'"[22] Five years after the draft riots, the memory of Seymour's alleged treason burned bright among

Republicans. Even if Seymour was not the hissing Copperhead haunting the Republican imagination, his political opponents insisted he was nonetheless fatally tainted by Copperhead opposition to the US Civil War.[23]

Nineteenth-century US presidential elections were usually raucous and rowdy. Stump orators played to the worst passions and prejudices of their audiences. Marches through towns could become unpleasant. People often transitioned from shouting at each other to fisticuffs. On election days, community pressure, as well as local toughs, frequently caused trouble at the polls, especially because the United States did not vote by secret ballot. During Reconstruction, paramilitary organizations in the US South, such as the Ku Klux Klan, practiced voter suppression. As they had done in 1856, 1860, and 1864, as well as the 1862 and 1866 midterm elections, and would do for the rest of the nineteenth century and part of the twentieth, Democrats ran a virulent white supremacy campaign. Democrat attack ads featured stereotypical depictions of African Americans lazily enjoying themselves while white men worked to support them and proclaimed that Republican policies favored African Americans at the expense of white people, albeit in cruder terms. They also accused Republicans of wanting to impose racial equality.

The tenor of the speeches from one-half of the Democratic ticket illustrated the deadly seriousness of the contest. Francis P. Blair Jr., son of Francis P. Blair Sr. and candidate for vice president, made a series of bitter addresses. Some of them explored the alleged consequences of Republican policies. During one speech, Blair stated that the army and the occupation of the US South cost more than $150 million. Great sums of money, he sneered, must be expended "in order to give the uneducated, semi-barbarous black people of the South the ascendency over the people of the white race." Did it benefit white northerners, he concluded, "to have this enormous sum levied in taxes upon the labor of the country in order to be squandered upon idle, worthless political negroes at the South."[24] This type of argument characterized most Democratic orations, although some orators included more racial epithets than Blair.

Blair moved beyond denunciations of alleged Republican malfeasance to even more dangerous ground in a St. Louis speech. According to one newspaper, "the assertion of Frank Blair in his St. Louis speech of Friday night, that if General Grant is elected President he will never leave the White House alive, makes a good deal of talk here. Some persons suppose he must have been drunk at the time, while others look upon it as a deliberate threat."[25] For a country less than four years removed from Lincoln's assassination, talk of assassination was profoundly disturbing. It risked opening wounds not fully healed from Lincoln's murder. Furthermore, it called to mind Lincoln's admonition that there can be no appeal from ballots to bullets in a democracy; when politicians fail at the polls, they are not supposed to reach for guns and assassinate opponents (or secede from the Union).[26]

Blair's friends dismissed the issue as Republican calumny. The *Cincinnati Daily Enquirer* complained Republicans misquoted Blair. Radical papers, specifically the *Cincinnati Gazette,* had Blair saying the following: "it [the Republic] becomes a mere appendage of the military chieftain who is lifted to power in the name of President, but who never will leave the Presidential mansion alive." In actuality, the offending language, taken verbatim from Blair's St. Louis speech, was as follows: "It [the Republic] becomes a mere appendage of the military chieftain who is lifted to power in the name of Presidency. But he will never leave the Presidential mansion as long as he lives."[27] Blair's friends insisted he *actually* meant Grant would rule for the rest of his life as a dictator and die of natural causes. Republicans understood Blair to threaten Grant's assassination.[28] Thomas Nast, the most gifted political cartoonist of the age, pilloried Blair in a cartoon entitled "Wilkes Booth the Second."[29] Nast depicted newspaper editor Marcus Pomeroy leading a veiled Blair to assassinate Grant. At least Porfirio Díaz, when he ran for president, had the decency never to call for the assassination of Benito Juárez or Sebastián Lerdo de Tejada. The same cannot, apparently, be said of Frank Blair.[30]

Republicans, to be fair, offered scathing indictments of Seymour. Henry Ward Beecher proclaimed that the election "will be a fair fight between rugged honesty and plausible craft."[31] Grant's old friend General William T. Sherman chuckled that Seymour's "is a bad nomination, and will be beaten all to pieces."[32] "There is not one Rebel to-day," thundered Horace Greeley, the sharp-tongued editor of the *New York Tribune,* "whose hands are red with the blood of Union soldiers, nor a plotter of treason who is not a partisan of Horatio Seymour, and ardently trying to elect him."[33] "The contrast and character between Grant and Seymour is very significant," argued a California newspaper. "The one is honest and free—the other dishonest and enslaved. The one fitly represents the new era of liberty and unshackled progress on which our country has entered—the other stands for and is bound by all the selfish schemes, passionate revenges and heretical theories which have so crippled us in the past."[34] Finally, a Detroit sheet claimed Seymour represented "all that was most malignant and persevering in home opposition to the success of the Union army" and deplored the fact that "some men propose to make this wretched demagogue President of the United States instead of Ulysses S. Grant."[35] Republicans proved as proficient at insulting their political foes as Democrats.

Thomas Nast devoted much of his time to pillorying Seymour. He depicted Seymour as, alternatively, a conniving, satanic figure; Mrs. Partington; Lady Macbeth; a pitiable fool; and a foul traitor. In "The Democratic Hell-Broth," Nast portrayed Seymour, Blair, and Wade Hampton of South Carolina as the witches from Shakespeare's Macbeth.[36] The "witches," according to W. A. Croffut's inspired adaptation of the Bard's words, concocted a brew composed of a Copperhead fang, Robert E. Lee's perjured tongue, the blood of freedmen from Camilla, and Frederick Douglass's chains. Seymour did not appear in "This Is a White Man's Government," arguably the most well-known 1868 Nast cartoon. Nast drew three figures representing the pillars of the Democratic Party: a thuggish Irishman who bore a closer resemblance to an ape than to a man, a wealthy capitalist, and a man resembling General Nathan Bedford Forrest with a CSA belt buckle. All three men placed their boots on the back of a prostrate African American soldier. The soldier clutched the US flag and reached for the ballot box. The Irishman carried a club labeled "A Vote," and the Confederate a knife labeled "The Lost Cause."[37]

In the United States, as in Mexico and Argentina, no national pronunciamiento or rebellion occurred during the elections of 1867 and 1868. The election featured heated words and, in Blair's case, a threat of assassination, but the losers did not seek to start a revolution, at least at the *national* level. However, "This Is a White Man's Government" revealed a critical point: the Confederate, resembling Forrest, represented the entire US South, where the Democratic Party attempted to exert control through force. Powerful paramilitary organizations like the Ku Klux Klan functioned as the military arm of the party. Forrest, the leader of the Klan, estimated a membership of forty thousand in Tennessee and more than a half million men throughout the states of the so-called Confederacy.[38] The Klan was a mass movement capable of widespread voter suppression and intimidation. Furthermore, Klansmen did not hesitate to murder their Black and white political opponents. One Republican sent a horrifying poem to the *New York Tribune* to illustrate the relationship between Democrats such as Blair and the KKK. The poem read "Blair, Blair, Black Sheep / Have you any wool? / Yes, my master, seven bags full— / Nigger scalps from Georgia, / Ku Klux got them all, / So many less nigger votes / Against us in the fall."[39]

Newspapers did not shy away from reporting Klan atrocities. "The peaceable portion of our population will be glad to hear that the wholesale slaughter of the loyal men of the South will be postponed until after the November election," one newspaper commented sarcastically. "The Southern rebels have promised to remain quiet until that time. Whatever assassination is necessary, will be done by the Ku-Klux Klan in a private way. Gen. Forrest and his friends have been admonished that they have been rather too hasty, and that they must not 'toot' their 'horn' until the election of Seymour and Blair has been secured."[40] Another paper commented, bitterly, that the KKK was "an organization for express purpose of answering argument by assassination."[41]

Answering argument by assassination become horrifyingly commonplace. In Louisiana, for instance, according to one Northern newspaper, "there exists a practical system of rebellion against the state and federal governments. Assassination and murder are the order of the day. The Ku Klux Klans have taken possession of the country, and loyal whites and blacks are running for their lives."[42] The *Boston Daily Advertiser* of October 19, 1868, reported the assassination of the sheriff and parish judge of St. Mary's Parish, Louisiana. They also noted the murder of a "negro preacher" and state senator named Randolph in Cokesbury, South Carolina. In addition, the Klan killed Deputy Sheriff J. Dollar and "a negro" in Arkansas.[43] Most disturbingly, these murders did not occasion much comment and, to far too many people, almost seemed routine. In a letter to James G. Taliaferro, D. E. Haynes stated: "I have met with the utmost feelings of rancor and revenge being hurled against me, for my political proclivities—And if I had the means of living any where I would leave here [St. Helena Parish]—I have to go Armed to my School room, for threats of assassination have been made against me."[44]

Emerson Bentley, a Northern transplant to Louisiana, recorded a remarkable episode in his diary about violence and courage: "A placard was posted up on the school house door: 'E. B. Beware! (dripping dagger, skull and bones, and coffin, painted on) K. K. K.' I pinned it to my breast and walked down Main Street as contentedly as ever, and with a feeling of pride, that this warning had been received While doing my duty as a man and as a supporter of a government that forgave rebels and overlooked their follies. I received curses as I passed from gentlemen (?)"[45] It took a special kind of courage to pin a

KKK warning to one's shirt and walk down Main Street, and Bentley defied the Klan at his peril. The accounts from newspapers might be dismissed as partisan propaganda—a standard argument white Southern ex-rebels frequently made—but the accounts of people who lived through the violence are harder to deny.

Violence and murder, specifically targeted against Black and white Republicans, became frighteningly common throughout the US South. A citizen, writing from Fulton County, Arkansas, noted "there is a Set of Soliders [or?] men of some kind in hear [sic] that is all over the country that calles [sic] them Selves Kuclks [sic] they are in the country in the Knight [sic] and when day comes there cant one of them found there is a great excitement a bout the election."[46] From Alabama, Dan Price informed Congressman Charles Pierce that the Klan did not go to ground following Grant's election. In fact, "on the night of the 5th Decr a band of Ku Klux went to the house of Dr Choutteau a true Radical of this county and fired at the Dr several times he being in his house." Price also noted that "they openly declare that they the Democrats intend to and will rule Ala. Congress and the laws to the contrary notwithstanding." He closed, rather plaintively, "dont forget us poor Devils Major and don't fail to remember the *Rebs.*"[47] Many such letters told similar stories of violence and terror.

In addition to assassinating individuals, usually in the dead of the night, large-scale massacres occurred in Camilla, Georgia, and Opelousas, Louisiana. On September 19, 1868, Democrats slaughtered African Americans and white Republicans at Camilla, Georgia.[48] In the aftermath of the massacre, Republican newspapers splashed the gory details across their pages. "The 'fearful Radical riot' at Camilla, Ga.," screamed the *New-York Commercial Advertiser,* "was a deliberate, preconcerted rebel butchery. It was another New Orleans massacre, inspired by the same devilish hate, planned and executed by the same identical class of unrepentant rebels."[49] Indeed, agreed the *Boston Journal,* "it only needs a casual perusal of the rebel account of the affair at Georgia to see that it was a cold-blooded, unprovoked massacre of Union men."[50] The *Richmond Whig and Advertiser,* on the other hand, a Democratic sheet, dismissed the massacre as "a negro riot."[51]

Massacre followed massacre. Barely a week and a half after Camilla, "another bloody butchery" occurred at Opelousas, in St. Landry Parish, Louisiana.[52] One of the articles Bentley clipped out of a newspaper to include in his diary argued, "the bloody affair in St. Landry Parish proves to have been an assault of the armed Democracy upon the Republicans of Opelousas, without provocation."[53] Democratic newspapers encouraged massacres by claiming that "there is a very dangerous condition of society in Opelousas. The Radical demagogues seem there more reckless and incendiary than in any other part of the State" and warning white men to beware and "keep your guns in order."[54] That is exactly what Democrats did. The results of the "riot" were telling: "it is estimated that over one hundred negroes were killed and about fifty wounded. The whites had four wounded but none killed."[55]

In response to efforts by Democrats to suppress Republican votes and win elections, the federal government under Andrew Johnson did little. Congress investigated massacres but, unsurprisingly, Johnson evinced little concern or desire to hunt down the perpetrators. Freedmen's Bureau agents lamented knowing exactly who committed the crimes and being unable to secure witnesses against them or uncertain if they could win guilty verdicts in Southern courts. These massacres were no less serious than caudillo rebellions in Argentina or pronunciamientos in Mexico, because they threatened the stability of the country and the individual states and made a mockery out of constitutional guarantees. Andrew Johnson could have learned something from watching how Presidents Mitre, Sarmiento, and Juárez handled rebellions.

Grant's victory in 1868, while a comfortable 214 to 80 in the electoral college, was much narrower in the popular vote: roughly 3,013,000 to 2,707,000. For many Republicans, this was alarmingly close. Even with all the tools in the Republican arsenal—denouncing Seymour as a traitor, harping on links between the Democratic Party and the rebels, lurid accounts of violence in the Southern states, and Grant as the savior of the Union—they could not even poll 53 percent of the popular vote! Looking at the electoral map, Republicans had additional reasons to worry: Louisiana and Georgia, not coincidentally both states that suffered large-scale massacres of Black and white Republicans, contributed their electoral votes to Seymour. For many people, this demonstration of the effectiveness of paramilitary violence was a point of particular concern. Four years down the road, in 1872, similar tactics might lock up the rest of the Southern states for the Democrats. With some gains in the lower North, Democrats could find a path to the presidency. In order to avoid this, Republicans had to strengthen Republican state governments in the US South while not losing sight of the Northern states. This would prove a tricky tightrope to walk.

Looking at the three elections in 1867–68, the inescapable conclusion is that the United States experienced the most disorder and violence. While no national pronunciamiento occurred in any of the three countries, the violence in Louisiana, Georgia, and other Southern states exceeded violence in Argentine provinces or Mexican states during the same period. In terms of why this happened, one is left with the inescapable conclusion that it is tied to the major difference between the United States and the other two nations—the role of racism and the legacy of slavery. The vanquished in each society felt that things were going out of kilter. This was particularly so for white Southern ex-rebels who made war to preserve slavery and found, by the end of the war, that this choice resulted in the destruction of their golden calf. The desire to restore an old hierarchy that put Black people back on the bottom rail of Southern society fueled violence in the United States during this period. Furthermore, some of the situation in the United States can be attributed to Johnson's lenient policies, particularly allowing the rebels back into the body politic so quickly, but also his general disinclination to stop the violence, a decided contrast with leaders in Mexico and Argentina. Whether U. S. Grant, Johnson's successor, would embrace the same leniency remained an open question. However, despite this very important difference, it is critical to note that all three countries experienced continued violence and violent episodes.

Failed Rebellions

Violence in the United States endured long after the election concluded. Congress eventually formed a committee to investigate Klan outrages. The printed testimony, along with the majority and minority reports, filled thirteen thick volumes.[56] While Johnson did little to stop violence in the US South, several governors took specific measures to suppress paramilitary organizations and reduce violence. In Tennessee, William G. Brownlow's State Guard helped subdue intimidation and violence.[57] In Texas, Edmund J. Davis and the state legislature established the Texas State Police to curb lawlessness.[58] In North Carolina, William Woods Holden fought the Klan in the Kirk-Holden War. However, the North Carolina Legislature impeached Holden and removed from office for his efforts.[59] In Argentina and Mexico, governors routinely led soldiers in battle and put down revolutions from the front lines. US governors, on the other hand, led from their statehouses. However, in their way, Brownlow, Davis, and Holden fought revolutionaries just as fiercely as Governor Rubi in Sinaloa and Governor Sarmiento in San Juan. The situations in the three countries mirrored each other because, at the state and local levels, the victors faced insurgencies determined to sow the ground with salt to deny them the fruits of their victories.

Andrew Johnson did little to stop the tide of violence. In December 1868, he issued another proclamation. This one declared "unconditionally and without reservation, to all and to every person who, directly or indirectly, participated in the late insurrection or rebellion a full pardon and amnesty for the offense of treason against the United States or of adhering to their enemies during the late civil war, with restoration of all rights, privileges, and immunities under the Constitution and the laws which have been made in pursuance thereof."[60] John C. Breckinridge welcomed Johnson's proclamation and returned to the United States from his exile in Canada.[61] Republicans and African Americans suffering from paramilitary violence were aghast.

Johnson's actions, coming at the tail end of his presidency, did not surprise anyone. People wondered whether Grant, the hero of the US Civil War and the man who famously declared in his letter of acceptance, "let us have peace," would allow violence to rage unchecked?[62] Grant understood that many Democrats and some Republicans remained skeptical about the seriousness of Klan outrages.[63] Attorney General Amos T. Akerman investigated reports of violence and found them serious enough to merit action. Akerman and Grant believed South Carolina the best place to attack the Klan.[64] Grant sought and received legislation from Congress, the Ku Klux Klan Acts, or the Enforcement Acts. This legislation gave Grant the tools he needed to destroy the Klan, including allowing him to suspend habeas corpus, which he did in a handful of South Carolina counties.[65] As one newspaper reported, immediately after the suspension of habeas corpus, "larger numbers of persons" went to the office of the US marshal "for the purpose of confessing themselves members of the Ku Klux organization, in the hope of escaping arrest and subsequent punishment."[66] Grant sent in federal solders, particularly cavalry, rather than relying on state militias. The soldiers rounded up suspected Klansmen. The suspects were tried in federal courts and many of the defendants fined or imprisoned. Grant's tactics broke the back of the KKK, which did not revive until the 1910s.[67]

Grant's political opponents derided him as a tyrant, a dictator, and a would-be Caesar. Grant, sneered the *Georgia Weekly Telegraph*, "is still absorbed in his South Carolina game, and evidently believes that the Ku-klux sensation will be trumps in the approaching Presidential campaign."[68] Rather than bringing peace, growled the *Richmond Whig and Advertiser,* Grant's administration has produced "Ku Klux bills, Enforcement acts, the assizes of Bond, the raiding of Grant's military, disfranchisement, arrests and murder itself, in cold blood, of peaceful citizens."[69] Republicans likely wondered if the newspaper confused Klan activities with government activities.

For African Americans and white Republicans, Grant's actions came as a tremendous relief. Grant demonstrated that, unlike his predecessor, he would act in the face of lawlessness and defend Black and white lives and rights. For a time, at least, Grant refused to allow violence to rage out of control in the United States. The problem came when state officials called on Grant again and again to repeat this performance. Grant's interference in South Carolina did not cost him his reelection bid in 1872. However, in 1873 and 1874, in the teeth of a vicious economic panic, Grant demonstrated different ideas about using the federal government and the army to interfere in the domestic affairs of the states. At that point, Democrat complaints about Grant's "violations" of the Constitution and alleged dictatorial tendencies began to sound more compelling.[70]

In Argentina, Sarmiento's 1868 victory did not extinguish the embers of Federale resistance. Understanding Sarmiento's presidency is the key to understanding why people, from Ricardo López Jordán to Bartolomé Mitre, rebelled against the national government. Sarmiento, as we have seen, promoted many different types of internal improvement and modernization. For some Argentines, his relentless drive toward modernization was neither desirable nor beneficial. As one scholar observed: "After Domingo F. Sarmiento became president in 1868, the contradictions of liberalism became more apparent. Continued military intervention and electoral fraud were the order of the day. The Sarmiento government was not democratic and despised the gaucho masses of the interior."[71] This analysis echoed Sarmiento's enemies, who delighted in comparing him to Rosas. They asserted that interventions in the provinces by the federal government and wars against caudillos were the trademarks of a tyrant. Such complaints echoed ways in which people in other countries defined their enemies. Díaz's Plan de La Noria suggested Juárez's reelection posed a threat to a nation. Blair and other Democrats ripped into Grant as a would-be despot and derided Kaiser Ulysses for breaking the Klan. Furthermore, these charges foreshadowed language that is discussed in the following chapter. People used exaggerated charges to feed claims that rebellions were unavoidable because their opponents threatened liberty and had to be removed at any cost. Modernization and internal improvement, programs promoted by Sarmiento, Juárez, and Republicans in the United States, as analyzed in chapter 4, threatened older ways of life and often prompted people to take up arms to stave off change.

In 1870 Sarmiento faced an ugly rebellion, as worrisome as the pronunciamientos Juárez faced in Mexico or the KKK insurgency in the United States. The rebellion occurred in Urquiza's province of Entre Ríos. Urquiza may have withdrawn from the battlefield after his defeat at Pavón because he had made an arrangement with Mitre to leave each other alone. If he made such a deal, it was a good one for Urquiza. He retired to Entre Ríos and ruled the province as governor. Urquiza chose not to support Peñaloza during the pacification of the interior. When the Paraguayan War began, Urquiza initially supported Mitre and mobilized men from Entre Ríos. His subordinates, General Ricardo López Jordán for example, told Urquiza that his men were prepared to fight Brazilians and Porteños, not Paraguayans. In other words, Jordán wanted to see a civil war within the Triple Alliance. Many of Urquiza's soldiers decided they did not want to fight and went home. Urquiza, who had facilitated the election of his nephew as governor in 1864, did not win enough electoral votes in 1868 to defeat Sarmiento, although he won all the electoral votes of Entre Ríos, Salta, and Santa Fe. At the same time, Urquiza was again elected governor of Entre Ríos, after overcoming support for López Jordán.

Urquiza respected public opinion, enunciated in the election of 1868, and did not encourage rebellions in the interior.[72] Furthermore, in July 1869, Urquiza sent Sarmiento a "valuable and curious present," a "magnificent embroidered smoking cap and dressing gown selected from among the numerous valuable articles which were taken by the English troops at the sacking of the summer Palace of the Emperor of China at Pekin in October 1860." The *Standard* believed this mark of esteem gratified Sarmiento.[73] Sarmiento and Urquiza's relationship had always been marked by alternating bouts of cooperation and conflict, and perhaps both saw advantages in trying to forge stronger links with each other.

Once in office, Sarmiento made a well-publicized visit to Entre Ríos to see Urquiza.[74] When he arrived, he embraced Urquiza and commented on "the pleasure of meeting again on the 18th anniversary of Urquiza's triumph over Rosas."[75] At a dinner in Sarmiento's honor, Urquiza paid careful attention to decorations. In the central patio stood "the four flags that won the day at Caseros, Argentine, Brazilian, Oriental, and Entre Riano. Large portrait of Sarmiento placed at one end of the patio, above the arches, surrounded with Argentine and other flags." Not only was Urquiza "pleased as punch," but after dinner "Sarmiento made a happy speech—remembered the glories of the 3d of February—alluded with great felicity to the political divisions in the Republic, hoping that the events of to-day would be an earnest of union and good will among all parties."[76] Urquiza and Sarmiento adroitly wrapped their meeting in the memory of their shared triumph over the tyrant Rosas.

Sarmiento and Urquiza also visited the San José colony in Entre Rios. Sarmiento praised the enterprise and dedication of the colonists and embraced Urquiza as a testament of friendship. As they left, the two men walked arm in arm, until they came to Urquiza's escort, cavalrymen dressed in uniforms from the Battle of Caseros. Sarmiento reminded the soldiers "that he had shared with them the fatigues and glories of Caseros; he pointed out to them the 'entente cordiale' that existed now between him and their brave commander Gen. Urquiza, the hero of that ever memorable day, and added that as their President and ancient companion in arms he relied upon them to support him and maintain peace in the Republic." Urquiza, in addition, addressed the soldiers, expressing his pleasure in entertaining Sarmiento and vowing, "as long as I have strength to raise this arm; and as long as President Sarmiento continues the policy he has so happily inaugurated, myself and mine will be devoted to support and respect his authority."[77] This was a charm offensive, by both Urquiza and Sarmiento, of the first magnitude. Both men realized the advantages of putting past antagonisms to rest and gloried in their shared participation in the defeat of Rosas at Caseros.

In terms of unifying the country, Urquiza made an excellent decision to meet with Sarmiento. What could look better, after all, then an old Federale and an old Unitario clasping hands across the bloody chasm? However, to Entre Riano Federales like López Jordán, Urquiza signed his own death warrant. As Argentine historian Felipe Pigna commented, Urquiza's "embrace of Sarmiento, the person responsible for the death of El Chacho, will cost Urquiza dearly."[78] Disgusted by the festival of cooperation and friendship between Urquiza and Sarmiento, López Jordán made his own plans.

In Argentina, as in the United States and Mexico, some people refused to let the ghosts of the past die. In all three nations, the intensity of their hatred for their enemies manifested itself in horrific acts of violence. On April 11, 1870, López Jordán sent a band of men to Urquiza's palace in Entre Ríos. Despite some obfuscating—López Jordán later claimed he intended to capture Urquiza but Urquiza started shooting—he ordered Urquiza's assassination. He also had Urquiza's sons, Justo Carmelo and Waldino, killed. Shortly thereafter, López Jordán assumed power as provisional governor of Entre Ríos. The *Standard* deplored the assassination and argued "the life of Gen. Urquiza was regarded as the pledge of peace in this Republic." Sarmiento "has, in the emergency, betrayed a very marked decision of character by sending up instantly to Entre Ríos 2500 men under the command of Gen. Emilio Mitre."[79] Another newspaper noted, several months later, "the conduct of President Sarmiento has been warmly applauded throughout the Republic."[80]

Newspapers throughout the United States printed news of Urquiza's assassination.[81] The *Herald*, for instance, wrote that the news "has come like a thunder clap in the midst of peace rejoicings still going on here." Sadly, the paper reported, "it appears to presage a general conflagration in La Plata by a union of the discontented 'federalists' of the Confederation with the insurrected 'blancos' of the Uruguayan republic against the law enforcing rule of Sarmiento, which threatens speedy annihilation of the power of those restless Gaucho chieftains."[82] The *New-Orleans Commercial Bulletin* reported that Urquiza "had figured largely in the wars and the politics of his country, and was very capable both as a soldier and a statesman."[83]

Sarmiento had a complex relationship with Urquiza. He denigrated him as a caudillo leading an illiterate peasant army when they marched to topple Rosas. And, at that point, Urquiza and Sarmiento were on the same side! Sarmiento distrusted Urquiza after the victory over Rosas at Caseros. Sarmiento and Mitre preferred to stay out of the Confederation. Sarmiento rejoiced at Urquiza's defeat at Pavón. In the final years of Urquiza's life, however, Sarmiento either came to a new understanding of the lion in winter, or perhaps he simply saw the sense in conciliating an old caudillo. Whatever the case, Sarmiento erupted in fury when he learned of Urquiza's assassination. He immediately directed an army to proceed to Entre Ríos. He also published a proclamation, addressed specifically to the people of Entre Ríos, but really for all Argentines. This odious act, Sarmiento thundered, covers the nation in disgrace. "Liberty has not the dagger for its instrument," he growled. Sarmiento urged all innocent citizens of Entre Ríos to distance themselves from the perpetrators of the crime.[84]

Two days later, the *Standard* sarcastically informed López Jordán that "the country is not going to split from Sarmiento" to join him. His revolution was "a mere passing cloud, and we have good reason to hope [it] will be the last revolution in these countries for many years."[85] The paper printed another Sarmiento proclamation. The national government, Sarmiento vowed, will never recognize López Jordán as governor of Entre Ríos. We refuse to do so, Sarmiento asserted, "for the sake of our Republican institutions, for the honor and dignity of mankind." The Argentine Constitution, Sarmiento explained, "gives to the National authorities powers," among which numbers the guarantee "to every province the enjoyment and full exercise of its institutions." Therefore, the government will save the honor and peace of Entre Ríos.[86] Although Sarmiento did not use the exact words, people in the United States would have understood his reasoning as securing to the province a republican form of government. Nevertheless, as Grant and Juárez discovered, one could attempt to secure each state/province a republican form of government, but people had very different ideas about what exactly that entailed.

Sarmiento's old acquaintance, Ignacio Rivas, now a general, led troops to Entre Ríos. Rivas, Emilio Conesa, Juan A. Gelly y Obes, and Emilio Mitre pursued López Jordán and fought the assassin in several engagements. López Jordán usually had more men than the generals he faced, but their troops were better armed and better trained.[87] As he fought the armies of the nation, the assassin also "sent an impertinent note to the National Senate, claiming that the murder of General Urquiza was a 'domestic occurrence in which the legislature of Entre Rios was sole judge,' as also the revolutions which elevated that individual to the position of Governor. He demands to be let alone, on peril of the constitution being declared a farce, and terrible consequences happening to his enemies."[88]

It might seem amusing that an assassin who killed his rivals and initiated a rebellion against the government offered a constitutionally based justification of his rebellion. However, such justifications became more and more common, as rebels and malcontents offered lists of diverse reasons about why they rebelled. López Jordán's rebellion came to a screeching halt after his defeat at the Battle of Ñaembé in January 1871. The would-be caudillo fled the country and exiled himself in Brazil. This was not the last time Sarmiento faced a rebellious Ricardo López Jordán. Sarmiento did not grant López Jordán amnesty. The assassin remained a threat because he left Argentina and sheltered himself elsewhere, not because the president pardoned him and allowed him to retire to Entre Ríos in peace.

As he attempted to modernize the nation, Sarmiento faced concerted opposition from López Jordán. Fortunately, Sarmiento's army proved better fighters than the caudillo's soldiers. Still, that did not change the fact that, like the United States and Mexico, Sarmiento faced a determined and hardy foe who wanted to see the restoration of the status quo antebellum. Sarmiento's response was the most forceful of the three leaders. Grant moved against the KKK, but he needed congressional legislation to facilitate his efforts and did not act unilaterally. Juárez was occasionally inconsistent about sending troops, although, more often than not, he did. Sarmiento, without hesitation, dispatched Mitre to Entre Ríos and ordered him to deal with the caudillo. When it wanted to, each government could suppress rebellions and put down violent bands of marauders. But, too often, they remained reluctant to punish rebels. Furthermore, as the following chapter demonstrates, some leaders eventually stopped suppressing rebellions because the political price for suppressing them became greater than the price for ignoring them.

In Mexico, Juárez also faced many violent episodes. Despite some inconsistency of response, the situation in Mexico matched that of the United States and Argentina: the state could and did put down pronunciamientos and revolutions. This chapter cannot discuss every episode that occurred during this period, so it highlights a handful of them to provide a panoramic view of state responses to violence in Mexico.

Tamaulipas became unsettled during this period. From Matamoros, Vice Consul Lucius Avery commented, in 1869, that Braulio Vargas and Servando Canales led a revolution.[89] Consul General Franklin Chase of Tampico also noted the presence of Canales and commented, "some sharp fighting has taken place between the revolted party, under the leadership of the notorious Canales, and the Government troops." The revolutionists, Chase fumed, left a wide swath of destruction in their wake. Fortunately, the federal government "sent two thousand troops from San Luis Potosi, into this State to operate with those previously sent for the aid and protection of the State Government, and also for the entire suppression of this above mentioned band of robbers and assassins."[90]

Loyalties proved fluid. For instance, "the troops at the Town of Altamira, serving under the rebel General Manuel M. Cuesta, suddenly pronounced against the said Cuesta in favor of the Supreme Government." The rebels against the rebels murdered Cuesta who had "refused to ratify a late convention agreed to between General Rocha on the part of the Government, and Canales." Someone, Chase wrote, paid "two desperate characters" five hundred dollars to assassinate Cuesta. "Peace may now be restored to the State of Tamaulipas," Chase commented, "but as many of the rebels have retired to their respective homes with their equipments, it will only be enjoyed for a brief period."[91] Chase identified a critical issue: the problem of leniency. Although the government broke up the rebellion, the rebels were not punished.[92]

Revolutionary disturbances continued in Tamaulipas. In 1870, the state legislature granted the governor "extraordinary powers to maintain order and protect the state from incursions on the border." The governor immediately doubled taxes to "place in the field a battalion of 800 men and two squadrons."[93] These measures proved sensible because, in late May, "the dissident Mexican General, Pedro Martinez has reached this vicinity with a force estimated at about 1000 men, said to be well armed and mounted, spreading misery and consternation in his course."[94] Martinez's force "retired from the immediate neighborhood" several days later, likely because "about two thousand government troops under command of General Rocha are on the march for this border." Avery concluded that "the near approach of the government troops, the firmness of the National Guard, and the failure to procure arms and ammunition in Brownsville, have induced Martinez to retire."[95]

Martinez did not retire terribly far and continued to besiege Matamoros. Eventually, "Gen. Miguel Palacios, Commanding the Garrison of this city, issued a proclamation declaring the city under Martial law."[96] Fortunately for everyone not a revolutionist, government troops suppressed the revolt on September 30. Like Sarmiento, Mitre, and Grant, Juárez sent a force to suppress an organized body of rebels determined to flout the law. They used martial law, a tactic that seemed high-handed, but it worked. However, despite suppressing the rebellion, Mexican authorities faced the problem of how to handle the rebels. Mostly they chose to let them go. This was a curiously squeamish tendency, but one that occurred frequently in the United States and less often in Argentina, Mexico's sister republics.

The election of 1867 did not produce a national pronunciamiento, but the state elections in Sinaloa sparked a revolution.[97] Governor Rubi, US Commercial Agent Isaac Sisson stated, "was declared newly elected by Congress." Immediately thereafter, "parties in the interior pronounced against him and declared for General Angel Martinez." Martinez controlled Mazatlán, but "Rubi has a force out side of the town; and a battle is expected every moment."[98] After "several small battles," Rubi withdrew to the mountains, and Martinez "declared himself Governor."[99] Like Louisiana in 1873–74, Sinaloa had two governors. However, the Mexican government proved more proactive about addressing the situation than the United States and sent three thousand men under General Corona to assist Rubi. "On Wednesday last they attacked the revolutionists headed by Martinez, about twelve miles from here and defeated them after a hard battle lasting forty five minutes. The loss on both sides about three hundred and fifty killed and wounded; The next morning Govr Rubi came in and immediately reassumed the duties of his office." Martinez, Sisson noted, "retired a short distance in the country and issued a proclamation acknowledging the supremacy of the general Government and gave notice that he was going to retire to private life."[100] Although the government dealt proactively with the revolution, they allowed one of the principals to retire to a quiet life and not answer for his actions.[101]

In Guerrero, malcontents did not even wait until Maximilian's execution before making their move. Vice Commercial Agent John A. Sutter Jr. described a "pronunciamento [sic] made, about three weeks ago, at Iguala, by Genl Jimenez of Tistla in this State, against Don Diego Alvarez, the legal Governor of the State of Guerrero, appointed by President Don Benito Juarez." Jimenez was no Conservative angry about the failure of the French Intervention. Rather, he commanded a brigade during the siege of Querétaro. "His present object," Sutter commented, "appears to be the overthrow of Genl Alvarez."[102] To put this into perspective, the Austrian Pretender was not even dead, and Guerrero faced a pronunciamiento from a man who commanded some of the troops who had besieged Maximilian at Querétaro.

Jimenez's pronunciamiento was not easily contained. Several weeks later, he defeated Álvarez near Iguala, although Álvarez still held Acapulco.[103] Sutter informed Admiral H. K. Thatcher, of the North Pacific Squadron, that Jimenez was "master of the interior of this state" and "appears to have at his command, at least for the present, more men and resources, than Genl D^n Diego Alvarez." Sutter feared Jimenez would "invade the entirely defenseless town of Acapulco with his ill governed hordes of soldiers."[104] A month later, Sutter grumbled that Guerrero was in status quo, Jimenez held the interior, and Álvarez the coast.[105] Jimenez and others did not care for the official appointed by Juárez and made their displeasure known the same way Servando Canales did in Tamaulipas—by rebelling. However, the federal government responded differently to rebellion in Guerrero than they did to rebellion in Sinaloa. "Although the Mexican Congress has declared in one of its first sessions, that Gen.l Diego Alvarez, the constitutional Governor of this State (Guerrero), is to be upheld against Gen.l Vicente Jimenez, who rebelled against his authority and holds the interior of the state, no energetic measures have as yet been taken to suppress the rebellion."[106] Perhaps the government's response was less energetic because of recovering from the trials of the French Intervention.

In 1868, the government sent 1,500 soldiers under General Francisco Arce to suppress the rebellion. Jimenez, Sutter reported, declared "he never will recognize General Diego Alvarez as Governor of this state and refuses to deliver up his arms, which, he says, do not belong to the Government."[107] When the government decided to suppress a rebellion, it usually did so with dispatch. After a few months, Arce ordered an election held for governor.[108] Several months later, Jimenez "was finally forced to surrender his arms to Genl Arce" and "left for the city of Mexico, where he is being tried for his misdeeds by a court-martial." Sutter joyfully reported that "all the troops throughout the state have been disbanded and peace and order have been so far restored, that the election for governor and members of the legislature of this state will come off on Sunday next."[109] Although no candidate obtained a majority, the state legislature decided between the two candidates with the highest number of votes: Álvarez and Arce. The legislature chose Arce.[110] This is how elections were supposed to work: parties compete, but no matter the outcome, nobody should appeal from ballots to bullets. Sadly, in all three countries, many people either did not understand or did not care about this point. Nevertheless, the victors could, and did, suppress violence, even if they did not always punish rebels. The point here is not that that all three countries became completely overwhelmed by violence and that all order disappeared, but that each one suffered similar violent episodes and that, for a time, governments could and did suppress violence.

The Elections of 1871 and 1872: Juárez and Grant before the People

In Mexico, the election of 1871 produced a national pronunciamiento. Juárez, who had been president for fourteen years, stood for reelection.[111] Some Mexicans believed the time had arrived for Juárez to leave office. Given that he led Mexico through two brutal conflicts, Juárez felt he had an indisputable claim to the presidency. President of the Supreme Court Sebastián Lerdo de Tejada and General Porfirio Díaz also thought they had some claim to the nation's grati- tude, not to mention the presidency. Because none of the candidates received a majority, Congress had to choose the president and that body selected Juárez.[112]

In the aftermath of Juárez's victory, and furious about his defeat, Porfirio Díaz retired to Oaxaca and issued a pronunciamiento, the Plan de la Noria. He opened the pronunciamiento by asserting, "forced and violent indefinite reelection of the federal executive, has placed in danger the national institu- tions." Díaz wrote, stirringly, that "the Constitution of 57 and electoral liberty will be our flag; less government and more liberties our program."[113] Díaz's pronunciamiento offered a serious and prolonged challenge to the federal gov- ernment, as rebels and malcontents swept through multiple states. This chal- lenge became fully as difficult to solve as the problem of paramilitary violence in the US South or caudillo resistance in Argentina. That said, the violence in Mexico and the United States differed in one respect; at this moment, rebels in the US sought to secure control of regions rather than claiming power at the national level.

Offering a fine-grained view of each state during this election is impossible. That said, several examples of rebellions illustrate how Díaz's pronunciamiento posed a serious threat to Mexico's stability. Consul A. Willard in Guaymas wor- ried about violence from other states bleeding into Sonora.[114] The garrison in Guaymas revolted to protest the electoral results. Malcontents headed for the town of Alamos "under the command of one Jesus Leyva (who proclaimed Porfirio Diaz as President of the Republic as the basis of said revolt)." They took Alamos without opposition, and the state troops melted before them. Governor Ignacio Pesqueira, with about six hundred soldiers, "is reported to be a short distance from Alamos and the news of a decisive action is daily ex- pected."[115] Sonora went from tranquility to open rebellion in a very short time.

Events moved just as quickly in other Mexican states. In Nuevo Leon, "General Geronimo [sic] Trevino, Governor of the State of Nuevo León, pro- nounced against the Government of President Juarez, and in favor of Gen. Deis [sic]." After occupying Monterey, Treviño advanced to Saltillo in Co- ahuila."[116] Saltillo surrendered to Treviño, and, subsequently, Treviño and Martinez pressed on to San Luis Potosí.[117] General Quiroga left Nuevo León for Tamaulipas, accompanied by eight hundred revolutionists, and occupied

Mier.[118] Although General Palacios, "who is favorable to President Juarez," held Matamoros, "it is more than probable that General Quiroga will capture this whole frontier as there are but few Government troops here."[119] In Nuevo Laredo, Commercial Agent Thomas Gilgan reported that "this place, since early in January last, has been occupied by forces in rebellion against the Government of President Juarez.[120]

Sinaloa, which had been wracked by violence before the election, did not receive a reprieve. Revolutionists took Mazatlán in November 1871 and "immediately appointed a Governor and Collector, and the General Government closed the Port." When the revolutionists controlled the city, Isaac Sisson commented, "we had six Governors and four Collectors." However, General Rocha captured Mazatlán in May 1872. Rocha "remained here about thirty days, opened the Port and appointed new officers. During that thirty days we had two Governors and two Collectors. General Rocha left Genl Flores here as Governor + Military Commander." In July, Flores was kidnapped "and taken into the Country, where they kept him about two weeks, then he bought himself off and returned. During those two weeks we had four Governors and one Collector." As if all this were not bad enough, revolutionists took Mazatlán again in August. "We have just received news," Sisson commented laconically, "that the Government forces are within three days march of this Port, so I suppose that in four days more we will change over again."[121]

In Guerrero, the pronunciado General Jimenez reappeared and rebelled against Governor Arce, for "real or imaginary wrongs, suffered by the former, at the hands of the latter." Apparently, the court-martial did not punish Jimenez, or at least not severely. Sutter complained that "all the officials, Municipal, State or Federal are quarreling amongst themselves, and for this very reason, none are supported by each other as they are, have any power or authority or authority, wherewith to make the Law and themselves respected."[122] By the end of the year, the political condition of the state improved because Jimenez and his rebels had been "either subdued, or driven out of the State, or taken prisoner and executed by the Federal troops, commanded by General Alvarez, sent by the Federal Government to the relief of the Governor of the State."[123] Jimenez was a serial pronouncer. In other words, he kept pronouncing and making trouble for Juárez. Unlike some of his fellow rebels, he managed to escape the fate he so richly deserved by taking advantage of Lerdo de Tejada's solution to the problems raised by the Plan de la Noria.[124] In this case, the Mexican government took a proactive approach toward the problem of violence and suppressed the rebellion. However, when it came to making people answer for their crimes, the Mexican government's record was mixed, at best, like that of the United States government. Argentine authorities did the best job in this regard.

Even in Mexico City, the administrative center of the nation, problems occurred after the election of 1871. Consul General Julius A. Skilton wrote that a portion of the garrison pronounced, "released about 800 criminals confined in the prison Known as Belen" and "captured the fortress on the south western edge of this City." Skilton noted, disconcertingly, that "prominent military characters in the Country already identified with revolutionary movements in this vicinity and in the pacific range of States are said to have been the leaders of the movement, and escaped." "There now exist," Skilton warned, "several considerable armed and mounted bands of anti-Juarez men in this immediate neighborhood and within sight of the Capital, who it is said proclaim General Diaz." To make matters still worse, "the public is suffering under a serious apprehension of impending general revolution."[125] Even in the one area of the country they should have had under the tightest lockdown, Liberals supporting Juárez faced unrest. Díaz's pronunciamiento generated a wave of violence, although that violence did not achieve its goal of placing Díaz in the presidential chair.

Mexico's election of 1871 featured an internecine war between two factions of Liberals. The US presidential election of 1872 also saw a rift in the Republican Party which Democrats attempted to exploit. Liberal Republicans adopted a rule-or-ruin approach and nominated Horace Greeley as their candidate, even before Grant's renomination. Greeley was perhaps a good man to appeal to disaffected Liberals, but not a winning candidate for most white Southern Democrats.[126] Nevertheless, hoping to capitalize on Republican disarray, Democrats co-opted the Liberal Republican Party by making Greeley their candidate for president. This ended badly for everyone involved with Greeley's candidacy. Grant won 286 electoral votes out of 352 and roughly 3,598,000 popular votes to Greeley's 2,834,700. The electoral map of 1872 did not, however, illustrate a permanent Republican majority. Some reconstructed states had been "redeemed," or taken over by Democrats. While Grant broke the back of the KKK, paramilitary violence continued, and new organizations sprung up to replace the Klan. Grant discovered, to his dismay, that cutting off one of the hydra's heads produced three more.

Republicans often proved overly sanguine about the state of affairs. Reflecting on the difference between 1868 and 1872, the *Wooster (OH) Republican* noted that while "the problem of reconstruction was a vital one" in 1868, by 1872, "the problem of reconstruction had been solved and solved ably." Even the domestic tranquility of the Southern states, "although occasionally disturbed by outbreaks of local lawlessness, is now happily founded upon a secure basis." The press, the paper continued, "no longer teems with sickening accounts of the atrocious violence of the Ku-Klux Klan." Had Blair and Seymour won in 1868, "what a wide prospect of confusion, violence, anarchy, misery and ruin, the Southern States would now present. The freedmen would have been dragooned, bludgeoned and oppressed. Civil authority would have perished. The Ku-Klux would have enjoyed unbridled license to plunder, burn, and murder."[127] While the Klan and other groups would likely have raged out of control under President Seymour, the line about "outbreaks of local lawlessness" should have received more attention. What could be done about these outbreaks? For that matter, had the "problem of reconstruction" really been solved?

Both parties charged each other with fraud and violence. "All reports from Georgia," one article wrote, "confirm the telegraphic statements of the Associated Press that in all parts of the State the colored voters were either driven violently from the polls or that the most outrageous means were resorted to to prevent them from voting." The paper used this to critique Greeley: "Almost the entire colored voting population, disfranchised by mob law, driven by violence from the polls, or excluded from them by equally outrageous devices, such as requiring 8,000 colored voters to vote at a single place—thus excluding three-fourths of them from any possible opportunity of voting—this is the 'conciliation' which Mr. Greeley has been preaching." Georgia Democrats, in other words, "have by a thoroughly organized system of terrorism and violence driven a large proportion of the colored voters of the South from the polls, and defrauded thousands of them by the most transparent tricks of despotic craft, of the right to vote."[128]

On the other hand, letters in the *New York Tribune* claimed Republicans the same sins. For one, "the frauds perpetuated at the late election in this state [Greensboro, North Carolina] and in Pennsylvania, will, I fear, have the effect to keep a large portion of the best people from going to the polls hereafter." The writer decried Republican fraud as a "hideous mockery." Another correspondent complained, "the United States Court machinery has been invoked to terrorize the Liberals of this State [Louisiana] into obedience and subjection." Another one noted, "throughout the State of Georgia there is great rejoicing and general surprise at the result of our State election" and "our Democratic friends are at a loss to know how such immense majorities have been obtained in counties that were considered close or doubtful, and how the Liberal ticket in counties with large colored majorities could be so handsomely elected."[129] Fraud and intimidation secured that result and became the watchword of many people of various political persuasions, throughout the Americas. As the following chapter notes, Democrats in the United States eventually became smarter about justifying violence. They never abandoned their crude, virulent racism, but they began to invoke themes like good government and decried fraud. Many northerners, growing ever more tired of Reconstruction, began to believe them. Similarly, Díaz men and Mitre's partisans in Argentina made a case for rebellion to secure good, honest government. But that was still in the future.

Conclusion

During this period, 1868–72, all three governments moved aggressively, if sometimes inconsistently, against episodes of violence and rebellions. Critically, the Grant, Juárez, and Sarmiento administrations had the will, the wherewithal, and the political capital to put down violence, at least when they chose to do so. Also critically, the violence in the three countries was not absolutely identical, but it was similar. Sometimes it took the form of small skirmishes. A white southerner attacked an African American or a white Republican. A brigand in Argentina or Mexico robbed a farmer of his goods. Small groups of men, either in the form of a paramilitary organization like the Ku Klux Klan, or a group of pronunciados, terrorized political opponents. Revolutionists captured, or attempted to capture, a town. There were also larger battles. Large groups of ex-rebels massacred African Americans and white Republicans at Opelousas, Louisiana, and Camilla, Georgia. Revolutionists pronounced against duly elected officials, seized cities, and challenged state governments. Sometimes, in Mexico and Argentina, they launched national rebellions. It would be a mistake to say that violence was universal, and this book does not, but it would also be a mistake to minimize the presence of violence and disorder in all three nations.

Facing this broadly similar violence, the three national governments responded in similar, albeit not identical ways. In Argentina, Sarmiento proved the most aggressive. Upon receiving news of Urquiza's assassination and López Jordán declaring himself governor of Entre Ríos, Sarmiento sent an army to crush the assassin. After a series of pitched battles, López Jordán fled to Brazil. In the United States, Andrew Johnson did nothing to tamp down the violence, but Ulysses S. Grant, his successor, took a hard line against the Ku Klux Klan in South Carolina. Although he did not prosecute the perpetrators of every violent episode, Grant secured congressional legislation and used the army like a scalpel against the KKK. In Mexico, Juárez did not respond to some uprisings and rebellions as quickly as Sarmiento did. However, when he responded, he usually sent sufficient force to quell the revolutionists. During this period, national governments showed that they could, and would, crush rebellions. This makes their failure to do so, discussed in the following chapter, all the more noteworthy.

How governments dealt with their rebels, pronunciados, and malcontents merits additional attention. In the United States, Grant and the attorney general prosecuted Klansmen in federal courts. This approach broke the organization and taught Klansmen, and former rebels more generally, that the government would act to suppress violence. However, trials and occupations were expensive and time-consuming. For a government looking to retrench, as the United States was after the Panic of 1873, these options became problematic. Furthermore, in the future, a hostile Democratic majority in Congress could easily hamstring Grant. In Mexico, the rebels and pronunciados were sometimes amnestied but were often left alone and never made to answer for their actions. This was the case in the United States as well for most of the rebels who participated in the US Civil War. This method had positive and negative elements. Positive because the government could claim benevolent motives and avoid looking like it longed to spill the blood of its citizens for their sins. Negative because people never answered for the crimes of murder and trying to overthrow local, state, or national governments. Dealing so lightly with malcontents encouraged serial pronouncers like Vicente Jimenez, Servando Canales, Porfirio Díaz, Wade Hampton, and El Chacho, not to mention scores of lesser-known men in all three countries to keep rebelling. Sarmiento's method, on the other hand, potentially had the opposite problem. Sarmiento never considered amnesty for López Jordán, and the assassin fled to Brazil. Sarmiento's treatment could be spun as heavy-handed and could inspire or induce others to rebel.

All three governments faced a similar problem: putting down rebellions, pacifying the rebels, and integrating them into the body politic. That is to say, after suppressing rebellions, they had to figure out what to do with the people who rebelled. Killing everyone was not an option as this would risk depopulating portions of the country. Thus, governments often reached for amnesty. But if amnesty sometimes worked in the short term by producing a lull in the violence, it was not, for this period at least, a good long-term solution. Still, if not that solution, what? The final chapter considers this question along with another one: why did governments suddenly take such a different approach, in the period 1872–80, to the problems of violence and rebellion than the approach they employed in this chapter?

7

Revolutions May Go Backward, 1872–1880

On July 18, 1872, President Benito Juárez of Mexico died of a heart attack. President of the Supreme Court Sebastián Lerdo de Tejada became interim president of an unsettled nation. Violence resulting from Porfirio Díaz's Plan de la Noria wracked the country. Upon learning of Juárez's death, some malcontents reevaluated the situation. In Mazatlán, "it is rumored upon authority that Genl Porfirio Diaz + Vega where [sic] in march for Mazatlan but hearing of the death of Prest. Juarez haltd and turned their columns back, declaring that they were only making war upon Juarez + his govt."[1] In Monterrey, seven thousand government troops faced off against five thousand revolutionists. However, "at present there is a short suspension of hostilities, owing to a new election for President having been ordered."[2]

President Lerdo quickly issued a proclamation promising to decree an immediate presidential election. The winner would serve a four-year term beginning in 1872 and ending in 1876.[3] In the same proclamation, Lerdo explained that he intended to promulgate "a decree of amnesty covering political crimes committed to this point, without excepting anyone."[4] Amnesty, he argued, was the only way to ensure no one lost their vote.[5] Lerdo's amnesty produced both a tremendous success and a stunning failure. Because his principal objective was to bring order out of chaos, amnesty, by and large, achieved that objective. Numerous people commented that the amnesty reduced violence, facilitated a fair election, and calmed the turbulent waters. It did not, by any means, stop all violence, but it curtailed the lion's share of disorder. Thus, amnesty accomplished all Lerdo hoped it would in the period immediately preceding and following the presidential election of 1872. Still, the very means by which amnesty achieved success created long-term problems. Lerdo's blanket pardon for all political crimes committed covered pronunciados like Díaz and Vicente Jimenez, among others, who took advantage of Lerdo's generosity. Granting amnesty to men like Díaz and Jimenez helped calm the country. However, like Mitre's treaty with El Chacho, it gave revolutionists a reprieve and a chance to plan their next revolution.

Violence and rebellions continued to occur in Mexico, the United States, and Argentina after 1872. However, unlike the period covered by the preceding chapter, national governments became less and less willing and/or able to contain violence. This chapter begins by analyzing violence in the period between Juárez's death and the tumultuous elections of 1876. Most of the violence generated by the Plan de la Noria evaporated, and Lerdo won the 1872 election handily. Díaz and his friends, however, bided their time for the next opportunity to lead a national pronunciamiento. In the United States, disaffected Democrats focused not on toppling the federal government but on "redeeming" their states. Louisiana's contested gubernatorial election of 1872–74 provided an arena to test strategies for overthrowing governments. Democrats then perfected their tactics in Mississippi in 1874–75. As a counterpoint, during Argentina's Revolution of 1874, Domingo F. Sarmiento and Nicolás Avellaneda confronted a profound challenge to their authority from an unexpected quarter, but they defeated the rebellion. The US and Mexican elections of 1876 highlighted the inability, or disinclination, of governments to contain violence at the state and national levels. Initiative passed to rebels who succeeded in achieving many, if not all, of their goals. This chapter concludes by discussing the elections of 1880 and the culmination of the paths taken by the United States, Mexico, and Argentina that led to an order that favored stability and discipline.

Biding Time and Perfecting Rebellion: 1872–1876

After Lerdo issued his amnesty decree, US officials noted that violence seemed to be abating. John A. Wolf sent an upbeat report from Minatitlan that Lerdo was "elected President of the United States of Mexico, allmost [sic] unanimously," and "Porfirio Diaz and General Treviño are about to be reinstated in their former positions." All appearances, Wolf stated, "look hopeful and promising for the future of Mexico." While local disturbances might continue, he predicted they would occur "on a much smaller scale as heretofore."[6] The state of affairs certainly improved in Minatitlan and elsewhere, but pardoning Díaz was a risky bet.

The violence that occurred after Lerdo's amnesty decree, like the rebellions in Louisiana and Mississippi, usually resulted from disputes over internal state affairs. For example, Governor Ignacio Pesqueira won reelection in the 1873 Sonora state elections.[7] Shortly thereafter, a pronunciamiento occurred over proposed reforms to the state constitution.[8] Pronunciados favored the reforms, whereas Pesqueira did not. The rebels seized Alamos and Pesqueira organized a force to defeat them. Consul A. Willard believed "this affair will be of short duration—as the state Govt appears to have strength sufficient to quell it."[9] Willard's prediction proved correct. By late October, malcontents abandoned Alamos without a fight.[10] Pesqueira led from the field in a way Governors Adelbert Ames of Mississippi and William P. Kellogg of Louisiana, despite having served in the military during the US Civil War, did not.

In Sonora, Governor Pesqueira had sufficient manpower to put down the rebellion. In other states, however, officials called on the federal government for assistance, with mixed results. In Matamoros, Juan N. Cortina and Juan Treviño Canales both ran for president of the ayuntamiento during the state elections.[11] Both men claimed victory. Cortina and his friends utilized force to take control of the office. Treviño Canales, with the backing of Governor Servando Canales, appealed to the state legislature, which "passed a decree Setting aside the Election under which Cortina pretended to hold the office." Cortina refused to accept this decision. Governor Canales raised a force to punish Cortina and "called on the General Government for assistance." The government ordered Cortina "to either relinquish his Military office or that of President of the Ayuntamiento." Lerdo also ordered "the Military Commander of this City to Sustain the Civil Authorities."[12] This was an odd episode, not least because Governor Servando Canales, who clearly suffered no punishment for his rebellions against Juárez, called on the federal government for help and Lerdo sustained him.[13]

The impeachment of Governor Victoriano Cepeda unsettled affairs in Coahuila.[14] The state legislature "referred the matter for decision to the federal government, requesting at the same time federal troops to enforce their authority as the legislature of Coahuila against governor Cepeda."[15] Unlike Lerdo's interference in the Cortina/Treviño Canales contest, this time the government "declined to interfer [sic] in a question which it considers as a local matter of the State in which it has no right to interfer [sic], and advised both parties to settle their difficulties peaceably amongst themselves."[16] "Dr. Salas, the governor appointed ad interim by the legislature," routed Cepeda and his followers during a skirmish at Candela.[17] Several months later, Commercial Agent William Schuchardt observed Coahuila "has a provisional governor appointed by the federal authorities, until members to the new legislature are elected who will decide the pending questions between Governor Cepeda and the old legislature."[18] Just as Grant refused to interfere when the North Carolina Legislature impeached William W. Holden, the Louisiana Legislature impeached Henry Clay Warmoth, and the Mississippi Legislature impeached Adelbert Ames, Lerdo also kept out of Coahuilan politics.

Finally, in La Paz, Consul David Turner reported that one hundred soldiers, under the command of Emiliano Ibarra "'pronounced,' made prisoners of their officers, of Governor Davalos, and of the principal Federal officers in the place. Not a shot was fired, nor a person hurt, and the whole thing was done so quietly that I know nothing of it untill [sic] I went to breakfast." According to Turner, Ibarra "pronounced only against Govr Davalos, that he recognized the General Government, and would account to it for his actions."[19] In other words, the pronunciados repudiated Governor Bibiano Dávalos, named Ibarra interim political chief, and proclaimed, numerous times, their fealty to the Constitution of 1857.[20] Soldiers brought in from Mazatlán defeated the rebels.[21] Like Díaz, Ibarra and his men proclaimed their loyalty to the Constitution of 1857 as they rebelled against unpopular officials. In other words, they believed themselves patriots protesting bad government.

The United States faced many difficulties of its own during this period, particularly in Louisiana.[22] During Reconstruction, tensions ran high between Republicans and Democrats as well as between different factions of the Republican Party. In 1868, Louisianans elected Henry Clay Warmoth governor. However, when the dissident Liberal Republicans bolted from the national Republican Party in 1872, the Louisiana Republican Party also split. Animosity between the Warmoth faction and the "Custom House Gang," mainly federal office holders and African Americans, resulted in an odd fusion party where all anti-Radical forces, including Warmoth's crowd, supported John McEnery, a Democrat.[23]

In 1872, Republicans ran US Senator William Pitt Kellogg against McEnery for governor.[24] Both men served as officers during the Civil War: Kellogg as a colonel in the Seventh Illinois Cavalry and McEnery as a captain in the Fourth Louisiana Infantry regiment, a rebel unit. The campaign quickly became heated. McEnery and Democrats cast the election as an opportunity to shatter Republican dominance.[25] Trouble arose, as in Matamoros, when the state tried to determine the victor of an election characterized by fraud and corruption. With Warmoth in control of the electoral machinery, "almost every device imaginable, fair or foul, was used to reduce Kellogg's vote and increase McEnery's."[26] Samuel B. Packard, the US marshal in New Orleans, complained to Attorney General George H. Williams that officials loyal to Warmoth defied election laws with impunity.[27]

The election resulted in two different vote totals. Republicans contended Kellogg won 72,890 votes to McEnery's 54,079. On the other hand, the Returning Board controlled by Warmoth certified McEnery as the winner with 65,579 votes to Kellogg's 55,973.[28] Because they did not control a Returning Board, Republicans went to US Circuit Court Judge Edward Durell, who supported Kellogg's application for an injunction against Warmoth.[29] Trying to make sense of the muddled situation, the *New York Tribune* wrote that "we may as well premise (1), that it is impossible for persons at a distance from the scene of conflict to get at the exact truth; and (2), that there is a great deal of rascality on both sides." The paper found the whole affair "a very miserable piece of business."[30]

The miserable piece of business became far more dangerous when both sides reinforced in preparation for a longer struggle. McEnery and the Democrats, armed with the certification from Warmoth's Board, prepared for his inauguration.[31] Kellogg and the Republicans, buttressed by the mantle of the federal judiciary, made their own preparations. Furthermore, the outgoing Republican-dominated legislature impeached Warmoth. Warmoth was automatically suspended from office and P. B. S. Pinchback, African American lieutenant governor and Kellogg supporter, became governor. Many Democrats believed Republicans stole the election.[32] McEnery's supporters buttressed this claim by portraying McEnery as victim of Republican meddling and the rightful governor of Louisiana.[33] In January, 1873, Louisiana inaugurated two governors and two legislatures.[34] The *Lowell (MA) Daily Citizen and News* observed "Kellogg and McEnery were both inaugurated yesterday, the latter drawing a large crowd at Lafayette Square."[35] Another Massachusetts paper commented, "the elections of Pinchback and McMillan as United States Senators from Louisiana by the Kellogg and McEnery Legislatures respectively, will precipitate the question of the legitimacy of those bodies upon the Senate."[36]

Louisiana's experiment in dual government lasted far longer than similar situations in Mexico. At first, McEnery attempted to appoint tax collectors and urged people not to pay taxes to Kellogg's collectors. "In so far as the validity of this performance goes," the *Weekly Louisianian* jeered, McEnery "might as well appoint a few for Mississippi, Maine or California or China. At home or abroad, all is the same; because as Mr. McEnery is neither in fact nor yet in law Governor of Louisiana."[37] When this scheme did not work, McEnery issued a proclamation calling up the militia.[38] He also unleashed the White League. Like the Ku Klux Klan, the White League was a paramilitary organization that existed throughout the US South.[39] However, Congress did not pass legislation targeting the White League, as they had with the Ku Klux Klan, and Grant did not send in the army to crush the organization.

McEnery's decision to sanction extralegal violence led to the Colfax and the Coushatta Massacres. The Colfax Massacre began as a conflict between officials appointed by Kellogg and disaffected McEnery supporters.[40] When the Republican officials raised a militia of African Americans to sustain their authority, White Leaguers and other McEnery supporters descended on Colfax. During the battle between the two groups, African Americans holed up in the courthouse while their opponents surrounded it. White Leaguers, who outnumbered the African Americans, set the courthouse on fire. The beleaguered African Americans surrendered, although this did not save them from White League barbarity. Many who escaped the fire were shot. Estimates of casualties ran from 100 to 150 African Americans, many of whom had been soldiers in the US Army. Most of McEnery's supporters fought in the rebel armies during the US Civil War.

The Colfax Massacre was "the most dramatic example of the anarchy that reigned throughout much of rural Louisiana."[41] President Grant, in his message to Congress, stated that the "butchery of citizens" at Colfax was "hardly surpassed by any acts of savage warfare."[42] Most McEnery supporters dismissed the massacre and focused on alleged African American depredations.[43] One newspaper commented, "the late fearful massacre of the blacks in their warlike array at Colfax in Grant parish, away up yonder on the Red River, does not appear in the least to have disturbed the reviving hilarity of New Orleans." The article concluded "matters are quiet in Louisiana, except four or five parishes."[44] Scholars also offered repugnant justifications, with one asserting that white southerners suffered under the "yoke of corruption" and "when they had attempted at the ballot-box to overturn it, they had been cheated." Therefore, "it was little wonder that the impetuous spirits among the people should be prompted to violence."[45] In other words, alleged bad government, either "negro misrule" or "carpetbag misrule," justified wholesale murder.[46]

General William H. Emory telegraphed Washington to ask if he should aid Kellogg. He received orders "to protect the state government from violence and overthrow only, and to use the military in aiding United States officials in serving processes." Furthermore, his superiors told him not to "interfere in local dissensions between the two parties, unless by order of the President, after a requisition by the Governor for troops has been made."[47] The federal government did little to stop the Colfax Massacre, but Kellogg also did not requisition troops.[48] In Tamaulipas, Governor Canales called on Lerdo for help, and Lerdo responded. In Coahuila, on the other hand, Governor Cepeda received no help from Lerdo, but his opponents were not revolutionists; they were forces loyal to the state legislature. Kellogg and Grant might have observed more closely the cooperative dynamic between Lerdo and Canales. After all, Kellogg faced a determined insurgency that repeatedly and ruthlessly appealed from ballots to bullets.

Appalled at the brutal violence and McEnery's intransigence, Kellogg and some Republicans began to discuss prosecuting McEnery for treason.[49] Kellogg's letter to Louisiana Attorney General A. P. Field stated that McEnery "and his aiders and abettors have continued to maintain their treasonable organization, and are still projecting and levying war against the Commonwealth, and that the recent massacre in Grant parish, if not directly planned and ordered by this man and his associates, was the result of their treasonable organization against the State government."[50] Terms like "guerilla warfare" and "anarchy" appropriately characterized the situation in Louisiana.[51] Articles reporting parishes ruled by mob law, with anarchy and bloodshed as the inevitable result, became commonplace.[52] Law and order broke down in Louisiana and the man responsible, McEnery, was never prosecuted or punished.

In some ways, Kellogg did not help matters. After contemplating treason prosecutions, he sent a remarkable series of letters to US Senator Oliver P. Morton, a Radical Republican from Indiana. Rather incredibly, in December 1873, Kellogg asserted, "except in a few distant border parishes where a number of desperate and lawless men inspired by the hope of some action by Congress favorable to them Continue to pursue the Bourbon policy of shooting colored men and occasionally a white republican with these exceptions good order prevails and the rights of all Citizens are protected irrespective of race and color."[53] The following month, Kellogg described the opposition as "a handful of played out city politicians who sit in his [McEnery's] back office & speculate on the chances of a new deal."[54] In addition, Kellogg asserted that "we have had no occasion to use the Federal troops for months" and stated, confidently, that "we are abundantly able to sustain ourselves in all respects without the intervention of the Federal authorities." He doubled down on this language, promising "so far as the state government is concerned I think no reasonable man can doubt that our ability to sustain ourselves is full and complete."[55] These ridiculously flawed assumptions gave politicians like Morton, if they believed Kellogg, an overly optimistic view of affairs in Louisiana.

It is unclear how Kellogg made these assertions with a straight face. Louisiana suffered a year and a half of violence. The White League perpetrated another massacre at Coushatta, in Red River Parish.[56] Capitalizing on fears of an African American mob, White Leaguers killed six white Republican officeholders and between five and twenty African Americans.[57] The *Inter Ocean* offered acidic condemnation, writing that McEnery "advised the people to hang all carpet-baggers and scalawags to the limbs of trees. This bloody and horrible tragedy is only one of many fruits of his advice."[58] Grant also condemned the massacre. Some of the victims, he intoned, "were republicans and officeholders under Kellogg. They were therefore doomed to death. Six of them were seized and carried away from their homes and murdered in cold blood. No one has been punished; and the conservative press of the State denounced all efforts to that end, and boldly justified the crime."[59]

These statements expose the farcical rhetoric of law and order the White League and McEnery's crowd utilized. They also suggest what "redemption" truly meant: the freedom to kill African Americans and white Republicans without consequence. However, even if their justifications were ludicrous, McEnery and his men demonstrated cognizance of certain political realities. Rather than simply shouting kill the [insert racial expletive], they wailed about fraud, bad government, and corruption, and used these issues to justify their appeal to violence. These denunciations of fraud, bad government, and corruption resonated with many people in the Northern states who grew sicker and sicker of Reconstruction. Additionally, the federal and state governments proved, for the most part, slow to respond to events. This is an important difference with Argentina and, to an extent, Mexico. Had either the federal or the state government taken a more active role in suppressing the White League, much of the violence could have been averted.

In September 1874, events came to a head. P. S. Armitage wrote to James C. Murphy that "the White League is growing both in numbers and boldness, They have got their artillery too, Well this looks like business—I hope there will be no bloodshed, but if Kellogg attempts any of his 'shenanigans,' give it to 'em hot and heavy."[60] Several weeks after the Coushatta Massacre, the Battle of Liberty Place, the crescendo of the protracted violence, occurred in New Orleans.[61] On September 14, 1874, McEnery's men seized the statehouse and Kellogg fled to the US Custom House. The Metropolitan Police, under the command of James Longstreet, fought a pitched battle with the White League in the streets of New Orleans.[62] White Leaguers, just like at Colfax, outnumbered their opponents and defeated them. Death tolls varied, but most reports agreed well over one hundred men, both White Leaguers and Metropolitans, were either killed or wounded.[63]

James C. Murphy wrote to his wife with details about the battle and what the battle meant for Louisiana. A US officer, he reported, "says he never saw more effective firing." Furthermore, "we were terribly in earnest and tried to do our work well. It is possible now that the Kellogg regime may be restored, but if the usurper does assume the office again it will be his death warrant."[64] In another letter, the second written that day, he commented, "I do not think the government will interfere from the present position of affairs." The people of New Orleans were orderly, and "the President cannot find tenable grounds for interference." Murphy told his wife, quite bluntly, that "if I had not participated in the victory I should have considered myself forever an outcast from our city. Now I have the honor and am proud to say that even though we *do* not redeem the State, I at least assisted in the noble effort."[65] Murphy's threats about what would happen to Kellogg if "the usurper" tried to resume his office were hardly bombast. Servando Canales might have felt sorry for Kellogg; whereas Lerdo answered his call for troops with dispatch, Grant proved tardy in aiding Kellogg.

At this juncture, the federal government finally intervened. Although the White Leaguers triumphed over the Metropolitans on September 14, within two days reinforcements compelled McEnery to surrender the statehouse. Kellogg, therefore, was reinstated.[66] As the *Cincinnati Enquirer* noted, "the Louisiana foolishness is brought to an end. At least it so appears. The lawless opponents of usurpation have, under protest, announced that they will subside."[67] The rebellion, it seemed, was finally over. The *Alexandria (VA) Gazette* noted, in addition, "five thousand troops can be concentrated in Louisiana within a week or ten days, including those already there, or in the vicinity. The number is about one-third of the active force of army, which nominally consists of 18,000 men."[68] The White League defeat proved momentary and the Republican victory pyrrhic. Despite Kellogg's talk of prosecuting the rebels, McEnery's only punishment was the scorn of some Republican newspapers. Indeed, two years later, during the chaos of the election of 1876, McEnery had the temerity to sign, as governor, the returns awarding Louisiana's electoral votes to the Democrat candidate, Samuel J. Tilden.[69]

Louisiana in 1872–74 faced a fierce internal conflict and grappled with important questions, specifically how to treat rebels who committed treason and attempted to overthrow governments, that had tremendous relevance for the fate of Reconstruction. The US government actually suppressed the rebellion, but they left the rebels unpunished. Several years later, in 1877, the same crowd again seized control of the state government. Kellogg did not issue an amnesty proclamation like Lerdo did, but that was basically what happened in Louisiana. Unlike some of the Mexican states, particularly Ignacio Pesqueira's Sonora, Kellogg did not have the ability to put down revolutions using the force at his command. The danger of amnesty and not punishing the rebels became ever more apparent.

Several months after the Battle of Liberty Place, Louisiana's state elections of 1874 created another problem. Democrats and Republicans each claimed a majority in the legislature. General Philip Sheridan removed several Democrat claimants to seats in the legislature, derided the White League as "banditti," and proposed to let the military arrest conspirators. As one historian commented, "while Louisiana Democrats were clearly up to no good, the idea of military trials of civilians and the image of federal soldiers evicting lawmakers from a legislative hall had a visceral impact on northern public opinion."[70] Despite the many sins of the Democrats, Grant and Sheridan seemed to be oppressive military chieftains intent on destroying the people's liberties. For many people, Grant and Sheridan's alleged crimes seemed far more disturbing than the actual crimes of the revolutionists. In addition, the Panic of 1873 hurt Grant and Republicans. People raged about hard times and punished the party in power at the polls. Democrat calls for retrenchment thus became even more seductive and their calls to pull troops out of the reconstructed states grew even more compelling. Revolutionists learned that framing their fight as resistance against tyranny resonated with many northerners, both Democrat and Republican. Ex-rebels went so far as adopting the Red Shirt as the symbol of white resistance, a symbol they borrowed from Garibaldi; another manifestation of reactionaries appropriating liberal ideas and symbols for illiberal ends. Grant found it ever-harder to justify interference when he knew it would redound to his discredit and hurt Republicans.

Louisiana was not the only disordered state in the United States in 1874. Vicksburg, Mississippi, also erupted in riots that led to the deaths of hundreds of African Americans. Grant deployed federal troops to restore order but at significant cost. For one "neither the federal government nor the state government could prevent a massacre or the overthrow of a duly elected sheriff." In addition, the paramilitary groups received confirmation that "an effective campaign of intimidation and violence could oust local Republican governments."[71] The strategies of the vanquished—tested in many states throughout the US South, most recently Louisiana—were ready for deployment during Mississippi's election of 1875, and, in the following year, the elections of 1876. Grant's interference not only showed the limits of state and national power to terrorists in Mississippi; it also angered many people throughout the United States. Former senator George Vickers of Maryland, for instance, wrote a furious letter to Senator Matthew W. Ransom of North Carolina. "Have we any State Governments, having rights which the Grant administration and the republican party, are bound to respect," he sputtered, sarcastically echoing the language of the *Dred Scott* decision. Vickers argued that Grant had no conception at all of the powers of the federal government.[72] Vickers, one voice among many denouncing Grant's interference, belonged to the Democratic Party. His dislike of Grant hardly began in 1875. Critically, though, as Republicans grew more skittish about the seemingly constant interference, Grant consequently became increasingly leery about interfering in Southern elections.

Mississippi, according to an article in the *New York Herald,* was a seething mess of contradictions. On the one hand, "peace and order prevail in all the counties." On the other, "the State courts do not punish murder, either of white or black," and "life is not held sacred, as it is in the North."[73] During the 1875 election, Democrats utilized the "Mississippi Plan," a continuation of the tactics employed in Louisiana and Vicksburg, to suppress Republican voting.[74]

They targeted white and Black Republicans and, through a mixture of violence, intimidation, economic coercion, bribery, and fraud, erased a Republican majority of thirty thousand and manufactured a thirty-thousand-vote majority for their party. Democrats in other states watched with glee. The *New York World* gloated that Governor Ames would likely be impeached.[75] The *New Hampshire Patriot*, reprinting an item from the *Philadelphia Times*, endorsed this view, stating "it was cruel of Pierrepont not to endorse his call for more troops. If Ames had gotten those soldiers all would be well."[76]

During Mississippi's brutal election of 1875, "direct appeals to President Grant brought attention to the political violence but little else."[77] Governor Ames sent a requisition to Grant for troops. Grant, however, did not send any. African American Congressman John R. Lynch of Mississippi offered one explanation for Grant's refusal. When Lynch asked Grant why he did nothing, Grant responded that his first instinct was to send troops to restore order. Indeed, according to Lynch, Grant was preparing the order when several Ohio Republicans called on him. They persuaded him not to help Mississippi by employing the following logic: "If the requisition of Governor Ames were honored, the Democrats would not only carry Mississippi, which would be lost to the Republicans in any event, but Democrat success in Ohio would, in that event, be an assured fact. If the requisition were not honored, it would make no change in the results in Mississippi but Ohio would be saved to the Republicans."[78] Grant yielded to this argument and sacrificed Mississippi for Ohio.[79]

Morally, Lynch's was the correct position. Politically, the Ohio Republicans were correct: no path existed to the White House for Republicans without Ohio. Politics, at least in this case, trumped morality. Grant no longer felt that he had sufficient political capital to justify interference. If he tried to prevent violence in Mississippi, he would doom Republican chances in Ohio in 1875 and 1876. Lerdo also looked ahead to the presidential election in 1876, but it seemed to factor less into his calculations about interference. In Argentina, however, the next presidential election was not until 1880, and Nicolás Avellaneda, elected in 1874, was not eligible to seek reelection. This gave him more freedom in how he dealt with rebels.

In 1874, Argentina stood thirteen years removed from Bartolomé Mitre's triumph at the Battle of Pavón. Therefore, Argentina was still a young nation when confronted with a serious rebellion driven by anger over the results of the presidential election of 1874.[80] This rebellion came from a most unexpected source: former president Bartolomé Mitre. Mitre attempted to elect Rufino de Elizalde as president in 1868 and grew irritated when Sarmiento won. By 1869, Mitre, now a senator in Congress from Buenos Aires, began to denounce Sarmiento's policies and programs.[81] He did this for several reasons. One, pragmatic politics. By opposing Sarmiento, Mitre could make himself a leader of the opposition and a candidate for president in 1874.[82] Two, Mitre did not agree with many of Sarmiento's policies. Three, he tapped into discontent evident among the elite. Consequently, "snobbery and elitism" marked Mitre's political movement, and Mitristas preferred oligarchy and conservatism.[83]

Mitre ran for president in 1874 against Nicolás Avellaneda, Sarmiento's friend and his minister of justice and public instruction. "With his followers in a minority throughout the country," one historian observed, "Mitre had little reason to believe that he could ever have won the election in the first place." However, "despite the odds against them, Mitre's followers claimed they would only lose the election if the government cheated."[84] Neither McEnery nor Mitre had compelling reasons for rebelling. In Louisiana, Democrats attempted to steal the election for McEnery and resorted to bullets when they failed. In Argentina, Avellaneda won the presidency with 146 electoral votes to Mitre's 79.[85] Some fraud likely occurred, as it did in most nineteenth-century elections, but Sarmiento did not steal the election for Avellaneda.

Mitre refused to accept the results, and news of his disgruntlement spread quickly. *La Estrella de Panama*, for instance, noted "there was much agitation in Buenos Aires because many feared a revolution on the part of the supporters of General Mitre."[86] Despite these rumblings, the *Standard* pointed out that Argentina had many reasons to be optimistic about the future: "never before in the annals of the country has there been so long an interval of tranquility, and the fact of the Chief Magistracy being now for a second time transferred in the constitutional manner shows how deeply grounded are the wishes of all parties to see the country advance, under whatever administration."[87] There is a world of difference between being angry about losing an election and attempting to overthrow a government. Mitre had every right to be disappointed. What he did next had no excuse. He and his supporters took up arms.

Some scholars dismiss the Revolution of 1874 as a farce by arguing that little support for the rebels existed and "the rebels proved spectacularly inept."[88] Such statements underestimate the threat the rebellion posed to Argentina. The *Standard*, on September 25, noted, "just as we go to press, we learn that

Congress has declared the Republic in state of siege."[89] The following day, it observed that the government had called out six regiments of the National Guard, numbering five thousand men, and Congress "sanctioned the calling out of all the National Guards of the Republic." Telegrams proclaiming the loyalty of the provinces of Jujuy, Salta, Corrientes, Catamarca, and Tucumán arrived in Buenos Aires.[90] US Minister Thomas O. Osborn informed the State Department that rebels disabled the gunboat *Uruguay* and utilized the gunboat *Paraná* to blockade Buenos Aires. Furthermore, according to Osborn, "there is no doubt that two of the divisions of the regular army have gone over to the insurgents."[91] The national government repaired the *Uruguay* and sent it out to hunt for the *Paraná*, still under the control of the revolutionists.[92] General Ignacio Rivas, one of Sarmiento's collaborators during the pacification of the interior in the early 1860s, joined the rebels. Rivas marched on Buenos Aires with four thousand men. Adolfo Alsina, the minister of war, led six thousand National Guards to oppose him.[93] In November, Osborn reported that "the situation here now appears to be critical" and noted that the government had a forty-thousand-man army in the field, with a fifteen-thousand-man reserve force at Rosario.[94]

Mitre's manifesto, issued in October 1874, justified his revolution. Reminding his fellow Argentines that he "never made use of either victory or power but for the public welfare" and "handed over the reins of power to the elect of the Nation," Mitre painted himself as a disinterested patriot. Furthermore, he noted, despite "iniquitous tactics," "notorious frauds," and "the violent action of the troops on the day of voting," he had urged his followers not to appeal to arms. Public authorities, he thundered, "winked at the fraud, shutting out the real representatives of the People, and accepting in their room the representatives of a daring forgery which nobody denied and everybody openly confessed." Mitre deplored the annihilation of Argentine liberties and claimed that the frauds of Sarmiento and Avellaneda made revolution a necessity.[95] Mitre, in other words, spoke McEnery and Díaz's language.

If Mitre's rebellion was more a farce than a threat, Sarmiento's actions were astonishingly out of proportion.[96] As with López Jordán's assassination of Urquiza, Sarmiento responded quickly and ferociously to internal disorder. Furthermore, Sarmiento told Osborn: "We are following the example of your Government in her late struggle for life; and we know we cannot go wrong. This government has the power to put down the rebellion, and she will put it down; at least I will do my full duty as President so long as I remain in the presidential chair."[97] Like Lincoln, Sarmiento vowed to suppress the rebellion in the interest of vindicating republican government.

In addition, Sarmiento's farewell address argued that the Revolution of 1874 was more than a passing annoyance. The revolutionists, Sarmiento observed, "conspired against the country, ruining its credit, destroying its wealth, and putting in jeopardy its railways, telegraphs and other works of civilization."[98] Sarmiento's description of how Argentina rallied to action also suggests a different picture of Mitre's rebellion: "The moment the telegraph announced the first alarm of civil war, 50,000 Argentines took up arms. Buenos Ayres is on foot with all its power, Santa Fe has 6000 armed men in the field, and Entre Rios, so long the patrimony of 'caudillos,' has 12,000 more ready for action."[99] In Argentina, the population of the country was only about two million people. In 1861, Lincoln called for seventy-five thousand volunteers initially out of a population of twenty-one million.[100] Many contemporaries considered the revolution a seminal event. One newspaper wrote that the "opinion in Montevideo about the Argentine revolution is that it will be a very long business, and possibly wind up in the most unlooked for manner."[101]

There were similarities, as well as differences, among the rebellions in Louisiana, Argentina, and Mexico. For one, Mitre's rebellion, as well as most of the rebellions in Mexico, occurred in a more compressed time span: anywhere from a few days to a handful of months. Kellogg, however, faced almost two years of guerrilla violence, culminating in a protracted battle. The response of each government likely had a critical effect in determining the length of each rebellion. In the aftermath of bloody civil wars, one would logically suspect that the federal government would try to nip violence in the bud. However, this was often not the case. In the United States, Grant certainly suppressed the Ku Klux Klan in South Carolina in 1871–72. However, he allowed the open wound in Louisiana to fester. After the Battle of Liberty Place, when he sent the army in to restore order, Grant paid a political price. Democrats delighted in deriding him as a would-be Caesar, and, combined with the economic woes of the Panic of 1873, Grant likely did not want to do anything that would add to Republican problems in the elections of 1875 and 1876. In Argentina, on the other hand, Sarmiento responded quickly and forcefully to internal turmoil. Whether that meant rushing an army to Entre Ríos to defeat Urquiza's assassin or suppressing a rebellion of discontented Mitristas, Sarmiento moved decisively. In Mexico, Lerdo's government whipsawed between intervening to suppress violence at the state level, such as when he helped Canales defeat Cortina in Tamaulipas, or taking a more hands-off approach, as with Governor Cepeda of Coahuila. It is no coincidence that shorter rebellions occurred in countries whose governments responded with force and alacrity.

Interestingly, where McEnery in Louisiana and most of the rebels in Mexico were not punished for their actions, Mitre and several of his supporters were tried before a council of war. The charges included desertion, disobeying orders, removing national troops from their posts, and taking up arms against the nation. Given the nature of these charges and of the revolution itself, the council of war dealt lightly with the rebels. They sentenced ex-Generals Mitre and Rivas, as well as ex-Colonels Ocampo, Gonsalez, Machado, and Murga to eight years in exile, ex-Colonel Vidal to six years in exile, and ex-Colonel Charras to three years in exile.[102]

Avellaneda offered amnesty to the rebels who laid down their arms during the revolution. He also chose to extend clemency toward the perpetrators and modified their sentences in order to "commemorate the glorious anniversary of our political emancipation." Avellaneda set Mitre, Gonsalez, Vidal, and Charras "at liberty without suffering the terms of exile." Rivas, Ocampo, and Murga were banished for eighteen months rather than eight years.[103] Mitre "returned to his home on the night of the 24th." Rivas, Ocampo, and Murga, on the other hand, "were shipped to Montevideo."[104] All in all, rather lenient penalties for attempting to overthrow a government.

Perhaps because Argentina had the strongest record in responding to internal disorder, Avellaneda felt he could mingle justice with mercy and not have his decision blow up in his face. Furthermore, where Lerdo issued his amnesty to calm turbulent waters and reduce violence, Avellaneda issued his from a position of strength: the state had already suppressed the rebellion and, perhaps, could afford to be merciful to the leaders. However, it may have sent the wrong message. Like McEnery, Mitre continued to be a viable political operator, although Mitre never again rose to the presidency. Unlike McEnery, Mitre did not become a serial pronouncer, but he did play a role in the Revolution of 1880. An important difference here concerns the fact that the Argentines were all relatively high-ranking military men. Many of McEnery's supporters were former soldiers, but he did not have significant support from officers in the regular army.

The Elections of 1876

The election of 1876 became a critical moment for both the United States and Mexico. In the United States, Republicans nominated Governor Rutherford B. Hayes of Ohio, who proved, in 1875, that Republicans could win Ohio even in a bad political climate. Democrats, on the other hand, nominated Governor Samuel J. Tilden of New York, the proponent of an amorphous program of "reform." Democrats had not controlled the presidency since the end of James Buchanan's term in 1861 and were sanguine about their chances of victory. Democrats accused Grant with lusting after a third term and played up charges of Caesarism.[105] Even with these handicaps, Republicans saw reasons for hope. Buoyed by their victory in Ohio in 1875 and working with a different set of tools and issues, such as the Catholic school question, Republicans believed they could win the election.

Democrats fretted about the presence of the army in the US South. In a letter to Senator Matthew Ransom, Jonathan Bragg complained about affairs in Alabama. "If our people are to be badgered & harassed by Sheridan & his myrmidons—under the advice & manipulation of Spencer & his deputy Marshals," Bragg growled, "one of two things will happen—either of which will produce consequences unpleasant to contemplate—Spencer & his marshals will be killed or driven away by force—or the people in disgust will stay at home & allow the election to go by default." Bragg claimed to speak for Alabama, Mississippi, and Louisiana.[106]

Republicans, on the other hand, considered troops absolutely necessary.[107] For example, D. A. Weber wrote to Governor Kellogg that "a number of petitions are being circulated among the Democrats for the removal of the US Soldiers stationed at Bayou Sara. Said petitions, I am informed, will be forwarded to Gen Augur by to-morrow's mail. Since the arrival of the troops we have enjoyed a perfect peace; and should they be ordered away from Bayou Sara, it would result [in] a renewal of all our troubles." Weber pleaded with Kellogg to implore Augur to leave the soldiers in place.[108] The election, as expected, proved contentious. Governor C. H. Brogden of North Carolina discussed with Grant the "extraordinary and exciting contest" in that state and how Republicans faced "the most powerful and unscrupulous opposition."[109] Democrats in South Carolina, Louisiana, and Florida—the last three Republican-controlled Southern states—utilized tactics recently perfected by

revolutionists in Louisiana and Mississippi and employed widespread intimidation, fraud, and murder. Thomas Nast, in a blistering cartoon, portrayed
the massacre of African Americans at Hamburg, South Carolina, as a Tilden-
approved policy of reform.[110]

On the evening of November 7, 1876, it looked like Tilden had won enough
electoral votes to become president. However, a question quickly arose: who
won South Carolina, Louisiana, and Florida's electoral votes? All three states
had Republican governors who controlled the returning boards. Realizing the
presidency rested on these electoral votes, hordes of "visiting statesmen," both
Republicans and Democrats, flooded into the three states. Ostensibly there
to supervise the counting and make sure everything was on the up-and-up, in
reality, the visiting statesmen spent most of their time trying to cajole, bribe,
or intimidate the returning boards. Neither party, despite sanctimonious deni-
als from the Democrats, refrained from corrupt behavior.[111] When the returning boards determined that Republicans won the electoral votes, Democrats
got up their own returning boards and, in Louisiana's case, had the old fraud
McEnery sign the returns. This was the context that led the *Nation* to argue
that the US South had been Mexicanized and that the Northern states may
have been as well.

In short succession, Congress faced a dilemma. Each state sent two different sets of returns, one awarding the electoral votes to Hayes and another
awarding them to Tilden. Democrats, who controlled the House of Representatives, claimed the House should decide the winner of the election because no
candidate had a majority in the electoral college. Republicans, who controlled
the Senate, claimed the president of the Senate should decide which set of returns counted. Threats of violence became legion. Most famously, hotheaded
Democrat Congressman Henry Watterson of Kentucky suggested Democrats
should march on Washington and inaugurate Tilden by force, if necessary.[112]
Congress established a fifteen-member electoral commission. In a series of
eight-to-seven votes, the commission awarded the disputed votes to Hayes,
giving him the presidency by a margin of one electoral vote.

According to some historians, quick thinking by some Republicans, the so-
called Compromise of 1877, saved the day. In this formulation, white Southern
Democrats went along with Hayes winning the presidential election. In turn,
Republicans promised to withdraw the troops protecting Governor Chamberlain in South Carolina and Governor Packard in Louisiana and allow Demo-

crats to "redeem" their states. Hayes would also appoint a Southern Democrat to his cabinet and would push for the construction of another transcontinental railroad in the Southern states. If a compromise occurred—and historians still debate this point—Republicans abandoned the final Republican-controlled states in the US South.[113] In a fair contest, especially in South Carolina, which had a majority African American population, Republicans would have won the elections. "Redemption," the word used to refer to the process whereby Democrats wrenched control of the Southern states away from Republicans, involved the overthrow of democratically elected governments, widespread voter suppression, significant levels of violence, and murder.

In Mexico, Lerdo de Tejada sought reelection in 1876. Porfirio Díaz consequently turned to his old weapon, the pronunciamiento. Díaz made one of the central declarations of his Plan de Tuxtepec, as he did with the Plan de la Noria, a denunciation of presidents being reelected.[114] Because Díaz pronounced months before the election, Mexico experienced rumblings of revolution before voting took place. Sometimes these tremors amounted to little. From Mérida, Consul Alphonse J. Lespinasse wrote that the government quelled a relatively limited insurrection.[115] In Guaymas, Consul A. Willard reported that about one thousand revolutionists controlled the town of Alamos, but the governor of Sonora, "with an equal number of men[,] is within a few leagues of said town, and a decisive battle is expected daily." Willard also noted that two Mexican vessels of war were due to arrive "with four hundred Federal troops, and instructions from the General Govt of Mexico to aid in restoring order in Sonora."[116] Unlike Grant in the United States, the Mexican government doubled down on restoring peace.

In other states, however, events raged out of control before the people even had a chance to vote. In Matamoros, for instance, a US diplomatic official reported that Díaz "has a Strong party Supposed to be favorable to another revolution," so the state government reinforced the city's garrison with several hundred additional soldiers."[117] Several months later, Díaz supposedly approached Matamoros with one thousand revolutionists. The federal government appointed General B. L de la Barra commander of military forces on the frontier. Barra quickly began organizing and arming the National Guard to defend Matamoros.[118] In an odd twist, both Juan N. Cortina and Servando Canales joined the pro-Díaz revolutionists, proving once again that revolutions, as politics, made for strange bedfellows.[119]

Things looked grim in other states as well, at least for Lerdo and the government forces. In Mier, Commercial Agent Marcus T. Milona reported that "the revolutionary forces under General Naranjo took possession of this city.[120] Lerdo placed Sinaloa under martial law and appointed General F. O. Acre military governor. While "the Capital of this State is in the hands of the revolutionary party," Arce "is confident of restoring order having lately received large reinforcements of government troops."[121] In Mexico City, Julius Skilton complained that revolutionists tampered with mailbags.[122] Silas Trowbridge reported the presence of a "formidable rebellion" in Veracruz and that pronunciados left a swath of destruction in their wake. Furthermore, "the gates of this city were closed early this morning, caused by the appearance of about 100 cavalry belonging to the pronunciados." Trowbridge concluded that "the military authorities here seem to have small faith in the constancy of their troops. Desertions to the rebels are frequent."[123] Finally, from Minatitlan, US Consul Solomon Sternberger noted that the city "was attacked by the enemy who has surrounded the town and burnt a large portion of it since. Yesterday the seventeenth the Government troops were reinforced to day they evacuate the place leaving it in hands of the Revolutionists."[124] Again, all this occurred before people even had a chance to cast their ballots.

Despite ever-increasing violence and revolution, Mexico held the presidential election. Lerdo claimed victory and the Mexican Congress concurred that he won the election. However, shortly thereafter, President of the Supreme Court José María Iglesias declared the election illegal because of fraud. A familiar story recurred. After voiding the election, Iglesias declared the presidency empty. As president of the Supreme Court, Iglesias claimed to be interim president of Mexico.[125] Thus, after the election, three contenders fought for the presidency: Lerdo, the democratically elected president; Iglesias, the president of the Supreme Court; and Díaz, the serial pronouncer. This was not a one-sided affair; Díaz, Lerdo, and Iglesias all had support in different regions of the country. Iglesias fled to Guanajuato and the protection of Governor Florencio Antillón.[126] The pattern of presidential succession in Mexico complicated the situation because of how Iglesias employed his power as president of the Supreme Court.

The decision of Iglesias to void the election, despite the manifestly self-interested motivations, provided additional respectability to the cause of the revolutionists. Díaz defeated an outnumbered pro-Lerdo force commanded by

Ignacio Alatorre in Tlaxcala, at the Battle of Tecoac. This proved to be a crucial moment because, after Alatorre's defeat, Lerdo retired from Mexico City, the first portion of a journey that would end in his exile in the United States. Alatorre's defeat also bolstered Díaz's claim to the presidency. Skilton reported, as a consequence of Lerdo leaving, "the complete occupation of the country—from Mexico to the Gulf by the revolutionary forces of General Porfirio Diaz."[127]

Revolutionists continued to gain strength. From Veracruz, Trowbridge noted that the tumultuous condition of the state had not eased. "The Man-of-War 'Libertad' has 'pronounced' and joined the rebellion," he reported. Furthermore, "twelve hundred 'pronunciados' are here and propose to take this city to-morrow night." He concluded: "We hear that Dias [sic] has taken Puebla and beaten Alatorre in a decisive manner near Apizaco. I have but little doubt that the rebellion will be successful."[128] Trowbridge was correct. Furthermore, General Arce failed to pacify Sinaloa. In January 1877, Díaz men occupied Mazatlán and Arce "asked and received the protection of this Consulate, where he still remains." In addition, "Jose Maria Iglesias with many of his partisans were passengers on the American Steamer 'Granada,' which sailed from this Port on the 19th inst for San Francisco, Cala."[129] Not only did a US consul protect a Mexican general, but the Lerdo and Iglesias partisans in Sinaloa bowed to the obvious and left Mexico for other destinations.[130]

Lerdo's government made a final effort in Guerrero. From Acapulco, John A. Sutter Jr. informed William Hunter that "the isthmus of Tehuantepec being in the power of the partisans of Porfirio Diaz, the Government of President Lerdo has declared the port of Salina Cruz closed to all commerce."[131] Lerdo's strategy involved interdicting ports in rebellion against the central government. When Sutter wrote to Hunter in January 1877, he noted the tragic development of events. Governor Diego Álvarez, after Lerdo left Mexico City, "considered it his duty to recognize, together with all the governors of the Northern and Western states, Mr. Iglesias" as president. However, "strictly adhering to the constitution, which he considers to be the Supreme law of the country, Gen¹ Alvarez never approved of the unconstitutional violent movement of Gen¹ Porfirio Dias [sic]." Fortunes of war favored Díaz, who, Sutter growled, conjured up a ghost from the past to haunt Guerrero: "He commissioned Gen¹ Jimenes [sic] one of his most zealous partisans and at the same time a personal enemy of Gen¹ Alzarez with a force of 2500 men to invade this state." Álvarez did not have enough soldiers to resist Jimenez, so he left the state capital and retired into the mountains to raise an army.[132] Two weeks later, Sutter commented, "the fugitive Ex president Lerdo and cabinet, having found a temporary asylum on board the [illegible word] ship 'Salvador' lay-ing at anchor in this port, will leave today for Panama."[133] Jimenez, the serial pronouncer who took advantage of Lerdo's amnesty, turned on the man who pardoned him to aid Díaz, another serial pronouncer.

Díaz's accession to the presidency did not stop the violence. A phenom-enon one might label "persistent Lerdismo" continued to operate. In other words, some people refused to accept Díaz's victory and continued to fight for Lerdo.[134] Most of them crouched down in the border states, sometimes strayed into the United States, and plotted revolutions. General Mariano Esco-bedo, Lerdo's minister of war, was one of the most prominent persistent Lerd-istas. A US diplomatic official informed the State Department that Escobedo "is still on the Texas border of the Rio Grande, with a considerable following of his former officers and Men" and "he and his Associates are believed to be Engaged in an Effort to re-establish the Government of Lerdo in Mexico."[135] No doubt the persistent Lerdistas appreciated the fact that replicating Díaz's methods allowed them to treat him to the same anxiety he caused Lerdo. Even though the efforts of this group ultimately came to naught, this was not the last time a group sought to topple Díaz by means of an invasion from the north.[136]

Violence did not immediately cease after 1876 or 1880 in any of the three countries. Díaz worked, during his first term as president in 1877–80 and his later terms, 1884–1911, to stamp out brigands and outlaws in the countryside.[137] Díaz became obsessed with securing order, something he shared with many people throughout the Americas. In the US South, and throughout the country more generally, African Americans suffered racist violence, including lynching and Jim Crow laws.[138] When movements such as the Populists threatened to upset the regional status quo, by creating alliances between white people and African Americans, ruling elites drove rhetorical wedges between these two groups. If that did not work, they got out the rifles. This led to events such as the Wilmington Massacre of 1898.[139] In Argentina, ruling elites attempted to keep a lid on radicalism to ensure the continuing stability of the conser-vative oligarchy. Violence did not completely cease, but, in some respects, it decreased. This decrease was due to new configurations of power in each of the three countries after 1880 and a preference for an order that emphasized stability and discipline.

1880

Given the length of presidential terms in each country and the years in which elections took place, 1880 was the first time all three countries had a presidential election in the same year. In the United States, both parties ran generals from the US Civil War. Republicans selected James A. Garfield; and Democrats, Winfield Scott Hancock. Although his margin in the popular vote was whisker thin, Garfield won handily in the electoral college. In comparison to the Reconstruction elections, 1868, 1872, and 1876, violence was present but much less pronounced.[140] Certainly Republicans waved the bloody shirt ferociously, and both parties engaged in fierce rhetoric, but when Hancock lost, disappointed Democrats did not appeal from ballots to bullets.

In Mexico, Porfirio Díaz, for the first and only time, did not seek reelection.[141] However, he stage-managed the election of one of his political associates, Manuel González. Although some people feared rebellion or unrest would occur, the election went off reasonably smoothly, with only sporadic instances of violence. From Mexico City, David Hunter Strother reported, "General Manuel Gonzalez took his seat as President of the Mexican Republic, amidst universal peace and tranquility and welcomed by public rejoicing and shouts of artillery; the first time, it is said, since the Reform of 1857, that a Ruler has been inaugurated in accordance with the prescribed Constitutional forms + with blank cartridges."[142] The scenes in the United States and Mexico stood in marked contrast to the tumult of earlier years.

In Argentina, however, the election of 1880 did not go smoothly at all. Long-standing tension between Buenos Aires and the other provinces exploded into violence. Many porteños deplored Avellaneda's election in 1874 because Avellaneda hailed from Tucumán and could not be counted on to watch out for the interests of Buenos Aires. Mitristas disliked Sarmiento and Alsina boosters contemplating the federalization of the city of Buenos Aires. In 1880, Avellaneda supported Julia A. Roca, also of Tucumán, against Governor Carlos Tejedor of Buenos Aires. When Roca won the election, Tejedor rebelled and took up arms.[143] Tejedor and the Buenos Aires forces fought several battles with the armies of the provinces and, after several months, surrendered. Mitre favored Tejedor's rebellion but did not take part, although he negotiated on behalf of the revolutionists, with Avellaneda. Both sides agreed to a general amnesty and Tejedor resigned his position as governor. Shortly thereafter, the Argentine

Congress passed a law federalizing the city of Buenos Aires. Tejedor's revolution, like Mitre's, ended without achieving its goals, but with a generous amnesty for the revolutionists.[144] The failure of Tejedor's revolution indicated that Argentina, like the United States and Mexico, had arrived at the culmination of a type of stability that dominated the life of each country for many decades.[145]

Conclusion

The situations in the United States, Mexico, and Argentina in the period 1862–80 were similar, although not identical. By bringing the experiences of the three countries together and analyzing them in comparative perspective, the chapters in part 2 reveal, through careful analysis of national elections, state and provincial elections, and violent episodes, that disorder and rebellions occurred in all three countries. True, in the United States in 1876 Tilden did not emulate Díaz by pronouncing and toppling the national government. However, while Democrats did not throw Hayes out of office, they "redeemed" Southern states through violence and terror, and their actions mirrored rebels, caudillos, and pronunciados in Mexico and Argentina. Most importantly, they got away with it and took the destiny of their region in hand.

In each of the three countries, by 1880, violence and disorder gave way to a particular type of stability and order. Historians of Latin America have discussed an important transformation that occurred at the end of the nineteenth century. As Hilda Sabato noted, "a rising creed put forward a concept of order that favored stability and discipline, rather than the active mobilization typical of elections and revolutions of old." Moreover, she found that republics in the United States, France, and Spanish America all sought to achieve order and stability to "avoid the volatility so characteristic of republics in the past."[146] James Sanders contended that "western industrial modernity" triumphed over "American republican modernity."[147] In the United States, many Republicans "came to the sober conclusion that retreating from the enforcement of Reconstruction was the only path toward preserving national stability and constitutional integrity."[148] In other words, Reconstruction failed to deliver its civil rights promise, but it pacified the US South, albeit at the expense of Black subjugation. Mexico and Argentina, too, won stability and reduced internal strife at the expense of large sectors of the population.

The stability and order achieved by 1880 in each nation compromised large groups of people. Republicans found it useful to wave the bloody shirt, but they basically wrote off the Southern states and focused on the Northern and Western states in order to win presidential elections. Redeemers in the Southern states rolled back many of the gains made during Reconstruction. A few years after, beginning in 1890, elites erected Jim Crow laws and resorted to violence and terror to maintain Jim Crow segregation.[149] In Argentina, Roca's election in 1880 initiated a period known as "el orden Conservador," or the Conservative order/oligarchy.[150] As historians have shown, ferment and disorder existed in Argentina, but not enough to topple this oligarchy. This Conservative order endured until the 1910s, when La Ley Sáenz Peña provided for universal, secret, and compulsory male suffrage. In 1916, the first election under the new law, Hipólito Yrigoyen's Unión Cívica Radical (the Radical Civic Union) won the election. In Mexico, Porfirio Díaz controlled the country from 1876 to 1911. Although he stepped aside in 1880, Díaz was reelected in 1884, 1888, 1892, 1896, 1900, 1904, and 1910. This period became known as the Porfiriato. Díaz offered order, stability, progress, and modernization, and all for a very small price: political freedom. Díaz could never fully erase dissent, but he made life unpleasant for dissenters.[151]

The role of violence in rolling back, or modifying, elements of reconstructions should not be discounted. In Mexico, even while declaring his love for the Constitution of 1857, Díaz's pronunciamientos invented reasons for rebelling and threw the country into chaos because of his own ambition. In the United States, lack of will by many Northern Republicans and a wave of violence in the US South rolled back advances made by Republican state governments during "Redemption" and paved the way for Jim Crow. In Argentina, Buenos Aires initially led the process to pacify the interior province, which produced a wave of violent resistance from gauchos and caudillos. However, the dominant position of Buenos Aires eroded by the late 1870s, to the point where Carlos Tejedor revolted, in an attempt to prevent the federalization of the city.

The racial animus of many white southerners toward African Americans and their white allies fed the hatred and violence of the vanquished in the US South. This is one of the chief differences between Argentina and Mexico, because Mexico and Argentina had abolished slavery considerably earlier than the United States had. However, race played an important role in the development of events in all three countries. Argentina launched campaigns against Native Americans in the 1870s and 1880s in an effort to open up more of the country to settlement. At the same time, the United States and Mexico worked together to curtail raiding by Native Americans. Furthermore, although Juárez was a Zapotec, many indigenous people in Mexico fought with the Conservatives and Imperialists—Tómas Mejía most prominently—because Liberal desire to break up communal landholdings did not bode well for them. Government action against tribal land also occurred in the United States with the Dawes Act. Race and racism, in other words, played a major role in the violence in the United States, but it is also important to remember that all three countries experienced similar patterns of violence. Indeed, looking at the Americas more broadly, many people, in all three nations, expressed qualms about the new worlds the victors attempted to create, the increased expenditures, and the costs of modernization. These fears, combined with racial fears and concerns, and the desire to re-create old hierarchies, played an important, if heretofore underanalyzed, role in the death of reconstructions and the paths that the United States, Mexico, and Argentina took to a certain type of stability.

Ultimately, 1880 represented an important moment in the political life of the Americas. During the 1850s and 1860s, the three republics in this study—the United States, Mexico, and Argentina—faced existential challenges from reactionary groups and their European allies. When the French Intervention ended in 1867, victorious Liberals celebrated overcoming these challenges and demonstrating, repeatedly, that republics could withstand severe internal crises. However, as part 2 has illustrated, violence did not cease after the guns fell silent. Internal factionalism rose to the forefront. Alliances pitting the vanquished and some discontented victors against other victors or groups of victors against each other became the norm. Different types of violence proliferated. By 1880, elites in the three nations had taken the destiny of each republic in hand and imposed their preferred brand of order. Rising concerns about African Americans and the rising tide of immigrants in the United States fueled a clear retreat from democracy and the advent of Jim Crow. Porfirio Díaz offered Mexicans order and stability, as long as people surrendered some of their liberties. Conservative oligarchs in Argentina also imposed order on the masses. Order and stability dominated each country for decades, until profound challenges arose in each republic in the twentieth century that shook the very foundations of this brand of order.

The seemingly boundless Pan-American dreams and cooperation of the 1860s and 1870s narrowed after 1880. The advent of Díaz to power in Mexico marked a turn in the US/Mexico relationship with US corporations gobbling up land and favors in Mexico and winning significant power from Díaz and his cronies. Similarly, the story of Argentina is often reduced to the flood of British capital that facilitated technological advancement. Pan-Americanism narrowed, focusing more on money and economics, and then suffered a major blow with the Spanish-Cuban-American War and, subsequently, decades of interventions by Presidents Theodore Roosevelt, William Howard Taft, and Woodrow Wilson. All three countries saw, in 1880 and beyond, the consolidation of the liberal state with glaring illiberal elements and narrower, but nevertheless persistent, ideas about Pan-American cooperation. Civil wars and reconstructions exhausted each nation. Perhaps, then, it is not surprising that many people accepted the seductive bargain—order and stability—without necessarily thinking through the heavy cost.

Conclusion

"BANANA REPUBLICS" & HIDDEN HISTORIES
OF COOPERATION

On January 6, 2021, a mob stormed the US Capitol. This would-be coup d'état demonstrated an important point that has appeared throughout this book, namely, that democracy and republicanism are fragile forces and are always under siege. One type of condemnation of January 6, 2021, merits note. Representative Mike Gallagher decried what occurred as "banana republic crap."[1] Former president George W. Bush made the same point, albeit more eloquently, when he called the events of January 6, 2021, "a sickening and heartbreaking sight" and explained that "this is how election results are disputed in a banana republic."[2] Observers noted the irony of using the term "banana republic" in this way. After all, United Fruit Company and the United States played a major role in extending corporate power into Latin America and shaping so-called "banana republics" in the late nineteenth and twentieth centuries. Nevertheless, many people agreed with Gallagher and Bush that the events of January 6, 2021, were indeed the stuff of "banana republics"; that is to say, the scenes one would expect to see in unstable and turbulent Latin American nations. Whatever the United States' flaws, this line of reasoning asserts, the US is not and never will be a "banana republic."

Ironically, despite the pearl-clutching about "banana republics," few people understood that, while violence in the Capitol in Washington, DC, was indeed relatively unusual, insurrections frequently occurred throughout the Americas during the period covered by this book (1860–80). To be sure, the United States avoided a pronunciamiento or a revolution at the national level (at least after 1865). However, white Southern ex-rebels used violence, fraud, and coercion to overthrow duly elected Republican state governments and "redeem" their states just as caudillos like El Chacho in Argentina and disaffected Liberals like Porfirio Díaz in Mexico turned to violence. If the measure of a "banana republic" is instability in elections, or the refusal of the losers to accept the results, it is important to note that both occurred in all three countries during the period examined by this book as well as in the intervening years. Ultimately, "banana republic" is a twentieth- and twenty-first-century equivalent of a term that cropped up during the period studied by this book—"Mexicanization." It reinforces for people in the United States an "us vs. them" mentality (things might be bad here, but at least we are not a banana republic). For Latin Americans, the term is a mark of US contempt and hypocrisy (especially given US complicity in facilitating the emergence of so-called "banana republics"). In other words, it reinforces pernicious distinctions among the nations of the New World.

The United States, contrary to what some may believe, does not exist in a bubble or in a vacuum. Attempting to analyze what happened in the United States without reference to the rest of the world is misguided, just as it is a mistake to omit the United States from world history. Furthermore, the tendency to frame what happened in the United States as unique or sui generis (whether during the country's Reconstruction or on January 6, 2021) is also a mistake. "Banana republic" enables bad thinking because it implies that, except for an occasional bout of misbehavior, the United States is profoundly different than Latin America. However, as this book has argued, placing the United States, Mexico, and Argentina alongside each other reveals a deeper and heretofore obscured American (hemispheric) history of violence, instability, and disorder. Each country faced a terrible civil war. Each country faced a determined insurgency as the victors attempted to knit their nations back together, insurgencies that employed similar methods and tactics. Finally, each country ultimately made the same devil's bargain in favor of a particular type of order and stability. Ultimately, this is a depressing and harrowing story, although more honest and forthright, particularly about the desire for order and stability in the Americas.

Ending the story on such a gloomy note, however, overlooks one of the key contributions of this book; namely, uncovering the hidden histories of Pan-American cooperation that existed during this period. *Civil Wars and Reconstructions in the Americas* draws on the words and actions of people throughout the Americas to illuminate an epic of Greater America.[3] By analyzing three violent conflicts—the Wars of Unification in Argentina, the War of the Reform

and French Intervention in Mexico, and the Civil War in the United States—
and the reconstructions that followed, this book explores a fascinating period
marked by heretofore underanalyzed cooperation among the three countries.
Indeed, 1860–80 was a moment of intense Pan-American cooperation. People
throughout the Americas saw the conflicts as interwoven, interconnected, or
parallel. People in all three nations, as they moved from civil war into reconstruction, engaged in similar discussions and struggles about the contours of
government and the political systems of their nations. The experiences of all
three nations fit into a larger struggle, both hemispheric and worldwide, that
pit republicanism and democracy against forces of reaction such as aristocracy,
monarchy, oligarchy, and conservatism.

Accounts of the intense Pan-American cooperation that existed during
this period hold tremendous contemporary relevance, particularly at a time
when US relations with Latin America are at a somewhat low ebb, although
nowhere near the nadir reached in the 1900s, 1910s, and early 1920s. Transnational warriors, particularly the Mexican, Argentine, US, and European soldiers
of freedom, who framed their individual conflicts and revolutions as part of a
much larger struggle between democracy and republicanism on the one hand
and the forces of reaction on the other, remind us that the histories of nations
do not stop at their borders. This period featured a dense web of links and
connections throughout the Atlantic World. Transnational warriors constantly
answered the call to fight on the side of the right throughout the Americas and
did so. Even reactionary transnational warriors framed their actions as some-
how serving freedom, although this seems risible to modern audiences. Nevertheless, illiberal soldiers understood just as well that events and forces transcended individual nations and that the world was interconnected. After the
US Civil War ended, many Mexicans who had already been encouraging the
United States to help redoubled their efforts and drew on the language of sister
republics and the Monroe Doctrine. People in the United States responded
and, together, these Americans (i.e., residents of the Americas) helped alter
the meaning of the Monroe Doctrine. In a powerful Pan-American alliance,
they defeated Maximilian, expelled the French, humbled Napoleon III, and
showed the world that republicanism and democracy, although fragile, could
defeat monarchism and aristocracy.

Pan-American cooperation continued long after Maximilian met his maker
at Querétaro. Mexicans and Argentines celebrated the Fourth of July. The vic-

tors in each nation collaborated in creating various types of internal improvements, particularly educational efforts, as they sought to create good citizens
and strengthen their republican experiments against illiberal forces. Many people, then and now, might be inclined to echo Alexis de Tocqueville's observation that the United States and the nations of Spanish America "will never
be linked in my mind."[4] However, this book illustrates another history of the
relationship between the United States, Mexico, and Argentina during a critical
period and one that people need to remember and understand today. Cooperation existed in the past, and there is no reason it cannot also exist in the present
and future. Policymakers throughout the hemisphere should learn the lessons
this period offers, namely, that cooperation and mutual understanding always
trump hatred and xenophobia.

People in the United States, Mexico, and Argentina, and, for that matter,
everyone in the Americas, should strive to understand these important moments of cooperation and friendship. They challenge us; if we can do it once,
why not again? Furthermore, it should never be a point of pride to deride one's
hemispheric neighbors as "banana republics" and strike a sanctimonious tone
that such things never happened in the United States, because, as this book reveals, they did. The history of Pan-American cooperation has been obscured,
in the intervening decades, by frequent US interventions, the Roosevelt Cor-
ollary to the Monroe Doctrine, and US support for right-wing dictatorships
during the Cold War. Nevertheless, the boundless Pan-American dreams that
this book analyzed never really died. Politicians often play to the lowest common denominator and appeal to hatred, xenophobia, and the fouler devils of
human nature. But this book shows that many people throughout the Americas
rejected this logic. Following their example, we can and should do so as well.
Cooperation can be difficult, to be sure, but it is always rewarding, especially
when we understand that the republics of the New World are not so different
and (as evidenced by January 6, 2021, and other events) that they still confront
the same struggles against the forces of reaction that they did a century and a
half ago. History is often more enlightening than inspiring, but the analysis of
Pan-American cooperation offered by this volume is both.

NOTES

Introduction: North and South (America)

1. McPherson, *The Battle Cry of Freedom*, 339–625; Hess, *The Civil War in the West*, 92–133; Cutrer, *Theater of a Separate War*, 133–210.

2. Guelzo, *Lincoln's Emancipation Proclamation*; Weber, *Copperheads*, 58–72; and McPherson, *The Battle Cry of Freedom*, 489–510.

3. Weber, *Copperheads*.

4. Abraham Lincoln [hereafter AL] to William S. Rosecrans [hereafter WSR], Jan. 5, 1863, in Basler, ed., *The Collected Works of Abraham Lincoln*, 9 vols., 6:39.

5. See "I can never forget, whilst I remember anything, that about the end of last year, and beginning of this, you gave us a hard earned victory which, had there been a defeat instead, the nation could scarcely have lived over" (AL to WSR, Aug. 31, 1863, in Basler, *Collected Works*, 6:424).

6. AL to Joseph Hooker, Jan. 26, 1863, in Basler, *Collected Works*, 6:78–79.

7. See Eller, *We Dream Together*.

8. Jones, *Blue and Gray Diplomacy*. Other bright spots became apparent in retrospect. For example, the Emancipation Proclamation generated anger during the 1862 midterm elections, but it also opened the doors to recruiting Black soldiers.

9. AL to Bartolome Mitre, Feb. 6, 1863, in Basler, *Collected Works*, 6:95.

10. See Morgan and Greene, "Introduction: The Present State of Atlantic History," 3–33.

11. See Sanders, *The Vanguard of the Atlantic World*; and Sabato, *Republics of the New World*.

12. Seventh and Last Debate with Stephen A. Douglas at Alton, Illinois, in Basler, *Collected Works*, 3:315.

13. Sarmiento, *Obras*, 27:7.

14. See Lang, *Contest of Civilizations*, 137.

15. For a recent study emphasizing the importance of cooperation in the US-Mexico borderlands, see González-Quiroga, *War and Peace on the Rio Grande Frontier*.

16. See Fitz, *Our Sister Republics*.

17. See Sexton, *The Monroe Doctrine*, for discussion of the Monroe Doctrine.

18. Crapol, *James G. Blaine*.

19. See Lang, *Contest of Civilizations*, 152; and Tucker, *Newest Born of Nations*.

20. See Fleche, *The Revolution of 1861*; and Tucker, *Newest Born of Nations*.

21. Dew, *Apostles of Disunion*.

22. Sabato, *Republics of the New World*, 116.

23. See Lang, *Contest of Civilizations*, 133, 137; and Downs, "The Mexicanization of American Politics."

24. For examples of transnational histories of the United States, see Bender, *A Nation among Nations;* Rauchway, *Blessed among Nations;* Tyrrell, *Transnational Nation;* and Sexton, *A Nation Forged by Crisis.*

25. Neely Jr., *The Civil War and the Limits of Destruction*, 72–108.

26. Kelley, *The Transatlantic Persuasion;* Butler, *Critical Americans;* McDaniel, *The Problem of Democracy in the Age of Slavery;* Rothera, "Our South American Cousin." For a later period, see Rodgers, *Atlantic Crossings.*

27. Hanna and Hanna, *Napoleon III and Mexico;* Schoonover, *Dollars over Dominion;* May, *The Union, The Confederacy, and the Atlantic Rim;* Kelly, "The North American Crisis of the 1860s"; and Doyle, *American Civil Wars.*

28. For abolitionism, see Blackett, *Building an Antislavery Wall;* Oldfield, *"Chords of Freedom";* Rugemer, *The Problem of Emancipation;* Clavin, *Toussaint Louverture and the American Civil War;* and McDaniel, *The Problem of Democracy.* For nationalism, see Doyle, *Nations Divided;* Doyle and Pamplona, *Nationalism in the New World;* and Quigley, *Shifting Grounds.*

29. See Owsley, *King Cotton Diplomacy;* Monaghan, *Diplomat in Carpet Slippers;* Jones, *Union in Peril;* Jones, *Abraham Lincoln and a New Birth of Freedom;* Jones, *Blue and Gray Diplomacy;* Foreman, *A World on Fire;* Bowen, *Spain and the American Civil War;* and Fry, *Lincoln, Seward, and U.S. Foreign Relations.*

30. Gleeson and Lewis, *The Civil War as Global Conflict;* Nagler, Doyle, and Gräser, *The Transnational Significance of the American Civil War;* and Doyle, *American Civil Wars.*

31. For work on the international dimensions of Reconstruction, see Sexton, "Toward a Synthesis of Foreign Relations in the Civil War Era, 1848–1877"; Smith, "The Past as a Foreign Country"; Summers, *The Ordeal of the Reunion*, 204–27; Zimmerman, "Reconstruction: Transnational History"; Prior, *Reconstruction in a Globalizing World;* Downs, *The Second American Revolution;* Prior, *Between Freedom and Progress;* and Link, *United States Reconstruction across the Americas.*

32. Some scholars want to abandon the term "Reconstruction" (see Downs and Masur, "Introduction: Echoes of War: Rethinking Post-Civil War Governance and Politics," in *The World the Civil War Made*, ed. Downs and Masur, 4). For the history of the term, see Prior, "Reconstruction, from Transatlantic Polyseme to Historiographical Quandary."

33. See Dunning, *Reconstruction: Political and Economic;* Fleming, *The Sequel of Appomattox;* Bowers, *The Tragic Era;* and Coulter, *The South during Reconstruction.* See also Smith and Lowery, *The Dunning School.* Du Bois, in *Black Reconstruction in America*, demonstrated the false nature of the Dunningite claims.

34. See Cox and Cox, "General O. O. Howard and the 'Misrepresented Bureau'"; McKitrick, *Andrew Johnson and Reconstruction;* Trefousse, *The Radical Republicans;* and Rose, *Rehearsal for Reconstruction.*

35. See McFeely, *Yankee Stepfather;* Benedict, *A Compromise of Principle;* Wiener, *Social Origins of the New South;* Litwack, *Been in the Storm So Long;* and Click, *Time Full of Trial.*

36. Foner, *Reconstruction.* See also Perman, "Eric Foner's Reconstruction." Perman wondered if anything remained to be said about Reconstruction. The answer, this book argues, is an emphatic yes.

37. Summers, *The Ordeal of the Reunion*, 204–27, pays some attention to international elements.

38. For the range of recent studies, see Schwalm, *A Hard Fight for We*; Faulkner, *Women's Radical Reconstruction*; Hogue, *Uncivil War*; Rosen, *Terror in the Heart of Freedom*; Cimbala and Miller, *The Great Task Remaining before Us*; and Genetin-Pilawa, *Crooked Paths to Allotment*.

39. Williams, *They Left Great Marks on Me*; Noe, *The Yellowhammer War*; Ross, *The Great New Orleans Kidnapping Case*; Nash, *Reconstruction's Ragged Edge*; Fitzgerald, *Reconstruction in Alabama*.

40. West, "Reconstructing Race"; Richardson, *West from Appomattox*; Paddison, *American Heathens*; Bottoms: *An Aristocracy of Color*; Smith, *Freedom's Frontier*; Arenson and Graybill, *Civil War Wests*; and Scharff, *Empire and Liberty*.

41. See Schwalm, *Emancipation's Diaspora*; and Stanley, *The Loyal West*.

42. For another study that uses both methodologies, see Sheehan-Dean, *Reckoning with Rebellion*.

43. For an argument in favor of transnational history, see Tyrrell, "American Exceptionalism in an Age of International History." For critiques, see McGerr, "The Price of the 'New Transnational History'"; and Fredrickson, "From Exceptionalism to Variability." See also Tyrrell, "Ian Tyrrell Responds." Tyrrell has published many transnational histories (see Tyrrell, *Woman's World/Woman's Empire*; Tyrrell, *True Gardens of the Gods*; Tyrrell, *Transnational Nation*; and Tyrrell, *Reforming the World*).

44. I borrow "imagined communities" from Anderson, *Imagined Communities*.

45. Fredrickson, "Comparative History," 462. Fredrickson used "American" when he meant "United States." See also Fredrickson, *White Supremacy*; Fredrickson, "Why the Confederacy Did Not Fight a Guerrilla War after the Fall of Richmond"; and Fredrickson, *The Comparative Imagination*.

46. For discussion of different types of comparisons, see Grew, "The Case for Comparing Histories"; Kolchin, *A Sphinx on the American Land*; and Kolchin, "Comparative Perspectives on Emancipation in the U.S."

47. Some historians favor comparative history (see Dal Lago, *Agrarian Elites*; Dal Lago, *William Lloyd Garrison and Giuseppe Mazzini*; and Dal Lago, *The Age of Lincoln and Cavour*).

48. Tannenbaum, *Slave and Citizen*; Elkins, *Slavery*; Klein, *Slavery in the Americas*; Hall, *Social Control in Slave Plantation Societies*; Kolchin, *Unfree Labor*; Genovese, "The South in the History of the Transatlantic World"; Penningroth, *The Claims of Kinfolk*; Tomich, *Through the Prism of Slavery*; Engerman, *Slavery, Emancipation, and Freedom*; Kaye, "The Second Slavery;" Foner, *Nothing but Freedom*; Woodward, "Emancipations and Reconstructions"; Holt, *The Problem of Freedom*; Cooper, Holt, and Scott, *Beyond Slavery*; Scott, *Degrees of Freedom*; and Kenny, *Contentious Liberties*.

49. To date, little work has been conducted on comparative reconstructions. See Bernstein, "South America Looks at North American Reconstruction"; Schivelbusch, *The Culture of Defeat*; Hahn, "The Politics of Black Rural Labourers in the Postemancipation South"; Kolchin, "Comparative Perspectives on Emancipation in the US South," and Rothera, "Our South American Cousin."

50. As the sources cited throughout this introduction indicate, usage of "American Civil War" is widespread.

51. See Kramer, "Power and Connection."

52. Hamill, *The Hidalgo Revolt*; Henderson, *The Mexican Wars for Independence*.

53. Hamnett, "Royalist Counterinsurgency and the Continuity of Rebellion."

54. Anna, *The Fall of the Royal Government in Mexico City*; Anna, *Spain and the Loss of America*; Anna, *The Mexican Empire of Iturbide*; and Anna, *Forging Mexico, 1821–1835*.

55. Rodríguez O, *"We Are Now the True Spaniards."* For other perspectives, see Van Young, *The Other Rebellion*; and Guardino, *The Time of Liberty*.

56. Anna, *Forging Mexico*; Costeloe, *The Central Republic in Mexico*.

57. Fowler, *Tornel and Santa Anna*; Fowler, *Santa Anna of Mexico*.

58. Vázquez and Meyer, *The United States and Mexico*; Wasserman, *Everyday Life and Politics*.

59. Hale, *Mexican Liberalism in the Age of Mora*; Sinkin, *The Mexican Reform*; Mallon, *Peasant and Nation*; Guardino, *Peasants, Politics and the Formation of Mexico's National State*; Thomson and LaFrance, *Patriotism, Politics, and Popular Liberalism*.

60. Mijangos y González, *The Lawyer of the Church*.

61. See Middlekauff, *The Glorious Cause*; Anderson, *Crucible of War*; Taylor, *The Internal Enemy*; and Taylor, *American Revolutions*.

62. Holton, *Unruly Americans*; Beeman, *Plain, Honest Men*; Maier, *Ratification*.

63. Armitage, *The Declaration of Independence*.

64. See Sellers, *The Market Revolution*; Wilentz, *The Rise of American Democracy*; and Howe, *What Hath God Wrought*.

65. Berlin, *Generations of Captivity*; Rothman, *Slave Country*.

66. Forbes, *The Missouri Compromise*; Hall, *Dividing the Union*.

67. See Newman, *The Transformation of American Abolitionism*; Laurie, *Beyond Garrison*; Laurie, *Rebels in Paradise*; and Sinha, *The Slave's Cause*.

68. Richards, *Gentlemen of Property and Standing*; Tomek, *Pennsylvania Hall*.

69. Smith, *The War with Mexico*; Schroeder, *Mr. Polk's War*; Pletcher, *The Diplomacy of Annexation*; Freehling, *The Road to Disunion*, vol. 1; Foos, *A Short, Offhand, Killing Affair*; Henderson, *A Glorious Defeat*; Greenberg, *A Wicked War*; Torget, *Seeds of Empire*; Guardino, *The Dead March*.

70. Hamilton, *Prologue to Conflict*.

71. Richards, *The Slave Power*.

72. Potter, *The Impending Crisis*; Fehrenbacher, *The Slaveholding Republic*.

73. Slaughter, *Bloody Dawn*; Barker, *The Imperfect Revolution*; Smith, *On the Edge of Freedom*; Murphy, *The Jerry Rescue*; Jackson, *Force and Freedom*.

74. Wunder and Ross, *The Nebraska-Kansas Act of 1854*.

75. Fehrenbacher, *Prelude to Greatness*; Gienapp, *The Origins of the Republican Party*.

76. Hoffer, *The Caning of Charles Sumner*; Freeman, *The Field of Blood*.

77. Etcheson, *Bleeding Kansas*; Epps, *Slavery on the Periphery*.

78. Fehrenbacher, *The Dred Scott Case*.

79. Ponce, *To Govern the Devil in Hell*.

80. Stauffer, *The Black Hearts of Men*; Reynolds, *John Brown*.

81. Holt, *The Election of 1860*; Dew, *Apostles of Disunion*.

82. Brown, *A Socioeconomic History of Argentina*; Rock, *Argentina*; Szuchman and Brown, *Revolution and Restoration*; Sheinin, *Argentina and the United States*.

83. Johnson, *Workshop of Revolution*.

84. Lynch, *San Martín.*

85. For Unitario hatred of Rosas, see Arana, *Juan Manuel de Rosas en la Historia Argentina,* 1:42; Udaondo, *Grandes hombres de nuestra patria,* 3:1026; Ramos, *Historia de la Nación Latino-americana,* 348; and Sawers, *The Other Argentina,* 6.

86. Lynch, *Argentine Dictator.*

87. Katra, *The Argentine Generation of 1837;* Shumway, *A Woman, a Man, a Nation.*

88. For studies focusing on Buenos Aires, see Szuchman, *Order, Family, and Community in Buenos Aires;* Sabato, *The Many and the Few;* and Shumway, *The Case of the Ugly Suitor.*

89. Adelman, *Republic of Capital.*

1. Transnational Warriors

My thanks to Mark E. Neely Jr. for suggesting this chapter title.

1. "No podrán ejercerse en la República los derechos politicos . . . por los que hayan aceptado empleos u honores de Gobiernos estranjeros, sin permiso del Congreso," Ley 346, Título 4, Artículo 8. For the text of the law, see the website maintained by Argentina's Ministro de Justicia y Derechos Humanos: http://servicios.infoleg.gob.ar/infolegInternet/anexos/45000-49999/488 54/norma.htm.

2. "D. Edelmiro Mayer solicita que el Congreso declare que está en el goce y uso de todos sus derechos de ciudadano" (*Congreso Nacional: Diario de Sesiones de la Cámara de Diputados, Año 1874,* 237).

3. For the debate in the Argentine Senate, see the speeches of Nicolás Avellaneda and Daniel Araoz, *República Argentina: Congreso Nacional: Cámara de Senadores, Sesiones de 1874,* 198–99.

4. *Congreso Nacional: Diario de Sesiones de la Cámara de Diputados, Año 1874,* 238. Del Valle and Leandro Alem later founded la Unión Cívica Radical. See Alonso, *Between Revolution and the Ballot Box.*

5. "Es una de las mas grandes de los tiempos modernos," and "que sin duda es también la guerra más santa de los tiempos modernos" (*Congreso Nacional: Diario de Sesiones de la Cámara de Diputados, Año 1874,* 238).

6. "Él es el representante de aquel amor inmenso sin límites, hácia todo lo que es republicano, hácia todo lo que es libre entre los americanos, desde la Patagonia hasta el Misisipi" (*Congreso Nacional: Diario de Sesiones de la Cámara de Diputados, Año 1874,* 238). A handwritten account of this session, in Argentina's Archivo General de la Nación, had del Valle say that "the services presented by Mr. Mayer to the cause of the liberty of man in the United States [and] to the independence of Mexico . . . these were not rendered to foreign Governments, but to the American cause" [Los servicios presentado por el Sr Mayer á la causa de la libertad del hombre en Est⁵ Un⁵ de la independencia de Méjico . . . estés no habían sido rendidos á Gobiernos estrangeros, sino á la causa Americana], Congreso Nacional, 1865–1867, Sala X, 30–5–02, AGN, Buenos Aires.

7. See "Héroes no mercenarios," *El Libre Pensador,* Feb. 17, 1881.

8. "En el pleno goce de sus derechos políticos" (*Congreso Nacional: Diario de Sesiones de la Cámara de Diputados, Año 1874,* 238; and *República Argentina: Congreso Nacional: Cámara de Senadores, Sesiones de 1874,* 198, 211).

9. See Forbes, *Manual for Patriotic Volunteer on Active Service in Regular and Irregular War.* Forbes intended the manual for "the use of the Italian (and all other) Liberals who are anxious to prepare themselves, in the shortest possible time, to take the field against the enemies of human progress" (1:vii).

10. For contemporary assessments, both positive and negative, see Gould, *Investigations in the Military and Anthropological Statistics of American Soldiers; Albany Evening Journal,* Nov. 12, 1861; "Address of Rev. Dr. Starrs," *New York Times,* Nov. 19, 1861; and Unknown to Sir, Feb. 12, 1865, Alexander Long Papers, Cincinnati Historical Society. For histories of Irish soldiers, see Bilby, *The Irish Brigade in the Civil War;* Creighton, *The Colors of Courage;* Tucker, *Irish Confederates;* Ural, *The Harp and the Eagle;* McCarthy, *Green, Blue and Grey;* Craughwell, *The Greatest Brigade;* Gleeson, *The Green and the Gray;* Keating; and Keating, *The Greatest Trial I Ever Had.* For histories of German soldiers, see Reinhart, *Two Germans in the Civil War;* Valuska and Keller, *Damn Dutch;* Creighton, *The Colors of Courage;* Kamphoefner and Helbich, *Germans in the Civil War;* Reinhart, *August Willich's Gallant Dutchmen;* and Keller, *Chancellorsville and the Germans.* Doyle, in *The Cause of All Nations,* observed that "a legacy of bias and language barriers have conspired to leave immigrant soldiers in the shadows of America's Civil War narrative" (160).

11. Consider the chapters in Ural, *Civil War Citizens.* Of seven essays, two focused on the Germans, two analyzed the Irish, one studied Jewish Confederates, one explored Native Americans, and the last discussed African Americans. That said, Latin American soldiers have not been completely ignored. See Thompson, *Mexican Texans in the Union Army;* Rosales, *Hispanic Confederates;* Tucker, *Cubans in the Confederacy;* de la Cova, *Cuban Confederate Colonel;* Thompson, *Tejanos in Gray;* Thompson, *A Civil War History of the New Mexico Volunteers and Militia;* and Thompson, *Tejano Tiger.*

12. Doyle, *The Cause of All Nations,* described how many people—Europeans, US citizens, and Latin Americans—saw the US Civil War as fraught with tremendous importance in terms of proving that democracy could survive such a concerted internal challenge as well as part of a larger worldwide struggle.

13. Hilda Sabato and James E. Sanders noted, quite correctly, that the vast majority of the world's republics were concentrated in the Americas and that Europeans looked to the Americas (not just the United States) (see Sabato, *Republics of the New World;* and Sanders, *Vanguard of the Atlantic World*).

14. One could also add other conflicts to this list. See, for example, Downs, *The Second American Revolution;* and Sheehan-Dean, *Reckoning with Rebellion.*

15. For discussions of freedom during this period, see Foner, *Nothing but Freedom;* Foner, *The Story of American Freedom;* Cooper, Holt, and Scott, *Beyond Slavery;* and Scott, *Degrees of Freedom.*

16. For classic discussions of republicanism, see Bailyn, *The Ideological Origins of the American Revolution;* Pocock, *The Machiavellian Moment;* and Rodgers, "Republicanism."

17. See Smith, *The Enemy Within.*

18. Neely Jr., *The Union Divided,* 182–83.

19. See Lynch, *Massacre in the Pampas;* Guardino, *The Time of Liberty;* and Delgado, *Making the Chinese Mexican.* For the United States, see Lee, *America for Americans.*

20. Jefferson cited in Peterson, *Thomas Jefferson and the New Nation,* 359.

21. It is useful to remember that mercenaries, adventurers, and idealists have fought, throughout history, for many reasons, in conflicts that ostensibly do not concern them (see Blaufarb,

"The Western Question"). During the US War for Independence, a number of Europeans fought alongside the revolutionists (see Lockhart, *The Drillmaster of Valley Forge;* Nash and Hodges, *Friends of Liberty;* Storozynski, *The Peasant Prince;* and Auricchio, *The Marquis: Lafayette Reconsidered*). In the same conflict, the British employed Hessian mercenaries to fight rebellious colonials (see Miller, *Dangerous Guests;* and Crytzer, *Hessians*). When white Southern rebels derided the Germans who fought for the United States in 1861–65 as mercenaries, they had this context in mind.

22. Sanders, *Vanguard of the Atlantic World,* 24.

23. Hibbert, *Garibaldi: Hero of Italian Unification,* 21–22. See also Billington, *Fire in the Minds of Men.*

24. See "República Oriental del Uruguay," *El Comercio,* July 13, 1843.

25. Lynch, *Argentine Dictator,* 275. Alexandre Dumas published a novel about the siege, *Montevideo o la nueva Troya.* It employed the same civilization/barbarism dichotomy as in Sarmiento's *Facundo.*

26. Riall, *Garibaldi,* 1. See also Scirocco, *Garibaldi.*

27. "El nombre de Garibaldi es inseparable del de Paz, Alsina, Velez, Mitre y tantos otros" (Sarmiento, *Obras,* 14:374).

28. See "News from South America," *Baltimore Sun,* Dec. 9, 1845; and "Interesting from the Argentina Confederation," *Tri-Weekly Ohio Statesman,* Apr. 20, 1846.

29. Sanders, *Vanguard of the Atlantic World,* 38. Sanders also analyzed the San Patricio Battalion, another group of transnational warriors (64–80). See also Miller, *Shamrock and Sword.*

30. A Mexican newspaper commented, on the possibility of Garibaldi returning to Uruguay to command the armies of the republic, that "Garibaldi will be a big man in the republic of Uruguay, but many of us fear that if he invades Argentine territory, General Rosas will make a big hangman" [Garibaldi, en la república del Uruguay, será un grande hombre; pero mucho nos tenemos que si penetrara alguna vez el territorio de la Argentina, el general Rosas lo haga un grande ahorcado] ("Proposicion," *El Universal,* Nov. 11, 1849). This never came to pass but highlighted Garibaldi as a warrior in two worlds.

31. It also facilitated the rise of Louis Napoleon, later Emperor Napoleon III.

32. Cited in Norman, *Revolutions in the Republican Imagination,* 3. See also Robertson, *Revolutions of 1848;* and Roberts, *Distant Revolutions.*

33. See Dal Lago, *William Lloyd Garrison and Giuseppe Mazzini,* 115, and McDaniel, *The Problem of Democracy,* 186.

34. See Gienapp, *The Origins of the Republican Party;* Honeck, *We Are the Revolutionists;* and Efford, *German Immigrants.*

35. See Trefousse, *Carl Schurz;* and Guelzo, *Gettysburg: The Last Invasion,* 166.

36. Downs, *Declarations of Dependence,* 92. See also Downs, "Anarchy at the Circumference"; and Downs and Downs, "Was Freedom Enough?"

37. "A Warrior's Career Ended," *New York Tribune,* Apr. 7, 1896. See the much terser, "he had served as a lieutenant under Kossuth and Garibaldi, and on the Union side in the civil war" ("Obituary," *New York Herald,* Apr. 7, 1896). See also "Major Hillebrandt Missing," *New York Herald,* Mar. 20, 1890.

38. "A Warrior's Career Ended," *New York Tribune,* Apr. 7, 1896.

39. "A Warrior's Career Ended," *New York Tribune,* Apr. 7, 1896.

40. After the US Civil War, Hillebrandt became an agent of the Bureau of Refugees, Freedmen, and Abandoned Lands (see Click, *Time Full of Trial;* Bradley, *Bluecoats and Tar Heels;* and Batchelor, *Race and Education in North Carolina*).

41. See Alduino and Coles, *Sons of Garibaldi in Blue and Gray;* and Doyle, *The Cause of All Nations,* 160–64, 170–73.

42. See Callahan, "The Confederate Diplomatic Archives," 2; Dunlap, *Augusta County, Virginia, in the History of the United States,* 19 and 21; and Hughes Jr. and Ware, *Theodore O'Hara,* 39.

43. "Col. Theodore O'Hara," *Mississippi Free Trader,* Dec. 6, 1853. See also "If we mistake not, Col. P. is one of the *proprietors and editors* of the Louisville *Times,* a whilom filibusterer of the rankest kind" (*Daily Missouri Republican,* June 13, 1853).

44. Chaffin, *Fatal Glory;* and May, *The Southern Dream of a Caribbean Empire.* For a different discussion see Gobat, *Empire by Invitation.*

45. See "Tribute to Merit," *New Orleans (LA) Daily Picayune,* June 25, 1850; "The Cuba Indictments," *Daily Globe,* July 2, 1850; Keehn, *Knights of the Golden Circle,* 153; and de la Cova, *Colonel Henry Theodore Titus,* 17–19, 22, and 25.

46. May, *Manifest Destiny's Underworld,* 56.

47. Kossuth was not universally admired (see "Letter from New York," *Mobile Register,* Aug. 2, 1859).

48. John T. Pickett to C. F. Henningson, Sept. 1852, Pickett Papers, LOC. Henningson, who was born in Brussels, participated in many Atlantic World conflicts. Like Pickett he joined the rebels during the US Civil War. Pickett's filibustering followed him for the rest of his life (see *Ohio State Journal,* Nov. 22, 1853).

49. Eichhorn, *Slavery and Liberty,* both quotes from page 91. Tucker, *Newest Born of Nations,* noted "northern support for Kossuth provided them [pro-filibuster white southerners] with an opportunity to draw parallels between the popular Lajos Kossuth and the Cuban filibuster Narciso López" (76). The constitution of the Order of the Lone Star, a pro-filibustering organization, pledged to "diffuse throughout the world the principle of liberty and republicanism" (Keehn, *Knights of the Golden Circle,* 197n31). In sum, the notion that filibusters could also be liberators and apostles of republicanism was a reasonably widespread, if nevertheless terribly flawed, idea.

50. Theodore O' Hara to John T. Pickett, Dec. 8, 1851, Pickett Papers, LOC.

51. Eyal, *The Young America Movement,* 94. See also Keehn, *Knights of the Golden Circle,* 8.

52. Zephaniah Kingsley, also a resident of the US South, came to a very different conclusion about Haiti. He "looked to Latin America to discover a true republicanism not tainted by the racism of the United States, seeing in Haiti—so often dismissed as barbarous—a superior civilization" (Sanders, *Vanguard of the Atlantic World,* 233).

53. Chatham Roberdeau Wheat, another transnational warrior with an odd trajectory, participated in filibustering expeditions, fought with Garibaldi in Sicily, and then with the rebels in the US Civil War (see Dufour, *Gallant Tiger;* Keehn, *Knights of the Golden Circle,* 153; and Tucker, *Newest Born of Nations,* 87–88).

54. See Doyle, *The Cause of All Nations,* 120–22.

55. For a broad study of Italians in exile, see Isabella, *Risorgimento in Exile.*

56. Sarmiento cited in Lynch, *Argentine Dictator,* 322. Sarmiento's relationship with Urquiza, explored in chapter 6, redefined the word "complicated."

57. "Letter from Buenos Ayres," *Charleston (SC) Courier,* May 17, 1852.

58. See "a contemptible chief—the traitor Hilario Lagos—collected upon the trenches of the city the forces of the country" ("Late and Interesting from South America," *Dallas (TX) Weekly Herald,* Oct. 29, 1853). This was a translation of a segment of a message from the government of Buenos Aires to the people.

59. In Mexico, Presidents Benito Juárez and Sebastián Lerdo de Tejada also utilized this tactic to stymie revolutionists. For Buenos Aires during this period, see Adelman, *Republic of Capital.*

60. For Spanish migration to Argentina, see Moya, *Cousins and Strangers.*

61. See El Comte del Cuerpo de Vol^s Españoles al Ministro de G y M, Febrero 9 de 1853; José Jaureguí al Señor Ministro de Guerra y Marina, Febrero 9 de 1853; and Ministro de Guerra y Marina al Comandante del cuerpo de Voluntarios Españoles D. José Jaureguí, Febrero 9 de 1853, all in Division Gobierno, 1404, Sala X, 18–08–02, Legiones, AGN, Buenos Aires.

62. Italian immigration to Argentina intensified after 1870 (see Baily, *Immigrants in the Land of Promise;* and Baily, "Italian Immigrants in Buenos Aires and New York City, 1870–1914").

63. For a sketch of Olivieri's life, see Bernardi, *La Vita del Colonnello Silvino Olivieri.* Riall wrote that Olivieri "spent the early 1850s leading an Italian legion in Buenos Aires against the dictator Rosas" (Riall, *Garibaldi,* 122). In actuality, Olivieri arrived after Rosas's defeat.

64. Mazzini admired Olivieri and wrote to a friend that "he will one day perhaps be our remplaçant for Garibaldi" (Riall, *Garibaldi,* 122). Olivieri died in 1856 and did not have a chance to become Garibaldi's replacement.

65. See Ministro de Guerra a Coronel Comte de la Legion Valiente, Junio 15 de 1853, Division Gobierno, 1404, Sala X, 18–08–02, Legiones, AGN, Buenos Aires.

66. "Ruego se sirva autorizarme a rendirle los mismos honores que se han hecho a los demas oficiales de Línea muertos por la Defensa de la Patria," Silvino Olivieri a José María Paz, Mayo 20 de 1853, Division Gobierno, 1404, Sala X, 18–08–02, Legiones, AGN, Buenos Aires. In a letter three months earlier, Olivieri spoke of Argentina as his "Segunda Patria" or second fatherland. See Silvino Olivieri a Exmo Señor Ministro de Guerra, 14 de Feb. de 1853, Division Gobierno, 1404, Sala X, 18–08–02, Legiones, AGN, Buenos Aires. Paz authorized Olivieri's request (see Paz to Olivieri, Mayo 20 de 1853, Division Gobierno, 1404, Sala X, 18–08–02, Legiones, AGN, Buenos Aires).

67. Many immigrants did not want to get caught up in wars (see Quigley, "Civil War Conscription," for immigrants in the United States who attempted to use their foreignness to avoid conscription).

68. Slatta, *Gauchos and the Vanishing Frontier,* 169. See also Riall, *Garibaldi,* 122–23.

69. "No hallándose ya la Patria en peligro y habiendo triunfado las leyes, y siendo la libertad una realidad" y "solo dejaron su trabajo para defender las instituciones del País" (Comte. de la Legion Valiente a Ministro de Guerra, Agosto [10?] de 1853, Division Gobierno, 1404, Sala X, 18–08–02, Legiones, AGN, Buenos Aires).

70. "Animado del buen deseo de ser util á esta Patria que adopto por mia, y cooperar por cuanto medio me sea posible en favor de la sagrada causa de la civilización y libertad" (José Jaureguí a Exmo. Señor, Enero 24 de 1853, Division Gobierno, 1404, Sala X, 18–08–02, Legiones, AGN, Buenos Aires).

71. "Soldados dedicados á defender las principios mas Sacro-Santos" (Olivieri a Ministro

de Guerra, Julio 15 de 1853, Division Gobierno, 1404, Sala X, 18–08–02, Legiones, AGN, Buenos Aires); and "Son bastantemente recompensados con la gloria de haber cooperado á la salvacion de la libertad de esta su segunda Patria" (Olivieri al Ministro de Guerra, Agosto 3 de 1853; Division Gobierno, 1404, Sala X, 18–08–02, Legiones, AGN, Buenos Aires).

72. "Los esfuerzos que hacen los Ytalianos y han hecho interiormente bajo las ordenes de V. S. para ser utiles de algún modo a la buena causa en el Rio de la Plata" (Olivieri al Ministro de Guerra, Junio 7 de 1853, Division Gobierno, 1404; Sala X, 18–08–02, Legiones, AGN, Buenos Aires).

73. Porteños did not have a monopoly on this language. Urquiza, in a proclamation of Feb. 1853, decried "men without virtue or patriotism," "hombres sin virtud ni patriotismo," who prolonged the horrors of war ("República Arjentina," *El Comercio*, Mar. 26, 1853).

74. See "Senator Wilson in New York," *New York Herald*, Oct. 4, 1860.

75. David Chambers to Abraham Lincoln [hereafter AL], Jan. 21, 1861, AL Papers, LOC. This sentiment was not universal (see "Victor Emanuel & Garibaldi represent Aristocracy, *Nobility of Italy*, they are at war against *the Population* of Italy. I would have them both shot," Charles G. Althusen to AL, Mar. 18, 1861, AL Papers, LOC).

76. Joseph Blanchard to AL, Mar. 28, 1861, AL Papers, LOC.

77. John Mitchel, upon hearing rumors about Garibaldi commanding a US army noted, "one would sincerely regret to hear of our gallant Italian being locked up in a Southern calaboose, as he certainly would be—or summarily lynched by Carolina citizens. Should he really go, however, I venture to beg for his life—for the sake of what he has elsewhere done; do not hang him, but, after having given him four dozen, send him back to us (Tucker, *Newest Born of Nations*, 159; see also 160–73).

78. Doyle, *The Cause of All Nations*, 17.

79. Giuseppe Garibaldi, Menotti Garibaldi, and Ricciotti Garibaldi to AL, Aug. 6, 1863, AL Papers, LOC.

80. Edward Yates to AL, May 4, 1864, AL Papers, LOC.

81. Although Garibaldi sometimes sacrificed republican goals and often evinced a streak of pragmatism, he remained for many a symbol of republicanism (see Sanders, *Vanguard of the Atlantic World*, 157–60).

82. Doyle explained that, in the aftermath of the debacle at Aspromonte, Garibaldi and his Red Shirts created a crisis in Europe that helped end secret plans in Great Britain and France to recognize the rebels in the United States (Doyle, *The Cause of All Nations*, 225–39).

83. Two decades after his return to Argentina, President Carlos Pellegrini appointed Mayer governor of the Territory of Santa Cruz (see "Shepherd Dogs of Patagonia," *Springfield [MA] Republican*, Dec. 4, 1894). In his spare time, Mayer translated Samuel Smiles, *Self Help* (London, 1866) into Spanish as *El Deber* (see *La Prensa*, Dec. 23, 1886; *La Prensa*, Dec. 29, 1886; and *La Prensa*, Dec. 30, 1886). See Bayly, *The Birth of the Modern World*, 319, 474, for a Japanese translation of *Self Help*.

84. W. Goodfellow to AL, Jan. 20, 1863, AL Papers, LOC. William Goodfellow was a US Methodist Episcopal missionary in Argentina (see "The Argentine Confederation," *New York Herald*, May 9, 1868; *The Gospel in All Lands*, 170, 553; and *Eighty-Eighth Annual Report of the American Bible Society*, 68–70).

85. W. Goodfellow to AL, Jan. 20, 1863, AL Papers, LOC. Mayer's testimonials do not appear in the Lincoln Papers.

86. See Sutherland, *African Americans at War,* 21.

87. Oscar W. Norton to "Sister L," in Norton, *Army Letters,* 217–18.

88. Dobak, *Freedom by the Sword,* 438–39.

89. See Sarmiento, *Vida de Abran Lincoln,* 222. Frances G. Crowley dismissed *Vida* as having "only a limited value for the modern reader. It is at best a popularization, drawn from random sources and translated into Spanish" (Crowley, *Domingo Faustino Sarmiento,* 147). Nicola Miller, in "'That Great and Gentle Soul': Images of Lincoln in Latin America," labeled the biography "pioneering (yet plagiarized)" (206). May, in *Slavery, Race, and Conquest in the Tropics,* noted that this "quickly written, widely recirculated and reprinted biography" helped "define Lincoln for decades in the minds of Latin American readers" (both quotes from 278).

90. Edelmiro Mayer, "Colored Troops," *Harper's Weekly,* June 27, 1863. The editors made "only such changes in his expressions as are absolutely essential."

91. Mayer, "Colored Troops." For slave soldiers, see Blanchard, *Under the Flags of Freedom.*

92. Mayer, "Colored Troops." This was incorrect. Lynch, *Argentine Dictator* and Andrews, *The Afro-Argentines of Buenos Aires,* contended that while Juan Manuel de Rosas was certainly not a populist, he made token concessions to Afro-Argentines, and some fought with him against the Unitarios. Mayer's dislike of Rosas led him to distort facts. See also Salvatore, *Wandering Paysanos,* 48; and Meisel, "The Fruits of Freedom."

93. For his service in Mexico, see Mayer, *Campaña y guarnicion.*

94. "Banished from Mexico," *New York Herald,* Apr. 7, 1869.

95. Adolfo and Federico were born in Cuba to a Cuban father. Their mother was a US citizen. When their father died in 1838, their mother relocated the family to Philadelphia. Both men returned to Cuba after the US Civil War.

96. See Scott, *Degrees of Freedom,* 96.

97. Cavada, *Libby Life.* See also "Libby Life," *Daily National Intelligencer,* June 18, 1864; "Northern Prisons for Rebels," *New Orleans (LA) Daily True Delta,* Aug. 13, 1864; and "New Publications," *Sacramento (CA) Daily Union,* Sept. 6, 1864.

98. Carlos Alvarez de la Mesa to Dear Fani, July 20, 1861, NYSMMVC, https://dmna.ny.gov/historic/reghist/civil/infantry/39thInf/deLaMesa/39thInf_Coll_deLaMesa_letters.htm.

99. Cited in Tucker, *Newest Born of Nations,* 167.

100. "Call of Col. Asboth upon the Hungarians in America," *New York Times,* May 3, 1861.

101. Zagonyi cited in Vida, *Hungarian Émigrés in the American Civil War,* 55.

102. Eichhorn, *Liberty and Slavery,* 123

103. Welsh cited in Doyle, *The Cause of All Nations,* 165.

104. Adolph Frick to Dear Mother and Sisters, May 11, 1862, in Kamphoefner and Helbich, *Germans in the Civil War,* 350.

105. August Horstmann to Parents, June 16, 1862, in Kamphoefner and Helbich, *Germans in the Civil War,* 122.

106. Doyle, *The Cause of All Nations,* 160. For another discussion of soldier motivations, see McPherson, *For Cause and Comrades.*

107. Grant, *Personal Memoirs of U.S. Grant,* 2:489.

108. Eichhorn, *Liberty and Slavery*, 128. See also Keehn, *Knights of the Golden Circle*, 153.

109. See Stevens, "Two Flags, One Cause"; de la Cova, *Cuban Confederate Colonel*; and Guterl, *American Mediterranean*. Chaffin, *Fatal Glory*, 78, contended Gonzales recruited Pickett and O'Hara.

110. See Frazier, *Blood and Treasure*, 41–42.

111. See Thompson, *Tejano Tiger*. Many Tejanos fought for the United States (see Valerio-Jiménez, "Although We Are the Last Soldiers").

112. Francis Preston Blair, Sr., Address to Jefferson Davis, Jan. 12, 1865, AL Papers, LOC.

113. These ideas were not limited to Blair. For rumors of Juárez being willing to welcome assistance from the Knights of the Golden Circle, a proslavery and profilibustering secret society, in the 1850s, see Keehn, *Knights of the Golden Circle*, 24, 40. Keehn made the problematic assertion that "if the U.S. sectional crisis hadn't intervened, one wonders whether Juárez and the Liberals would have changed their mind and invited the Knights to establish a Mexican colony as a counterbalance against French intervention" (Keehn, *Knights of the Golden Circle*, 188).

114. Romero cultivated the Blairs because of their connections, but his goal was a free Mexico, not one run by Jefferson Davis.

115. Francis Preston Blair, Sr., to AL, Feb. 8, 1865, AL Papers, LOC. William A. Blair considered Francis Preston Blair's a "dubious solution" that Lincoln "quickly shoved aside" (Blair, "Finding the End of America's Civil War," 1758, 1759). Doyle labeled it a "half-mad tour de force" and a "bizarre plan" (Doyle, *The Cause of All Nations*, 286). It is hard to dispute either assessment.

116. Harris, "The Hampton Roads Peace Conference."

117. Doyle, *The Cause of All Nations*, 288. Stephens achieved infamy for stating that the cornerstone of the rebel government rested on idea that "the negro is not equal to the white man" (see Schott, *Alexander H. Stephens of Georgia*, 334; and Doyle, *The Cause of All Nations*, 35–37).

118. Francis Preston Blair, Sr., to AL, Feb. 22, 1865, AL Papers, LOC.

119. Pope Pius IX denounced the Constitution of 1857 and compared Mexican Liberals to "Giuseppe Garibaldi and Guiseppe Mazzini, all godless enemies of the church" (Doyle, *The Cause of All Nations*, 114).

120. The failure of Napoleon's New World schemes did not immediately result in his downfall. That came several years later at the hands of the Iron Chancellor, Otto von Bismarck.

121. For Confederate exiles to other places see Griggs, *The Elusive Eden;* Dawsey and Dawsey, *The Confederados;* Harter, *The Lost Colony of the Confederacy;* Simmons Jr., *Confederate Settlements in British Honduras;* Jarnagin, *A Confluence of Transatlantic Networks;* and Wolnisty, *A Different Manifest Destiny.* John Dooley, a US rebel in a Northern prison camp, noted that some of his fellow inmates were "trying to gain some knowledge of the Spanish tongue in order, as they say, to seek their fortunes in Mexico should the worst come to the worst" (Curran, *John Dooley's Civil War*, 326).

122. Journal Entry of May 6, 1865, in the Mary Elizabeth Mitchell Journal, #1917-z, SHC, UNC-CH.

123. See Rolle, *The Lost Cause;* Davis, *Fallen Guidon;* O'Flaherty, *General Jo Shelby;* Sellmeyer, *Jo Shelby's Iron Brigade;* Arthur, *General Jo Shelby's March;* and Wahlstrom, *The Southern Exodus to Mexico.*

124. Historians often cite President Vicente Guerrero's 1829 decree as the end of slavery in

Mexico, but that decree was later revoked and slavery ended in 1837 (see Torget, *Seeds of Empire*, 305).

125. J. E. Harrison to Gordon Granger, June 21, 1865, Carter-Harrison Family Papers, Baylor University.

126. To be fair, Shelby possibly preferred fighting for Juárez. His men, however, voted to seek shelter with Maximilian (see Arthur, *General Jo Shelby's March*).

127. Thomas Alexander Hamilton to Hamilton Yancey, Mar. 10, 1866, Benjamin C. Yancey Papers, SHC, UNC-CH.

128. See chapter 2.

129. Rable, *Damn Yankees!*, analyzed the many ways white southerners demonized their opponents. This fierce hatred prolonged the war and also likely made some rebels unwilling to face life under the hated Yankees and more willing to flee to foreign countries.

130. Abraham Lincoln, "Annual Message to Congress," Dec. 1, 1862, in Basler, *Collected Works*, 5:537.

131. Dietrich Gerstein to Dear Brother, Jan. 1, 1863, in Kamphoefner and Helbich, *Germans in the Civil War*, 281.

132. See J. Frank Cumming to J. A. J. Creswell, Aug. 23, 1865, John A. J. Creswell Papers; LOC; and Rothera, "The Men Are Understood to Have Been Generally Americans, in the Employ of the Liberal Government."

2. Sister Republics and the Monroe Doctrine

1. Olliff, *Reforma Mexico*, explored US involvement in Mexico in the 1850s. The United States offered minor aid during the Buchanan years, but rapprochement really began following Lincoln's inauguration (see Pletcher, *Rails, Mines, and Progress;* and Schoonover, *Dollars over Dominion*). For the US War with Mexico, see Smith, *The War with Mexico;* Schroeder, *Mr. Polk's War;* Pletcher, *The Diplomacy of Annexation;* Freehling, *The Road to Disunion, vol. 1;* Foos, *A Short, Offhand, Killing Affair;* Henderson, *A Glorious Defeat;* Greenberg, *A Wicked War;* Torget, *Seeds of Empire;* and Guardino, *The Dead March*.

2. Ocampo to Matías Romero, Dec. 22, 1860, AL Papers, LOC.

3. Romero cited in *Mexican Lobby*, 3. See also *Sixteenth-President-in-Waiting*, 218, 220–21, and 236.

4. For a recent discussion of progress during this period, see Prior, *Between Freedom and Progress*.

5. Edward Conner [hereafter EC] to William H. Seward [hereafter WHS], June 12, 1865, Reel 1, Volume 1, DUSC-Guaymas.

6. *Biographical Sketch of Andrew Johnson,* 8 and 11.

7. Many Europeans wanted to see the United States defeat the rebels (see Doyle, *The Cause of All Nations*).

8. *Biographical Sketch of Andrew Johnson,* 11.

9. *Biographical Sketch of Andrew Johnson,* 11. The crowd responded to this line with "great applause."

10. For the Monroe Doctrine, see Perkins, *A History of the Monroe Doctrine;* and Sexton, *The Monroe Doctrine.*

11. Stampp famously labeled Andrew Johnson "the last Jacksonian" (see Stampp, *The Era of Reconstruction*).

12. Histories of Reconstruction usually foreground domestic and minimize international elements (see the discussion in the introduction of this work).

13. Trefousse, *Andrew Johnson,* 261. Interestingly, Seward placed a memo on Lincoln's desk in April 1861 advocating declaring war on France or Spain in order to spark nationalism in the US South and cause the Confederacy to come running home (see WHS to Abraham Lincoln, Apr. 1, 1861, AL Papers, LOC). For Seward's evolving Mexican policy, see Callahan, *Evolution of Seward's Mexican Policy.*

14. See "Visit of General Rosecrans to the Legislature," *Salem (MA) Register,* May 15, 1865; and "Speaker Colfax on 'The Next War,'" *Springfield (MA) Weekly Republican,* Sept. 2, 1865. Readers will note some differences between this chapter and my article "The Men Are Understood to Have Been Generally Americans, in the Employ of the Liberal Government." My thanks to Don Doyle for pushing me to rethink Seward's approach to Mexico.

15. Francis Preston Blair, Sr. to Andrew Johnson, Aug. 1, 1865, in *Papers of Andrew Johnson* [hereafter *PAJ*], 8:523.

16. Horace Maynard to Andrew Johnson, July 18, 1865, in *PAJ,* 8:430.

17. Horace Maynard to Andrew Johnson, July 18, 1865, in *PAJ,* 8:431n4.

18. Schoonover, *Mexican Lobby,* 98.

19. See Doyle, "Reconstruction and Anti-imperialism," for a recent account of Seward's approach to Mexico.

20. The point of this chapter is not to say that Seward deserves X percent of the credit and Grant deserves Y percent, but to argue that there was a broad impulse in the United States to help Mexico and that Mexicans adeptly played on this impulse. Dogged Mexican resistance and US assistance ultimately defeated the French and the Imperialists.

21. See "Nathan C. Brooks coined the term 'sister republics' following the Mexican-American War in an attempt to justify the U.S. incursion into Mexico" (Seijas and Frederick, *Spanish Dollars and Sister Republics,* 156). In fact, as Fitz, *Sister Republics* demonstrated, this language began decades earlier.

22. See Edward Lee Plumb [hereafter ELP] to My Dear Romero, May 10, 1865, Volume 6, Plumb Papers, LOC.

23. ELP to Charles Sumner [hereafter CS], Jan. 26, 1864, Volume 6;,Plumb Papers, LOC.

24. See U. S. Grant [hereafter USG] to P. H. Sheridan, May 17, 1865, in Sheridan, *Personal Memoirs,* 2:209.

25. Sheridan, *Personal Memoirs,* 2:210.

26. Sheridan, *Personal Memoirs,* 2:210.

27. USG to Andrew Johnson, June 19, 1865, in *PAJ,* 8:257.

28. J. M. Schofield to Major-General Sherman, May 4, 1865, in *The War of the Rebellion,* Series I, Volume XLVII, Part III, 392 [hereafter *OR*].

29. See Rolle, *The Lost Cause;* Davis, *Fallen Guidon;* O'Flaherty, *General Jo Shelby;* Sellmeyer, *Jo Shelby's Iron Brigade;* Arthur, *General Jo Shelby's March;* and Wahlstrom, *The Southern Exodus to Mexico.*

30. August Horstmann to Dear Parents, July 16, 1864, in Kamphoefner and Helbich, *Germans in the Civil War*, 128. See also August Horstmann to Dearest Parents, June 23, 1865, ibid., 129; and Victor Klausmeyer to Unknown, Apr. 4, 1865, ibid., 239.

31. USG to Andrew Johnson, July 15, 1865, in *PAJ*, 8:410. Governor William G. Brownlow of Tennessee agreed with Grant (see "Gov Brownlow on the Negro," *Springfield (MA) Weekly Republican*, Oct. 14, 1865).

32. The only full-length biography of Romero is Bernstein, *Matías Romero*.

33. In 1865 alone, Romero lobbied Andrew Johnson, William H. Seward, Ulysses S. Grant, William T. Sherman, John Schofield, John Conness, Thaddeus Stevens, Elihu Washburne, Samuel S. Cox, Godlove Orth, Jacob Howard, Robert C. Schenck, Nathaniel Banks, Schuyler Colfax, Zachariah Chandler, Benjamin F. Wade, James McDougall, John Logan, James Beekman, Thurlow Weed, James Gordon Bennett, Montgomery Blair, William Dennison, James Speed, Philip H. Sheridan, and Francis Preston Blair Sr. (see Schoonover, *Mexican Lobby*, 50–113).

34. Schoonover estimated Romero wrote from five hundred to seven hundred dispatches each year, totaling more than a million words (Schoonover, *Mexican Lobby*, x).

35. Miller, "Matías Romero," 228.

36. See Schofield, *Forty-Six Years in the Army*, 378–93; and Connelly, *John M. Schofield*, 182–86. Romero sounded out William T. Sherman, but he "was determined to retire to private life." Romero also almost asked Sheridan, but "he was valuable in his strategic position as commander of the Department of the Gulf" (Miller, "Matías Romero," both quotes from 242).

37. Schoonover, *Mexican Lobby*, 100; Schofield, *Forty-Six Years in the Army*, 379.

38. Schofield, *Forty-Six Years in the Army*, 378.

39. Schofield, *Forty-Six Years in the Army*, 378.

40. Schofield, *Forty-Six Years in the Army*, 381.

41. Schofield, *Forty-Six Years in the Army*, 381.

42. Schofield, *Forty-Six Years in the Army*, 382.

43. Schofield, *Forty-Six Years in the Army*, 385.

44. Schofield, *Forty-Six Years in the Army*, 393.

45. Miller, "Matías Romero," 244.

46. Schoonover, *Mexican Lobby*, 102.

47. Schoonover, *Mexican Lobby*, 103.

48. Schoonover, *Mexican Lobby*, 103.

49. Chance, *José María de Jesús Carvajal*, explored Carvajal and Wallace's attempts to purchase arms for Mexico. The information I present here expands the picture.

50. This commission entitled Wallace to "all the authorities, rights, privileges, and emoluments, incident to such a commission, according to the laws and Customs of the Mexican service" (José M. J. Carvajal [hereafter JMJC] to Lew Wallace [hereafter LW], Apr. 26, 1865, Box 1, Folder 3, Oliver P. Morton Papers, ISL).

51. JMJC to LW, Apr. 26, 1865, Box 1, Folder 3, Oliver P. Morton Papers, ISL. Wallace sent copies of his correspondence with Carvajal to Morton in 1868 when he sought compensation from Mexico.

52. LW to JMJC, Apr. 27, 1865, Box 1, Folder 3, Morton Papers, ISL.

53. LMJC to LW, Apr. 29, 1865, Box 1, Folder 3, Morton Papers, ISL.

54. LW to General [Carvajal], Apr. 30, 1865, Box 1, Folder 3, Morton Papers, ISL. Wal-

lace's tenure in Mexico proved unpleasant. He did not command troops and was horrified by a pronunciamiento against Carvajal. Wallace spent years dunning the Mexican government for compensation.

55. Grant believed Wallace performed poorly at the Battle of Shiloh and told Romero "failure and discredit" marked Wallace's endeavors (Schoonover, *Mexican Lobby*, 100). See also Woodworth, "Intolerably Slow"; and Mortenson, *Politician in Uniform*. Romero and Carvajal worked together to sell bonds (see "New Mexican Scheme," *New York World*, Oct. 23, 1865).

56. This would have violated the terms of Wallace and Carvajal's agreement.

57. Wallace to Grant, Jan. 14, 1865, in *OR*, Series I, Volume LXVIII, 512.

58. Mortenson, *Politician in Uniform*, 166. Language like this suggests that Seward was right to be concerned about the possibility of some forms of intervention in Mexico degenerating into a land grab.

59. Miller, "Lew Wallace and the French Intervention in Mexico," both quotes on 50.

60. Miller, "Herman Strum: Hoosier Secret Agent for Mexico," 1-2.

61. Cited in Miller, *Arms across the Border*, 34.

62. "The Mexican Excitement," *Philadelphia (PA) Inquirer*, May 12, 1865. This paper quoted a New York paper and referred to New York City, not Philadelphia.

63. "The Latest Phases of the Mexican Question," *San Francisco (CA) Bulletin*, June 5, 1865.

64. Miller, "The American Legion of Honor in Mexico," 241.

65. R. H. Milroy to Andrew Johnson, May 8, 1865, Reel 14, Andrew Johnson Papers, LOC.

66. "Mexican Emigrations," *San Francisco (CA) Bulletin*, Oct. 11, 1866.

67. Miller, "The American Legion of Honor in Mexico," 231.

68. Sanders, *Vanguard of the Atlantic World*, 144.

69. ELP to CS, Jan. 26, 1864, Volume 6, Plumb Papers, LOC.

70. For a recent discussion of the Black Decree see Neely Jr., *The Civil War and the Limits of Destruction*, 72-108.

71. ELP to CS, Oct. 26, 1865, Plumb Papers, LOC.

72. ELP to N. P. Banks and CS, Apr. 4, 1866, Volume 7, Plumb Papers, LOC.

73. *Dinner to Señor Matías Romero*, 19. See also *Banquet to Señor Matias Romero*.

74. "The Reception of George Thompson," *Lowell (MA) Daily Citizen and News*, Mar. 3, 1864. See also "Presentation of a Sword to General Hooker at the Union League Club," *Sacramento (CA) Daily Union*, June 28, 1865.

75. Juárez replied, "my government will take peculiar care to cultivate with diligent assiduity the cordial and frank relations which now happily bind the two Republics" ("Further from Mexico" (*New Orleans (LA) Daily Picayune*, June 13, 1861. Corwin's had been one of the loudest voices opposing the US War with Mexico in 1846-48.

76. Joseph C. Breckinridge to Robert J. Breckinridge, Nov. 27, 1865, Box 244, Breckinridge Family Papers, LOC.

77. See "A Steam Line of Guaymas," *San Francisco (CA) Daily Evening Bulletin*, Apr. 10, 1861; and "Communication with Guaymas," *Sacramento (CA) Daily Union*, Apr. 13, 1861. One of California's senators, James McDougall, detested the French presence in Mexico and worked with Romero.

78. "Dangers on the Isthmus of Panama," *New York Herald*, June 21, 1861.

79. "The Celebration of Washington's Day," *Springfield (MA) Republican*, Mar. 1, 1862.

80. "A Voice from the South," *Sacramento (CA) Daily Union*, July 21, 1862.

81. "Mr. Corwin's Return to the United States," *New York World*, May 27, 1864.

82. "A Desperate Hope," *Cleveland (OH) Daily Plain Dealer*, June 23, 1864. "Shoddy" referred to poorly manufactured supplies for the army and suggested all Republicans were corrupt war profiteers.

83. See also "The Boot on the Wrong Foot," *Wisconsin Daily Patriot*, Oct. 22, 1864. For Republicans using Maximilian to attack Copperheads, see "Union Meeting in Sidney," *Cincinnati (OH) Daily Commercial*, Aug. 1, 1863.

84. "The Arrival of Napoleon's Puppet," *Sacramento (CA) Daily Union*, July 11, 1864.

85. See "The Republic of Mexico," *Coos Republican*, Nov. 21, 1865; "Pulpit Gems," *Philadelphia (PA) Daily Age*, Dec. 9, 1865; and "The French-Mexican Question," *Savannah (GA) National Republican*, Mar. 27, 1866.

86. "The United States and Mexico," *New York Evening Post*, July 27, 1865. See also "The Monroe Doctrine," *New York World*, July 13, 1865; and "The 'Signs,'" *Pittsfield (MA) Sun*, July 20, 1865, for anti-French speeches by Montgomery Blair and James Harlan.

87. "Last Night's Report," *Janesville (WI) Daily Gazette*, July 28, 1863. See also "Important from Mexico," *Milwaukee (WI) Daily Sentinel*, July 29, 1863; "The Empire in Mexico," *New York Herald*, July 29, 1863; and "Important from Mexico," *Wisconsin Daily Patriot*, July 30, 1863.

88. "Interesting from Mexico," *Sacramento (CA) Daily Union*, Aug. 8, 1863. See also "Later and Important News from Mexico," *San Francisco (CA) Daily Evening Bulletin*, Aug. 7, 1863.

89. "The Monroe Doctrine," *New Orleans (LA) Daily True Delta*, June 26, 1864. See also *Arguments in Favor of the Enforcement of the Monroe Doctrine*, a series of essays on the Monroe Doctrine dedicated to Bordon.

90. "La causa del republicanismo en Méjico es la causa de la América" and "si Méjico sucumbe y la influencia y poder de los Estados Unidos es anulado, toda está perdido para siempre" ("La Causa de Méjico es la Causa de la América," *El Nuevo Mundo*, Apr. 28, 1865).

91. See "Mexico was underrepresented in the popular excitement in part because its rural and grassroots insurgency peaked in the early 1810s, when US onlookers were distracted by their second war with Britain, and because when Mexico finally declared independence in the early 1820s, it did so as a monarchy" (Fitz, *Sister Republics*, 15).

92. On a different note, Sanders commented that in the period before 1898 "the public sphere viewed the United States not as a distant and distinct society to be imitated (as was the case with Europe under cultural modernity), but as an essentially similar sister republic" (Sanders, *Vanguard of the Atlantic World*, 80).

93. See "New York Items," *Providence (RI) Evening Press*, Nov. 16, 1865; and "By Telegraph," *Albany (NY) Argus*, Nov. 17, 1865.

94. "Mexico," *Albany (NY) Evening Journal*, Nov. 18, 1865.

95. "About Mexico," *New Mexico Press*, Nov. 21, 1865.

96. ELP to CS, Apr. 23, 1867, Volume 7, Plumb Papers, LOC.

97. Schoonover, *Mexican Lobby*, 100.

98. Sheridan, *Personal Memoirs*, 214–15.

99. J. E. P. Doyle to Andrew Johnson, Oct. 12, 1867, Reel 29, Andrew Johnson Papers, LOC.

100. Thompson, *Cortina,* 167.

101. Thompson, *Cortina,* 152. See also "It is said that several of those prisoners [from Cortina's band] are natives of the United States" (Franklin Chase [hereafter FC] to WHS, May 8, 1866, Reel 4, Volume 8, DUSC-Tampico). See also Marquis de Lafayette Lane [hereafter MDLL] to WHS, Nov. 2, 1865, Reel 9, Volume 9, DUSC-Veracruz, for a report that US deserters fought with Cortina.

102. For the bitter history between Cortina and Texans, see Collins, *Texas Devils.*

103. Sheridan, *Personal Memoirs,* 216.

104. Sheridan, *Personal Memoirs,* 224–26. For a broader discussion, see Miller, *Arms across the Border.*

105. See Miller, "The American Legion of Honor in Mexico."

106. See J. Frank Cumming to J. A. J. Creswell, Feb. 7, 1864; John A. J. Creswell Papers, LOC.

107. "An Old Timer," *Tombstone (AZ) Prospector,* Dec. 1, 1890.

108. "Samuel Brannan in Mexico," *San Francisco (CA) Evening Bulletin,* Aug. 23, 1880.

109. A. Willard to J. C. B. Davis, Mar. 16, 1870, Reel 2, Volume 2, DUSC-Guaymas.

110. Dobak, *Freedom by the Sword,* 438–39. Dobak added, "Mayer never faced punishment for his breach of neutrality" (439).

111. Lewis S. Ely [hereafter LSE] to WHS, Aug. 22, 1864, Reel 3, Volume 5, DUSC-Acapulco.

112. See *Executive Documents,* 9:42.

113. FC to WHS, Apr. 27, 1864, Reel 4, Volume 7, DUSC-Tampico. Other people had no trouble believing Mexicans would fight (see "a Matamoras letter of June 16th, to the Era, mentions the rumor that 7,000 French soldiers are on the way there from Vera Cruz. The Mexicans at Tamaulipas and Matamoras will give them a warm reception, and will fight them to the last" ("By Telegraph," *Baltimore Sun,* July 31, 1863).

114. Lucius Avery to WHS, Oct. 26, 1865, Reel 3, Volume 8, DUSC-Matamoros. See also Dobak, *Freedom by the Sword,* 451; and "From the Rio Grande," *New-York Daily Tribune,* Sept. 12, 1865.

115. Schoonover, *Mexican Lobby,* 97–98. Grant gave Mussey permission to leave the United States to serve in Mexico.

116. F. B. Elmer [hereafter FBE] to WHS, Apr. 9, 1866, Reel 1, Volume 1, DUSC–La Paz.

117. FBE to WHS, May 1, 1866, and FBE to WHS, July 3, 1866, Reel 1, Volume 1, DUSC–La Paz.

118. FBE to WHS, Reel 1, Volume 1, DUSC–La Paz.

119. Sutter Jr., *The Sutter Family,* 59.

120. Sutter Jr., *The Sutter Family,* 55. Sutter's life, like that of his famous father, has been distorted by exaggerations, tall tales, and fanciful inventions. Ottley was very careful about analyzing such stories.

121. See Sutter's angry report about Montenegro's threat to bombard Acapulco if the Liberals attacked his forces (John A. Sutter Jr to WHS, Sept. 12, 1866, Reel 3, Volume 5, DUSC-Acapulco).

122. Geo. F Bowman to WHS, Oct. 14, 1866, Reel 3, Volume 5, DUSC-Acapulco. On a note following this report, someone (Seward?) wrote: "Notify the Commercial Agent, Mr. Cole, that the public interests imperatively require his presence at his post immediately. Instruct him to report at what time he will return and on his arrival to resume charge of the post, and investigate and report to the Dept the facts and proceedings adverted to in the letter of which a copy is enclosed."

123. Geo M. Hedges [hereafter GMH] to WHS, Oct. 24, 1866, Reel 3, Volume 5, DUSC-Acapulco. See also GMH to General Montenegro, Oct. 22, 1866, enclosed in this dispatch.

124. GMH to WHS, Oct. 24, 1866, Reel 3, Volume 5, DUSC-Acapulco.

125. Gilbert M. Cole [hereafter GMC] to WHS, Oct. 28, 1866, Reel 3, Volume 5, DUSC-Acapulco.

126. GMC to WHS, Nov. 16, 1866, Reel 3, Volume 5, DUSC-Acapulco.

127. See GMC to WHS, Dec. 7, 1866, Reel 3, Volume 5, DUSC-Acapulco.

128. GMC to WHS, Feb. 23, 1867, Reel 3, Volume 5, DUSC-Acapulco.

129. GMC to WHS, May 7, 1867, Reel 3, Volume 5, DUSC-Acapulco.

130. EC to WHS, Apr. 29, 1865, Reel 1, Volume 1, DUSC-Guaymas.

131. Consular records provide an unparalleled look into the working of diplomacy, but they can be frustratingly vague. I could not find the man Conner mentioned elsewhere in the historical record.

132. The State Department removed Lewis S. Ely in 1864 and B. W. Sanders in 1865.

133. The United States prosecuted filibusterers under the Neutrality Act (see May, *Manifest Destiny's Underworld,* 52).

134. On Pan-Americanism, see Frazer, "Latin American Projects to Aid Mexico during the French Intervention."

135. ELP to Benito Juárez, Aug. 15, 1867, Plumb Papers, LOC.

3. What to the Mexican and the Argentine Is the Fourth of July?

The chapter title references Frederick Douglass's famous 1852 speech "What to the Slave Is the Fourth of July?" (see Foner, *Frederick Douglass*). My thanks to Jadwiga M. Biskupska for suggesting this title.

1. *The Assassination of Abraham Lincoln,* all quotes from 629. For slightly different wording, see G. Méndez to B. W. Sanders [hereafter BWS], July 4, 1865, Reel 2, Volume 2, DUSC-Tabasco.

2. For two considerations, see Ferris, "The Relations of the United States with South America during the American Civil War," 76; and Kelly, "The Lost Continent of Abraham Lincoln," 241. For Fourth of July celebrations in the United States, see Travers, *Celebrating the Fourth;* Waldstreicher, *In the Midst of Perpetual Fetes;* Altschuler and Blumin, *Rude Republic;* Neely Jr., *Lincoln and the Triumph of the Nation,* 9–14; and Criblez, *Parading Patriotism.*

3. See also "Later from Mexico," *Wilmington Daily Journal,* Mar. 20, 1860; "Important from Mexico," *New York Evening Post,* Mar. 20, 1860; "Mejico—Importante," *Diario de la Marina,* Mar. 23, 1860; "The Naval Action of Sixth March," *Harper's Weekly,* Mar. 31, 1860; and "Domestic Intelligence," *Harper's Weekly,* Apr. 7, 1860.

4. Franklin Chase [hereafter FC] to Lewis Cass [hereafter LC], Mar. 3, 1860, Reel 3, Volume 6, DUSC-Tampico.

5. Decree of Juan José de la Garza, July 3, 1860, Reel 3, Volume 6, DUSC-Tampico. In a letter sent the following day, Chase thanked Garza for "the honors you are now conferring upon the flag of the United States" (FC to Juan José de la Garza, July 4, 1860, Reel 3, Volume 6, DUSC-Tampico).

6. Garza's decree said nothing about a serenade by a military band. Perhaps this was a last-minute addition.

7. FC to LC, July 5, 1860, Reel 3, Volume 6, DUSC-Tampico.

8. Chase routinely criticized Garza. For instance, he complained about his arbitrary and despotic acts (FC to William L. Marcy [hereafter WLM], Feb. 21, 1856, Reel 2, Volume 4, DUSC-Tampico). He asserted that Garza committed atrocities against US citizens in Tampico (FC to LC, Apr. 27, 1858, Reel 3, Volume 5, DUSC-Tampico). He also complained that Garza extorted money from merchants (FC to John Appleton, Sept. 29, 1858, Reel 3, Volume 5, DUSC-Tampico). Chase praising Garza was a major transformation in their relationship.

9. "The United States Ship Lancaster," *New York Commercial Advertiser,* Aug. 10, 1861. See also "Gleanings by Mails," *Philadelphia (PA) Inquirer,* Aug. 12, 1861; and "The U.S. Ship Lancaster," *Dollar Newspaper* (Phildadelphia, PA), Aug. 14, 1861. I found no mention of this event in the Acapulco consular records.

10. "Letter from Mexico," *Sacramento (CA) Daily Union,* Aug. 10, 1861. Morrell did not say anything about this event in his despatches to the State Department.

11. M. M. Kimmey [hereafter MMK] to William H. Seward [hereafter WHS], Sept. 21, 1863, Reel 1, Volume 2, DUSC-Monterrey.

12. "Affairs in Mexico," *New York Herald,* Aug. 16, 1863. The italics appeared in the original version. This except came from *La Bandera.* That paper noted, "we are in receipt of full files of the *Independencia Mejicano* (Juarez news organ) from San Luis Potosi."

13. John Xantus [hereafter JX] to WHS, July 8, 1863, Reel 1, Volume 1, DUSC-Manzanillo.

14. JX to WHS, July 8, 1863, Reel 1, Volume 1, DUSC-Manzanillo.

15. In 1866, Marcus Otterbourg attempted something similar (see "Confederate Exiles Celebrating the Fourth of July," *Richmond (VA) Whig,* July 24, 1866; "Mexico," *New York Herald,* July 23, 1866; "Ah! Indeed!," *Philadelphia (PA) Inquirer,* July 24, 1866; "The Fourth of July in Mexico," *Baltimore Sun,* July 24, 1866; "Mexico," *New York World,* July 25, 1866; and "Foreign Gossip," *Chilton (WI) Times,* Aug. 11, 1866. A year earlier, Otterbourg offered to arrest rebels emigrating to Mexico (see Marcus Otterbourg to WHS, July 11, 1865, Reel 6, Volume 11, DUSC–Mexico City).

16. In 1916, San Juan Batista changed its name to Villahermosa.

17. See "unlike so many of the individuals who had represented US interests in Tabasco, he manifested an intellectual curiosity that ranged beyond scrutinizing ship manifests" (Rugeley, *The River People in Flood Time,* 250).

18. BWS to WHS, July 8, 1865, Reel 2, Volume 2, DUSC-Tabasco. See also Rugeley, *The River People in Flood Time,* 251.

19. See "however flattering to national pride, Sanders understood the self-interest behind such displays" (Rugeley, *The River People in Flood Time,* 252).

20. BWS to WHS, July 8, 1865, Reel 2, Volume 2, DUSC-Tabasco.

21. Felipe J. Serra et al, [hereafter FJS] et al., to BWS, July 4, 1865, Reel 2, Volume 2, DUSC-Tabasco.

22. BWS to FJS et al., July 4, 1865, Reel 2, Volume 2, DUSC-Tabasco.

23. BWS to FJS et al., July 4, 1865, Reel 2, Volume 2, DUSC-Tabasco.

24. Anti-Semitic comments occurred frequently during this period (see Neely Jr., *The Union Divided,* 155–58).

25. BWS to G. Méndez, July 4, 1865, Reel 2, Volume 2, DUSC-Tabasco.

26. Notation on FJS to BWS, July 4, 1865, Reel 2, Volume 2, DUSC-Tabasco.

27. The letter did not appear with the other papers from the State Department file on Tabasco.

28. BWS to WHS, Jan. 11, 1866, Reel 2, Volume 2, DUSC-Tabasco.

29. This was not the first celebration during the Era of Civil Wars and Reconstructions (see "The War in South America," *Public Ledger,* Sept. 3, 1859; and "Fourth of July at Pergamino," *The Standard,* July 26, 1864).

30. By "Provincial Government," the paper meant the government of Buenos Aires.

31. "The 4th July Banquet," *The Standard,* July 6, 1865.

32. Mitre commanded the Argentine army during the War of the Triple Alliance and could not attend.

33. "The 4th July Banquet," *The Standard,* July 6, 1865. See also Leroux, "Sarmiento's Self-Strengthening Experiment," 59.

34. This celebration appeared frequently in US newspapers (see "Fourth of July in Buenos Ayres," *New York Evening Post,* Sept. 4, 1865; "Fourth of July at Buenos Ayres," *Liberator,* Sept. 1, 1865; "From South America," *New-York Daily Tribune,* Sept. 5, 1865; "From South America," *Philadelphia [PA] Inquirer,* Sept. 5, 1865; "The Fourth of July in South America—The Celebration in Buenos Ayres," *Providence [RI] Evening Press,* Sept. 5, 1865; and *New-Orleans Times,* Sept. 15, 1865).

35. *The Standard* printed articles analyzing the meaning of the Fourth of July (see, all in *The Standard:* "The Fourth of July," July 11, 1865; "The Fourth of July, 1866," July 4, 1866; "The Fourth of July," July 4, 1867; "The Fourth of July," July 4, 1868; "Fourth of July," July 4, 1869; "The Fourth of July, 1870," July 6, 1870; "The Fourth of July," July 4, 1871; "Fourth of July," July 4, 1872; and "Fourth of July," July 4, 1874).

36. "The Fourth of July: On Board the Kate Sergent," *The Standard,* July 10, 1867.

37. "The Fourth July Celebration," *The Standard,* July 10, 1867.

38. "The Fourth of July in Rosario, Grand Banquet," *The Standard,* July 12, 1868. See also "Editor's Table," *The Standard,* July 11, 1868.

39. See also "Important from Cordoba," *The Standard,* July 11, 1871; and "Review for Europe," *The Standard,* July 15, 1873.

40. "Ninth of July in Asuncion: Grand Argentine Banquet," *The Standard,* July 23, 1869.

41. For Sarmiento's involvement in another celebration, see the conclusion to this chapter.

42. "Como las trompetas de Jericó derribaban murallas" and "desmoronarse el edificio social antiguo" (Domingo F. Sarmiento, "El 4 de Julio de los Estados Unidos," in Sarmiento, *Obras,* 22:15). Osborn hosted gatherings in previous years (see "Editor's Table," *The Standard,* July 3, 1874).

43. I agree with David M. K. Sheinin that, "although frequently punctuated by episodic conflict, the history of US-Argentine relations is one of cooperative interaction" (Sheinin, *Argentina and the United States,* 4).

44. On June 7, 1867, the *Tacony* refused to allow Antonio López de Santa Anna to land in Veracruz and use the city as the foundation of a new sphere of influence for Santa Anna (see Fowler, *Santa Anna of Mexico,* 334–35).

45. E. H. Saulnier [hereafter EHS] to WHS, July 13, 1867, Reel 10, Volume 10, DUSC-Veracruz.

46. FC to Frederick W. Seward [hereafter FWS], July 5, 1867, Reel 5, Volume 9, DUSC-Tampico. Chase did not include any decrees or correspondence with Pavón.

47. "Mexico," *New-York Tribune,* July 23, 1868. See also "Mexico," *New York Herald,* July 25, 1868.

48. "Telegraphic News from All Parts of the World," *New York Herald,* July 24, 1868.

49. "Mexico," *New York Herald,* July 25, 1868. Nebraska, the thirty-seventh state, joined the Union on March 1, 1867.

50. "Detailed News from Mexico," *Helena (MT) Weekly Herald,* July 30, 1868. See also "Mexico," *Detroit Tribune,* July 31, 1868. The only mention Commercial Agent Isaac Sisson made of a Fourth of July celebration was in 1867 (see IS to FWS, Aug. 15, 1867, Reel 3, Volume 3, DUSC-Mazatlán).

51. "Mexico," *Philadelphia (PA) Inquirer,* Aug. 21, 1868; italics in original.

52. Charles Moye [hereafter CM] to Hamilton Fish [hereafter HF], July 5, 1869, Reel 1, Volume 1, DUSC-Chihuahua.

53. "Mexico," *Cincinnati Commercial Tribune,* July 23, 1869. See also "Mexico," *Boston Daily Advertiser,* July 23, 1869.

54. "Mexico," *New York Herald,* July 25, 1869. See also "Mexico," *New York Herald,* July 18, 1869.

55. Julius Noureau [hereafter JN] to Hon. Second Assistant Secretary of State, Jan. 10, 1872, Reel 1, DUSC–San Luis Potosi.

56. JN to William Hunter [hereafter WH], July 10, 1872, Reel 1, DUSC–San Luis Potosi. When Noureau resigned his position in 1873, the Commercial Agency closed until 1882, precluding further comments about July Fourth celebrations in San Luis Potosí.

57. General M. de la Peña to Warner P. Sutton [hereafter WPS], July 3, 1880, Reel 6, Volume 15, DUSC-Matamoros.

58. WPS to General M. de la Peña, July 8, 1880, Reel 6, Volume 15, DUSC-Matamoros. There is no indication why Sutton did not respond until July 8.

59. WPS to WH, July 14, 1880, Reel 6, Volume 15, DUSC-Matamoros.

60. A. Willard [hereafter AW] to J. C. B. Davis, July 6, 1869, Reel 2, Volume 2, DUSC-Guaymas.

61. AW to HF, July 5, 1870, Reel 2, Volume 2, DUSC-Guaymas.

62. "Los convidados manifestaron en elocuentes frases de sincera amistad sus simpatías por el pueblo gigante que marcha á la cabeza de la civilización" and "Willard expresó sus ardientes deseos de ver á México grande y feliz" ("El Dia 4 del Corriente," *La Asociación del Pueblo,* July 15, 1870, Reel 2, Volume 2, DUSC-Guaymas).

63. "Durante la comida hubo mil muestras" and "de mútuas simpatías y sincera amistad, probando con esto una vez más la perfecta armonía que existe entre los ciudadanos de ambas repúblicas" ("El Dia 4 del Corriente," *La Asociación del Pueblo,* July 15, 1870, Reel 2, Volume 2, DUSC-Guaymas).

64. AW to WH, July 6, 1871, Reel 2, Volume 2, DUSC-Guaymas. See also AW to WH, July 7, 1872, AW to WH, July 6, 1874, and AW to WH, July 6, 1875, all in Reel 3, Volume 3, DUSC-Guaymas.

65. AW to WH, July 5, 1873, Reel 3, Volume 3, DUSC-Guaymas.

66. A. F. Garrison [hereafter AFG] to WH, July 10, 1876, Reel 4, Volume 4, DUSC-Guaymas.

67. AW to WH, July 5, 1880, Reel 5, Volume 5, DUSC-Guaymas. See also AW to WH, July 6, 1877, AW to WH, July 5, 1878, and AW to WH, July 5, 1879, all in Reel 4, Volume 4, DUSC-Guaymas.

68. AW to WH, Feb. 23, 1872, Reel 2, Volume 2, DUSC-Guaymas. See Young, "Red Men, Princess Pocahontas, and George Washington," for Washington's Birthday in a border town several decades later.

69. AFG to WH, Mar. 10, 1873, Reel 3, Volume 3, DUSC-Guaymas.

70. AW to WH, Feb. 23, 1875, Reel 3, Volume 3, DUSC-Guaymas; AW to WH, Feb. 23, 1876, Reel 4, Volume 4, DUSC-Guaymas; and AW to WH, Mar. 5, 1867, Reel 4, Volume 4, DUSC-Guaymas.

71. See chapter 7.

72. Blum, *Reforging the White Republic*, 215.

73. Doyle and Pamplona, *Nationalism in the New World*, argued that the Americas have been neglected in discussions of nationalism and that the American experience can benefit a general understanding of nationalism. This chapter proposes a way that nationalism in the Americas might contribute to a discussion of nationalism more generally.

74. Xenophobia and nativism were also issues in Argentina (see Lynch, *Massacre in the Pampas*). However, anti-US sentiment in the pre-1861 period was not nearly as strong in Argentina as it was in Mexico.

75. George L. MacManus [hereafter GLM] to LC, Jan. 28, 1859, Reel 1, Volume 1, DUSC-Chihuahua.

76. GLM to LC, July 12, 1859, Reel 1, Volume 1, DUSC-Chihuahua.

77. General James H. Carleton denounced McManus as a traitor with "open and avowed secession proclivities" (James H. Carleton to WHS, Feb. 20, 1863, Reel 1, Volume 1, DUSC-Chihuahua).

78. See Reuben W. Creel to WHS, Mar. 6, 1865, Reel 1, Volume 1, DUSC-Chihuahua.

79. See Joseph Knotts to WH, no date, and Louis H. Scott to WH, Apr. 4, 1877, Reel 1, Volume 2, DUSC-Chihuahua.

80. Charles P. Stone to LC, Jan. 17, 1859, Reel 1, Volume 1, DUSC-Guaymas.

81. Farrelly Alden [hereafter FA] to Captain William D. Porter [hereafter WDP], Oct. 25, 1859, Reel 1, Volume 1, DUSC-Guaymas.

82. FA to WDP, Nov. 18, 1859, Reel 1, Volume 1, DUSC-Guaymas.

83. FA to WDP, Nov. 21, 1859, Reel 1, Volume 1, DUSC-Guaymas.

84. William L. Baker to WHS, Nov. 18, 1861, Reel 1, Volume 1, DUSC-Guaymas.

85. Rollin C. M. Hoyt to HF, Feb. 24, 1871, Reel 1, Volume 2, DUSC-Minatitlan.

86. John A. Wolf to Hon. Second Assistant Secretary of State, Sept. 18, 1872, Reel 2, Volume 2, DUSC-Minatitlan.

87. During the US Civil War, Governor Santiago Vidaurri enacted friendly policies toward rebels (see MMK to WHS, Sept. 21, 1863, Reel 1, Volume 1, DUSC-Monterrey; and Tyler, *Santiago Vidaurri and the Southern Confederacy*).

88. Joseph Ulrich to Hon Second Assistant Secretary of State, July 12, 1873, Reel 2, Volume 3, DUSC-Monterrey. Ulrich warned that these attacks were a portent of things to come.

89. John Weber [hereafter JW] to WH, July 16, 1877, Reel 3, Volume 4, DUSC-Monterrey. The Know-Nothings, a US nativist political party, won impressive victories in the mid-1850s.

90. JW to WH, Aug. 16, 1879, Reel 3, Volume 4, DUSC-Monterrey.

91. Thomas Sprague [hereafter TS] to WLM, Apr. 7, 1856, Reel 1, Volume 1, DUSC–La Paz.

92. TS to WLM, June 26, 1856, Reel 1, Volume 1, DUSC–La Paz.

93. F. B. Elmer [hereafter FBE] to WHS, Sept. 30, 1863, Reel 1, Volume 1, DUSC–La Paz.

94. FBE to WHS, Mar. 3, 1865, Reel 1, Volume 1, DUSC–La Paz.

95. FBE to WHS, Apr. 10, 1867, Reel 1, Volume 1, DUSC–La Paz.

96. David Turner [hereafter DT] to Hon. Second Asst. Secretary of State, Jan. 30, 1871, Reel 2, Volume 2, DUSC–La Paz.

97. DT to Hon. Second Asst. Secretary of State, May 29, 1875, Reel 2, Volume 2, DUSC–La Paz. Turner included the translation in his despatch.

98. DT to Hon. Second Asst. Secretary of State, July 19, 1875, Reel 2, Volume 2, DUSC–La Paz.

99. For nativism and xenophobia during US Reconstruction, see Paddison, *American Heathens*; Bottoms: *An Aristocracy of Color*; and Smith, *Freedom's Frontier*.

100. Criblez, *Parading Patriotism*, noted that foreigners in the US Midwest, usually Germans, but sometimes Irish, faced threats from nativist mobs.

101. FJS et al, to BWS July 4, 1865, Reel 2, Volume 2, DUSC-Tabasco.

102. "Fourth of July in Chile," *The Standard*, July 6, 1873.

4. Visions of the Victors

1. "Educar la masa de la población suramericana, es mi empresa" (Domingo Faustino Sarmiento [hereafter DFS], "Estado de las Repúblicas Sudamericanas á Mediados del Siglo," in Sarmiento, *Obras*, 16:92, 91). For similar language in reference to the United States, see McDaniel, *The Problem of Democracy*, 110.

2. For Sarmiento and education, see Leroux, "Sarmiento's Self-Strengthening Experiment"; and Rothera, "Our South American Cousin." For education and reform, see Butler, "Lincoln as the Great Educator."

3. For transnational and global history, see Tyrrell, "American Exceptionalism in an Age of International History"; McGerr, "The Price of the 'New Transnational History'"; Tyrrell, "Ian Tyrrell Responds"; Thelen, "Of Audiences, Borderlands, and Comparisons"; Fredrickson, "From Exceptionalism to Variability"; Bender, *Rethinking American History in a Global Age*; Seigel, "Beyond Compare"; "AHR Conversation: On Transnational History"; Tyrrell, "Reflections on the Transnational Turn in United States History: Theory and Practice"; Zimmerman, *Alabama in Africa*; "Forum: Teaching the Civil War Era in Global Context: A Discussion"; and "Interchange: Globalizations and Its Limits between the American Revolution and the Civil War."

4. For an early discussion of South Americans and Reconstruction, see Bernstein, "South America Looks at North American Reconstruction." For analysis of a broader community of reformers, see McDaniel, *The Problem of Democracy*.

5. *Harper's Weekly* quoted in Butler, *Critical Americans*, 89.

6. For education and political parties in the United States, see Baker, *Affairs of Party*. For an overview covering the antebellum period, see Neem, *Democracy's Schools*. There are far too many studies of education in all three countries to cite in this note.

7. "Editor's Table," *The Standard*, Feb. 23, 1881. Lewis Hanke proclaimed that Sarmiento would always be remembered as "'a soldier in the never-ceasing battle for the liberty of men's

minds,' who considered the schoolroom the most important battlefield in America" (Hanke, *South America*, 76). Although the scholarly literature concerning Sarmiento is vast, his biographers have yet to appreciate the ways that a specific pattern of developments in the United States influenced him (see Guerra, *Sarmiento: Sus Vidas i sus Obras*; Rojas, *El Profeta de la Pampa*, 525; Correas, *Sarmiento and the United States*; Bunkley, *Vida de Sarmiento*; and Campobassi, *Sarmiento y su época*). Two exceptions are Rippy, "Yankee Teachers and the Founding of Argentina's Elementary School System"; and Dorn, "Sarmiento, the United States, and Public Education."

8. As a young man, Sarmiento read widely in an attempt to better his situation (see Sarmiento, *Obras*, 3:1–346).

9. See Rock, *Argentina*. The centralist/federalist division in Argentine politics appeared in Mexican and US politics as well. For Mexico, see Hale, *Mexican Liberalism in the Age of Mora*. In the United States, Federalists, Whigs, and Republicans often opted for a stronger central government, whereas Jeffersonian Republicans and Democrats usually favored a weaker central government and stronger state governments. However, examples exist of Federalists, Whigs, and Republicans preferring a weaker central government and Jeffersonian Republicans and Democrats embracing a stronger one (see Karp, *This Vast Southern Empire*, for analysis of how slaveholders, supposedly proponents of limited government, created an aggressive foreign policy of slavery).

10. Both sides frequently referred to the other as "savages" (see de la Fuente, *Children of Facundo*).

11. See Lynch, *Argentine Dictator*.

12. Most Argentine historians contend that, after 1861, the old labels (Unitarios and Federales) fell into disfavor. De la Fuente's *Children of Facundo* argued that the old labels persisted.

13. "El mas bárbaro representante de la barbarie" ("Edificios y fondos de Escuelas," in Sarmiento, *Obras*, 24:173).

14. Sarmiento's reading included Benjamin Franklin's autobiography and works by John Stuart Mill. Importantly, Sarmiento did not agree with Mill on every point. In *On Liberty*, Mill argued for mandatory education but also wrote that "if the government would make up its mind to *require* for every child a good education, it might save itself the trouble of *providing* one" (Mill, *On Liberty*, 190). Sarmiento firmly believed the government should play an active role in providing education and creating good citizens.

15. Characterizing the political ideology of the Federales is not easy. Burns, *The Poverty of Progress*, called them populists and folk leaders. Lynch, *Argentine Dictator*, argued the opposite. Shumway, *The Invention of Argentina*, illustrated many varieties of Federalism.

16. See Oria, "La literatura argentina durante la época de Rosas"; and Katra, *The Argentine Generation of 1837*.

17. "Centenares de alumnos arjentinos cuentan en su seno los colejios de Francia, Chile, Brasil, Norte-América, Inglaterra, i aun España. Ellos volverán luego a realizar en su patria las instituciones que ven brillar en todos esos Estados libres; i pondrán su hombro para derrocar al tirano semi-bárbaro" (Sarmiento, *Obras*, 7:224).

18. Sarmiento quoted in Bailey and Nasatir, *Latin America*, 394–95.

19. *Life in the Argentine Republic in the Days of Tyrants*, 272.

20. "La instrucción primaria es la medida de la civilización de un pueblo. Donde es incompleta, donde yace abandonada . . . hay un pueblo semi bárbaro, sin luces, sin costumbres, sin industria, sin progresos" (Sarmiento, *Obras*, 28:28). See also Sarmiento, *Obras*, 28:69, 215, 283, 372, and 367.

21. Helper, *The Impending Crisis of the South.*

22. Sumner, *The Barbarism of Slavery;* Higginson, *Out-Door Papers,* 108–9.

23. See Basler, *Collected Works,* 2:121–32; 3:1–37; 5:198 and 518–37; 6:537; and 8:183–84.

24. See "Civilization and Barbarism," *Baltimore Gazette and Daily Advertiser,* Jan. 1, 1831; "The Barbarism of the Day," *Albany (NY) Evening Journal,* July 28, 1857; *Public Ledger,* Aug. 13, 1861; and *New York Herald,* Dec. 5, 1861.

25. For useful discussions see Mazlish, *Civilization and Its Contents;* and Bowden, *The Empire of Civilization.*

26. Because *Facundo* was published in 1845 and not translated into English until 1868, scholars assume people in the United States did not know about it. However, David T. Haberly argued that an article about gauchos published in the *Atlantic Monthly* in 1858 communicated the gist of *Facundo* to the US reading public (see Haberly, "Facundo in the United States").

27. See "Chile," *El Siglo Diez y Nueve,* July 28, 1844; and "Ortografía Chilena," *El Comercio,* Aug. 31, 1844.

28. "He visto sus millones de campesinos, proletarios i artesanos viles, degradados, indignos de ser contados entre los hombres" (Sarmiento, *Obras,* 5:384).

29. "¿Por qué no vemos levantarse de nuevo el jenio de la civilizacion europea, que brillaba ántes" (Sarmiento, *Obras,* 7:179). James Sanders noted that letrados like Sarmiento "tended to look to Europe for validation," which was true of Sarmiento's early years but not of the post-1848 period, when he found much more to admire in the United States (Sanders, *Vanguard of the Atlantic World,* 146).

30. See Sarmiento, *Travels in the United States in 1847.*

31. "El gran reformador de la educacion primaria. Viajero como yo en busca de métodos i sistemas por Europa" (Sarmiento, *Obras,* 5:446–48).

32. Mary Mann noted, years later, that Sarmiento "could not speak English then and I talked with him in French one whole day" (see Mary Mann to Henry Barnard, July 21, 1865, in Luiggi, "Some Letters of Sarmiento and Mary Mann," 189).

33. Sarmiento, *Obras,* 29:446–50.

34. Sarmiento, *Obras,* 5:446.

35. By this point, Sarmiento spoke English and did not have to converse in French (see Mary Mann to Henry Barnard, Sept. 18, 1866, in Luiggi, "Some Letters of Sarmiento and Mary Mann," 198).

36. See Genova, "Sarmiento's *Vida de Horacio Mann.*"

37. "Que completaron la Independencia proclamada en 1776, por la libertad del esclavo y la educacion del pueblo" (Sarmiento, *Obras,* 22:20). See the discussion of this celebration in chapter 3.

38. "Hace tiempo que una de las preocupaciones del público es la mejora de las escuelas" ("Edificios de escuelas," in Sarmiento, *Obras,* 18:162).

39. Shumway, *The Invention of Argentina,* 81.

40. Shumway, *The Invention of Argentina,* 85.

41. Szuchman, "Childhood Education and Politics in Nineteenth-Century Argentina," 119–20.

42. "La tendencia de las reformas modernas en el sistema de escuelas se dirige á ocupar mas mujeres que hombres en la enseñanza porque cuestan menos y son mas aptas que los hom-

bres para manejar niños pequeños" ("Beneficencia Pública," July 16, 1856, in Sarmiento, *Obras,* 24:373).

43. "Educar á los pueblos bien y barato es hacerlo por medio de la mujer" and "Se puede utilizar creando un medio de educación para todos los niños en general" ("La caridad y el estado," Oct. 19, 1857, in Sarmiento, *Obras,* 18:128).

44. "Un día ha de llegar en que en una escuela de varones y de mujeres se enseñe todo por mujeres," Oct. 19, 1857, in Sarmiento, *Obras,* 18:128).

45. See Sklar, *Catharine Beecher;* and Boydston, Kelley, and Margolis, *The Limits of Sisterhood.*

46. See Mann, *A Few Thoughts on the Powers and Duties of Women,* 65; and Mann, *Life of Horace Mann,* 424.

47. DFS to Benjamin C. Yancey [hereafter BCY], July 18, 1859, Benjamin C. Yancey Papers, SHC, UNC-CH.

48. BCY to DFS, July 19, 1859, Yancey Papers.

49. Numerous scholars have analyzed the connection between education and citizenship (see Boonshoft, *Aristocratic Education,* 49).

50. "Governor's Message," *San Francisco (CA) Evening Bulletin,* Jan. 6, 1859.

51. "Education of the Masses," *Austin (TX) State Gazette,* Aug. 20, 1859. Some people worried that the wrong type of education, such as too much emphasis on "foreign literature" and the history of other countries, would produce mediocre citizens (see "American Education," *New Orleans (LA) Daily Picayune,* Dec. 26, 1844).

52. See Schwaller, *The Church in Colonial Latin America;* and Schwaller, *The History of the Catholic Church in Latin America.*

53. Schweiger, "The Literate South: Reading before Emancipation," table 2, 333.

54. See "Governor's Message," *The Crisis,* Jan. 9, 1862.

55. See "Address of Mr. Wise to His Constituents," *Baltimore Sun,* Feb. 29, 1844.

56. Schweiger, "The Literate South," 333.

57. Schweiger, "The Literate South," 333. The fact that the literacy rate was this high among enslaved people was impressive, given widespread opposition to literate slaves.

58. See Sumner, *The Barbarism of Slavery.*

59. Douglass, *My Bondage and My Freedom,* 151–62.

60. McPherson, *The Political History of the United States of America, during the Great Rebellion,* 286. The House of Representatives passed Crittenden's resolution, and the Senate passed a resolution offered by Senator Andrew Johnson of Tennessee with very similar wording.

61. See, for example, Berlin, Fields, Miller, Reidy, and Rowland, *Slaves No More;* Williams, *I Freed Myself;* and Reidy, *Illusions of Emancipation.*

62. See Manning, *Troubled Refuge;* Silkenat, *Driven from Home;* and Taylor, *Embattled Freedom.*

63. Butler, *Butler's Book,* 209–10.

64. Butler, *Butler's Book,* 256–64.

65. Frederick Douglass, "How to End the War," *Douglass' Monthly,* May 1861.

66. Frederick Douglass, "Men of Color, To Arms!," *Douglass' Monthly,* Mar. 1863. See also Emberton, "Only Murder Makes Men."

67. See McPherson, *The Negro's Civil War;* Cornish, *The Sable Arm;* Glatthaar, *Forged in Bat-*

tle; Berlin, Reidy, and Rowland, *Freedom's Soldiers;* Smith, *Black Soldiers in Blue;* Wilson, *Campfires of Freedom;* Reid, *Freedom for Themselves;* and Egerton, *Thunder at the Gates.*

68. See Taylor, *Embattled Freedom,* 41.

69. For a recent study of movement in the Southern states during the US Civil War, see Sternhell, *Routes of War.*

70. For the classic study, see Powell, *New Masters.* For other discussions, see Smith, *The Enemy Within,* 154–74 and Frazier, *Blood on the Bayou.*

71. The military contained people with very different mind-sets, although even those who never abandoned their racial prejudices could still be liberators (see Teters, *Practical Liberators*).

72. See Eaton, *Grant, Lincoln and the Freedmen* for the reminiscences of John Eaton, one of the most important and sympathetic officials toward the freedpeople.

73. See Faulkner, *Women's Radical Reconstruction.*

74. For Northern abolitionists and the freedpeople, see Schwalm, *A Hard Fight for We;* and Hunter, *Bound in Wedlock.*

75. Rose, *Rehearsal for Reconstruction;* Saville, *The Work of Reconstruction;* Click, *Time Full of Trial;* Taylor, *Embattled Freedom.*

76. "The Contrabands at Fortress Monroe," *New Hampshire Sentinel,* Nov. 14, 1861.

77. Sanders, *Vanguard of the Atlantic World,* 129.

78. For discussions of education during this period, see Kolchin, *First Freedom,* 79–106; Morris, *Reading, 'Riting, and Reconstruction;* Anderson, *The Education of Blacks in the South;* Jones, *Soldiers of Light and Love;* Williams, "Commenced to Think Like a Man"; Williams, *Self-Taught;* Span, *From Cotton Field to Schoolhouse;* Butchart, *Schooling the Freed People;* and Behrend, *Reconstructing Democracy.*

79. Jones, *Soldiers of Light and Love,* both quotes on 3.

80. Green, *Educational Reconstruction,* 16. See Heinrich and Harding, *From Slave to Statesman,* for an African American teacher in Virginia.

81. See, for example, "Normal School for Negroes," *Flake's Bulletin,* Dec. 14, 1866.

82. See Mary Mann to Henry Barnard, July 21, 1865, and Mary Mann to Henry Barnard, July 21, 1865, in Luiggi, "Some Letters of Sarmiento and Mary Mann," 188–89 and 189.

83. Sarmiento sent Henry Barnard a copy of *Facundo* published in French (see DFS to Henry Barnard, July 28, 1865, in Luiggi, "Some Letters of Sarmiento and Mary Mann," 190–91).

84. "Al día siguiente comí con Waldo Emerson, á quien había mandado el *Facundo.* Este libro me sirve de medio de introducción. Si ser Ministro no vale para todos, ser educacionista es ya un gran título á la benevolencia de este pueblo de profesores y de maestros; pero todavía me queda en reserva el *Facundo* que es mi cañón Parrot. Nada le resiste" (DFS to Señora Aurelia Velez, Oct. 15, 1865, in Sarmiento, *Obras,* 29:67).

85. See Rockland, *Travels in the United States in 1847,* 51. Mary Mann commented, in the preface to her translation of *Facundo,* that "when R. W. Emerson read the book, he told Colonel Sarmiento that if he would write thus for our public, he would be read" (Mann, *Life in the Argentine Republic,* xii).

86. "La Atenas americana" (DFS to Señora doña Juana Manso, June 10, 1865, in Sarmiento, *Obras,* 29:36). This phrase was not unique to Sarmiento (see "Miscellany," *The Farmer's Cabinet,* Nov. 14, 1844; "The Great New England Wide Awake Demonstration," *Providence (RI) Evening Press,* Oct. 17, 1860; and Caroline Winterer, *The Culture of Classicism*).

87. Sarmiento was also interested in other elements of Reconstruction (see "Reconstruccion del Sur" and "Irradiacion de Civilizacion," in Sarmiento, *Obras*, 29:120–27, 128–37, two articles he wrote for *El Zonda* in 1866).

88. Behrend, *Reconstructing Democracy*, 121; see also 2–3, 8–9, 45, 59, and 130.

89. "Han nombrado *superintendentes* de la *aid societies* en el Sud, y estos calculado que se necesitan por lo pronto *quince mil escuelas* y *quince mil maestras*, y todas las sociedades se han puesto en movimiento para obtenerlas . . . Ya se han contratado *ochocientas maestras*, ciento cincuenta de ellas costeadas y contratadas por la de New York solamente" (DFS to Señora doña Juana Manso, June 10, 1865, in Sarmiento, *Obras*, 29:35–36). For more on Juana Manso, see Guerrero, *Mujeres de Sarmiento*, 75–105; and Fletcher, "Juana Manso," 108–20.

90. "Una niña se trasladó á la Carolina del Sur y se puso ella sola al frente de una plantación de algodón de trescientos negros á quienes no solamente educaba sino que les enseñaba el ejercicio de las armas sin perder nunca su prestigio de señorita" (DFS to Señora Juana Manso, Oct. 15, 1867, in Sarmiento, *Obras*, 29:220).

91. "Mientras se debate esta cuestión, *quince mil escuelas*, que los domingos serán dominicales para adultos, habrán en pocos años borrados el pecado original de la absoluta ignorancia en el Sur, y los negros libertos estarán luego más adelantados que nosotros blancos" (Sarmiento, *Obras*, 29:37).

92. "Cien niñas bostonianas, á la cabeza de otras tantas escuelas en Buenos Aires, ó en las Provincias, crearían todo el sistema de enseñanza de Massachusetts, con su eficiencia, su extensión y su realidad" (DFS to Señora Doña María Manso, Apr. 21, 1865, in Sarmiento, *Obras*, 29:23).

93. "No sería hermoso espectáculo . . . ver llegar á Buenos Aires . . . cuarenta muchachas rubias, modestas sin gazmoñería, virtuosas, de esa virtud práctica, útil, social, que prepara una madre á una familia futura, maestras de escuela, bostonianas, colonas de educación y de republicanismo" (DFS to Señora Doña María Manso, Apr. 21, 1865, in Sarmiento, *Obras* 29:25).

94. See Taylor, *Reminiscences of My Life in Camp*; Stevenson, *The Journals of Charlotte Forten Grimké*; and Stevenson, "Considering the War from Home and the Front."

95. Jones, "Civilization and Barbarism and Sarmiento's Indian Policy," 41.

96. See Rothera, "Our South American Cousin." For Hotze, see Bonner, "Slavery, Confederate Diplomacy, and the Racialist Mission of Henry Hotze."

97. Taylor, *Embattled Freedom*, 190.

98. Green, *Educational Reconstruction*, offered numerous evidences proving this point.

99. "Setecientas maestras norte americanas en la República Argentina ó en Chile, repararían en diez años el estrago de tres siglos" (DFS to Señor Redactor de "La Patria" de Valparaíso, Oct. 1, 1865, in Sarmiento, *Obras*, 30:78–79.

100. Rojas, "Presidencia Sarmiento. Vicepresidencia Adolfo Alsina."

101. Luiggi, *65 Valiants*, 17. See also "Compulsory Education," *Springfield (OH) Globe-Republic*, Nov. 13, 1886; "South American Women," *New York Tribune*, Apr. 14, 1901; "Many School Teachers," *El Paso (TX) Herald*, May 1, 1915; and "Teachers' Exploit of '80s is Recalled," *New York Times*, Aug. 6, 1933. This number did not match Sarmiento's optimistic estimate of seven hundred teachers because Sarmiento had high standards and wanted a certain type of woman to teach (blond, white, and young). In addition, some women decided, upon further reflection, that teaching in Argentina would not work for them.

102. See table 1.4 in Engerman and Sokoloff, *Economic Development in the Americas Since 1500*, 28–29.

103. Hale, *Mexican Liberalism in the Age of Mora*.

104. Thomson and LaFrance, *Patriotism, Politics, and Popular Liberalism in Nineteenth-Century Mexico*, 19.

105. See Sinkin, *The Mexican Reform*.

106. Sinkin, *The Mexican Reform*.

107. See Vaughan, *The State, Education, and Social Class in Mexico*; Hale, *The Transformation of Liberalism in Late Nineteenth-Century Mexico*; Vaughan, *Cultural Politics in Revolution*; and Dawson, *Indian and Nation in Revolutionary Mexico*.

108. See Bailey, *¡Viva Cristo Rey!*; Meyer, *The Cristero Rebellion*; and Stauffer, *Victory on Earth or in Heaven*.

109. See Kurtz, *Excommunicated from the Union*. For Catholic service during the US Civil War, see Conyngham, *Soldiers of the Cross*.

110. Nast published two versions of this cartoon. "The American River Ganges" (*Harper's Weekly*, Sept. 30, 1871) included several figures from New York City's Tweed Ring where "The American River Ganges" (*Harper's Weekly*, May 8, 1875) replaced them with generic figures.

111. See Holt, *By One Vote*, 50–53 and 140–42.

112. Pope Pius IX was widely condemned as one of the most reactionary popes. His reign "would be remembered as a rebellion against everything modern" (Doyle, *The Cause of All Nations*, 262).

113. Szurmuk, *Women in Argentina*, 128n2.

114. See Verhoeven, *Transnational Anti-Catholicism*. For Bismarck, see Efford, *German Immigrants, Race, and Citizenship in the Civil War Era*.

115. "Argentine Schools," *New York-Herald Tribune*, July 30, 1889.

116. Bayly, *The Birth of the Modern World*, 317. See also "A Sacrilegious Act in Buenos Ayres Holy Week," *Irish World and American Industrial Liberator*, June 2, 1894.

117. Crowley, *Domingo Faustino Sarmiento*.

118. "La Base de la democracia," in Sarmiento, *Obras* 29:232.

119. Teachers in the United States who taught freedpeople encountered opposition from many white southerners because of their objectives, not their religious backgrounds (see Rose, *Rehearsal for Reconstruction*; and Zuczek, *State of Rebellion*). Disagreements among Protestant denominations frequently occurred in the United States.

120. See Taylor, *The Transportation Revolution: 1815–1860*; Sellers, *The Market Revolution*; John, *Spreading the News*; Stokes and Conway, *The Market Revolution in America*; Larson, *Internal Improvement*; and Howe, *What Hath God Wrought*.

121. For a recent discussion of internal improvement, see Prior, *Between Freedom and Progress*.

122. Crassweller, *Perón and the Enigmas of Argentina*, 42.

123. Hodge, "Benjamin Apthorp Gould and the Founding of the Argentine National Observatory."

124. Oszlak, *La formación del estado argentino*.

125. Rock, *Argentina*, 145.

126. William Wheelwright to the Secretary of State, Apr. 10, 1869, Reel 1, Volume 1, DUSC-Rosario.

127. See Curry, *Blueprint for Modern America;* and Richardson, *The Greatest Nation of the Earth.*

128. The Revenue Act authorized a 3 percent tax on incomes above eight hundred dollars; the Legal Tender Act created "greenbacks"; the Homestead Act made homesteads of 160 acres available at low cost; and the Revenue Act of 1862 established the office of the Commissioner of Internal Revenue, levied excise taxes, and created a progressive income tax.

129. See Foner, *Reconstruction;* and Summers, *The Ordeal of the Reunion.*

130. See White, *Railroaded,* 37–38.

131. Matías Romero al Secretario de Relaciones Exteriores, Marzo 22 de 1882, Caja 2, Expediente 9, Relaciones Exteriores, 1882 Marzo, 50, AGN, Mexico City.

132. Wasserman, *Everyday Life and Politics in Nineteenth-Century Mexico.*

133. A. Willard to William Hunter, Mar. 31, 1873, Reel 3, Volume 3, DUSC-Guaymas. For additional discussion of railroads and mines, see Truett, *Fugitive Landscapes*

134. See Helper, *The Impending Crisis of the South;* Fredrickson, introduction to *The Impending Crisis of the South;* Bailey, *Hinton Rowan Helper;* and Brown, *Southern Outcast.*

135. "New Publications," *Daily Inter Ocean,* July 16, 1881. See also "The News in Brief," *Philadelphia (PA) Inquirer,* Oct. 7, 1881. For a scathing attack against the project, see "The Three Americas," *Dallas (TX) Weekly Herald,* Mar. 23, 1882.

136. See Hinton Rowan Helper to Señor Romero, Mar. 15, 1882, and Matías Romero to Hinton Rowan Helper, Mar. 22, 1882, in Caja 2, Expediente 9, Relaciones Exteriores, 1882 Marzo, 50, AGN, Mexico City. For additional discussion of the railroad, see also M. Romero al Secretario de Relaciones Exteriores, Junio 14 de 1882, in Caja 2, Expediente 19, Relaciones Exteriores, 1882, 432, AGN, Mexico City.

137. Hobsbawm, *The Age of Capital: 1848–1875,* 29–68.

138. See Sinkin, *The Mexican Reform.* For Indigenous challenges to and appropriations of Liberal policies, see Mallon, *Peasant and Nation;* and Thomson and La France, *Patriotism, Politics, and Popular Liberalism in Nineteenth-Century Mexico.*

139. See Beck, *Columns of Vengeance;* Kelman, *A Misplaced Massacre;* Lahti, *Wars for Empire;* and Lahti, *Soldiers in the Southwest Borderlands.*

140. See Genetin-Pilawa, *Crooked Paths to Allotment.*

141. James H. Bell to B. H. Epperson, Feb. 22, 1865, Box 2D106, Benjamin Holland Epperson Papers; Briscoe Center, UTA.

142. Tocqueville, *"Democracy in America" and Two Essays on America,* 264.

143. Downs, "The Mexicanization of American Politics." For additional discussion of this issue, see also Pike, *The United States and Latin America* and chap. 5 of this book.

144. Edward Lee Plumb to Charles Sumner, July 26, 1867, Volume 7, Plumb Papers, LOC.

145. Bolton, "The Epic of Greater America."

5. The Problem of Order (Not Mexicanization)

1. "The South American Louisiana," *Chicago Tribune,* Oct. 16, 1874.

2. See chapter 7 for discussion of both episodes.

3. Comparative analysis of violence, disorder, and politics is largely absent in the scholarly

literature discussing the United States during Reconstruction. James K. Hogue commented that "Louisiana in 1877 resembled the new Latin American republics in their first generation after independence," but he did not develop this observation (Hogue, *Uncivil War,* 177). See also Elliott, "Nation-Building Begins at Home." Tunnell, *Crucible of Reconstruction* and Nystrom, *New Orleans after the Civil War,* did not mention violence in Argentina.

4. For a recent treatment of violence and US Reconstruction, see Egerton, *The Wars of Reconstruction.*

5. There are many fine studies of violence during and after US Reconstruction, but they rarely look beyond the borders of the United States. See Rable, *But There Was No Peace;* Williams, *The Great South Carolina Ku Klux Klan Trials 1871–1872;* Hahn, *A Nation under Our Feet;* Lemann, *Redemption;* Martinez, *Carpetbaggers, Cavalry, and the Ku Klux Klan;* Budiansky, *The Bloody Shirt;* Keith, *The Colfax Massacre;* Lane, *The Day Freedom Died;* Williams, *They Left Great Marks on Me;* Emberton, *Beyond Redemption;* Downs, *After Appomattox;* and Parsons, *Ku-Klux.*

6. Zarco cited in Sanders, *Vanguard of the Atlantic World,* 134.

7. Sanders, *Vanguard of the Atlantic World,* 149.

8. For a recent discussion, see Downs, "The Mexicanization of American Politics."

9. Cited in Lang, *Contest of Civilizations,* 137

10. Worth cited in Lang, *Contest of Civilizations,* 380

11. "Arrest Them!," *Dallas (TX) Weekly Herald,* Jan. 13, 1877.

12. "What Is 'Mexicanization'?" *The Nation,* Dec. 21, 1876, 365.

13. "What Is 'Mexicanization'?" *The Nation,* Dec. 21, 1876, 365.

14. "What Is 'Mexicanization'?" *The Nation,* Dec. 21, 1876, 365–66, quote on 366.

15. See Lynch, *Caudillos in Spanish America,* for order and caudillos in Latin America. See Graham, *Patronage and Politics in Nineteenth-Century Brazil* for the problem of order in Brazil. See Lynch, *Argentine Dictator;* de la Fuente, *Children of Facundo;* Salvatore, *Wandering Paysanos;* Sabato, *The Many and the Few;* Lynch, *Massacre in the Pampas;* Adelman, *Republic of Capital;* and Oszlak, *La formación del estado argentino* for the problem of order in Argentina. See Perry, *Juárez and Díaz;* Sinkin, *The Mexican Reform;* and Berry, *The Reform in Oaxaca* for the problem of order in Mexico.

16. For excellent analysis of the US election of 1876, see Holt, *By One Vote.*

17. For discussion of pronunciamientos, see Fowler, *Forceful Negotiations;* Fowler, *Malcontents, Rebels, and Pronunciados;* Fowler, *Celebrating Insurrection;* and Fowler, *Independent Mexico.*

18. Julius Noureau to William Hunter, Apr. 7, 1871, Reel 1, DUSC–San Luis Potosi.

19. Fowler, *Malcontents,* x. See also Sabato, *Republics of the New World,* 112.

20. Fowler, *Malcontents,* xxiv.

21. Erika Pani, "Intervention and Empire: Politics as Usual," in Fowler, *Malcontents,* 251.

22. Argentina has provinces, whereas the United States and Mexico have states. The title of this section references US Congressman Thaddeus Stevens's idea about Reconstruction. Stevens believed rebel states were "conquered provinces" and could be treated any way the victors liked. Some Argentines also subscribed to the idea that conquered provinces could be treated differently and that interventions, in the name of liberty, were not a bad idea.

23. "Un ave fénix parecía renacer de las cenizas de la guerra civil" (Oszlak, *La formación del estado argentino,* 88).

24. De la Fuente, *Children of Facundo,* 164.

25. See "es lo mas razonable y justo que, pr su parte, Contribuyan con algo a los gastos de una grra hecha tan solo en su apoyo y para libertarlas del despotismo que las oprime" (WP to IR, Jan. 3, 1862, Sala X, 02-02-02, Archivo del Gen. Dr. I. Rivas, 1857–1877, 143, AGN, Buenos Aires).

26. See "es necesario, al mismo tiempo, no aceptar, por motivo alguno la Continuación de Videla en el Gob° de la Provincia" (WP to IR, Jan. 3, 1862, Sala X, 02-02-02, Archivo del Gen. Dr. I. Rivas, 1857–1877, 143, AGN, Buenos Aires. News had not reached Paunero that Videla resigned the governorship on January 2, 1862.

27. DFS to IR, Jan. 6, 1862; Sala X, 02-02-02, Archivo del Gen. Dr. I. Rivas, 1857–1877, 143, AGN, Buenos Aires. Sarmiento replaced Federalist Francisco Díaz, who fled after Urquiza's defeat at Pavón. For Sarmiento as governor, see Guerra, *Sarmiento: Sus vidas i sus obras,* 211–30; Moreno, *Radiografía de Sarmiento,* 235–50; Gálvez, *Vida de Sarmiento,* 330–74; and Campobassi, *Sarmiento y su época,* 1:517–53.

28. See "habiendo desaparecido en la noche del 2 al 3 del presente, el poder que rejia de hecho esta Provincia i que surgió del triunfo del barbaro Saa, las autoridades derrocadas por él, fueron inmediatamente restablecidas" (SC to IR, Jan. 5, 1862, Sala X, 02-02-02, Archivo del Gen. Dr. I. Rivas, 1857–1877, 143, AGN, Buenos Aires). The advance of porteño armies broke the power of Federale Juan Saá.

29. See "Mi Gobierno, Señor Coronel, nunca ha opuesto resistencia á la consolidacion de la libertad e instituciones creadas por la Constitucion reformada" (DAV to IR, Jan. 25, 1862, Sala X, 02-02-02, Archivo del Gen. Dr. I. Rivas, 1857–1877, 143, AGN, Buenos Aires). Juan A. Gelly y Obes, a friend of Mitre and soon to be minister of war, also complimented Rivas on his progress (see JAGyO to IR, Jan. 28, 1862; Sala X, 02-02-02, Archivo del Gen. Dr. I. Rivas, 1857–1877, 143, AGN, Buenos Aires).

30. See "las manifestaciones mas entusiastas de profundo respeto y gratitud con que, ese noble pueblo, ha recibido á los Solos de Bs Ays" and "Esta conducta generosa y patriota no me sorprende ni me estrana. Ella es muy propia y muy digna del heroico pueblo de Sn Juan, mártir, tantas veces, del despotismo y de su amor fanatico pr la libertad" (WP to IR, Feb. 6, 1862, Sala X, 02-02-02, Archivo del Gen. Dr. I. Rivas, 1857–1877, 143, AGN, Buenos Aires).

31. See "los salteños, esos vándalos de la República se ponen en armas contra Tucuman, y amenazan decididamente su frontera, en union con los de Catamarca, y el Chacho" (WP to IR, Feb. 6, 1862, Sala X, 02-02-02, Archivo del Gen. Dr. I. Rivas, 1857–1877, 143, AGN, Buenos Aires).

32. See "La influencia brutal de Peñaloza" y "que hoy se adhiere al pensamiento de todas las Provincias libres iniciado por Bs. Ayres, de organizar la República sobre la base de la Constitucion reformada," WP to Patricio Llanos, Feb. 24, 1862, Sala X, 02-02-02, Archivo del Gen. Dr. I. Rivas, 1857–1877, 143, AGN, Buenos Aires.

33. Paunero commented that the uprising of a group of montoneras disordered La Rioja. See WP to IR, Feb. 26, 1862, Sala X, 02-02-02, Archivo del Gen. Dr. I. Rivas, 1857–1877, 143, AGN, Buenos Aires.

34. See AS to IR, Mar. 7, 1862, Sala X, 02-02-02, Archivo del Gen. Dr. I. Rivas, 1857–1877, 143, AGN, Buenos Aires.

35. The United States and Mexico also experienced brutal guerrilla violence during their respective civil wars and reconstructions.

36. See D. F. Sarmiento to Bartolomé Mitre, Apr. 10, 1862, in *Sarmiento-Mitre Correspondencia 1846–1868,* 71. Sarmiento sent Mitre many letters about this subject.

37. De la Fuente, *Children of Facundo,* 1.

38. See WP to IR, Apr. 17, 1862, Sala X, 02-02-02, Archivo del Gen. Dr. I. Rivas, 1857–1877, 143, AGN, Buenos Aires.

39. Governor Juan Barbeito of San Luis also complained about Peñaloza (see JB to IR, May 4, 1862, Sala X, 02-02-02, Archivo del Gen. Dr. I. Rivas, 1857–1877, 143, AGN, Buenos Aires).

40. See "la Provᵃ de Sⁿ Luis, ocupada en parte por las fuerzas del Caudillejo [*sic*] Angel V. Peñaloza, los que pudieron amenazar tambien á esta ó la de Mendoza pᵃ revivir los restos federales qᵉ han podido mantenerse en sus territorios á la sombra de nuestra politica tolerante" (DFS to IR, Apr. 19, 1862, Sala X, 02-02-02, Archivo del Gen. Dr. I. Rivas, 1857–1877, 143, AGN, Buenos Aires).

41. See Fellman, *Inside War,* 95–97.

42. "San Luís taken and re-taken," *The Standard,* May 10, 1862. In May 1862, Mitre was governor and interim president of Argentina. He won the election of 1862 and began his six-year term as president in October 1862.

43. See "nosotros no podamos mantener el orden en cada provincia, cuando Rosas ha podido hacerlo toda la vida" (WP to IR, May 10, 1862, Sala X, 02-02-02, Archivo del Gen. Dr. I. Rivas, 1857–1877, 143, AGN, Buenos Aires).

44. See "no quitar ni poner gobernadores; nuestra misión es puramente militar y, á lo único que puede atender se es á sostener y apoyar los Gobiernos legales" (WP to IR, June 3, 1862, Sala X, 02-02-02, Archivo del Gen. Dr. I. Rivas, 1857–1877, 143, AGN, Buenos Aires).

45. For additional discussion, see chapter 7.

46. "Monthly Review for British Packet," *The Standard,* May 29, 1862.

47. Rock, "The Collapse of the Federalists."

48. "Peñaloza," *The Standard,* May 12, 1863.

49. "Sandes and Penaloza," *The Standard,* June 18, 1863.

50. "The Rosario Mails," *The Standard,* Oct. 4, 1863.

51. "The Rosario Mails," *The Standard,* Oct. 29, 1863. See also "French Packet Review," *The Standard,* Nov. 11, 1863; and "The 'Situation,'" *The Standard,* Nov. 18, 1862.

52. "Glorious News. The Chacho Is Dead. Long Live Mitre," *The Standard,* Nov. 26, 1863. This account included reports from Irrazabal and Sarmiento.

53. "From South America," *New York World,* Jan. 27, 1864.

54. "South American Affairs," *New York World,* Mar. 10, 1864.

55. For a definition of "estado de sitio," see "state of siege means 'extraordinary facilities,' placing the security, liberty and life of each of us at the caprice of one man" ("The State Prisoners," *The Standard,* Aug. 3, 1866). The difference between "estado de sitio" and the suspension of habeas corpus was, at least according to Sarmiento, negligible (see "El Estado del Sitio Según el Doctor Rawson," in Sarmiento, *Obras* 31:65).

56. Shumway, *The Invention of Argentina,* 231. See also "Penaloza's alias the Chacho's Death," *The Standard,* Dec. 1, 1863.

57. Shumway, *The Invention of Argentina,* 228. See also Guerra, *Sarmiento,* 219.

58. The Argentine Constitution discussed "estado de sitio" in Primera Parte, Capítulo Único,

Art. 23; Segunda Parte, Sección Primera, Capítulo Segundo, Art. 53; Segunda Parte, Sección Primera, Capítulo Cuarto, Art. 67; and Segunda Parte, Sección Segunda, Capítulo Tercero, Art. 86, http://pdba.georgetown.edu/Constitutions/Argentina/arg1853.html#seccionsegundacap3.

59. See "las provincias no ejercen el Poder delegado a la Nación," Sección Tercera, Capítulo Segundo, Artículo 108, http://pdba.georgetown.edu/Constitutions/Argentina/arg1853.html# titulo2.

60. See Rawson, *El Estado de sitio según la Constitución Argentina;* and Sarmiento, "El Estado de sitio según El Doctor Rawson," in Sarmiento, *Obras,* 31:61–110.

61. See C. Galván Moreno, *Radiografía de Sarmiento,* 235–50; and Gálvez, *Vida de Sarmiento,* 37.

62. Rawson—"¿No tema V.E. que el Gobierno Nacional cimente el despotismo en el *estado de sitio?*" Sarmiento—"Temo por el contrario que la *anarquía por falta de poder* . . . traiga el despotismo, por la subversión de gobiernos ilustrados y bien intencionados, pero destituidos de los medios de garantir la sociedad" (in Sarmiento, *Obras,* 31:105). Rawson and Sarmiento were both Unitarios. Their fight was analogous to conflicts between Moderate and Radical Republicans in the United States or among factions of Liberals in Mexico.

63. This justification mirrored that of people in the United States who spoke of helping each state secure a republican form of government.

64. "To Erastus Corning and Others," June 12, 1863, in Basler, *Collected Works,* 6:266. For Vallandigham, see Klement, *The Limits of Dissent,* 156–212.

65. "La siguiente carta . . . será de mucha consecuencia en las Republicas Sud-americanas, donde la opinión de hombres ilustrados vacila, en cuanto a las facultades del Ejecutivo para conservar la tranquilidad en tiempos de conmoción o invasión" (Sarmiento, *Vida de Abran Lincoln,* 199).

66. Downs made this point for the United States in *After Appomattox.*

67. Lee's surrender did not mark the end of the war. Joseph E. Johnston surrendered to William T. Sherman in North Carolina several weeks later. In the Trans-Mississippi, Stand Watie did not surrender until late June 1865.

68. See Masur, *Lincoln's Last Speech.*

69. "Last Public Address," Apr. 11, 1865, in Basler, *Collected Works,* 8:404. See also Abraham Lincoln to Michael Hahn, Mar. 13, 1864, in Basler, *Collected Works,* 7:243.

70. Booth cited in Burlingame, *Abraham Lincoln,* 2:811.

71. Dew, *Apostles of Disunion.*

72. For hatred and demonization during the US Civil War, see Rable, *Damn Yankees!*

73. "President Johnson's Amnesty Proclamation," *New York Times,* May 30, 1865.

74. "Proclamation 135—Reorganizing a Constitutional Government in North Carolina," May 29, 1865, The American Presidency Project, http://www.presidency.ucsb.edu/ws/?pid=72403. Johnson later urged William Sharkey to disarm the Radicals by adopting such a measure.

75. Many Republicans considered this madness. See "is there no way to arrest the insane course of the President in 'Reconstruction'" and "if something is not done the president will be crowned king before Congress meets!" (Thaddeus Stevens to Charles Sumner, June 14, 1865, Reel 4, Thaddeus Stevens Papers).

76. Why Johnson pardoned the old elite, when he, as a poor white man, fiercely hated them, has never been fully answered. The best reason was that, although Johnson wanted to humiliate

them, he felt they could take the destiny of the region in hand. In other words, racism trumped class resentment.

77. See Foner, *Nothing But Freedom*, 6–7.

78. Congress established the Bureau in March, 1865.

79. Petition of Colored Citizens, Aug. 2, 1865, *The Freedmen's Bureau Online*, http://www.freed mensbureau.com/alabama/mobilepetition.htm.

80. Report of the Assistant Commissioner for the State of Alabama, *The Freedmen's Bureau Online*, http://www.freedmensbureau.com/alabama/alaoutrages.htm.

81. Registered Report of Murders and Outrages, Sept. 1866–July 1867, *The Freedmen's Bureau Online*, http://www.freedmensbureau.com/texas/brenhamoutrages.htm.

82. Registered Report of Murders and Outrages, Sept. 1866–July 1867, *The Freedmen's Bureau Online*, http://www.freedmensbureau.com/texas/shermanoutrages2.htm. See also Blair, *The Record of Murders and Outrages*.

83. The Ku Klux Klan coalesced in 1866 and 1867. Other paramilitary groups existed during this period (see Parsons, *Ku-Klux*).

84. Jas. S. Havron to W. Turner, July 7, 1867, in Havron, James Scott, Papers, 1848–1849, TSLA. The date of this collection is misleading—the papers go through 1867.

85. See Ash, *A Massacre in Memphis*; and Hollandsworth Jr., *An Absolute Massacre*.

86. For Fort Pillow, see Cimprich, *Fort Pillow*; Ward, *River Run Red*; and Tap, *The Fort Pillow Massacre*.

87. For discussion of the Klan, see chapter 6.

88. For discussion of other paramilitary groups, see chapter 7.

89. See Trefousse, *Andrew Johnson*, 262–67.

90. Duff Green to Andrew Johnson [hereafter AJ], Nov. 15, 1866, Reel 25, Johnson Papers, LOC. Clingman was a North Carolina congressman and senator before the US Civil War and a brigadier general in the rebel army.

91. A. R. Johnstone to AJ, Nov. 4, 1866, Reel 25, Johnson Papers, LOC

92. Thomas Powell to AJ, Jan. 5, 1867, Reel 25, Johnson Papers, LOC. Many such examples exist in the Johnson Papers; these are just a few.

93. "Response to a Serenade," Nov. 10, 1864, in Basler, *Collected Works*, 8:101.

94. See Reuben W. Creel [hereafter RWC] to William H. Seward [hereafter WHS], Aug. 18, 1866, Reel 1, Volume 1, DUSC-Chihuahua.

95. See Cadenhead Jr., *Jesús González Ortega and Mexican National Politics*; and Hamnett, *Juárez*.

96. RWC to WHS, Jan. 26, 1864, Reel 1, Volume 1, DUSC-Chihuahua.

97. Ortega, some have suggested, did not have the military materiel to fight the French.

98. RWC to WHS, Mar. 2, 1864, Reel 1, Volume 1, DUSC-Chihuahua. See also RWC to James H. Carleton, Feb. 3, 1864, Reel 1, Volume 1, DUSC-Chihuahua.

99. Chief Justice Salmon P. Chase might have behaved very different during Andrew Johnson's impeachment trial if the same succession pattern had been in place in the United States. Johnson himself might have behaved differently had he been constitutionally obligated to go before the people in 1865–66 to seek election to a full term.

100. These efforts were of a piece with attempts by the so-called Confederacy to meddle in Northern politics and strengthen the Copperheads (antiwar Democrats) in the United States.

101. Lucius Avery to WHS, Sept. 18, 1866, Reel 3, Volume 8, DUSC-Matamoros.

102. Franklin Chase [hereafter FC] to Frederick W. Seward [hereafter FWS], Dec. 28, 1866, Reel 4, Volume 8, DUSC-Tampico.

103. FC to WHS, Jan. 17, 1867, Reel 5, Volume 9, DUSC-Tampico.

104. FC to WHS, Feb. 15, 1867, Reel 5, Volume 9, DUSC-Tampico.

105. Liberal General Mariano Escobedo had Maximilian pinned down at Querétaro.

106. FC to FWS, Apr. 15, 1867, Reel 5, Volume 9, DUSC-Tampico.

107. FC to FWS, May 20, 1867, Reel 5, Volume 9, DUSC-Tampico.

108. FC to FWS, June 17, 1867, Reel 5, Volume 9, DUSC-Tampico.

109. Not unlike Lincoln, who, after delivering the Gettysburg Address, had to stymie an illegal Democratic takeover of the US House of Representatives (see Belz, "The Etheridge Conspiracy of 1863").

110. Marcus Otterbourg [hereafter MO] to FWS, Dec. 10, 1866, Reel 6, Volume 11, DUSC–Mexico City. See also RWC to WHS, Aug. 18, 1866, Reel 1, Volume 1, DUSC-Chihuahua.

111. MO to FWS, Jan. 17, 1867, Reel 6, Volume 12, DUSC–Mexico City.

112. "Nuevos manejos de Gonzalez Ortega," La Sociedad, Jan. 16, 1867, in MO to FWS, Jan. 17, 1867, Reel 6, Volume 12, DUSC–Mexico City.

113. For one Conservative troublemaker, see Brittsan, Popular Politics and Rebellion in Mexico.

114. The vast majority of Liberals supported Maximilian's execution. Conservatives did not, but they were already unhappy with Juárez. This was a surprising comment from Chase because he was usually an astute observer of Mexican affairs. Seward and many European liberals, however, pleaded for Maximilian's pardon. Díaz would pronounce against Juárez four years later and against Lerdo de Tejada, Juárez's successor, nine years later.

115. FC to FWS, July 31, 1867, Reel 5, Volume 9, DUSC-Tampico.

116. Charles Moye to WHS, June 3, 1867, Reel 1, Volume 1, DUSC-Chihuahua.

117. E. H. Saulnier to WHS, Oct. 1, 1867. and EHS to WHS, Oct. 14, 1867, Reel 10, Volume 10, DUSC-Veracruz.

118. US authorities executed Henry Wirz, the commandant of Andersonville Prison, for his treatment of prisoners, not for treason.

6. Suppressing Rebellions and Punishing Rebels, 1867–1872

1. Puebla was the site of the May 5, 1862, Liberal victory over the French.

2. Charles W. Brink to William H. Seward [hereafter WHS], Feb. 8, 1869, Reel 7, Volume 13, DUSC–Mexico City.

3. E. H. Saulnier to WHS, Feb. 8, 1869, Reel 11, Volume 11, DUSC-Veracruz.

4. "Mexico," New York Herald, Mar. 15, 1869.

5. See Sabato, Republics of the New World, 120.

6. McLynn, "The Argentine Presidential Election of 1868," 303.

7. "Argentine Confederation," New York Herald, May 21, 1868.

8. "Editor's Table," The Standard, Jan. 3, 1868. Elizalde spoke at the 1865 July Fourth celebration (see chapter 3).

9. "Review for Europe," The Standard, Feb. 23, 1868.

10. "Mas adelante publicamos una carta del general Mitre al redactor de la *Nacion*. Segun ella, el programa de Sarmiento es contra el país; la candidatura de Alsina es contrabando y la de Urquiza inadmisible" ("Republica Arjentina," *La Voz de Chile y de las Republicas Americanas,* Feb. 25, 1868).

11. "South America," *New York World,* May 16, 1868. See also "Review for Europe," *The Standard,* Mar. 11, 1868; and "Republica Argentina," *La Voz de Chile y de las Republicas Americanas,* May 12, 1868.

12. McLynn, "The Argentine Presidential Election of 1868," 304.

13. See McLynn, "Consequences for Argentina of the War of Triple Alliance"; Whigham, *The Paraguayan War;* Kraay and Whigham, *I Die with My Country;* and Whigham, *The Road to Armageddon.*

14. Rock, *Argentina,* 130.

15. "Argentine Confederation," *New York Herald,* May 21, 1868.

16. See "South America," *New York Herald,* July 1, 1868; "Telegraph to Morning Papers," *Providence (RI) Evening Press,* July 1, 1868; and "Telegraphic News," *Albany (NY) Argus,* July 2, 1868. *The Standard,* on the other hand, believed Elizalde "the candidate who had most chance of success" (see "Review for Europe," *The Standard,* May 12, 1868).

17. McLynn, "The Argentine Presidential Election of 1868," 320. See also "The Elections for President and Vice-President," *The Standard,* July 12, 1868. "Editor's Table," *The Standard,* Apr. 7, 1868, predicted, on the basis of a report from a paper in Uruguay, 94 for Urquiza, 34 for Sarmiento, and 28 for Elizalde. The electoral votes from Corrientes and Tucumán were not counted (see "Escrutinio de la Eleccion del Presidente," in *Congreso Nacional. Cámara de Senadores. Sesion de 1868,* 360–62).

18. Wm. Wheelwright to WHS, July 8, 1868; Ree1, Volume 1, DUSC-Rosario.

19. See "Argentine Confederation," *New York Herald,* Sept. 15, 1868; "By Atlantic Telegraph," *Public Ledger,* Sept. 15, 1868; and "The Paraguayan War," *New York Herald,* Sept. 21, 1868.

20. "Argentine Confederation," *New York Herald,* Dec. 7, 1868. See also "South America," *Philadelphia (PA) Inquirer,* Dec. 7, 1868; and "Cable Dispatches," *Eastern Argus (Portland, ME),* Dec. 7, 1868.

21. See Franklin, "Election of 1868."

22. "Horatio Seymour Nominated," *Detroit (MI) Tribune,* July 17, 1868. See Bernstein, *The New York City Draft Riots.*

23. For a recent treatment of Seymour, see Harris, *Two Against Lincoln.*

24. "Blair at Pittsburg," *Cincinnati (OH) Daily Gazette,* Oct. 1, 1868.

25. "By Telegraph," *Boston Daily Advertiser,* Oct. 19, 1868. See also *Boston Daily Advertiser,* Oct. 19, 1868, "Various Items," *Lowell (MA) Daily Citizen and News,* Oct. 19, 1868; and Summers, *A Dangerous Stir.*

26. "Message to Congress in Special Session," July 4, 1861, in Basler, *Collected Works* 4:439.

27. "The Latest Infamous Radical Forgery—The Gazette," *Cincinnati (OH) Daily Enquirer,* Oct. 20, 1868.

28. See "The Latest News," *Missouri Democrat,* Oct. 19, 1868; and "Latest by Telegraph," *Cincinnati (OH) Daily Gazette,* Oct. 20, 1868.

29. "Wilkes Booth the Second," *Harper's Weekly,* Nov. 7, 1868.

30. Parrish, however, considered the comment a "purported Blair remark" (Parrish, *Frank Blair,* 256).

31. "Mr. Beecher on Grant and Chase," *New York Evening Post,* July 11, 1868. This article was widely reprinted (see "Beecher on the Presidency," *Cincinnati [OH] Daily Gazette,* July 13, 1868; "Letter from Henry Ward Beecher," *Saint Paul [MN] Daily Press,* July 15, 1868; *Leavenworth [KS] Bulletin,* July 17, 1868; and "Letter from Henry Ward Beecher," *Daily State Register* [Des Moines, IA], July 21, 1868).

32. "In General," *Boston Daily Advertiser,* July 15, 1868.

33. "The Presidency," *New York Tribune,* July 15, 1868.

34. "Grant to the West," *Sacramento (CA) Daily Union,* July 16, 1868.

35. "The Men and the Issue," *Detroit (MI) Tribune,* July 17, 1868.

36. "The Democratic Hell Broth," *Harper's Weekly,* Oct. 31, 1868.

37. "This Is a White Man's Government," *Harper's Weekly,* Sept. 5, 1868.

38. For the Ku Klux Klan, see Trelease, *White Terror;* Nelson, *Iron Confederacies;* and Parsons, *Ku-Klux.*

39. Parrish labeled this poem "scurrilous" (Parrish, *Frank Blair,* 256), but Blair's strident rhetoric about resisting Republican tyranny encouraged Klan violence.

40. "A Lull in the War," *Troy (NY) Weekly Times,* Sept. 12, 1868. See also "Gen. Forrest and the Ku-Klux Klan," *Troy (NY) Weekly Times,* Sept. 12, 1868.

41. "Shall the Flag Protect Wherever It Waves," *Jamestown (NY) Journal,* Sept. 18, 1868.

42. "A Seymour Rebellion in Louisiana," *Connecticut Courant,* Aug. 15, 1868.

43. "Southern News," *Boston Daily Advertiser,* Oct. 19, 1868.

44. D. E. Haynes to James G. Taliaferro, Mar. 20, 1868, Box 3, Folder 1, James G. Taliaferro and Family Papers, LSU.

45. Emerson Bentley Diary; Folder 3, Emerson Bentley Papers, ULL. Bentley included the question mark as a comment on the "gentlemen" who cursed him.

46. Henry L. Darling [Fulton Co., Arkansas] to Martha J. Darling, Nov. 15, 1868, Folder 4, Galloway Family Papers, TSLA

47. Dan Price [Livingston, Sumter Co., AL] to C. W. Pierce, Dec. 21, 1868; Dan Price Letter, MSS 3713, Box SC0088, Special Collections, Hoole Library, University of Alabama.

48. See "The Georgia Massacre," *Troy (NY) Weekly Times,* Sept. 26, 1868 and *Quincy (MA) Whig and Republican,* Oct. 1, 1868. Hence the reference in "The Democratic Hell-Broth" to the blood of freedmen spilled at Camilla.

49. "The Georgia Massacre," *New-York Commercial Advertiser,* Sept. 22, 1868.

50. "The Georgia Massacre," *Boston Journal,* Sept. 23, 1886.

51. "The Negro Mob in Georgia," *Richmond (VA) Whig and Advertiser,* Sept. 25, 1868.

52. "More Results of Democratic Teachings," *New-York Commercial Advertiser,* Oct. 7, 1868.

53. Emerson Bentley Diary, Folder 3, Emerson Bentley Papers, ULL.

54. New Orleans (LA) *Daily Picayune,* Sept. 18, 1868.

55. "The War of Races," *New-Orleans Commercial Bulletin,* Oct. 5, 1868.

56. See *Report of the Joint Select Committee to Inquire into the Condition of Affairs in the Late Insurrectionary States.*

57. See Severance, *Tennessee's Radical Army.*

58. See Crouch and Brice, *The Governor's Hounds.*

59. See "North Carolina," *New York Herald,* Dec. 18, 1870; "By Overland Telegraph," *Stockton (CA) Daily Evening Herald,* Dec. 20, 1870; "Holden and Kirk," *New York World,* Feb. 20, 1871; "North Carolina," *Cincinnati (OH) Daily Enquirer,* Feb. 21, 1871; and "The Impeachment of Gov. Holden," *Wheeling (WV) Daily Intelligencer,* Mar. 23, 1871. In 2011, the North Carolina Senate pardoned Holden.

60. Andrew Johnson, "Proclamation Granting Full Pardon and Amnesty," Dec. 25, 1868, http://www.presidency.ucsb.edu/ws/?pid=72360.

61. Breckinridge's correspondents were also happy (see J. B. Beck to JCB, Dec. 25, 1868; Mary [S?]. Bullock to JCB, Dec. 25, 1868; J. A. Early to JCB, Dec. 1868; Saml K. Hays to JCB, Dec. 25, 1868; and Wm. Preston Johnston to JCB, Jan. 8, 1868 [1869]; all in Box 264, Papers of the Breckinridge Family, LOC.

62. See Simpson, *Let Us Have Peace.*

63. See "The President's Ku Klux Message," *New York Herald,* Jan. 14, 1871.

64. Martinez, *Carpetbaggers, Cavalry and the Ku Klux Klan;* Williams, *The Great South Carolina Ku Klux Klan Trials;* Zuczek, *State of Rebellion.*

65. See "The Ku Klux Rebellion," *New York Herald,* Oct. 18, 1871; "The Ku-Klux," *New-York Tribune,* Oct. 18, 1871; and "The South Carolina Ku-Klux," *Wilmington (DE) Daily Commercial,* Oct. 18, 1871.

66. "The South Carolina Ku Klux," *New York Herald,* Oct. 18, 1871.

67. That said, some Klansmen later joined other paramilitary organizations.

68. "Military Prisoners-Piling on the Agony," *Georgia Weekly Telegraph,* Apr. 30, 1872.

69. "From Washington," *Richmond (VA) Whig and Advertiser,* May 10, 1872. See also "The Blunder of the Emperor," *Richmond (VA) Whig and Advertiser,* Oct. 27, 1871.

70. For additional discussion, see chapter 7.

71. Richmond, *Carlos Pellegrini and the Crisis of the Argentine Elites,* 4. See also Romero, *A History of Argentine Political Thought,* 155, 159.

72. "Editor's Table," *The Standard,* July 31, 1868.

73. "Editor's Table," *The Standard,* July 2, 1869.

74. "Editor's Table," *The Standard,* Jan. 6, 1870.

75. "The President's Tour," *The Standard,* Feb. 6, 1870.

76. "The President's Tour," *The Standard,* Feb. 8, 1870. I transcribed this article exactly as it appeared.

77. "The President's Tour," *The Standard,* Feb. 12, 1870.

78. "El abrazo con Sarmiento, el principal responsable de la muerte del Chacho, le costará muy caro a Urquiza" (Pigna, "Justo José de Urquiza," https://www.elhistoriador.com.ar/justo-jose-de-urquiza/).

79. "The Death of Gen. Urquiza," *The Standard,* Apr. 16, 1870. See also "Assassination of General Urquiza" and "The Late Gen. Urquiza," both in *The Standard,* Apr. 16, 1870.

80. "Argentine Confederation," *New York Tribune,* June 15, 1870.

81. See "Summary of the News," *New York World,* May 14, 1870; "South America," *New York Herald,* May 14, 1870; "News of the Morning," *Sacramento (CA) Daily Union,* May 25, 1870; *Albany (NY) Evening Journal,* May 24, 1870; "The Assassination of Urquiza," *Boston Daily Journal,*

May 24, 1870; *The Farmer's Cabinet*, June 2, 1870; and "Editorial Notes," *Weekly Alta Californian*, June 4, 1870.

82. "Central and South America," *New York Herald*, May 21, 1870. For fears Urquiza's assassination would lead to a new war, see "Latest News by Mail," *New Orleans (MA) Daily Picayune*, May 29, 1870.

83. *New-Orleans (LA) Commercial Bulletin*, May 25, 1870. See also "A President Removed from South America," *Cincinnati (OH) Daily Enquirer*, May 25, 1870; and "South American News," *Cincinnati (OH) Daily Gazette*, May 25, 1870.

84. "Latest from Entre Rios," *The Standard*, Apr. 19, 1870.

85. "The Entre-Riano Revolution," *The Standard*, Apr. 21, 1870.

86. "The President's Proclamation to the People," *The Standard*, Apr. 21, 1870.

87. At the climactic Battle of Ñaembé, López Jordán had roughly seven thousand men, whereas Governor Santiago Baibiene of Corrientes and Lieutenant Colonel Julio Argentino Roca had about three thousand. That did not stop Baibiene and Roca from crushing López Jordán.

88. "The Rebellion in the Argentine Republic," *New York World*, Sept. 13, 1870.

89. Lucius Avery [hereafter LA] to the Secretary of State, May 19, 1869, Reel 3, Volume 9, DUSC-Matamoros. See also Thompson, *Cortina*.

90. Franklin Chase [hereafter FC] to Frederick W. Seward [hereafter FWS], Sept. 30, 1868, Reel 5, Volume 9, DUSC-Tampico. For another report on the brutality of the fighting, see FC to WHS, Feb. 23, 1869, Reel 5, Volume 9, DUSC-Tampico.

91. FC to Hamilton Fish [hereafter HF], Oct. 19, 1869, Reel 5, Volume 9, DUSC-Tampico.

92. See Julius Noureau to William Hunter [hereafter WH], Apr. 7, 1871, Reel 1, DUSC–San Luis Potosi.

93. LA to J.C.B. Davis [hereafter JCBD], Feb. 15, 1870, Reel 4, Volume 10, DUSC-Matamoros.

94. LA to JCBD, May 27, 1870, Reel 4, Volume 10, DUSC-Matamoros. For complaints about confusion because of war and revolutions, see LA to JCBD, June 4, 1870, Reel 4, Volume 10, DUSC-Matamoros.

95. LA to JCBD, June 9, 1870, Reel 4, Volume 10, DUSC-Matamoros.

96. Thomas F. Wilson [hereafter TFW] to HF, June 10, 1870, Reel 4, Volume 10, DUSC-Matamoros.

97. See Isaac Sisson [hereafter IS] to FWS, Nov. 18, 1867, Reel 3, Volume 3, DUSC-Mazatlán.

98. IS to FWS, Feb. 1, 1868, Reel 3, Volume 3, DUSC-Mazatlán.

99. IS to FWS, Mar. 16, 1868, Reel 3, Volume 3, DUSC-Mazatlán.

100. IS to FWS, Apr. 22, 1868, Reel 3, Volume 3, DUSC-Mazatlán.

101. See IS to FWS, Apr. 3, 1869, Reel 3, Volume 3, DUSC-Mazatlán; A. Willard [hereafter AW] to Hon. Secretary of State, Apr. 15, 1869; AW to Hon. Secretary of State, Apr. 29, 1869; and AW to HF, June 30, 1869, all in Reel 2, Volume 2, DUSC-Guaymas; and *The American Annual Cyclopaedia and Register of Important Events of the Year 1869*, 9:441.

102. John A. Sutter, Jr. [hereafter JAJS] to WHS, June 17, 1867, Reel 3, Volume 5, DUSC-Acapulco.

103. JASJ to WHS, June 30, 1867, Reel 3, Volume 5, DUSC-Acapulco. See also JASJ to WHS, Aug. 25, 1867, Reel 3, Volume 5, DUSC-Acapulco.

104. JASJ to Admiral H. K. Thatcher, Aug. 24, 1867, Reel 3, Volume 5, DUSC-Acapulco. See also JASJ to WHS, Aug. 25, 1867, Reel 3, Volume 5, DUSC-Acapulco.

105. JASJ to WHS, Sept. 30, 1867, Reel 3, Volume 5, DUSC-Acapulco.

106. JASJ to WHS, Dec. 31, 1867, Reel 3, Volume 5, DUSC-Acapulco.

107. JASJ to WHS, Mar. 31, 1868, Reel 3, Volume 6, DUSC-Acapulco.

108. JASJ to WHS, June 30, 1868, Reel 3, Volume 6, DUSC-Acapulco.

109. JASJ to WHS, Sept. 30, 1868, Reel 3, Volume 6, DUSC-Acapulco.

110. JASJ to WHS, Dec. 31, 1868, Reel 3, Volume 6, DUSC-Acapulco.

111. Mexico's Constitution of 1857 did not prohibit reelection. Nevertheless, Díaz, in 1871 and 1876, made antireelectionism the basis of his pronunciamientos.

112. See AW to WH, June 3, 1871, Reel 2, Volume 2, DUSC-Guaymas.

113. "La reelección indefinida, forzosa y violenta, del ejecutivo federal, ha puesto en peligro las instituciones nacionales," and "'Constitución de 57 y libertad electoral' será nuestra bandera; 'Menos gobierno y más libertades,' nuestro programa" (*Plan de la Noria*, Nov. 9, 1871, https://arts.st-andrews.ac.uk/pronunciamientos/dates.php?f=y&pid=1011&m=11&y=1871).

114. AW to WH, Sept. 30, 1871, Reel 2, Volume 2, DUSC-Guaymas. See also AW to WH, Nov. 16, 1871, Reel 2, Volume 2, DUSC-Guaymas.

115. AW to WH, Nov. 16, 1871, Reel 2, Volume 2, DUSC-Guaymas.

116. TFW to WH, Nov. 13, 1871, Reel 4, Volume 10, DUSC-Matamoros.

117. TFW to WH, Jan. 5, 1872, Reel 4, Volume 10, DUSC-Matamoros.

118. TFW to WH, Jan. 5, 1872, Reel 4, Volume 10, DUSC-Matamoros. See also Charley Mayer to WH, Jan. 1, 1872, Reel 1, DUSC-Mier.

119. TFW to WH, Jan. 5, 1872, Reel 4, Volume 11, DUSC-Matamoros. See also "Mexico," unidentified clippling, Caja 2/Expediente 5/1876/No. 144, México Independiente/Gobierno y Relaciones Exteriores/R. E./54912/Caja 2, AGN, Mexico City.

120. Thomas Gilgan [hereafter TG] to WH, Apr. 3, 1872, Reel 1, Volume 1, DUSCO–Nuevo Laredo. See also TG to WH, May 20, 1872, and TG to WH, June 22, 1872, both in Reel 1, Volume 1, DUSCO–Nuevo Laredo.

121. IS to Hon. Second Asst. Secretary of State, Oct. 10, 1872, Reel 4, Volume 4, DUSC-Mazatlán.

122. JASJ to the Honorable Second Assistant Secretary of State, Jan. 20, 1871, Reel 3, Volume 6, DUSC-Acapulco. See also Jacobs, *Ranchero Revolt*.

123. JASJ to WH, Oct. 3, 1871, Reel 3, Volume 6, DUSC-Acapulco.

124. See chapter 7.

125. Julius A. Skilton to Hon. Second Assistant Secretary of State, Aug. 30, 1871, Reel 6, Volume 12, DUSC–Mexico City.

126. For two interpretations of the Liberal Republicans, see Sproat, *The Best Men;* and Slap, *The Doom of Reconstruction.*

127. "Reconstruction in 1868–72," *Wooster (OH) Republican,* Apr. 11, 1872.

128. "Democratic Terrorism in Georgia," *Saint Paul (MN) Daily Press,* Oct. 8, 1872.

129. "The Political Situation in the South," *New-York Tribune,* Oct. 17, 1872.

7. Revolutions May Go Backward, 1872–1880

1. A. F. Garrison to William Hunter [hereafter WH], Aug. 15, 1872, Reel 3, Volume 3, DUSC-Guaymas.

2. Charles Winslow to WH, Aug. 19, 1872, Reel 1, Volume 1, DUSC-Guerrero.

3. See "Numero 41. Manifesto del C. Presidente de la Republica," in *Recopilación de Leyes,* XVI:283–87.

4. "Un decreto de amnistía por los delitos políticos cometidos hasta aquí, sin excepción de persona alguna" ("Numero 41. Manifesto del C. Presidente de la Republica," in *Recopilación de Leyes,* XVI:284).

5. For both decrees. see "Numero 42. Amnistia" y "Numero 43. Elecciones Para Presidentes de la Republica," in *Recopilación de Leyes,* XVI:289–92.

6. John A. Wolf to Hon. Second Assistant Secretary of State, Nov. 12, 1872, Reel 2, Volume 2, DUSC-Minatitlan. See also John C. Huston to Second Assistant Secretary of State, Dec. 31, 1872, Reel 1, Volume 2, DUSC-Chihuahua; and Lucius Avery [hereafter LA] to WH, Oct. 1, 1873, Reel 1, DUSC-Camargo.

7. A. Willard [hereafter AW] to WH, June 22, 1873, Reel 3, Volume 3, DUSC-Guaymas.

8. AW to WH, Sept. 30, 1873, Reel 3, Volume 3, DUSC-Guaymas.

9. AW to WH, Oct. 2, 1873, Reel 3, Volume 3, DUSC-Guaymas.

10. AW to WH, Oct. 21, 1873, Reel 3, Volume 3, DUSC-Guaymas. State troops defeated a pronunciamiento in 1875 (see AW to WH, Sept. 8, 1875, Reel 3, Volume 3, DUSC-Guaymas).

11. Thomas F. Wilson [hereafter TFW] to WH, Dec. 22 1873, Reel 4, Volume 11, DUSC-Matamoros.

12. TFW to WH, Apr. 18, 1874, Reel 5, Volume 12, DUSC-Matamoros. See also Jerry Thompson, *Cortina,* 219–21.

13. For fears of a pronunciamiento in Monterrey, following a gubernatorial election, see Joseph Ulrich to Hon. Second Assistant Secretary of State, July 12, 1873, Reel 2, Volume 3, DUSC-Monterrey and TFW to WH, Sept. 22, 1875, Reel 5, Volume 12, DUSC-Matamoros.

14. Wm. Schuchardt [hereafter WS] to Hon. Second Assistant Secretary of State, Aug. 29, 1873, Reel 1, Volume 2, DUSC–Piedras Negras.

15. WS to Hon. Second Assistant Secretary of State, Sept. 17, 1873, Reel 1, Volume 2, DUSC–Piedras Negras.

16. WS to Hon. Second Assistant Secretary of State, Sept. 17, 1873, Reel 1, Volume 2, DUSC–Piedras Negras.

17. WS to Hon. Second Assistant Secretary of State, Oct. 21, 1873, Reel 1, Volume 2, DUSC–Piedras Negras' and "Coahuila," *El Siglo Diez y Nueve,* Nov. 5, 1873.

18. WS to Hon. Second Assistant Secretary of State, Feb. 13, 1874, Reel 1, Volume 2, DUSC–Piedras Negras.

19. David Turner [hereafter DT] to Hon. Second Assistant Secretary of State, June 3, 1875, Reel 2, Volume 2, DUSC–La Paz.

20. Plan in DT to Hon. Second Assistant Secretary of State, June 25, 1875, Reel 2, Volume 2, DUSC–La Paz. See also Bancroft, *The Works of Hubert Howe Bancroft,* 14:413.

21. DT to Hon. Second Assistant Secretary of State, July 19, 1875, Reel 2, Volume 2, DUSC–La Paz.

22. During the US Civil War, Lincoln used Louisiana as a laboratory to test his Reconstruction policy (see McCrary, *Abraham Lincoln and Reconstruction;* Cox, *Lincoln and Black Freedom;* and Harris, *With Charity for All*). In his last public address, Lincoln defended the reconstructed government in Louisiana (see chapter 5).

23. Taylor, *Louisiana,* 110. See also Taylor, *Louisiana Reconstructed,* 209–313; Reed, *David French Boyd,* 115–69; and Dawson, *Army Generals and Reconstruction,* 133–82.

24. For background on McEnery, see "A Well Deserved Compliment," *New Orleans (LA) Daily Picayune,* July 17, 1872; "Our Candidate for Governor," *New Orleans (LA) Daily Picayune,* July 26, 1872; Johnson, *The Twentieth Century Biographical Dictionary of Notable Americans;* Trefousse, *Historical Dictionary of Reconstruction,* 142; and Cowan and McGuire, *Louisiana Governors,* 110–13. For background on Kellogg, see Trefousse, *Historical Dictionary,* 120; C. Howard Nichols, "William Pitt Kellogg," 172–76; and Cowan and McGuire, *Louisiana Governors,* 114–18.

25. See "Political Meetings," *New Orleans (LA) Daily Picayune,* July 26, 1872; "The Campaign," *Cincinnati (OH) Daily Gazette,* Aug. 29, 1872; and "The Young Democrats," *New Orleans Daily Picayune,* July 11, 1872.

26. Taylor, *Louisiana: A History,* 110.

27. S. B. Packard to George H. Williams, in McPherson, *A Hand-Book of Politics for 1874,* 100. See also "probably, though not certainly, McEnery received a majority of the ballots that went into the boxes; probably, but again not certainly, in an honest election Kellogg would have had a majority" (Taylor, *Louisiana,* 110).

28. These numbers come from McPherson, *A Hand-Book of Politics for 1874,* 228.

29. See "Warmoth and His Returning Board," *Cincinnati (OH) Daily Gazette,* Nov. 18, 1872 and "Kellogg vs. Warmoth," *New Orleans (LA) Daily Picayune,* Nov. 28, 1872.

30. "The Louisiana Quarrel," *New York Tribune,* Dec. 7, 1872. See also "the election was a gigantic fraud, and there no reliable returns of its result. Kellogg obtained possession of the office, and in my opinion has more right to it than his competitor" ("President Grant's Special Message on Affairs in the State of Louisiana, Jan. 13, 1875," in McPherson, *A Hand-Book of Politics for 1876,* 33).

31. See "the Democrats, having stolen the election originally, were outraged that it was stolen back" (Taylor, *Louisiana,* 110).

32. "President Grant," *Indianapolis Sentinel,* Dec. 18, 1872; "The Louisiana Troubles," *San Francisco (CA) Evening Bulletin,* Dec. 20, 1872; "The Duty of Our People," *New Orleans (LA) Daily Picayune,* Dec. 31, 1872; "Mass Meeting in St. Mary," *New Orleans Daily Picayune,* Jan. 2, 1873; and "The Conflict in Louisiana," *Baltimore Sun,* Jan. 7, 1873.

33. See "Political Notes," *New York Tribune,* Dec. 31, 1872.

34. See Ridpath and Buell, *History of the United States,* 201.

35. "Various Items," Lowell (MA) *Daily Citizen and News,* Jan. 14, 1873.

36. "Political Jottings," *Boston Evening Journal,* Jan. 16, 1873. The Senate declined to seat both men.

37. "Mr. John McEnery," *Weekly Louisianian,* Jan. 25, 1873. See also "Proclamation by the Governor," *New Orleans (LA) Daily Picayune,* Feb. 18, 1873.

38. "More Troubles Threatened," *New York Herald,* Feb. 27, 1873. See also "This Evening's Dis-

patches," *San Francisco (CA) Daily Evening Bulletin,* Feb. 27, 1873; "Bayonet Logic," *Indianapolis (IN) Sentinel,* Mar. 7, 1873; and "The Garroted State," *Albany (NY) Argus,* Mar. 21, 1873.

39. For differences between paramilitary and vigilante organizations, see Hogue, *Uncivil War,* 11–12.

40. See Keith, *The Colfax Massacre;* and Lane, *The Day Freedom Died.*

41. Foner, *Reconstruction.*

42. McPherson, *A Hand-Book of Politics for 1876,* 33.

43. See "Mass meeting to Organize the People's League of Louisiana," *New Orleans (LA) Daily Picayune,* Apr. 15, 1873; "To the Editor of the Picayune," *New Orleans (LA) Daily Picayune,* Apr. 29, 1873; and "Treason in Louisiana," *New Orleans (LA) Daily Picayune,* May 1, 1873.

44. "Signs of Peace at New Orleans," *New York Herald,* Apr. 23, 1873.

45. Rhodes, *History of the United States,* 7:176.

46. A historical marker at the site explains that the "Colfax Riot" "marked the end of carpet-bag misrule in the South." This offensive language reveals a woefully outdated interpretation of the Colfax Massacre. The marker was removed in May 2021.

47. "By Telegraph," *New York Evening Post,* Apr. 19, 1873.

48. To be fair, the government prosecuted some of the murderers and won convictions. However, in *US v. Cruikshank,* the Supreme Court overturned these convictions.

49. See "This Morning's Dispatches," *San Francisco (CA) Daily Evening Bulletin,* Apr. 25, 1873; "Kellogg," *New Orleans (LA) Daily Picayune,* Apr. 28, 1873; and "Treason in Louisiana," *New Orleans (LA) Daily Picayune,* May 1, 1873.

50. "Treason in Louisiana," *New Orleans (LA) Daily Picayune,* May 1, 1873. Kellogg directed Field to "spare no effort in this prosecution," but McEnery was never tried for treason. The *New Orleans (LA) Daily Picayune* sneered, in their commentary, "we presume, that the gibbet is to be erected in the streets of New Orleans, to signalize and support his usurpation."

51. See also "Kellogg's four years were almost a period of guerrilla warfare in Louisiana" (Taylor, *Louisiana,* 111).

52. "The Louisiana Troubles," *The Elevator,* May 10, 1873.

53. William Pitt Kellogg to Sir [OPM], Dec. 8, 1873, Folder 8, Box 1, Oliver P. Morton Papers, ISL.

54. William Pitt Kellogg to Dear Sir [OPM], Jan. 7, 1874, Folder 9, Box 1, Oliver P. Morton Papers, ISL.

55. William Pitt Kellogg to My dear Sir [OPM], Feb. 23, 1874, Folder 9, Box 1, Oliver P. Morton Papers, ISL

56. See *Inter Ocean,* Aug. 20, 1874.

57. See Tunnell, ed., *Carpetbagger from Vermont,* 133–61; and Tunnell, *Edge of the Sword,* 184–231.

58. "The Reign of Hate," *Inter Ocean,* Sept. 2, 1874. See also "Colonel McEnery may justly be charged as directly and mainly responsible for most of the horrid murders committed in north Louisiana" ("Penitent and General Notes," *Massachusetts Spy,* Oct. 2, 1874).

59. McPherson, *A Hand-Book of Politics for 1876,* 33. See also Grant's angry avowal that "the spirit of hatred and violence is stronger than law" (McPherson, *A Hand-Book of Politics for 1876,* 34).

60. Phil to My dear Boy, Sept. 4, 1874; Folder 86, Murphy Family Papers, HNOC.

61. For background, see "Revolution," *New York Herald,* Sept. 15, 1874; "The Louisiana Troubles," *Alexandria Gazette,* Sept. 18, 1874; "Louisiana," *Cincinnati (OH) Enquirer,* Sept. 18, 1874; "From Louisiana," *Augusta (GA) Chronicle,* Sept. 18, 1874; "The War Ended," *Washington, DC, Daily Critic,* Sept. 18, 1874; "Exit Penn," *Inter Ocean,* Sept. 18, 1874; "Civil War in New Orleans," *Richmond (VA) Whig,* Sept. 18, 1874; and "Louisiana," *New York Herald,* Sept. 27, 1874.

62. Longstreet, a former rebel general, had become a Republican. This is a good reminder that not all rebels stayed rebels (see "Penitent and General Notes," *Massachusetts Spy,* Oct. 2, 1874).

63. "Revolution," *New York Herald,* Sept. 15, 1874.

64. JMC to Dear Wife, Sept. 17, 1874; Folder 87; Murphy Family Papers, HNOC.

65. JMC to Dear Wife, Sept. 17, 1874; Folder 88; Murphy Family Papers, HNOC.

66. "The Latest News," *Public Ledger,* Sept. 18, 1874. See also "Squelched," *Sioux City (IA) Daily Journal,* Sept. 18, 1874; "Louisiana," *Columbian Register,* Sept. 26, 1874.

67. "Louisiana," *Cincinnati (OH) Enquirer,* Sept. 18, 1874.

68. "The Louisiana Troubles," *Alexandria (VA) Gazette,* Sept. 18, 1874.

69. Holt, *By One Vote.*

70. Tunnell, *Edge of the Sword,* 230.

71. Behrend, *Reconstructing Democracy,* 211.

72. George W. Vickers to Matthew W. Ransom, Jan. 26, 1875, Matt W. Ransom Papers, SHC, UNC-CH.

73. "Mississippi," *New York Herald,* June 7, 1875.

74. See Lemann, *Redemption.*

75. "Summary of the News," *New York World,* Nov. 2, 1875. Ames was impeached in 1876 but cut a deal with Democrats: he resigned his office and the legislature dropped the charges.

76. *New Hampshire Patriot,* Nov. 10, 1875.

77. Behrend, *Reconstructing Democracy,* 233.

78. See Lynch, *Reminiscences of an Active Life,* 174; and Chernow, *Grant,* 817–18. Republicans won the 1875 Ohio gubernatorial election.

79. See "for Lynch, the precise words of each exchange (the authentic reconstruction of the past) were not as important as his memory of the event and its meaning for the present" (Behrend, "Facts, Memories, and History," 94).

80. Elías José Palti contended that the Revolution of 1874 has been obscured by events after 1880 (see Palti, *El momento romántico,* 138n45). See also Villar, *Nueva historia Argentina,* 3:938–39; Levene, *Lecciones de historia Argentina,* 2:527–28; Chávez, *Historia del país de los Argentinos,* 279; Rennie, *The Argentine Republic,* 120–21; de Gandía, *Historia de la República Argentina en el siglo XIX,* 774; Davis, *Makers of Democracy in Latin America,* 59; Bailey and Nasatir, *Latin America,* 395; Keen and Wasserman, *A History of Latin America,* 218; Richmond, *Carlos Pellegrini and the Crisis of the Argentine Elites,* 7; Romero, *A History of Argentine Political Thought,* 156–57; and Benjamín García Holgado, *De Mitre a Roca,* 27–28.

81. Rock, *State Building and Political Movements in Argentina.*

82. Per the Constitution of 1853, presidents of Argentina could not succeed themselves, but nothing barred a president from serving nonconsecutive terms.

83. Rock, *State Building,* 82.

84. Rock, *State Building,* 83–84.

85. See "Resultado del escrutinio de la eleccion para Presidente y Vicepresidente de la Nación Argentina," *Congreso Nacional: Cámara de Senadores: Sesiones de 1874,* 289–92; and "Editor's Table," *The Standard,* Aug. 8, 1874.

86. "Mucha ajitacion habia en Buenos Aires; algunos temian una revolucion de parte de los partidarios del jeneral Mitre" ("Sud America," *La Estrella de Panama,* Sept. 16, 1874).

87. "*Review for Europe,*" *The Standard,* Sept. 15, 1874. This article should remind US historians of the rhetoric about the "Revolution of 1800" in which the US Federalist John Adams lost the election of 1800 to Democratic-Republican Thomas Jefferson. Jefferson's election ended twelve years of Federalist control of the presidency, but Adams handed power over to Jefferson. The system, as in Argentina, worked. As Sarmiento explained, Argentina and the United States traveled the same path; they just happened to be at different points on that path.

88. Rock, *State Building,* 85–86; see also 131.

89. "Editor's Table," *The Standard,* Sept. 25, 1874.

90. "The Situation," *The Standard,* Sept. 26, 1874.

91. Thomas O. Osborn [hereafter TOO] to Hamilton Fish [hereafter HF], Sept. 29, 1874, in *Papers Relating to the Foreign Relations of the United States,* 1:5.

92. TOO to HF, Oct. 5, 1874, in *Papers Relating to the Foreign Relations of the United States,* 1:6–7.

93. TOO to HF, Oct. 13, 1874, in *Papers Relating to the Foreign Relations of the United States,* 1:9–10.

94. TOO to HF, Nov. 13, 1874, in *Papers Relating to the Foreign Relations of the United States,* 1:17.

95. "Manifesto of Gen. Mitre," *The Standard,* Oct. 11, 1874.

96. For Sarmiento reviewing troops, see "The Situation," *The Standard,* Oct. 10, 1874.

97. TOO to HF, Oct. 5, 1874, in *Papers Relating to the Foreign Relations of the United States,* 1:6.

98. "Farewell Address of President Sarmiento," *The Standard,* Oct. 10, 1874.

99. "Farewell Address of President Sarmiento" *The Standard,* Oct. 10, 1874.

100. Under the terms of the Militia Act of 1792, amended in 1795, the militia Lincoln called up could only serve for three months.

101. "Commercial News," *The Standard,* Nov. 14, 1874.

102. "Sentence," May 19, 1875, in TOO to HF, June 7, 1875 in *Papers Relating to the Foreign Relations of the United States,* 1:34–35.

103. "Government decree," May 24, 1875, in TOO to HF, June 7, 1875 in *Papers Relating to the Foreign Relations of the United States,* 1:35. Rivas was eventually reinstated (see Luis M. Campos to Mi Señor D. Ygnacio Rivas, June 5, 1877; Sala X, 02-02-02, Archivo del Gen. Dr. I. Rivas, 1857–1877, 143, AGN, Buenos Aires).

104. TOO to HF, June 7, 1875, in *Papers Relating to the Foreign Relations of the United States,* 1:34.

105. One of Senator Ransom's correspondents thought the third term point was a giant humbug. See "the papers have been making a great noise about the 3d term—I have never believed that Grant expected the nomination for a 3d Term. I was never a Greely man—I hope the Democrats will do better this year" (G. W. Brooks to Matthew W. Ransom, Feb. 26, 1876, the Matt W. Ransom Papers, SHC, UNC-CH).

106. Jonathan Bragg to Matthew W. Ransom, Jan. 20, 1876, Matt W. Ransom Papers, SHC, UNC-CH.

107. For troops in the US South, see Downs, *After Appomattox.*

108. D. A. Weber to WPK, Mar. 6, 1876, Box 6, Folder 39A, William Pitt Kellogg Papers, LSU.

109. C. H. Brogden to U.S. Grant, Dec. 11, 1876, Matt W. Ransom Papers, SHC, UNC-CH.

110. "The Bloody Shirt Reformed," *Harper's Weekly,* Aug. 12, 1876.

111. Holt, *By One Vote,* discussed Democrats' efforts to steal an electoral vote in Oregon. For a brilliant discussion of the Potter Committee's investigation of the Election of 1876 see Fairclough, *Bulldozed and Betrayed.*

112. The *Detroit (MI) Weekly Tribune,* Jan. 18, 1877; "Political Notes," *Easton (MD) Gazette,* Jan. 20, 1877; "Henry Watterson's Flip-Flop," *Indianapolis (IN) Daily Sentinel,* Feb. 17, 1877; and "General News," *Idaho Avalanche,* Mar. 3, 1877. See also Margolies, *Henry Watterson and the New South.*

113. See Woodward, *Reunion and Reaction;* Peskin, "Was There a Compromise of 1877?"; and Woodward, "Yes, There Was a Compromise of 1877." Greg Downs's "Mapping Occupations" website made it very clear that the army did not leave the South, but stayed, albeit in diminished numbers (Downs and Nesbit, *Mapping Occupation,* https://www.mappingoccupation.org/).

114. See https://arts.st-andrews.ac.uk/pronunciamientos/dates.php?f=y&pid=1611&m=1&y=1876. Given Díaz's course later in life, this strident antireelectionism cannot help but seem ironic.

115. Alphonse J. Lespinasse [hereafter AJL] to WH, Mar. 10, 1876, Reel 1, Volume 2, DUSC-Merida. See also AJL to WH, Apr. 28, 1876; AJL to WH, Aug. 4, 1876; AJL to WH, Dec. 5, 1876; AJL to WH, Jan. 5, 1877; and AJL to WH, Jan. 16, 1877; all in Reel 1, Volume 2, DUSC-Merida.

116. AW to WH, Feb. 10, 1876, Reel 4, Volume 4, DUSC-Guaymas. See also AW to WH, Jan. 17, 1876, Reel 4, Volume 4, DUSC-Guaymas.

117. TFW to HF, Jan. 8, 1876, Reel 5, Volume 12, DUSC-Matamoros.

118. TFW to WH, Mar. 23, 1876, Reel 5, Volume 12, DUSC-Matamoros.

119. Officials in Tampico and Nuevo Laredo also reported revolutionary disturbances. See Edmund Johnson to WH, Mar. 30, 1876, Reel 6, Volume 11, DUSC-Tampico; and James J. Haynes to WH, Mar. 15, 1876, Reel 1, Volume 1, DUSCO–Nuevo Laredo.

120. Marcus T. Milona to WH, Apr. 22, 1876; DUSC-Mier.

121. E. G. Kelton [hereafter EGK] to HF, July 21, 1876, Reel 4, Volume 4, DUSC-Mazatlán. See also Julius A. Skilton [hereafter JAS] to Hon. Second Assistant Secretary of State, July 14, 1876, Reel 8, Volume 15, DUSC–Mexico City.

122. JAS to Hon. Second Assistant Secretary of State, Mar. 15, 1876, Reel 8, Volume 15, DUSC–Mexico City.

123. Silas T. Trowbridge [hereafter STT] to WH, Apr. 11, 1876, Reel 12, Volume 12, DUSC-Veracruz.

124. Solomon Sternberger [hereafter SS] to Hon. Sec. Assistant Secretary of State, Apr. 18, 1876, Reel 2, Volume 2, DUSC-Minatitlan. See also SS to Hon. Sec. Assistant Secretary of State, June 20, 1876, Reel 2, Volume 2, DUSC-Minatitlan.

125. See JAS to Hon. Second Assistant Secretary of State, Oct. 30, 1876, Reel 8, Volume 15, DUSC–Mexico City.

126. JAS to Hon. Second Assistant Secretary of State, Oct. 30, 1876, Reel 8, Volume 15, DUSC–Mexico City.

127. JAS to Hon. Second Assistant Secretary of State, Nov. 28, 1876, Reel 8, Volume 15,

DUSC–Mexico City. See also JAS to HF, Dec. 7, 1876, JAS to Hon. Second Assistant Secretary of State, Dec. 30, 1876, both in Reel 8, Volume 15, DUSC–Mexico City.

128. STT to WH, Nov. 21, 1876, Reel 12, Volume 12, DUSC-Veracruz. Trowbridge referred to the Battle of Tecoac.

129. EGK to WH, Jan. 20, 1877, Reel 4, Volume 4, DUSC-Mazatlán.

130. See also EGK to WH, Feb. 14, 1877, Reel 4, Volume 4, DUSC-Mazatlán.

131. John A. Sutter, Jr. [hereafter JASJ] to WH, Nov. 27, 1876, Reel 4, Volume 7, DUSC-Acapulco.

132. JASJ to WH, Jan. 11, 1877, Reel 4, Volume 7, DUSC-Acapulco.

133. JASJ to WH, Jan. 25, 1877, Reel 4, Volume 7, DUSC-Acapulco. See also JASJ to WH, Mar. 14, 1877, Reel 4, Volume 7, DUSC-Acapulco.

134. See the newspaper clippings in Caja 2, Expediente 5, 1876, No 144, México Independiente/Gobierno y Relaciones Exteriores/R. E./54912/Caja 2, AGN, Mexico City.

135. TFW to WH, Nov. 15, 1877, Reel 5, Volume 13, DUSC-Matamoros.

136. See Young, *Catarino Garza's Revolution on the Texas-Mexico Border.*

137. See Vanderwood, *Disorder and Progress.*

138. See Campney, *This Is Not Dixie.*

139. See Prather, *We Have Taken a City;* and Cecelski and Tyson, *Democracy Betrayed.*

140. Lause, *The Civil War's Last Campaign* discussed violent outbursts at Weaver rallies.

141. Díaz had the Constitution of 1857 amended in 1878 to prohibit presidents serving consecutive terms. In 1887, he had it amended again to allow permit a president serving two consecutive terms. In 1892, he had it amended again to remove all provisions about reelection.

142. David H. Strother to WH, Dec. 28, 1880, Reel 9, Volume 17, DUSC–Mexico City.

143. See "Revolution Ended," *Salt Lake (UH) Weekly Tribune,* July 10, 1880; Alonso, *Between Revolutions and the Ballot Box;* and Sabato, *Buenos Aires en armas.*

144. See Yablon, "Disciplined Rebels: The Revolution of 1880 in Buenos Aires."

145. Tejedor later served in the Chamber of Deputies from 1894–1898. See B. W. Green to WH, July 28, 1880, and B. W. Green to WH, July 29, 1880, both in Reel 1, Volume 1, DUSC-Córdoba.

146. Sabato, *Republics of the New World,* first quote 197, second quote 207.

147. Sanders, *Vanguard of the Atlantic World.*

148. Lang, *Contest of Civilizations,* 396.

149. See Woodward, *The Strange Career of Jim Crow;* Perman, *Struggle for Mastery;* Calhoun, *From Bloody Shirt to Full Dinner Pail;* and White, *The Republic for Which It Stands.*

150. See Botana, *El orden conservador;* and Richmond, *Carlos Pellegrini and the Crisis of the Argentine Elites.*

151. Matthews, *The Civilizing Machine;* Buffington, *A Sentimental Education for the Working Man;* and Neufeld, *The Blood Contingent.*

Conclusion: "Banana Republics" and Hidden Histories of Cooperation

1. "'Banana Republic Crap': Some Republicans Turn on Trump over Capitol Violence," *U.S. News and World Report,* Jan. 6, 2021.

2. Statement by President George W. Bush on Insurrection at the Capitol, Jan. 6, 2021, George W. Bush Presidential Center, https://www.bushcenter.org/about-the-center/newsroom/press-releases/2021/statement-by-president-george-w-bush-on-insurrection-at-the-capitol.html.

3. Bolton, "The Epic of Greater America."

4. De Tocqueville, *Democracy in America,* 264.

BIBLIOGRAPHY

Manuscript Collections

Abbreviations in square brackets indicate usage in notes.

Archivo General de la Nación, Buenos Aires [AGN, Buenos Aires]
    Archivo del Gen. Dr. I. Rivas, 1857–1877, Sala X, 02-02-02
    Congreso Nacional, 1865–1867, Sala X, 30-5-02
    División Gobierno, Legiones, Sala X, 18-08-02
Archivo General de la Nación, Mexico City [AGN, Mexico City]
    México Independiente/Gobierno y Relaciones Exteriores/R. E./54912
Baylor University, The Texas Collection
    Carter-Harrison Family Papers, Accession #316
Cincinnati Historical Society, Cincinnati, Ohio
    Alexander Long Papers, Cincinnati Historical Society
Indiana State Library, Indiana Division, Manuscript Section
    Oliver P. Morton Papers, 1855–1909, L113
Library of Congress, Washington, DC [LOC]
    Breckinridge Family Papers, 1752–1965
    John A. J. Creswell Papers
    Andrew Johnson Papers
    Abraham Lincoln Papers
    John T. Pickett Papers, 1822–1884
    Edward Lee Plumb Papers, 1825–1903
    Thaddeus Stevens Papers
Louisiana State University, Baton Rouge, Hill Memorial Library Special Collections
    James G. Taliaferro and Family Papers, MSS 1047
    William Pitt Kellogg Papers, MSS 195
New Orleans, Louisiana, Williams Research Center, The Historic New Orleans Collection
    Murphy Family Papers, MSS 270

New York State Military Museum and Veterans Research Center
  Captain Carlos Alvarez de la Mesa Collection
Tennessee State Library and Archives, Nashville
  Galloway Family Papers, 1832–1889; MF 1117
  Havron, James Scott, Papers, 1848–1849; Ac. No. 1364; Small Collections
  IV-D-5
University of Alabama, Hoole Library Special Collections
  Dan Price Letter, MSS 3713
University of Louisiana, Lafayette, Special Collections
  Emerson Bentley Papers; Coll. 94
University of North Carolina at Chapel Hill, Wilson Library, The Southern Historical
Collection
  Mary Elizabeth Mitchell Journal, #1917-z
  Matt W. Ransom Papers, #2615
  Benjamin C. Yancey Papers, #2594
University of Texas at Austin, Dolph Briscoe Center for American History
  Benjamin Holland Epperson Papers, 1834–1876

Printed Primary Sources

Arguments in Favor of the Enforcement of the Monroe Doctrine, Contained in His Annual Message of 1823; And its application to our relations with our Sister Republic of Mexico, in 1864. New Orleans: Era Book and Job Office, 1864.

Bancroft, Hubert H. *The Works of Hubert Howe Bancroft.* San Francisco: History Company, 1888.

Banquet to Señor Matias Romero, Envoy Extraordinary and Minister Plenipotentiary from Mexico to the United States, by the Citizens of New York. October 2, 1867. New York: Hosford and Sons, 1867.

Basler, Roy P., ed. *The Collected Works of Abraham Lincoln.* 9 vols. New Brunswick, NJ: Rutgers University Press, 1953.

Bernardi, Gaetan. *La Vita del Colonnello Silvino Olivieri.* Naples: Stamperia e Cartiere del Fibreno, 1861.

Biographical Sketch of Andrew Johnson, of Tennessee, Together with his Speech at Nashville, June 10, 1864, and his Letter Accepting the Nomination as Vice President of the United States, Tendered him by the National Union Convention. Washington, DC: Union Congressional Committee, 1864.

Burlingame, Michael, ed. *Sixteenth-President-in-Waiting: Abraham Lincoln and the Springfield Dispatches of Henry Villard, 1860–1861.* Carbondale: Southern Illinois University Press, 2018.

Butler, Benjamin Franklin. *Butler's Book: Autobiography and Personal Reminiscences of Major-General Benjamin F. Butler.* Boston: A. M. Thayer, 1892.

Cavada, Federico Fernández. *Libby Life: Experiences of a Prisoner of War in Richmond, Virginia, 1863–1864.* Philadelphia: King and Baird, 1864.

Congreso Nacional. Cámara de Senadores. Sesion de 1868. Buenos Aires: Imprenta del Orden, 1869.

Congreso Nacional: Diario de Sesiones de la Cámara de Diputados, Año 1874. Buenos Aires: Imprenta Especial Para Obras, 1875.

Conyngham, David Power. *Soldiers of the Cross, the Authoritative Text: The Heroism of Catholic Chaplains and Sisters in the American Civil War.* Edited by David J. Endres and William B. Kurtz. Notre Dame, IN: University of Notre Dame Press, 2019.

Curran, Robert Emmett, ed. *John Dooley's Civil War: An Irish American's Journey in the First Virginia Infantry Regiment.* Knoxville: University of Tennessee Press, 2012.

Dinner to Señor Matías Romero, Envoy Extraordinary and Minister Plenipotentiary from Mexico, on the 29th of March, 1864. New York, 1866.

Douglass, Frederick. *My Bondage and My Freedom.* New York: Miller, Orton and Mulligan, 1855.

Dumas, Alexandre. *Montevideo o la nueva Troya.* Buenos Aires: Los Libros de Mirasol, 1961.

Eaton, John. *Grant, Lincoln and the Freedmen.* New York: Longmans, Green, 1907.

Eighty-Eighth Annual Report of the American Bible Society, 1904: Together with a List of Auxiliary Societies, Their Officers, and an Appendix. New York: American Bible Society, 1904.

Executive Documents Printed by Order of the House of Representatives during the Second Session of the Thirty-Sixth Congress, 1860–'61. Washington, DC: GPO, 1861.

Foner, Philip S., ed. *Frederick Douglass: Selected Speeches and Writings.* Chicago: Lawrence Hill, 1999.

Forbes, Hugh. *Manual for Patriotic Volunteer on Active Service in Regular and Irregular War. Being the Art and Science of Obtaining and Maintaining Liberty and Independence.* New York: W. H. Tinson, 1855.

Gould, Benjamin Apthorp. *Investigations in the Military and Anthropological Statistics of American Soldiers.* New York: Hurd and Houghton, 1869.

Graf, LeRoy P., and Ralph W. Haskins, eds. *The Papers of Andrew Johnson.* 16 vols. Knoxville: University of Tennessee Press, 1967–2000.

Grant, Ulysses S. *Personal Memoirs of U. S. Grant.* 2 vols. New York: Charles L. Webster, 1886.

Helper, Hinton Rowan. *The Impending Crisis of the South.* 1857. Edited by Earl Schenck Miers. New York: Crowell-Collier, 1963.

———. *The Impending Crisis of the South: How to Meet It.* 1857. Cambridge, MA: Harvard University Press, 1968.

Higginson, Thomas Wentworth. *Out-Door Papers*. Boston: Ticknor and Fields, 1863.

Johnson, Rossiter. *The Twentieth Century Biographical Dictionary of Notable Americans.* Boston: The Biographical Society, 1904.

Kamphoefner, Walter D., and Wolfgang Helbich, eds. *Germans in the Civil War: The Letters They Wrote Home.* Chapel Hill: University of North Carolina Press, 2006.

Keating, Ryan W., ed. *The Greatest Trial I Ever Had: The Civil War Letters of Margaret and Thomas Cahill.* Athens: University of Georgia Press, 2017.

Life in the Argentine Republic in the Days of Tyrants; or Civilization and Barbarism. Translated by Mary Tyler Peabody Mann. New York: Hurd and Houghton, 1868.

Luiggi, Alice Houston. "Some Letters of Sarmiento and Mary Mann." *Hispanic American Historical Review* 32, no. 2 (May 1952): 187–211.

Lynch, John R. *Reminiscences of an Active Life: The Autobiography of John Roy Lynch.* 1970. Edited by John Hope Franklin. Jackson: University Press of Mississippi, 2008.

Mann, Horace. *A Few Thoughts on the Powers and Duties of Women. Two Lectures.* Syracuse, NY: Hall, Mills, 1853.

Mann, Mary Tyler Peabody. *Life of Horace Mann.* Boston: Walker, Fuller, 1865.

Mayer, Edelmiro. *Campaña y guarnicion: Memorias de un militar argentino en el ejército republicano de Benito Juárez.* 1891. Mexico City: Secretario de Hacienda y Credito Publico, 1972.

McPherson, Edward. *A Hand-Book of Politics for 1874: Being a Record of Important Political Action, National and State, From July 15, 1872 to July 15, 1874.* Washington, DC: Solomons and Chapman, 1874.

———. *A Hand-Book of Politics for 1876: Being a Record of Important Political Action, National and State, From July 15, 1874 to July 15, 1876.* Washington, DC: Solomons and Chapman, 1876.

———. *The Political History of the United States of America, during the Great Rebellion.* Washington, DC: Philp and Solomons, 1865.

Mill, John Stuart. *On Liberty.* London: John W. Parker and Son, 1859.

Norton, Oscar Wilcox. *Army Letters 1861–1865.* Chicago: O. L. Deming, 1903.

Papers Relating to the Foreign Relations of the United States, Transmitted to Congress with the Annual Message of the President, December 5, 1875. Washington, DC: GPO, 1875.

Rawson, Guillermo. *El Estado de Sitio Según la Constitución Argentina.* Buenos Aires: Imprenta de la Soc. Tipográfica Bonaerense, 1863.

Recopilación de Leyes, Decretos y Providencias de los Poderes Legislativo y Ejecutivo de la Union. Mexico City: Imprenta del Gobierno, 1873.

Reinhart, Joseph R., ed. *August Willich's Gallant Dutchmen: Civil War Letters from the 32nd Indiana Infantry.* Kent, OH: Kent State University Press, 2006.

———, ed. *Two Germans in the Civil War: The Diary of John Daeuble and the Letters of Gottfried Rentscheler.* Knoxville: University of Tennessee Press, 2004.

Report of the Joint Select Committee to Inquire into the Condition of Affairs in the Late Insurrectionary States. Washington, DC: GPO, 1872.

República Argentina: Congreso Nacional: Cámara de Senadores, Sesiones de 1874. Buenos Aires: Compañía Sud-Americana de Billetes de Banco, 1986.

Sarmiento, Domingo F. *Facundo: Civilization and Barbarism.* Translated by Kathleen Ross. Berkeley: University of California Press, 2003.

———. *Obras de D. F. Sarmiento.* Edited by A. Belin Sarmiento. 53 vols. Buenos Aires: Imprenta y Litografía Mariano Moreno, 1897.

———. *Travels in the United States in 1847.* Translated by Michael Aaron Rockland. Princeton, NJ: Princeton University Press, 1970.

———. *Vida de Abran Lincoln, décimo sesto presidente de los Estados Unidos.* New York: D. A. Appleton, 1866.

Sarmiento-Mitre Correspondencia 1846–1868. Buenos Aires: Imprenta de Coni Hermanos, 1911.

Schofield, John M. *Forty-Six Years in the Army.* New York: Century, 1897.

Schoonover, Thomas D., ed. *Mexican Lobby: Matías Romero in Washington 1861–1867.* Lexington: University Press of Kentucky, 2014.

Sheridan, Philip H. *Personal Memoirs of Philip Henry Sheridan.* 1888. 2 vols. New York: D. Appleton, 1902.

Smiles, Samuel. *Self Help.* London, 1866.

Stevenson, Brenda, ed. *The Journals of Charlotte Forten Grimké.* New York: Oxford University Press, 1988.

Sumner, Charles. *The Barbarism of Slavery: Speech of Hon. Charles Sumner, on the Bill for the Admission of Kansas as a Free State.* Washington, DC: Buell and Blanchard, Printers, 1860.

Sutter, John A., Jr. *The Sutter Family and the Origins of Gold-Rush Sacramento.* 1943. Edited by Allan R. Ottley. Norman: University of Oklahoma Press, 2002.

Taylor, Susie King. *Reminiscences of My Life in Camp with the 3rd United States Colored Troops Late 1st S. C. Volunteers.* Boston: Published by the Author, 1902.

The American Annual Cyclopaedia and Register of Important Events of the Year 1869. New York: D. Appleton, 1870.

The Assassination of Abraham Lincoln, Late President of the United States of America, and the Attempted Assassination of William H. Seward, Secretary of States and Frederick W. Seward, Assistant Secretary, on the Evening of the 14th of April, 1865. Expressions of Condolence and Sympathy Inspired by These Events. Washington, DC: GPO, 1867.

The Gospel in All Lands: Representing the Missionary Society of the Methodist Episcopal Church. Methodist Episcopal Church, 1887.

Tocqueville, Alexis de. *"Democracy in America" and Two Essays on America.* Translated by Gerald E. Bevan. London: Penguin, 2003.

US War Department. *The War of the Rebellion: A Compilation of the Official Records of the Union and Confederate Armies.* 129 vols. Washington, DC: GPO, 1880–1901.

Consular Records

Argentina: Despatches from US Consul Locations:
  Córdoba (DUSC-Córdoba)
  Rosario (DUSC-Rosario)
Mexico: Despatches from US Consul Locations:
  Acapulco (DUSC-Acapulco)
  Camargo (DUSC-Camargo)
  Chihuahua (DUSC-Chihuahua)
  Guaymas (DUSC-Guaymas)
  Guerrero (DUSC-Guerrero)
  La Paz (DUSC-LP)
  Manzanillo (DUSC-Manzanillo)
  Matamoros (DUSC-Matamoros)
  Mazatlán (DUSC-Mazatlán)
  Merida (DUSC-Merida)
  Mexico City (DUSC-MC)
  Mier (DUSC-Mier)
  Minatitlan (DUSC-Minatitlan)
  Monterrey (DUSC-Monterrey)
  Officials in Nuevo Laredo (DUSCO-NL)
  Piedras Negras (DUSC-PN)
  San Luis Potosi (DUSC-SLP)
  Tabasco (DUSC-Tabasco)
  Tampico (DUSC-Tampico)
  Veracruz (DUSC-Veracruz)

Newspapers and Periodicals

Albany (NY) Argus
Albany (NY) Evening Journal
Alexandria (VA) Gazette
Augusta (GA) Chronicle
Baltimore (MD) Gazette and Daily Advertiser

Baltimore (MD) Sun

Boston (MA) Daily Advertiser

Boston (MA) Daily Journal

Charleston (SC) Courier

Chicago (IL) Tribune

Chilton (WI) Times

Cincinnati (OH) Commercial Tribune

Cincinnati (OH) Daily Commercial

Cincinnati (OH) Daily Enquirer

Cincinnati (OH) Daily Gazette

Cleveland (OH) Plain Dealer

Columbian Register (New Haven, CT)

Connecticut Courant (Hartford)

Coos Republican (Lancaster, NH)

The Crisis (Columbus, OH)

Lowell (MA) Daily Citizen and News

Washington, DC, Daily Critic

San Francisco (CA) Daily Evening Bulletin

Stockton (CA) Daily Evening Herald

Wilmington (NC) Daily Journal

Daily Missouri Democrat (St. Louis)

Daily Missouri Republican (St. Louis)

Daily National Intelligencer (Washington, DC)

Des Moines (IA) Daily State Register

Dallas (TX) Weekly Herald

Detroit (MI) Tribune

Diario de la Marina (Havana, Cuba)

Dollar Newspaper (Philadelphia, PA)

Douglass' Monthly (Rochester, NY)

Eastern Argus (Portland, ME)

Easton (MD) Gazette

El Comercio (Lima, Peru)

The Elevator (San Francisco, CA)

El Libre Pensador (Buenos Aires, Argentina)

El Nuevo Mundo (San Francisco, CA)

El Paso (TX) Herald

El Siglo Diez y Nueve (Mexico City, Mexico)

El Universal (Mexico City, Mexico)

Farmer's Cabinet (Philadelphia, PA)

Flake's Bulletin (Galveston, TX)

Georgia Weekly Telegraph (Macon)

Harper's Weekly (New York)

Helena (MT) Weekly Herald

Idaho Avalanche (Silver City)

Indianapolis (IN) Sentinel

Inter Ocean (Chicago, IL)

Irish World and American Industrial Liberator (New York)

Jamestown (NY) Journal

Janesville (WI) Daily Gazette

La Estrella de Panama (Panama City, Panama)

La Prensa (Buenos Aires, Argentina)

La Voz de Chile y de las Republicas Americanas (San Francisco, CA)

Leavenworth (KS) Bulletin

The Liberator (Boston, MA)

Lowell (MA) Daily Citizens and News

Massachusetts Spy (Worcester)

Milwaukee (WI) Daily Sentinel

Mississippi Free Trader (Natchez)

Mobile (AL) Register

The Nation (New York)

New Hampshire Patriot (Concord)

New Hampshire Sentinel (Keene)

New Mexico Press (Albuquerque)

New-Orleans (LA) Commercial Bulletin

New Orleans (LA) Daily Picayune

New Orleans (LA) Daily True Delta

New-Orleans (LA) Times

New York Commercial Advertiser

New York Evening Post

New York Herald

New York Times

New York Tribune

New York World

Ohio State Journal (Columbus)

Philadelphia (PA) Daily Age

Philadelphia (PA) Inquirer

Pittsfield (MA) Sun

Providence (RI) Evening Press

Public Ledger (Philadelphia, PA)
Quincy (IL) Whig and Republican
Richmond (VA) Whig
Sacramento (CA) Daily Union
Saint Paul (MN) Daily Press
Salem (MA) Register
Salt Lake Weekly Tribune (Salt Lake City, UT)
San Francisco (CA) Evening Bulletin
Savannah (GA) National Republican
Sioux City (IA) Daily Journal
Springfield (MA) Weekly Republican
Springfield (OH) Globe-Republic
The Standard (Buenos Aires, Argentina)
State Gazette (Austin, Texas)
Tombstone (AZ) Prospector
Tri-Weekly Ohio Statesman (Columbus)
Troy (NY) Weekly Times
Weekly Alta Californian (San Francisco)
Weekly Louisianan (New Orleans)
Wheeling (WV) Daily Intelligencer
Wilmington (DE) Daily Commercial
Wisconsin Daily Patriot (Madison)
Wooster (OH) Republican

Secondary Sources

Adelman, Jeremy. *Republic of Capital: Buenos Aires and the Legal Transformation of the Atlantic World.* Stanford, CA: Stanford University Press, 1999.

"AHR Conversation: On Transnational History." *American Historical Review* 111 (Dec. 2006): 1441–64.

Alduino, Frank W., and David J. Coles. *Sons of Garibaldi in Blue and Gray: Italians in the American Civil War.* Youngstown, NY: Cambria, 2007.

Alonso, Paula. *Between Revolution and the Ballot Box: The Origins of the Argentine Radical Party.* Cambridge: Cambridge University Press, 2000.

Altschuler, Glen C., and Stuart M. Blumin. *Rude Republic: Americans and Their Politics in the Nineteenth Century.* Princeton, NJ: Princeton University Press, 2000.

Anderson, Benedict. *Imagined Communities: Reflections on the Origins and Spread of Nationalism.* London: Verso, 1983.

Anderson, Fred. *Crucible of War: The Seven Years' War and the Fate of the Empire in British North America, 1754–1766.* New York: Knopf, 2000.

Anderson, James D. *The Education of Blacks in the South, 1860–1935.* Chapel Hill: University of North Carolina Press, 1988.

Andrews, George Reid. *The Afro-Argentines of Buenos Aires, 1800–1900.* Madison: University of Wisconsin Press, 1980.

Anna, Timothy E. *The Fall of the Royal Government in Mexico City.* Lincoln: University of Nebraska Press, 1978.

———. *Forging Mexico, 1821–1835.* Lincoln: University of Nebraska Press, 1998.

———. *The Mexican Empire of Iturbide.* Lincoln: University of Nebraska Press, 1990.

———. *Spain and the Loss of America.* Lincoln: University of Nebraska Press, 1983.

Arana, Enrique. *Juan Manuel de Rosas en la historia Argentina: Creador y sostén de la unidad nacional: Rosas y la política exterior con otros estudios.* 3 vols. Buenos Aires: Instituto Panamericano de Cultura, 1954.

Arenson, Adam, and Andrew R. Graybill, eds. *Civil War Wests: Testing the Limits of the United States.* Oakland: University of California Press, 2015.

Armitage, David. *The Declaration of Independence: A Global History.* Cambridge, MA: Harvard University Press, 2007.

Arthur, Anthony. *General Jo Shelby's March.* New York: Random House, 2010.

Ash, Stephen V. *A Massacre in Memphis: That Race Riot That Shook the Nation One Year after the Civil War.* New York: Hill and Wang, 2013.

Auricchio, Laura. *The Marquis: Lafayette Reconsidered.* New York: Vintage, 2014.

Bailey, David C. *¡Viva Cristo Rey! The Cristero Rebellion and the Church-State Conflict in Mexico.* Austin: University of Texas Press, 1974.

Bailey, Helen Miller, and Abraham P. Nasatir. *Latin America: The Development of Its Civilization.* Englewood Cliffs, NJ: Prentice-Hall, 1960.

Bailey, Hugh C. *Hinton Rowan Helper: Abolitionist-Racist.* Tuscaloosa: University of Alabama Press, 1965.

Baily, Samuel L. *Immigrants in the Land of Promise: Italians in Buenos Aires and New York City, 1870–1914.* Ithaca, NY: Cornell University Press, 1999.

———. "Italian Immigrants in Buenos Aires and New York City, 1870–1914: A Comparative Analysis of Adjustment." In *Mass Migration to Modern Latin America,* edited by Baily and Eduardo José Míguez, 69–80. Wilmington, DE: Scholarly Resources, 2003.

Bailyn, Bernard. *The Ideological Origins of the American Revolution.* Cambridge, MA: Harvard University Press, 1967.

Baker, Jean H. *Affairs of Party: The Political Culture of Northern Democrats in the Mid-Nineteenth Century.* 1983. New York: Fordham University Press, 1998.

Barker, Gordon S. *The Imperfect Revolution: Anthony Burns and the Landscape of Race in Antebellum America.* Kent, OH: Kent State University Press, 2010.

Batchelor, John E. *Race and Education in North Carolina: From Segregation to Desegregation.* Baton Rouge: Louisiana State University Press, 2015.

Bayly, C. A. *The Birth of the Modern World: 1780–1914.* Malden, MA: Blackwell, 2004.

Beck, Paul N. *Columns of Vengeance: Soldiers, Sioux, and the Punitive Expeditions, 1863–1864.* Norman: University of Oklahoma Press, 2013.

Beeman, Richard. *Plain, Honest Men: The Making of the American Constitution.* New York: Random House, 2009.

Behrend, Justin. "Facts, Memories, and History: John R. Lynch and the Memory of Reconstruction in the Age of Jim Crow." In *Remembering Reconstruction: Struggles over the Meaning of America's Most Turbulent Era,* edited by Carole Emberton and Bruce E. Baker, 84–108. Baton Rouge: Louisiana State University Press, 2017.

———. *Reconstructing Democracy: Grassroots Black Politics in the Deep South after the Civil War.* Athens: University of Georgia Press, 2015.

Belz, Herman. "The Etheridge Conspiracy of 1863: A Projected Conservative Coup." *Journal of Southern History* 36 (Nov. 1970): 549–67.

Bender, Thomas. *A Nation among Nations: America's Place in World History.* New York: Hill and Wang, 2006.

———, ed. *Rethinking American History in a Global Age.* Berkeley: University of California Press, 2002.

Benedict, Michael Les. *A Compromise of Principle: Congressional Republicans and Reconstruction, 1863–1869.* New York: Norton, 1974.

Berlin, Ira. *Generations of Captivity: A History of African American Slaves.* Cambridge, MA: Harvard University Press, 2003.

Berlin, Ira, Barbara J. Fields, Steven F. Miller, Joseph P. Reidy, and Leslie S. Rowland. *Slaves No More: Three Essays on Emancipation and the Civil War.* Cambridge: Cambridge University Press, 1992.

Berlin, Ira, Joseph P. Reidy, and Leslie S. Rowland. *Freedom's Soldiers: The Black Military Experience in the Civil War.* Cambridge: Cambridge University Press, 1998.

Bernstein, Harry. *Matías Romero: 1837–1898.* Mexico: Fondo de Cultura Económica, 1973.

———. "South America Looks at North American Reconstruction." In *New Frontiers of the American Reconstruction,* edited by Harold M. Hyman, 87–104. Urbana: University of Illinois Press, 1966.

Bernstein, Iver. *The New York City Draft Riots: Their Significance for American Society and Politics in the Age of the Civil War.* New York: Oxford University Press, 1990.

Berry, Charles R. *The Reform in Oaxaca, 1856–1876: A Microhistory of the Liberal Revolution.* Lincoln: University of Nebraska Press, 1981.

Bilby, Joseph G. *The Irish Brigade in the Civil War: The 69th New York and Other Irish Regiments of the Army of the Potomac.* Conshohocken, PA: Combined Publishing, 1995.

Billington, James H. *Fire in the Minds of Men: Origins of the Revolutionary Faith*. New Brunswick, NJ: Transaction, 1999.

Blackett, R. J. M. *Building an Antislavery Wall: Black Americans in the Atlantic Abolition Movement, 1830–1860*. Baton Rouge: Louisiana State University Press, 1983.

Blair, William A. "Finding the End of America's Civil War." *American Historical Review* 120 (Dec. 2015): 1753–66.

———. *The Record of Murders and Outrages: Racial Violence and the Fight over Truth at the Dawn of Reconstruction*. Chapel Hill: University of North Carolina Press, 2021.

Blanchard, Peter. *Under the Flags of Freedom: Slave Soldiers and the War of Independence in Spanish South America*. Pittsburgh, PA: University of Pittsburgh Press, 2008.

Blaufarb, Rafe. "The Western Question: The Geopolitics of Latin American Independence." *American Historical Review* 112 (June 2007): 742–63.

Blum, Edward J. *Reforging the White Republic: Race, Religion, and American Nationalism 1865–1898*. Baton Rouge: Louisiana State University Press, 2005.

Bolton, Herbert E. "The Epic of Greater America." *American Historical Review* 38 (April 1933): 448–74.

Bonner, Robert E. "Slavery, Confederate Diplomacy, and the Racialist Mission of Henry Hotze." *Civil War History* 51 (2005): 288–316.

Boonshoft, Mark. *Aristocratic Education and the Making of the American Republic*. Chapel Hill: University of North Carolina Press, 2020.

Botana, Natalio R. *El orden conservador: La política argentina entre 1880 y 1916*. Buenos Aires: Sudamericana, 1977.

Bottoms, D. Michael. *An Aristocracy of Color: Race and Reconstruction in California and the West*. Norman: University of Oklahoma Press, 2013.

Bowden, Brett. *The Empire of Civilization: The Evolution of an Imperial Idea*. Chicago: University of Chicago Press, 2009.

Bowen, Wayne H. *Spain and the American Civil War*. Columbia: University of Missouri Press, 2011.

Bowers, Claude G. *The Tragic Era: The Revolution after Lincoln*. New York: Houghton Mifflin, 1929.

Boydston, Jeanne, Mary Kelley, and Anne Margolis. *The Limits of Sisterhood: The Beecher Sisters on Women's Rights and Woman's Sphere*. Chapel Hill: University of North Carolina Press, 1988.

Bradley, Mark L. *Bluecoats and Tar Heels: Soldiers and Civilians in Reconstruction North Carolina*. Lexington: University Press of Kentucky, 2009.

Brittsan, Zachary. *Popular Politics and Rebellion in Mexico: Manuel Lozada and La Reforma, 1855–1876*. Nashville, TN: Vanderbilt University Press, 2015.

Brown, Jonathan C. *A Socioeconomic History of Argentina, 1776–1860*. Cambridge: Cambridge University Press, 1979.

Budiansky, Stephen. *The Bloody Shirt: Terror after the Civil War.* New York: Penguin, 2008.

Buffington, Robert W. *A Sentimental Education for the Working Man: The Mexico City Penny Press, 1900–1910.* Durham, NC: Duke University Press, 2015.

Bunkley, Allison Williams. *Vida de Sarmiento.* Buenos Aires: Editorial Universitaria de Buenos Aires, 1966.

Burlingame, Michael. *Abraham Lincoln: A Life.* Baltimore, MD: Johns Hopkins University Press, 2008.

Burns, E. Bradford. *The Poverty of Progress: Latin America in the Nineteenth Century.* Berkeley: University of California Press, 1980.

Butchart, Ronald E. *Schooling the Freed People: Teaching, Learning, and the Struggle for Black Freedom, 1861–1876.* Chapel Hill: University of North Carolina Press, 2010.

Butler, Leslie. *Critical Americans: Victorian Intellectuals and Transatlantic Liberal Reform.* Chapel Hill: University of North Carolina Press, 2007.

———. "Lincoln as the Great Educator: Opinion and Educative Liberalism in the Civil War Era." In *The Transnational Significance of the American Civil War,* edited by Jörg Nagler, Don H. Doyle, and Marcus Gräser, 49–66. London: Palgrave Macmillan, 2016.

Cadenhead, Ivie E., Jr. *Jesús González Ortega and Mexican National Politics.* Fort Worth: Texas Christian University Press, 1972.

Calhoun, Charles W. *From Bloody Shirt to Full Dinner Pail: The Transformation of Politics and Governance in the Gilded Age.* New York: Hill and Wang, 2010.

Callahan, James Morton. "The Confederate Diplomatic Archives—The Pickett Papers." *South Atlantic Quarterly* 2 (Jan. 1903): 1–9.

———. *Evolution of Seward's Mexican Policy.* Morgantown: West Virginia University, 1908.

Campney, Brent M. S. *This Is Not Dixie: Racist Violence in Kansas, 1861–1927.* Urbana: University of Illinois Press, 2015.

Campobassi, José. *Sarmiento y su época.* Buenos Aires: Editorial Losada, 1975.

Cecelski, David, and Timothy B. Tyson, eds. *Democracy Betrayed: The Wilmington Race Riot of 1898 and Its Legacy.* Chapel Hill: University of North Carolina Press, 1998.

Chaffin, Tom. *Fatal Glory: Narciso López and the First Clandestine U.S. War against Cuba.* 1996. Baton Rouge: Louisiana State University Press, 2003

Chance, Joseph E. *José María de Jesús Carvajal: The Life and Times of a Mexican Revolutionary.* San Antonio, TX: Trinity University Press, 2006.

Chávez, Fermín. *Historia del país de los Argentinos.* Buenos Aires: Ediciones Teoría, 1967.

Chernow, Ron. *Grant.* New York: Penguin, 2017.

Cimbala, Paul A., and Randall M. Miller, eds. *The Great Task Remaining before Us: Reconstruction as America's Continuing Civil War.* New York: Fordham University Press, 2010.

Cimprich, John. *Fort Pillow: A Civil War Massacre and Public Memory.* Baton Rouge: Louisiana State University Press, 2005.

Clavin, Matthew J. *Toussaint Louverture and the American Civil War: The Promise and Peril of a Second Haitian Revolution.* Philadelphia: University of Pennsylvania Press, 2010.

Click, Patricia. *Time Full of Trial: The Roanoke Island Freedmen's Colony, 1862–1867.* Chapel Hill: University of North Carolina Press, 2001.

Collins, Michael L. *Texas Devils: Rangers and Regulars on the Lower Rio Grande, 1846–1861.* Norman: University of Oklahoma Press, 2008.

Connelly, Donald B. *John M. Schofield and the Politics of Generalship.* Chapel Hill: University of North Carolina Press, 2006.

Cooper, Frederick, Thomas C. Holt, and Rebecca J. Scott, eds. *Beyond Slavery: Explorations of Race, Labor, and Citizenship in Postemancipation Societies.* Chapel Hill: University of North Carolina Press, 2000.

Cornish, Dudley Taylor. *The Sable Arm: Black Troops in the Union Army, 1861–1865.* 1956. Lawrence: University Press of Kansas, 1987.

Correas, Edmundo. *Sarmiento and the United States.* Gainesville: University of Florida Press, 1961.

Costeloe, Michael P. *The Central Republic in Mexico, 1835–1846: Hombres de Bien in the Age of Santa Anna.* Cambridge: Cambridge University Press, 1993.

Coulter, E. Merton. *The South during Reconstruction 1865–1877.* Baton Rouge: Louisiana State University Press, 1947.

Cowan, Walter Greaves, and Jack B. McGuire. *Louisiana Governors: Rulers, Rascals, and Reformers.* Jackson: University Press of Mississippi, 2008.

Cox, John, and LaWanda Cox. "General O. O. Howard and the 'Misrepresented Bureau.'" *Journal of Southern History* 10 (Nov. 1944): 447–60.

Cox, LaWanda. *Lincoln and Black Freedom: A Study in Presidential Leadership.* Columbia: University of South Carolina Press, 1981.

Crapol, Edward P. *James G. Blaine: Architect of Empire.* Wilmington, DE: Scholarly Resources, 2000.

Crassweller, Robert D. *Perón and the Enigmas of Argentina.* New York: Norton, 1987.

Craughwell, Thomas J. *The Greatest Brigade: How the Irish Brigade Cleared the Way to Victory in the American Civil War.* Beverly, MA: Fair Winds, 2011.

Creighton, Margaret S. *The Colors of Courage: Gettysburg's Forgotten History: Immigrants, Women, and African Americans in the Civil War's Defining Battle.* New York: Basic, 2005.

Criblez, Adam. *Parading Patriotism: Independence Day Celebrations in the Urban Midwest, 1826–1876.* DeKalb: Northern Illinois University Press, 2013.

Crouch, Barry A., and Donaly E. Brice. *The Governor's Hounds: The Texas State Police, 1870–1873.* Austin: University of Texas Press, 2011.

Crowley, Frances G. *Domingo Faustino Sarmiento.* New York: Twayne, 1972.

Crytzer, Brady J. *Hessians: Mercenaries, Rebels, and the War for British North America.* Yardley, PA: Westholme, 2015.

Curry, Leonard P. *Blueprint for Modern America: Nonmilitary Legislation of the First Civil War Congress.* Nashville, TN: Vanderbilt University Press, 1968.

Cutrer, Thomas W. *Theater of a Separate War: The Civil War West of the Mississippi River, 1861–1865.* Chapel Hill: University of North Carolina Press, 2017.

Dal Lago, Enrico. *The Age of Lincoln and Cavour: Comparative Perspectives on Nineteenth-Century American and Italian Nation-Building.* New York: Palgrave Macmillan, 2015.

———. *Agrarian Elites: American Slaveholders and Southern Italian Landowners, 1815–1861.* Baton Rouge: Louisiana State University Press, 2005.

———. *William Lloyd Garrison and Giuseppe Mazzini: Abolition, Democracy, and Radical Reform.* Baton Rouge: Louisiana State University Press, 2013.

Davis, Edwin Adams. *Fallen Guidon: The Saga of Confederate General Jo Shelby's March to Mexico.* College Station: Texas A&M University Press, 1995.

Davis, Harold E. *Makers of Democracy in Latin America.* New York: Cooper Square, 1968.

Dawsey, Cyrus B., and James M. Dawsey, eds. *The Confederados: Old South Immigrants in Brazil.* Tuscaloosa: University of Alabama Press, 1998.

Dawson, Alexander. *Indian and Nation in Revolutionary Mexico.* Tucson: University of Arizona Press, 2004.

Dawson, Joseph G., III. *Army Generals and Reconstruction: Louisiana, 1862–1877.* Baton Rouge: Louisiana State University Press, 1982.

De Gandía, Enrique. *Historia de la República Argentina en el siglo XIX.* Buenos Aires: Angel Estrada y Cía. S.A., 1940.

De la Cova, Antonio Rafael. *Colonel Henry Theodore Titus: Antebellum Soldier of Fortune and Florida Pioneer.* Columbia: University of South Carolina Press, 2016.

———. *Cuban Confederate Colonel: The Life of Ambrosio José Gonzales.* Columbia: University of South Carolina Press, 2003.

De la Fuente, Ariel. *Children of Facundo: Caudillo and Gaucho Insurgency during the Argentine State-Formation Process (La Rioja, 1853–1870).* Durham, NC: Duke University Press, 2000.

De la Teja, Jesús F., ed. *Lone Star Unionism, Dissent, and Resistance: Other Sides of Civil War Texas.* Norman: University of Oklahoma Press, 2016.

Delgado, Grace Peña. *Making the Chinese Mexican: Global Migration, Localism, and Exclusion in the U.S.-Mexico Borderlands.* Stanford, CA: Stanford University Press, 2012.

Dew, Charles B. *Apostles of Disunion: Southern Secession Commissioners and the Causes of the Civil War.* Charlottesville: University Press of Virginia, 2001.

Dobak, William A. *Freedom by the Sword: The U.S. Colored Troops, 1862–1867.* Washington, DC: Center of Military History, 2011.

Dorn, Georgette Magassy. "Sarmiento, the United States, and Public Education." In *Sarmiento and His Argentina,* edited by Joseph T Criscenti, 77–89. Boulder, CO: Lynne Rienner, 1993.

Downs, Gregory P. *After Appomattox: Military Occupation and the Ends of War.* Cambridge, MA: Harvard University Press, 2015.

———. "Anarchy at the Circumference: Statelessness and the Reconstruction of Authority in Emancipation North Carolina." In *After Slavery: Race, Labor, and Citizenship in the Reconstruction South,* edited by Bruce E. Baker and Brian Kelly, 98–121. Gainesville: University Press of Florida, 2013.

———. *Declarations of Dependence: The Long Reconstruction of Popular Politics in the South, 1861–1908.* Chapel Hill: University of North Carolina Press, 2011.

———. "The Mexicanization of American Politics: The United States' Transnational Path from Civil War to Stabilization." *American Historical Review* 117 (April 2012): 387–409.

———. *The Second American Revolution: The Civil War–Era Struggle over Cuba and the Rebirth of the American Republic.* Chapel Hill: University of North Carolina Press, 2019.

Downs, Gregory P., and James Downs. "Was Freedom Enough?" In *The New York Times: Disunion: A History of the Civil War,* edited by Ted Widmer with Clay Risen and George Kalogerakis, 52–55. New York: Oxford University Press, 2016.

Downs, Gregory P., and Kate Masur, eds. *The World the Civil War Made.* Chapel Hill: University of North Carolina Press, 2015.

Doyle, Don H., ed. *American Civil Wars: The United States, Latin America, Europe, and the Crisis of the 1860s.* Chapel Hill: University of North Carolina Press, 2017.

———. *Nations Divided: America, Italy, and the Southern Question.* Athens: University of Georgia Press, 2002.

———. "Reconstruction and Anti-imperialism: The United States and Mexico." In *United States Reconstruction Across the Americas,* edited by William A. Link. Gainesville: University Press of Florida, 2019.

———. *The Cause of All Nations: An International History of the American Civil War.* New York: Basic, 2015.

Doyle, Don H., and Marco Antonio Pamplona, eds. *Nationalism in the New World.* Athens: University of Georgia Press, 2006.

Du Bois, W. E. B. *Black Reconstruction in America: 1860–1880.* New York: Harcourt, Brace, 1935.

Dufour, Charles L. *Gallant Tiger: The Life of Roberdeau Wheat.* Baton Rouge: Louisiana State University Press, 1957.

Dunlap, Boutwell. *Augusta County, Virginia, in the History of the United States.* Frankfort, KY: State Journal Company, 1918.

Dunning, William A. *Reconstruction: Political and Economic 1865–1877*. New York: Harper and Brothers, 1907.

Efford, Alison Clark. *German Immigrants, Race, and Citizenship in the Civil War Era*. Cambridge: Cambridge University Press, 2013.

Egerton, Douglas R. *Thunder at the Gates: The Black Regiments That Redeemed America*. New York: Basic, 2016.

———. *The Wars of Reconstruction: The Brief, Violent History of America's Most Progressive Era*. New York: Bloomsbury Press, 2014.

Eichhorn, Niels. *Liberty and Slavery: European Separatists, Southern Secession, and the American Civil War*. Baton Rouge: Louisiana State University Press, 2019.

Elkins, Stanley M. *Slavery: A Problem in American Institutional and Intellectual Life*. Chicago: University of Chicago Press, 1959.

Eller, Anne. *We Dream Together: Dominican Independence, Haiti, and the Fight for Caribbean Freedom*. Durham, NC: Duke University Press, 2016.

Elliott, Mark. "Nation-Building Begins at Home." *Review in American History* 35 (June 2007): 239–46.

Emberton, Carole. *Beyond Redemption: Race, Violence, and the American South after the Civil War*. Chicago: University of Chicago Press, 2013.

———. "'Only Murder Makes Men': Reconsidering the Black Military Experience." *Journal of the Civil War Era* 2 (Sept. 2012): 369–93.

Engerman, Stanley L. *Slavery, Emancipation, and Freedom: Comparative Perspectives*. Baton Rouge: Louisiana State University Press, 2007.

Engerman, Stanley L., and Kenneth L. Sokoloff. *Economic Development in the Americas since 1500: Endowments and Institutions*. Cambridge: Cambridge University Press, 2012.

Epps, Kristen. *Slavery on the Periphery: The Kansas-Missouri Border in the Antebellum and Civil War Eras*. Athens: University of Georgia Press, 2016.

Etcheson, Nicole. *Bleeding Kansas: Contested Liberty in the Civil War Era*. Lawrence: University Press of Kansas, 2004.

Eyal, Yonatan. *The Young America Movement and the Transformation of the Democratic Party 1828–1861*. Cambridge: Cambridge University Press, 2007.

Fairclough, Adam. *Bulldozed and Betrayed: Louisiana and the Stolen Elections of 1876*. Baton Rouge: Louisiana State University Press, 2021.

Faulkner, Carol. *Women's Radical Reconstruction: The Freedmen's Aid Movement*. Philadelphia: University of Pennsylvania Press, 2004.

Fehrenbacher, Don E. *The Dred Scott Case: Its Significance in American Law and Politics*. New York: Oxford University Press, 1978.

———. *Prelude to Greatness: Lincoln in the 1850s*. Stanford, CA: Stanford University Press, 1962.

———. *The Slaveholding Republic: An Account of the United States Government's Relations to Slavery.* New York: Oxford University Press, 2001.

Fellman, Michael. *Inside War: The Guerrilla Conflict in Missouri during the American Civil War.* New York: Oxford University Press, 1989.

Ferris Nathan L. "The Relations of the United States with South America during the American Civil War." *Hispanic American Historical Review* 21 (Feb. 1941): 51–78.

Fitz, Caitlin. *Our Sister Republics: The United States in an Age of American Revolutions.* New York: Norton, 2016.

Fitzgerald, Michael W. *Reconstruction in Alabama: From Civil War to Redemption in the Cotton South.* Baton Rouge: Louisiana State University Press, 2017.

Fleche, Andre M. *The Revolution of 1861: The American Civil War in the Age of Nationalist Conflict.* Chapel Hill: University of North Carolina Press, 2012.

Fleming, Walter L. *The Sequel of Appomattox.* New Haven, CT: Yale University Press, 1919.

Fletcher, Lea. "Juana Manso: Una voz en el desierto." In *Mujeres y cultura en la Argentina del siglo XIX,* edited by Fletcher, 108–20. Buenos Aires: Feminaria Editora, 1994.

Foner, Eric. *Nothing but Freedom: Emancipation and Its Legacy.* Baton Rouge: Louisiana State University Press, 1983.

———. *Reconstruction: America's Unfinished Revolution, 1863–1877.* New York: Harper and Row, 1988.

———. *The Story of American Freedom.* New York: Norton, 1998.

Foos, Paul. *A Short, Offhand, Killing Affair: Soldiers and Social Conflict during the Mexican American War.* Chapel Hill: University of North Carolina Press, 2001.

Forbes, Robert Pierce. *The Missouri Compromise and Its Aftermath: Slavery and the Meaning of America.* Chapel Hill: University of North Carolina Press, 2007.

Foreman, Amanda. *A World on Fire: Britain's Crucial Role in the American Civil War.* New York: Random House, 2010.

"Forum: Teaching the Civil War Era in Global Context: A Discussion." *Journal of the Civil War Era* 5 (March 2015): 126–53.

Fowler, Will, ed. *Celebrating Insurrection: The Commemoration and Representation of the Nineteenth-Century Mexican Pronunciamiento.* Lincoln: University of Nebraska Press, 2013.

———, ed. *Forceful Negotiations: The Origins of the Pronunciamiento in Nineteenth-Century Mexico.* Lincoln: University of Nebraska Press, 2011.

———. *Independent Mexico: The Pronunciamiento in the Age of Santa Anna, 1828—1855.* Lincoln: University of Nebraska Press, 2016.

———, ed. *Malcontents, Rebels, and Pronunciados: The Politics of Insurrection in Nineteenth-Century Mexico.* Lincoln: University of Nebraska Press, 2012.

———. *Santa Anna of Mexico.* Lincoln: University of Nebraska Press, 2007.

———. *Tornel and Santa Anna: The Writer and the Caudillo, Mexico 1795–1853.* Westport, CT: Greenwood, 2000.

Franklin, John Hope. "Election of 1868." In *History of American Presidential Elections, 1789–1968,* edited by Arthur M. Schlesinger Jr., 1247–300. New York: Chelsea House, 1971.

Frazer, Robert W. "Latin American Projects to Aid Mexico during the French Intervention." *Hispanic American Historical Review* 28, no. 3 (Aug. 1948): 377–88.

Frazier, Donald S. *Blood and Treasure: Confederate Empire in the Southwest.* College Station: Texas A&M University Press, 1995.

———. *Blood on the Bayou: Vicksburg, Port Hudson, and the Trans-Mississippi.* Buffalo Gap, TX: State House Press, 2015.

Fredrickson, George M. "Comparative History." In *The Past before Us: Contemporary Historical Writings in the United States,* edited by Michael Kammen, 457–73. Ithaca, NY: Cornell University Press, 1980.

———. *The Comparative Imagination: On the History of Racism, Nationalism, and Social Movements.* Berkeley: University of California Press, 2000.

———. "From Exceptionalism to Variability: Recent Developments in Cross-National Comparative History." *Journal of American History* 82 (Sept. 1995): 587–604.

———. Introduction to *The Impending Crisis of the South: How to Meet It,* by Hinton Rowan Helper. 1857. Cambridge, MA: Harvard University Press, 1968.

———. *White Supremacy: A Comparative Study in American and South African History.* New York: Oxford University Press, 1981.

———. "Why the Confederacy Did Not Fight a Guerrilla War after the Fall of Richmond: A Comparative View." *35th Annual Robert Fortenbaugh Memorial Lecture.* Gettysburg, PA: Gettysburg College, 1996.

Freehling William W. *The Road to Disunion. Vol. 1: Secessionists at Bay, 1776–1854.* New York: Oxford University Press, 1990.

Freeman, Joanne B. *The Field of Blood: Violence in Congress and the Road to the Civil War.* New York: Farrar, Straus and Giroux, 2018.

Fry, Joseph A. *Lincoln, Seward, and U.S. Foreign Relations in the Civil War Era.* Lexington: University Press of Kentucky, 2009.

Gálvez, Manuel. *Vida de Sarmiento: El hombre de autoridad.* Buenos Aires: Emecé 1945.

Genetin-Pilawa, C. Joseph. *Crooked Paths to Allotment: The Fight over Federal Indian Policy after the Civil War.* Chapel Hill: University of North Carolina Press, 2012.

Genova, Thomas. "Sarmiento's *Vida de Horacio Mann:* Translation, Importation, and Entanglement." *Hispanic Review* 82 (Winter 2014): 21–41.

Genovese, Eugene D. "The South in the History of the Transatlantic World." In *What Made the South Different,* edited by Kees Gispen, 3–18. Jackson: University Press of Mississippi, 1990.

Gienapp, William E. *The Origins of the Republican Party, 1852–1856.* New York: Oxford University Press, 1987.

Glatthaar, Joseph T. *Forged in Battle: The Civil War Alliance of Black Soldiers and White Officers.* Baton Rouge: Louisiana State University Press, 1990.

Gleeson, David T. *The Green and the Gray: The Irish in the Confederate States of America.* Chapel Hill: University of North Carolina Press, 2013.

Gleeson, David T., and Simon Lewis, eds. *The Civil War as Global Conflict: Transnational Meanings of the American Civil War.* Columbia: University of South Carolina Press, 2014.

Gobat, Michel. *Empire by Invitation: William Walker and Manifest Destiny in Central America.* Cambridge, MA: Harvard University Press, 2018.

González-Quiroga, Miguel Ángel. *War and Peace on the Rio Grande Frontier, 1830–1880.* Norman: University of Oklahoma Press, 2020.

Graham, Richard. *Patronage and Politics in Nineteenth-Century Brazil.* Stanford, CA: Stanford University Press, 1990.

Green, Hilary. *Educational Reconstruction: African American Schools in the Urban South, 1865–1890.* New York: Fordham University Press, 2016.

Greenberg, Amy S. *A Wicked War: Polk, Clay, Lincoln, and the 1846 U.S. Invasion of Mexico.* New York: Vintage, 2012.

Grew, Raymond. "The Case for Comparing Histories." *American Historical Review* 85 (Oct. 1980): 763–82.

Griggs, William Clark. *The Elusive Eden: Frank McMullen's Confederate Colony in Brazil.* Austin: University of Texas Press, 1987.

Guardino, Peter F. *The Dead March: A History of the Mexican-American War.* Cambridge, MA: Harvard University Press, 2017.

———. *Peasants, Politics and the Formation of Mexico's National State.* Stanford, CA: Stanford University Press, 1996.

———. *The Time of Liberty: Popular Political Culture in Oaxaca, 1750–1850.* Durham, NC: Duke University Press, 2005.

Guelzo, Allen C. *Gettysburg: The Last Invasion.* New York: Random House, 2013.

———. *Lincoln's Emancipation Proclamation: The End of Slavery in America.* New York: Simon and Schuster, 2004.

Guerra, J. Guillermo. *Sarmiento: Sus vidas i sus obras.* Santiago de Chile: Imprenta Elzeviriana, 1901.

Guerrero, César H. *Mujeres de Sarmiento.* Buenos Aires: Artes Gráficas, 1960.

Guterl, Matthew Pratt. *American Mediterranean: Southern Slaveholders in the Age of Emancipation.* Cambridge, MA: Harvard University Press, 2008.

Haberly, David T. "Facundo in the United States: An Unknown Reading." *Ciberletras: Revista de crítica literaria y de cultura* 14 (2005): n.p.

Hahn, Steven. *A Nation under Our Feet: Black Political Struggles in the Rural South from Slavery to the Great Migration*. Cambridge, MA: Harvard University Press, 2003.

———. "The Politics of Black Rural Labourers in the Postemancipation South." In *The American South and the Italian Mezzogiorno*, edited by Enrico Dal Lago and Rick Halpern, 112–31. New York: Palgrave Macmillan, 2002.

Hale, Charles A. *Mexican Liberalism in the Age of Mora, 1821–1853*. New Haven, CT: Yale University Press, 1968.

———. *The Transformation of Liberalism in Late Nineteenth-Century Mexico*. Princeton, NJ: Princeton University Press, 1989.

Hall, Gwendolyn Midlo. *Social Control in Slave Plantation Societies: A Comparison of St. Domingue and Cuba*. Baltimore, MD: Johns Hopkins University Press, 1971.

Hall, Matthew W. *Dividing the Union: Jesse Burgess Thomas and the Making of the Missouri Compromise*. Carbondale: Southern Illinois University Press, 2016.

Hamill, Hugh M. *The Hidalgo Revolt: Prelude to Mexican Independence*. Gainesville: University of Florida Press, 1966.

Hamilton, Holman. *Prologue to Conflict: The Crisis and Compromise of 1850*. Lexington: University Press of Kentucky, 1964.

Hamnett, Brian R. *Juárez*. London: Longman, 1994.

———. "Royalist Counterinsurgency and the Continuity of Rebellion: Guanajuato and Michoacán, 1813–1820." *Hispanic American Historical Review* 62 (Feb. 1982): 19–48.

Hanke, Lewis. *South America*. Princeton, NJ: Van Nostrand, 1967.

Hanna, Alfred J., and Kathryn A. Hanna. *Napoleon III and Mexico: American Triumph over Monarchy*. Chapel Hill: University of North Carolina Press, 1971.

Harris, William C. "The Hampton Roads Peace Conference: A Final Test of Lincoln's Presidential Leadership." *Journal of the Abraham Lincoln Association* 21, no. 1 (Winter 2000): 30–61.

———. *Two Against Lincoln: Reverdy Johnson and Horatio Seymour, Champions of the Loyal Opposition*. Lawrence: University Press of Kansas, 2017.

———. *With Charity for All: Lincoln and the Restoration of the Union*. Lexington: University Press of Kentucky, 1997.

Harter, Eugene C. *The Lost Colony of the Confederacy*. College Station: Texas A&M University Press, 2000.

Heinrich, Robert, and Deborah Harding, eds. *From Slave to Statesman: The Life of Educator, Editor, and Civil Rights Activist Willis M. Carter of Virginia*. Baton Rouge: Louisiana State University Press, 2016.

Henderson, Timothy J. *A Glorious Defeat: Mexico and Its War with the United States*. New York: Hill and Wang, 2007.

———. *The Mexican Wars for Independence*. New York: Hill and Wang, 2009.

Hess, Earl J. *The Civil War in the West: Victory and Defeat from the Appalachians to the Mississippi.* Chapel Hill: University of North Carolina Press, 2012.

Hibbert, Christopher. *Garibaldi: Hero of Italian Unification.* 1965. Reprint. New York: St. Martin's, 2008.

Hobsbawm, Eric. *The Age of Capital: 1848–1875.* London: Weidenfeld and Nicolson, 1975.

Hodge, John E. "Benjamin Apthorp Gould and the Founding of the Argentine National Observatory." *The Americas* 28 (Oct. 1971): 152–75.

Hoffer, Williamjames Hull. *The Caning of Charles Sumner: Honor, Idealism, and the Origins of the Civil War.* Baltimore, MD: Johns Hopkins University Press, 2010.

Hogue, James K. *Uncivil War: Five New Orleans Street Battles and the Rise and Fall of Radical Reconstruction.* Baton Rouge: Louisiana State University Press, 2006.

Holgado, Benjamín García. *De Mitre a Roca: Política, sociedad y economía 1860–1904.* Buenos Aires: Editorial El Coloquio, 1975.

Hollandsworth, James G., Jr. *An Absolute Massacre: The New Orleans Race Riot of July 30, 1866.* Baton Rouge: Louisiana State University Press, 2001.

Holt, Michael F. *By One Vote: The Disputed Presidential Election of 1876.* Lawrence: University Press of Kansas, 2008.

———. *The Election of 1860: "A Campaign Fraught with Consequences."* Lawrence: University Press of Kansas, 2017.

Holt, Thomas C. *The Problem of Freedom: Race, Labor, and Politics in Jamaica and Britain, 1832–1938.* Baltimore, MD: Johns Hopkins University Press, 1992.

Holton, Woody. *Unruly Americans and the Origins of the Constitution.* New York: Hill and Wang, 2007.

Honeck, Mischa. *We Are the Revolutionists: German-Speaking Immigrants and American Abolitionists after 1848.* Athens: University of Georgia Press, 2011.

Howe, Daniel Walker. *What Hath God Wrought: The Transformation of America, 1815–1848.* New York: Oxford University Press, 2007.

Hughes, Nathaniel Cheairs, Jr., and Thomas Clayton Ware. *Theodore O'Hara: Poet-Soldier of the Old South.* Knoxville: University of Tennessee Press, 1998.

Hunter, Tera. *Bound in Wedlock: Slave and Free Black Marriage in the Nineteenth Century.* Cambridge, MA: Harvard University Press, 2017.

"Interchange: Globalizations and Its Limits between the American Revolution and the Civil War." *Journal of American History* 103 (Sept. 2016): 400–433.

Isabella, Maurizio. *Risorgimento in Exile: Italian Émigrés and the Liberal International in the Post-Napoleonic Era.* New York: Oxford University Press, 2009.

Jackson, Kellie Carter. *Force and Freedom: Black Abolitionists and the Politics of Violence.* Philadelphia: University of Pennsylvania Press, 2019.

Jacobs, Ian. *Ranchero Revolt: The Mexican Revolution in Guerrero.* Austin: University of Texas Press, 1982.

Jarnagin, Laura. *A Confluence of Transatlantic Networks: Elites, Capitalism, and Confederate Migration to Brazil.* Tuscaloosa: University of Alabama Press, 2008.

Jenkins, Philip. *Hoods and Shirts: The Extreme Right in Pennsylvania, 1925–1950.* Chapel Hill: University of North Carolina Press, 1997.

John, Richard R. *Spreading the News: The American Postal System from Franklin to Morris.* Cambridge, MA: Harvard University Press, 1995.

Johnson, Lyman L. *Workshop of Revolution: Plebeian Buenos Aires and the Atlantic World, 1776–1810.* Durham, NC: Duke University Press, 2011.

Jones, Howard. *Abraham Lincoln and a New Birth of Freedom: The Union and Slavery in the Diplomacy of the Civil War.* Lincoln: University of Nebraska Press, 1999.

———. *Blue and Gray Diplomacy: A History of Union and Confederate Foreign Relations.* Chapel Hill: University of North Carolina Press, 2010.

———. *Union in Peril: The Crisis over British Intervention in the Civil War.* Chapel Hill: University of North Carolina Press, 1992.

Jones, Jacqueline. *Soldiers of Light and Love: Northern Teachers and Georgia Blacks, 1865–1875.* 1980. Athens: University of Georgia Press, 1992.

Jones, Kristine L. "Civilization and Barbarism and Sarmiento's Indian Policy." In *Sarmiento and His Argentina,* edited by Joseph T Criscenti, 35–43. Boulder, CO: Lynne Rienner, 1993.

Karp, Matthew. *This Vast Southern Empire: Slaveholders at the Helm of American Foreign Policy.* Cambridge, MA: Harvard University Press, 2016.

Katra, William H. *The Argentine Generation of 1837: Echeverría, Alberdi, Sarmiento, Mitre.* Madison, NJ: Fairleigh Dickinson University Press, 1996.

Kaye, Anthony E. "The Second Slavery: Modernity in the Nineteenth-Century South and the Atlantic World." *Journal of Southern History* 75 (Aug. 2009): 627–50.

Keating, Ryan W. *Shades of Green: Irish Regiments, American Soldiers, and Local Communities in the Civil War Era.* New York: Fordham University Press, 2017.

Keehn, David C. *Knights of the Golden Circle: Secret Empire, Southern Secession, Civil War.* Baton Rouge: Louisiana State University Press, 2013.

Keen, Benjamin, and Mark Wasserman. *A History of Latin America.* Boston: Houghton Mifflin, 1988.

Keith, LeeAnna. *The Colfax Massacre: The Untold Story of White Power, Black Terror, and the Death of Reconstruction.* New York: Oxford University Press, 2008.

Keller, Christian B. *Chancellorsville and the Germans: Nativism, Ethnicity, and Civil War Memory.* New York: Fordham University Press, 2010.

Kelley, Robert. *The Transatlantic Persuasion: The Liberal Democratic Mind in the Age of Gladstone.* New York: Knopf, 1969.

Kelly, Patrick J. "The Lost Continent of Abraham Lincoln." *Journal of the Civil War Era* 9 (June 2019): 223–48.

———. "The North American Crisis of the 1860s." *Journal of the Civil War Era* 2 (Sept. 2012): 337–68.

Kelman, Ari. *A Misplaced Massacre: Struggling over the Memory of Sand Creek.* Cambridge, MA: Harvard University Press, 2013.

Kenny, Gail L. *Contentious Liberties: American Abolitionists in Post-Emancipation Jamaica, 1834–1866.* Athens: University of Georgia Press, 2010.

Klein, Herbert S. *Slavery in the Americas: A Comparative Study of Virginia and Cuba.* Chicago: University of Chicago Press, 1967.

Klement, Frank L. *The Limits of Dissent: Clement L. Vallandigham and the Civil War.* New York: Fordham University Press, 1998.

Kolchin, Peter. "Comparative Perspectives on Emancipation in the US South: Reconstruction, Radicalism, and Russia." *Journal of the Civil War Era* 2 (June 2012): 203–32.

———. *First Freedom: The Responses of Alabama's Blacks to Emancipation and Reconstruction.* Westport, CT: Greenwood, 1972.

———. *A Sphinx on the American Land: The Nineteenth-Century South in Comparative Perspective.* Baton Rouge: Louisiana State University Press, 2003.

———. *Unfree Labor: American Slavery and Russian Serfdom.* Cambridge, MA: Harvard University Press, 1987.

Kraay, Hendrik, and Thomas L. Whigham, eds. *I Die with My Country: Perspectives on the Paraguayan War, 1864–1870.* Lincoln: University of Nebraska Press, 2004.

Kramer, Paul A. "Power and Connection: Imperial Histories of the United States in the World." *American Historical Review* 116 (Dec. 2011): 1348–91.

Kurtz, William B. *Excommunicated from the Union: How the Civil War Created a Separate Catholic America.* New York: Fordham University Press, 2016.

Lahti, Janne, ed. *Soldiers in the Southwest Borderlands, 1848–1886.* Norman: University of Oklahoma Press, 2017.

———. *Wars for Empire: Apaches, the United States, and the Southwest Borderlands.* Norman: University of Oklahoma Press, 2017.

Lane, Charles. *The Day Freedom Died: The Colfax Massacre, the Supreme Court, and the Betrayal of Reconstruction.* New York: Henry Holt, 2008.

Lang, Andrew F. *A Contest of Civilizations: Exposing the Crisis of American Exceptionalism in the Civil War Era.* Chapel Hill: University of North Carolina Press, 2021.

Larson, John Lauritz. *Internal Improvement: National Public Works and the Promise of Popular Government in the Early United States.* Chapel Hill: University of North Carolina Press, 2001.

Laurie, Bruce. *Beyond Garrison: Antislavery and Social Reform.* Cambridge: Cambridge University Press, 2005.

———. *Rebels in Paradise: Sketches of Northampton Abolitionists.* Amherst: University of Massachusetts Press, 2015.

Lause, Mark A. *The Civil War's Last Campaign: James B. Weaver, the Greenback-Labor Party, and the Politics of Race and Section.* Lanham, MD: University Press of America, 2001.

Lee, Erika. *America for Americans: A History of Xenophobia in the United States.* New York: Basic, 2019.

Lemann, Nicholas. *Redemption: The Last Battle of the Civil War.* New York: Farrar, Straus and Giroux, 2006.

Leroux, Karen. "Sarmiento's Self-Strengthening Experiment: Americanizing Schools for Argentine Nation-Building." In *Teaching America to the World and the World to America,* edited by Richard Garlitz and Lisa Jarvinen, 51–71. New York: Palgrave Macmillan, 2012.

Levene, Ricardo. *Lecciones de Historia Argentina.* Buenos Aires: J. Lajouane, 1937.

Link, William A., ed. *United States Reconstruction across the Americas.* Gainesville: University Press of Florida, 2019.

Litwack, Leon. *Been in the Storm So Long: The Aftermath of Slavery.* New York: Random House, 1979.

Lockhart, Paul. *The Drillmaster of Valley Forge: The Baron de Steuben and the Making of the American Army.* New York: HarperCollins, 2008.

Luiggi, Alice Houston. *65 Valiants.* Gainesville: University of Florida Press, 1965.

Lynch, John. *Argentine Dictator: Juan Manuel de Rosas, 1829–1852.* New York: Oxford University Press, 1981.

———. *Caudillos in Spanish America, 1800–1850.* New York: Oxford University Press, 1992.

———. *Massacre in the Pampas, 1872: Britain and Argentina in the Age of Migration.* Norman: University of Oklahoma Press, 1998.

———. *San Martín: Argentine Soldier, American Hero.* New Haven, CT: Yale University Press, 2009.

Maier, Pauline. *Ratification: The People Debate the Constitution, 1787–1788.* New York: Simon and Schuster, 2010.

Mallon, Florencia E. *Peasant and Nation: The Making of Postcolonial Mexico and Peru.* Berkeley: University of California Press, 1995.

Manning, Chandra. *Troubled Refuge: Struggling for Freedom in the Civil War.* New York: Knopf, 2016.

Margolies, Daniel S. *Henry Watterson and the New South: The Politics of Empire, Free Trade, and Globalization.* Lexington: University Press of Kentucky, 2006.

Martinez, J. Michael. *Carpetbaggers, Cavalry and the Ku Klux Klan: Exposing the Invisible Empire during Reconstruction.* Lanham, MD: Rowman and Littlefield, 2007.

Masur, Louis P. *Lincoln's Last Speech: Wartime Reconstruction and the Crisis of Reunion.* New York: Oxford University Press, 2015.

Matthews, Michael. *The Civilizing Machine: A Cultural History of Mexican Railroads, 1876–1910*. Lincoln: University of Nebraska Press, 2013.

May, Robert E. *Manifest Destiny's Underworld: Filibustering in Antebellum America*. Chapel Hill: University of North Carolina Press, 2002.

———. *Slavery, Race, and Conquest in the Tropics: Lincoln, Douglas, and the Future of Latin America*. Cambridge: Cambridge University Press, 2013.

———. *The Southern Dream of a Caribbean Empire*. Baton Rouge: Louisiana State University Press, 1973.

———, ed. *The Union, The Confederacy, and the Atlantic Rim*. West Lafayette, IN: Purdue University Press, 1995.

Mazlish, Bruce. *Civilization and Its Contents*. Stanford, CA: Stanford University Press, 2004.

McCarthy, Cal. *Green, Blue and Grey: The Irish in the American Civil War*. Cork, Ireland: Collins, 2009.

McCrary, Peyton. *Abraham Lincoln and Reconstruction: The Louisiana Experiment*. Princeton, NJ: Princeton University Press, 1978.

McDaniel, W. Caleb. *The Problem of Democracy in the Age of Slavery: Garrisonian Abolitionists and Transatlantic Reform*. Baton Rouge: Louisiana State University Press, 2013.

McFeely, William S. *Yankee Stepfather: General O. O. Howard and the Freedmen*. New Haven, CT: Yale University Press, 1968.

McGerr, Michael. "The Price of the 'New Transnational History.'" *American Historical Review* 96 (Oct. 1991): 1056–67.

McKitrick, Eric L. *Andrew Johnson and Reconstruction*. New York: Oxford University Press, 1960.

McLynn, F. J. "The Argentine Presidential Election of 1868." *Journal of Latin American Studies* 11 (Nov. 1979): 303–23.

———. "Consequences for Argentina of the War of Triple Alliance 1865–1870." *The Americas* 41 (July 1984): 81–98.

McPherson, James M. *The Battle Cry of Freedom: The Civil War Era*. New York: Oxford University Press, 1988.

———. *For Cause and Comrades: Why Men Fought in the Civil War*. New York: Oxford University Press, 1997.

———. *The Negro's Civil War: How American Blacks Felt and Acted during the War for the Union*. New York: Pantheon, 1965.

Meisel, Seth. "'The Fruits of Freedom': Slaves and Citizens in Early Republican Argentina." In *Slaves, Subjects, and Subversives: Blacks in Colonial Latin America*, edited by Jane G. Landers and Barry M. Robinson, 273–305. Albuquerque: University of New Mexico Press, 2006.

Meyer, Jean A. *The Cristero Rebellion: The Mexican People between Church and State 1926—1929.* Cambridge: Cambridge University Press, 1976.

Middlekauff, Robert. *The Glorious Cause: The American Revolution, 1763–1789.* New York: Oxford University Press, 1982.

Mijangos y González, Pablo. *The Lawyer of the Church: Bishop Clemente de Jesús Munguía and the Clerical Response to the Mexican Liberal Reforma.* Lincoln: University of Nebraska Press, 2015.

Miller, Ken. *Dangerous Guests: Enemy Captives and Revolutionary Communities during the War for Independence.* Ithaca, NY: Cornell University Press, 2014.

Miller, Nicola. "'That Great and Gentle Soul' Images of Lincoln in Latin America." In *The Global Lincoln,* edited by Richard Carwardine and Jay Sexton, 206–22. Oxford: Oxford University Press, 2011.

Miller, Robert Ryal. "The American Legion of Honor in Mexico." *Pacific Historical Review* 30, no. 3 (Aug. 1961): 229–41.

———. *Arms across the Border: United States Aid to Juárez during the French Intervention in Mexico.* Philadelphia, PA: American Philosophical Society, 1973.

———. "Herman Strum: Hoosier Secret Agent for Mexico." *Indiana Magazine of History* 58, no. 1 (March 1962): 1–15.

———. "Lew Wallace and the French Intervention in Mexico." *Indiana Magazine of History* 59, no. 1 (March 1963): 31–50.

———. "Matías Romero: Mexican Minister to the United States during the Juárez-Maximilian Era." *Hispanic American Historical Review* 45, no. 2 (May 1965): 228–45.

———. *Shamrock and Sword: The St. Patrick's Battalion in the U.S.–Mexican War.* Norman: University of Oklahoma Press, 1989.

Monaghan, Jay. *Diplomat in Carpet Slippers: Abraham Lincoln Deals with Foreign Affairs.* Indianapolis, IN: Bobbs-Merrill, 1945.

Moreno, C. Galván. *Radiografía de Sarmiento: Amplia visión de su sida y de su obra.* Buenos Aires: Editorial Claridad, 1938.

Morgan, Philip D., and Jack P. Greene. "Introduction: The Present State of Atlantic History." In *Atlantic History: A Critical Appraisal,* edited by Jack P. Greene and Morgan, 3–33. New York: Oxford University Press, 2009.

Morris, Robert C. *Reading, 'Riting, and Reconstruction: The Education of Freedmen in the South.* Chicago: University of Chicago Press, 1981.

Mortenson, Christopher R. *Politician in Uniform: General Lew Wallace and the Civil War.* Norman: University of Oklahoma Press, 2019.

Moya, Jose C. *Cousins and Strangers: Spanish Immigrants in Buenos Aires, 1850–1930.* Berkeley: University of California Press, 1998.

Murphy, Angela F. *The Jerry Rescue: The Fugitive Slave Law, Northern Rights, and the American Sectional Crisis.* New York: Oxford University Press, 2016.

Nagler, Jörg, Don H. Doyle, and Marcus Gräser, eds. *The Transnational Significance of the American Civil War.* New York: Palgrave Macmillan, 2016.

Nash, Steven E. *Reconstruction's Ragged Edge: The Politics of Postwar Life in the Southern Mountains.* Chapel Hill: University of North Carolina Press, 2016.

Neely, Mark E., Jr. *The Civil War and the Limits of Destruction.* Cambridge, MA: Harvard University Press, 2007.

———. *Lincoln and the Triumph of the Nation: Constitutional Conflict in the American Civil War.* Chapel Hill: University of North Carolina Press, 2011.

———. *The Union Divided: Party Conflict in the Civil War North.* Cambridge, MA: Harvard University Press, 2002.

Neem, Johann N. *Democracy's Schools: The Rise of Public Education in America.* Baltimore, MD: Johns Hopkins University Press, 2017.

Nelson, Scott Reynolds. *Iron Confederacies: Southern Railways, Klan Violence, and Reconstruction.* Chapel Hill: University of North Carolina Press, 1999.

Neufeld, Stephen B. *The Blood Contingent: The Military and the Making of Modern Mexico, 1876–1911.* Albuquerque: University of New Mexico Press, 2017.

Newman, Richard. *The Transformation of American Abolitionism: Fighting Slavery in the Early Republic.* Chapel Hill: University of North Carolina Press, 2002.

Nichols, C. Howard. "William Pitt Kellogg." In *The Louisiana Governors: From Iberville to Edwards,* edited by Joseph G. Dawson III, 172–76. Baton Rouge: Louisiana State University Press, 1990.

Noe, Kenneth W., ed. *The Yellowhammer War: The Civil War and Reconstruction in Alabama.* Tuscaloosa: University of Alabama Press, 2013.

Norman, Matthew David. "Revolutions in the Republican Imagination: American Perceptions of the 1848–49 Revolutions in Europe." PhD diss., University of Illinois, 2006.

Nystrom, Justin. *New Orleans after the Civil War: Race, Politics, and a New Birth of Freedom.* Baltimore, MD: Johns Hopkins University Press, 2010.

O'Flaherty, Daniel. *General Jo Shelby: Undefeated Rebel.* Chapel Hill: University of North Carolina Press, 2000.

Oldfield, J. R. *"Chords of Freedom": Commemoration, Ritual and British Transatlantic Slavery.* Manchester, UK: Manchester University Press, 2007.

Olliff, Donathan C. *Reforma Mexico: A Search for Alternatives to Annexation, 1854–1861.* Tuscaloosa: University of Alabama Press, 1981.

Oria, José A. "La literatura argentina durante la epoca de Rosas (1829–1852)." In *Historia de la nación Argentina,* edited by Ricardo Levene, 359–87. Buenos Aires: Academia Nacional de la Historia, 1951.

Oszlak, Oscar. *La formación del estado argentino.* Buenos Aires: Editorial de Belgrano, 1982.

Owsley, Frank L. *King Cotton Diplomacy: Foreign Relations of the Confederate States of America.* Chicago: University of Chicago Press, 1931.

Paddison, Joshua. *American Heathens: Religion, Race, and Reconstruction in California.* Berkeley: University of California Press, 2012.

Palti, Elías José. *El momento romántico: Nación, historia y lenguajes politicos en la Argentina del siglo XIX.* Buenos Aires: Eudeba, 2009.

Pani, Erika. "Intervention and Empire: *Politics as Usual.*" In *Malcontents, Rebels, and Pronunciados: The Politics of Insurrection in Nineteenth-Century Mexico,* edited by Will Fowler, 236–54. Lincoln: University of Nebraska Press, 2012.

Parrish, William E. *Frank Blair: Lincoln's Conservative.* Columbia: University of Missouri Press, 1998.

Parsons, Elaine Frantz. *Ku-Klux: The Birth of the Klan during Reconstruction.* Chapel Hill: University of North Carolina Press, 2015.

Penningroth, Dylan. *The Claims of Kinfolk: African American Property and Community in the Nineteenth-Century South.* Chapel Hill: University of North Carolina Press, 2003.

Perkins, Dexter. *A History of the Monroe Doctrine.* Boston: Little, Brown, 1963.

Perman, Michael. "Eric Foner's Reconstruction: A Finished Revolution." *Reviews in American History* 17, no. 1 (March 1989): 73–78.

———. *Struggle for Mastery: Disfranchisement in the South, 1888–1908.* Chapel Hill: University of North Carolina Press, 2001.

Perry, Laurens Ballard. *Juárez and Díaz: Machine Politics in Mexico.* De Kalb: Northern Illinois University Press, 1978.

Peskin, Allan. "Was There a Compromise of 1877?" *Journal of American History* 60 (June 1973): 63–75.

Peterson, Merrill D. *Thomas Jefferson and the New Nation: A Biography.* New York: Oxford University Press, 1970.

Pigna, Felipe. "Justo José de Urquiza." *El Historiador.* https://www.elhistoriador.com.ar/justo-jose-de-urquiza/.

Pike, Frederick B. *The United States and Latin America: Myths and Stereotypes of Civilization and Nature.* Austin: University of Texas Press, 1992.

Pletcher, David M. *The Diplomacy of Annexation: Texas, Oregon, and the Mexican War.* Columbia: University of Missouri Press, 1973.

———. *Rails, Mines, and Progress: Seven American Promoters in Mexico, 1867–1911.* Ithaca, NY: Cornell University Press, 1958.

Pocock, J. G. A. *The Machiavellian Moment: Florentine Political Thought and the American Republican Tradition.* Princeton, NJ: Princeton University Press, 1975.

Ponce, Pearl T. *To Govern the Devil in Hell: The Political Crisis of Territorial Kansas.* DeKalb: Northern Illinois University Press, 2014.

Potter, David. *The Impending Crisis: America before the Civil War: 1848–1861.* Completed and edited by Don E. Fehrenbacher. New York: HarperCollins, 1976.

Powell, Lawrence N. *New Masters: Northern Planters during the Civil War and Reconstruction.* New Haven, CT: Yale University Press, 1980.

Prather, H. Leon. *We Have Taken a City: Wilmington Racial Massacre and the Coup of 1898.* Rutherford, NJ: Associated University Press, 1984.

Prior, David. *Between Freedom and Progress: The Lost World of Reconstruction Politics.* Baton Rouge: Louisiana State University Press, 2019.

———. "Reconstruction, from Transatlantic Polyseme to Historiographical Quandary." In *Reconstruction in a Globalizing World,* edited by Prior, 172–208. New York: Fordham University Press, 2018.

———, ed. *Reconstruction in a Globalizing World.* New York: Fordham University Press, 2018.

Quigley, Paul. "Civil War Conscription and the International Boundaries of Citizenship." *Journal of the Civil War Era* 4 (Sept. 2014): 373–97.

———. *Shifting Grounds: Nationalism and the American South 1848–1865.* New York: Oxford University Press, 2012.

Rable, George C. *But There Was No Peace: The Role of Violence in the Politics of Reconstruction.* Athens: University of Georgia Press, 1984.

———. *Damn Yankees! Demonization and Defiance in the Confederate South.* Baton Rouge: Louisiana State University Press, 2015.

Ramos, Jorge Abelardo. *Historia de la nación Latinoamericana.* Buenos Aires: A. Peña Lillo, 1968.

Rauchway, Eric. *Blessed among Nations: How the World Made America.* New York: Hill and Wang, 2006.

Reed, Germaine M. *David French Boyd: Founder of Louisiana State University.* Baton Rouge: Louisiana State University Press, 1977.

Reid, Richard M. *Freedom for Themselves: North Carolina's Black Soldiers in the Civil War Era.* Chapel Hill: University of North Carolina Press, 2008.

Reidy, Joseph P. *Illusions of Emancipation: The Pursuit of Freedom and Equality in the Twilight of Slavery.* Chapel Hill: University of North Carolina Press, 2019.

Rennie, Ysabel F. *The Argentine Republic.* New York: Macmillan, 1945.

Reynolds, David S. *John Brown, Abolitionist: The Man Who Killed Slavery, Sparked Civil War, and Seeded Civil Rights.* New York: Vintage, 2005.

Rhodes, James F. *History of the United States: From the Compromise of 1850 to the McKinley-Bryan Campaign of 1896.* New York: Macmillan, 1920.

Riall, Lucy. *Garibaldi: Invention of a Hero.* New Haven, CT: Yale University Press, 2007.

Richards, Leonard L. *Gentlemen of Property and Standing: Anti-Abolition Mobs in Jacksonian America.* New York: Oxford University Press, 1971.

———. *The Slave Power: The Free North and Southern Domination, 1780–1860.* Baton Rouge: Louisiana State University Press, 2000.

Richardson, Heather Cox. *The Greatest Nation of the Earth: Republican Economic Policies during the Civil War.* Cambridge, MA: Harvard University Press, 1997.

———. *West from Appomattox: The Reconstruction of American after the Civil War.* New Haven, CT: Yale University Press, 2007.

Richmond, Douglas W. *Carlos Pellegrini and the Crisis of the Argentine Elites, 1880–1916.* New York: Praeger, 1989.

Ridpath, John Clark, and J. W. Buell. *History of the United States: Epochs of Nationality, War, and Greatness.* Washington, DC: American History Society, 1900.

Rippy, J. Fred. "Yankee Teachers and the Founding of Argentina's Elementary School System." *Hispanic American Historical Review* 24 (Feb. 1944): 166–69.

Roberts, Timothy Mason. *Distant Revolutions: 1848 and the Challenge to American Exceptionalism.* Charlottesville: University of Virginia Press, 2009.

Robertson, Priscilla. *Revolutions of 1848: A Social History.* Princeton, NJ: Princeton University Press, 1952.

Rock, David. *Argentina 1516–1987: From Spanish Colonization to Alfonsín.* Berkeley: University of California Press, 1987.

———. "The Collapse of the Federalists: Rural Revolt in Argentina 1863–1876." *Estudios Interdisciplinarios de América Latina y el Caribe* 9, no. 2 (July–Dec. 1998): 5–20.

———. *State Building and Political Movements in Argentina, 1860–1916.* Stanford, CA: Stanford University Press, 2002.

Rodgers, Daniel T. *Atlantic Crossings: Social Politics in a Progressive Age.* Cambridge, MA: Harvard University Press, 1998.

———. "Republicanism: The Career of a Concept." *Journal of American History* 79 (June 1992): 11–38.

Rodríguez O, Jaime E. *"We Are Now the True Spaniards": Sovereignty, Revolution, Independence, and the Emergence of the Federal Republic of Mexico, 1808–1824.* Stanford, CA: Stanford University Press, 2012.

Rojas, Nerio. "Presidencia Sarmiento. Vicepresidencia Adolfo Alsina (1868–1874)." In *Historia Argentina,* edited by Roberto Levillier, 2873–2922. Buenos Aires: Plaza y Janés S. A., 1968.

Rojas, Ricardo. *El Profeta de la Pampa.* Buenos Aires: Editorial Losada, 1945.

Rolle, Andrew F. *The Lost Cause: The Confederate Exodus to Mexico.* Norman: University of Oklahoma Press, 1965.

Romero, José Luis. *A History of Argentine Political Thought.* Translated by Thomas F. McGann. Stanford, CA: Stanford University Press, 1963.

Rosales, John O'Donnell. *Hispanic Confederates.* Baltimore, MD: Genealogical Publishing, 1997.

Rose, Willie Lee. *Rehearsal for Reconstruction: The Port Royal Experiment*. Athens: University of Georgia Press, 1964.

Rosen, Hannah. *Terror in the Heart of Freedom: Citizenship, Sexual Violence, and the Meaning of Race in the Postemancipation South*. Chapel Hill: University of North Carolina Press, 2009.

Ross, Michael A. *The Great New Orleans Kidnapping Case: Race, Law, and Justice in the Reconstruction Era*. New York: Oxford University Press, 2014.

Rothera, Evan C. "'The Men Are Understood to Have Been Generally Americans, in the Employ of the Liberal Government': Civil War Veterans and Mexico, 1865–1867." In *The War Went On: Reconsidering the Lives of Civil War Veterans*, edited by Brian Matthew Jordan and Rothera, 37–60. Baton Rouge: Louisiana State University Press, 2020.

———. "Our South American Cousin: Domingo F. Sarmiento and Education in Argentina and the United States." In *Reconstruction in a Globalizing World*, edited by David Prior, 21–49. New York: Fordham University Press, 2018.

Rothman, Adam. *Slave Country: American Expansion and the Origins of the Deep South*. Cambridge, MA: Harvard University Press, 2005.

Rugeley, Terry. *The River People in Flood Time: The Civil Wars in Tabasco, Spoiler of Empires*. Stanford, CA: Stanford University Press, 2014.

Rugemer, Edward Bartlett. *The Problem of Emancipation: The Caribbean Roots of the American Civil War*. Baton Rouge: Louisiana State University Press, 2008.

Sabato, Hilda. *Buenos Aires en armas: La revolución de 1880*. Buenos Aires: Siglo XXI, 2008.

——— *The Many and the Few: Political Participation in Republican Buenos Aires*. Stanford, CA: Stanford University Press, 2001.

———. *Republics of the New World: The Revolutionary Political Experiment in 19th-Century Latin America*. Princeton, NJ: Princeton University Press, 2018.

Salvatore, Ricardo D. *Wandering Paysanos: State Order and Subaltern Experience in Buenos Aires During the Rosas Era*. Durham, NC: Duke University Press, 2003.

Sanders, James E. *The Vanguard of the Atlantic World: Creating Modernity, Nation, and Democracy in Nineteenth-Century Latin America*. Durham, NC: Duke University Press, 2014.

Saville, Julie. *The Work of Reconstruction: From Slave to Wage Labor in South Carolina, 1860–1870*. Cambridge: Cambridge University Press, 1994.

Sawers, Larry. *The Other Argentina: The Interior and National Development*. Boulder, CO: Westview, 1996.

Scharff, Virginia, ed. *Empire and Liberty: The Civil War and the West*. Oakland: University of California Press, 2015.

Schivelbusch, Wolfgang. *The Culture of Defeat: On National Trauma, Mourning, and Recovery*. New York: Henry Holt, 2001.

Schoonover, Thomas D. *Dollars over Dominion: The Triumph of Liberalism in Mexican–United States Relations, 1861–1867*. Baton Rouge: Louisiana State University Press, 1978.

Schott, Thomas E. *Alexander H. Stephens of Georgia: A Biography*. Baton Rouge: Louisiana State University Press, 1988.

Schroeder, John H. *Mr. Polk's War: American Opposition and Dissent, 1846–1848*. Madison: University of Wisconsin Press, 1973.

Schwaller, John F., ed. *The Church in Colonial Latin America*. Wilmington, DE: Scholarly Resources, 2000.

———. *The History of the Catholic Church in Latin America: From Conquest to Revolution and Beyond*. New York: New York University Press, 2011.

Schwalm, Leslie A. *Emancipation's Diaspora: Race and Reconstruction in the Upper Midwest*. Chapel Hill: University of North Carolina Press, 2009.

———. *A Hard Fight for We: Women's Transition from Slavery to Freedom in South Carolina*. Urbana: University of Illinois Press, 1997.

Schweiger, Beth Barton. "The Literate South: Reading Before Emancipation." *Journal of the Civil War Era* 3 (Sept. 2013): 331–59.

Scirocco, Alfonso. *Garibaldi: Citizen of the World: A Biography*. Translated by Allan Cameron. Princeton, NJ: Princeton University Press, 2007.

Scott, Rebecca J. *Degrees of Freedom: Louisiana and Cuba After Slavery*. Cambridge, MA: Harvard University Press, 2005.

Seigel, Micol. "Beyond Compare: Comparative Method after the Transnational Turn." *Radical History Review* 91 (Winter 2005): 62–90.

Seijas, Tatiana, and Jake Frederick. *Spanish Dollars and Sister Republics: The Money That Made Mexico and the United States*. Lanham, MD: Rowman and Littlefield, 2017.

Sellemeyer, Deryl. *Jo Shelby's Iron Brigade*. Gretna, LA: Pelican, 2007.

Sellers, Charles. *The Market Revolution: Jacksonian America, 1815–1846*. New York: Oxford University Press, 1991.

Severance, Benjamin H. *Tennessee's Radical Army: The State Guard and Its Role in Reconstruction, 1867–1869*. Knoxville: University of Tennessee Press, 2005.

Sexton, Jay. *The Monroe Doctrine: Empire and Nation in Nineteenth-Century America*. New York: Hill and Wang, 2011.

———. *A Nation Forged by Crisis: A New American History*. New York: Basic, 2018.

———. "Toward a Synthesis of Foreign Relations in the Civil War Era, 1848–1877." *American Nineteenth Century History* 5 (Autumn 2004): 50–73.

Sheehan-Dean, Aaron. *Reckoning with Rebellion: War and Sovereignty in the Nineteenth Century*. Gainesville: University Press of Florida, 2020.

Sheinin, David M. K. *Argentina and the United States: An Alliance Contained*. Athens: University of Georgia Press, 2006.

Shumway, Jeffrey M. *The Case of the Ugly Suitor and Other Histories of Love, Gender, and Nation in Buenos Aires*. Lincoln: University of Nebraska Press, 2005.

———. *A Woman, a Man, a Nation: Mariquita Sánchez, Juan Manuel de Rosas, and the Beginnings of Argentina*. Albuquerque: University of New Mexico Press, 2019.

Shumway, Nicolas. *The Invention of Argentina*. Berkeley: University of California Press, 1991.

Silkenat, David. *Driven from Home: North Carolina's Refugee Crisis*. Athens: University of Georgia Press, 2016.

Simmons, Donald C., Jr. *Confederate Settlements in British Honduras*. Jefferson, NC: MacFarland, 2001.

Simpson, Brooks. *Let Us Have Peace: Ulysses S. Grant and the Politics of War and Reconstruction, 1861–1868*. Chapel Hill: University of North Carolina Press, 1991.

Sinha, Manisha. *The Slave's Cause: A History of Abolition*. New Haven, CT: Yale University Press, 2016.

Sinkin, Richard N. *The Mexican Reform, 1855–1876: A Study in Liberal Nation-Building*. Austin: University of Texas Press, 1979.

Sklar, Kathryn Kish. *Catharine Beecher: A Study in American Domesticity*. New Haven, CT: Yale University Press, 1973.

Slap, Andrew L. *The Doom of Reconstruction: The Liberal Republicans in the Civil War Era*. New York: Fordham University Press, 2006.

Slatta, Richard W. *Gauchos and the Vanishing Frontier*. Lincoln: University of Nebraska Press, 1983.

Slaughter, Thomas P. *Bloody Dawn: The Christiana Riot and Racial Violence in the Antebellum North*. New York: Oxford University Press, 1991.

Smith, David G. *On the Edge of Freedom: The Fugitive Slave Issue in South Central Pennsylvania, 1820–1870*. New York: Fordham University Press, 2013.

Smith, John David, ed. *Black Soldiers in Blue: African American Troops in the Civil War Era*. Chapel Hill: University of North Carolina Press, 2002.

Smith, John David, and J. Vincent Lowery, eds. *The Dunning School: Historians, Race, and the Meaning of Reconstruction*. Lexington: University Press of Kentucky, 2013.

Smith, Justin Harvey. *The War with Mexico*. New York: Macmillan, 1919.

Smith, Mark M. "The Past as a Foreign Country: Reconstruction, Inside and Out." In *Reconstructions: New Perspectives on the Postbellum United States*, edited by Thomas J. Brown, 117–40. New York: Oxford University Press, 2006.

Smith, Michael Thomas. *The Enemy Within: Fears of Corruption in the Civil War North*. Charlottesville: University of Virginia Press, 2011.

Smith, Stacey L. *Freedom's Frontier: California and the Struggle over Unfree Labor, Emancipation, and Reconstruction*. Chapel Hill: University of North Carolina Press, 2013.

Span, Christopher M. *From Cotton Field to Schoolhouse: African American Education in Mississippi, 1862–1875*. Chapel Hill: University of North Carolina Press, 2009.

Sproat, John G. *The Best Men: Liberal Reformers in the Gilded Age*. New York: Oxford University Press, 1968.

Stampp, Kenneth M. *The Era of Reconstruction, 1865–1877.* New York: Knopf, 1965.

Stanley, Matthew E. *The Loyal West: Civil War and Reunion in Middle America.* Urbana: University of Illinois Press, 2016.

Stauffer, Brian A. *Victory on Earth or in Heaven: Mexico's Religionero Rebellion.* Albuquerque: University of New Mexico Press, 2019.

Stauffer, John. *The Black Hearts of Men: Radical Abolitionists and the Transformation of Race.* Cambridge, MA: Harvard University Press, 2001.

Sternhell, Yael A. *Routes of War: The World of Movement in the Confederate South.* Cambridge, MA: Harvard University Press, 2012.

Stevens, Michel Wendell. "Two Flags, One Cause—A Cuban Patriot in Gray: Ambrosio José Gonzales." In *Cubans in the Confederacy: José Agustín Quintero, Ambrosio José Gonzales, and Loreta Janeta Velazquez,* edited by Phillip Thomas Tucker, 143–224. Jefferson, NC: McFarland, 2002.

Stevenson, Brenda. "Considering the War from Home and the Front: Charlotte Forten's Civil War Dairy Entries." In *Civil War Writing: New Perspectives on Iconic Texts,* edited by Gary W. Gallagher and Stephen Cushman, 170–99. Baton Rouge: Louisiana State University Press, 2019.

Stokes, Melvyn, and Stephen Conway, eds. *The Market Revolution in America: Social, Political, and Religious Expressions, 1800–1880.* Charlottesville: University Press of Virginia, 1996.

Storozynski, Alex. *The Peasant Prince: Thaddeus Kosciuszko and the Age of Revolutions.* New York: St. Martin's, 2009.

Summers, Mark Wahlgren. *A Dangerous Stir: Fear, Paranoia, and the Making of Reconstruction.* Chapel Hill: University of North Carolina Press, 2009.

———. *The Ordeal of the Reunion: A New History of Reconstruction.* Chapel Hill: University of North Carolina Press, 2014.

Sutherland, Jonathan D. *African Americans at War: An Encyclopedia.* Santa Barbara, CA: ABC-CLIO, 2004.

Szuchman, Mark D. "Childhood Education and Politics in Nineteenth-Century Argentina: The Case of Buenos Aires." *Hispanic American Historical Review* 70 (Feb. 1990): 109–38.

———. *Order, Family, and Community in Buenos Aires, 1810–1860.* Stanford, CA: Stanford University Press, 1988.

Szuchman, Mark D., and Jonathan C. Brown, eds. *Revolution and Restoration: The Rearrangement of Power in Argentina, 1776–1860.* Cambridge: Cambridge University Press, 1994.

Szurmuk, Mónica. *Women in Argentina: Early Travel Narratives.* Gainesville: University Press of Florida, 2000.

Tannenbaum, Frank. *Slave and Citizen.* Boston: Beacon, 1946.

Tap, Bruce. *The Fort Pillow Massacre: North, South, and the Status of African Americans in the Civil War Era.* New York: Routledge, 2014.

Taylor, Alan. *American Revolutions: A Continental History, 1750–1804.* New York: Norton, 2016.

———. *The Internal Enemy: Slavery and War in Virginia, 1772–1832.* New York: Norton, 2013.

Taylor, Amy Murrell. *Embattled Freedom: Journeys through the Civil War's Slave Refugee Camps.* Chapel Hill: University of North Carolina Press, 2018.

Taylor, George Rogers. *The Transportation Revolution: 1815–1860.* 1951. New York: Routledge, 2015.

Taylor, Joe Gray. *Louisiana: A History.* New York: Norton, 1984.

———. *Louisiana Reconstructed: 1863–1877.* Baton Rouge: Louisiana State University Press, 1974.

Teters, Kristopher A. *Practical Liberators: Union Officers in the Western Theater during the Civil War.* Chapel Hill: University of North Carolina Press, 2018.

Thelen, David. "Of Audiences, Borderlands, and Comparisons: Toward the Internationalization of American History." *Journal of American History* 79 (Sept. 1992): 432–62.

Thompson, Jerry D. *A Civil War History of the New Mexico Volunteers and Militia.* Albuquerque: University of New Mexico Press, 2015.

———. *Cortina: Defending the Mexican Name in Texas.* College Station: Texas A&M University Press, 2007.

———. *Mexican Texans in the Union Army.* El Paso: Texas Western Press, 1986.

———. *Tejano Tiger: José de los Santos Benavides and the Texas-Mexican Borderlands, 1823–1891.* Fort Worth: Texas Christian University Press, 2017.

———, ed. *Tejanos in Gray: Civil War Letters of Captains Joseph Rafael de la Garza and Manuel Yturri.* College Station: Texas A&M University Press, 2011.

Thomson, Guy P. C., and David G. LaFrance. *Patriotism, Politics, and Popular Liberalism in Nineteenth-Century Mexico.* Wilmington, DE: Scholarly Resources, 1999.

Tomek, Beverly C. *Pennsylvania Hall: A "Legal Lynching" in the Shadow of the Liberty Bell.* New York: Oxford University Press, 2013.

Tomich, Dale W. *Through the Prism of Slavery: Labor, Capital, and the World Economy.* Lanham, MD: Rowman and Littlefield, 2004.

Torget, Andrew J. *Seeds of Empire: Cotton, Slavery, and the Transformation of the Texas Borderlands, 1800–1850.* Chapel Hill: University of North Carolina Press, 2015.

Travers, Len. *Celebrating the Fourth: Independence Day and the Rites of Nationalism in the Early Republic.* Amherst: University of Massachusetts Press, 1997.

Trefousse, Hans L. *Andrew Johnson: A Biography.* New York: Norton, 1989.

———. *Carl Schurz: A Biography.* Knoxville: University of Tennessee Press, 1982.

———. *Historical Dictionary of Reconstruction*. Westport, CT: Greenwood, 1991.

———. *The Radical Republicans: Lincoln's Vanguard for Racial Justice*. Baton Rouge: Louisiana State University Press, 1969.

Trelease, Allen W. *White Terror: The Ku Klux Klan Conspiracy and Southern Reconstruction*. Baton Rouge: Louisiana State University Press, 1995.

Truett, Samuel. *Fugitive Landscapes: The Forgotten History of the U.S.–Mexico Borderlands*. New Haven, CT: Yale University Press, 2006.

Tucker, Ann L. *Newest Born of Nations: European Nationalist Movements and the Making of the Confederacy*. Charlottesville: University of Virginia Press, 2020.

Tucker, Philip Thomas, ed. *Cubans in the Confederacy: José Agustín Quintero, Ambrosio José Gonzales, and Loreta Janeta Velazquez*. Jefferson, NC: McFarland, 2002.

———. *Irish Confederates: The Civil War's Forgotten Soldiers*. Abilene, TX: McWhiney Foundation Press, 2006.

Tunnell, Ted., ed. *Carpetbagger from Vermont: The Autobiography of Marshall Harvey Twitchell*. Baton Rouge: Louisiana State University Press, 1989.

———. *Crucible of Reconstruction: War, Radicalism, and Race in Louisiana, 1862–1877*. Baton Rouge: Louisiana State University Press, 1984.

———. *Edge of the Sword: The Ordeal of Carpetbagger Marshall H. Twitchell in the Civil War and Reconstruction*. Baton Rouge: Louisiana State University Press, 2001.

Tyler, Ronnie C. *Santiago Vidaurri and the Southern Confederacy*. Austin: Texas State Historical Association, 1973.

Tyrrell, Ian. "American Exceptionalism in an Age of International History." *American Historical Review* 96 (Oct. 1991): 1031–55.

———. "Ian Tyrrell Responds." *American Historical Review* 96 (Oct. 1991): 1068–72.

———. "Reflections on the Transnational Turn in United States History: Theory and Practice." *Journal of Global History* 4 (Nov. 2009): 453–74.

———. *Reforming the World: The Creation of America's Moral Empire*. Princeton, NJ: Princeton University Press, 2010.

———. *Transnational Nation: United States History in Global Perspective Since 1789*. New York: Palgrave Macmillan, 2007.

———. *True Gardens of the Gods: Californian-Australian Environmental Reform, 1860–1930*. Berkeley: University of California Press, 1999.

———. *Woman's World/Woman's Empire: The Woman's Christian Temperance Union in International Perspective, 1880–1930*. Chapel Hill: University of North Carolina Press, 1991.

Udaondo, Enrique. *Grandes hombres de nuestra patria*. 3 vols. Buenos Aires: Editorial Pleamar, 1968.

Ural, Susannah, J., ed. *Civil War Citizens: Race, Ethnicity, and Identity in America's Bloodiest Conflict*. New York: New York University Press, 2010.

———. *The Harp and the Eagle: Irish American Volunteers and the Union Army, 1861–1865.* New York: New York University Press, 2006.

Valerio-Jiménez, Omar S. "'Although We Are the Last Soldiers': Citizenship, Ideology, and Tejano Unionism." In *Lone Star Unionism, Dissent, and Resistance: Other Sides of Civil War Texas,* edited by Jesús F. de la Teja, 123–45. Norman: University of Oklahoma Press, 2016.

Valuska, David L., and Christian B. Keller. *Damn Dutch: Pennsylvania Germans at Gettysburg.* Mechanicsburg, PA: Stackpole, 2004.

Vanderwood, Paul J. *Disorder and Progress: Bandits, Police, and Mexican Development.* Lincoln: University of Nebraska Press, 1981.

Van Young, Eric. *The Other Rebellion: Popular Violence, Ideology, and the Mexican Struggle for Independence.* Stanford, CA: Stanford University Press, 2001.

Vaughan, Mary Kay. *Cultural Politics in Revolution: Teachers, Peasants, and Schools in Mexico, 1930–1940.* Tucson: University of Arizona Press, 1997.

———. *The State, Education, and Social Class in Mexico, 1880–1928.* DeKalb: Northern Illinois University Press, 1982.

Vázquez, Josefina Zoraida, and Lorenzo Meyer. *The United States and Mexico.* Chicago: University of Chicago Press, 1985.

Verhoeven, Timothy. *Transnational Anti-Catholicism: France and the United States in the Nineteenth Century.* New York: Palgrave Macmillan, 2010.

Vida, István Kornél. *Hungarian Émigrés in the American Civil War: A Historical and Biographical Dictionary.* Jefferson, NC: McFarland, 2012.

Villar, Jorge Caldas. *Nueva Historia Argentina.* Buenos Aires: Editorial Juan C. Granda, 1968.

Wahlstrom, Todd W. *The Southern Exodus to Mexico: Migration across the Borderlands after the American Civil War.* Lincoln: University of Nebraska Press, 2015.

Waldstreicher, David. *In the Midst of Perpetual Fetes: The Making of American Nationalism, 1776–1820.* Chapel Hill: University of North Carolina Press, 1997.

Ward Andrew. *River Run Red: The Fort Pillow Massacre in the American Civil War.* New York: Penguin, 2005.

Wasserman, Mark. *Everyday Life and Politics in Nineteenth-Century Mexico: Men, Women, and War.* Albuquerque: University of New Mexico Press, 2000.

Weber, Jennifer L. *Copperheads: The Rise and Fall of Lincoln's Opponents in the North.* New York: Oxford University Press, 2006.

West, Elliott. "Reconstructing Race." *Western Historical Quarterly* 34 (Spring 2003): 6–26.

Whigham, Thomas L. *The Paraguayan War. Vol. 1: Causes and Early Conduct.* Lincoln: University of Nebraska Press, 2002.

———. *The Road to Armageddon: Paraguay Versus the Triple Alliance, 1866–1870.* Calgary, Alberta: University of Calgary Press, 2017.

White, Richard. *Railroaded: The Transcontinentals and the Making of Modern America.* New York: Norton, 2011.

———. *The Republic for Which It Stands: The United States during Reconstruction and the Gilded Age, 1865–1896.* New York: Oxford University Press, 2017.

Wiener, Jonathan. *Social Origins of the New South: Alabama, 1860–1885.* Baton Rouge: Louisiana State University Press, 1978.

Wilentz, Sean. *The Rise of American Democracy: Jefferson to Lincoln.* New York: Norton, 2005.

Williams, David. *I Freed Myself: African American Self-Emancipation in the Civil War Era.* Cambridge: Cambridge University Press, 2014.

Williams, Heather Andrea. "'Commenced to Think Like a Man': Literacy and Manhood in African American Civil War Regiments." In *Southern Manhood: Perspectives on Masculinity in the Old South,* edited by Craig Thompson Friend and Lorri Glover, 196–219. Athens: University of Georgia Press, 2004.

———. *Self-Taught: African American Education in Slavery and Freedom.* Chapel Hill: University of North Carolina Press, 2005.

Williams, Kidada E. *They Left Great Marks on Me: African American Testimonies of Racial Violence from Emancipation to World War I.* New York: New York University Press, 2012.

Williams, Lou Faulkner. *The Great South Carolina Ku Klux Klan Trials, 1871–1872.* Athens: University of Georgia Press, 1996.

Wilson, Keith P. *Campfires of Freedom: The Camp Life of Black Soldiers during the Civil War.* Kent, OH: Kent State University Press, 2002.

Winterer, Caroline. *The Culture of Classicism: Ancient Greece and Rome in American Intellectual Life, 1780–1910.* Baltimore, MD: Johns Hopkins University Press, 2001.

Wolnisty, Claire M. *A Different Manifest Destiny: U.S. Southern Identity and Citizenship in Nineteenth-Century America.* Lincoln: University of Nebraska Press, 2020.

Woodward, C. Vann. "Emancipations and Reconstructions: A Comparative Study." In *The Future of the Past: Historical Writings,* 145–66. New York: Oxford University Press, 1989.

———. *Reunion and Reaction: The Compromise of 1877 and the End of Reconstruction.* New York: Oxford University Press, 1966.

———. *The Strange Career of Jim Crow.* New York: Oxford University Press, 1955.

———. "Yes, There Was a Compromise of 1877." *Journal of American History* 60 (June 1973): 215–23.

Woodworth, Steven E. "Intolerably Slow: Lew Wallace's March to the Battlefield." In *The Shiloh Campaign,* edited by Woodworth, 77–95. Carbondale: Southern Illinois University Press, 2009.

Wunder, John R., and Joann M. Ross, eds. *The Nebraska-Kansas Act of 1854.* Lincoln: University of Nebraska Press, 2008.

Yablon, Ariel. "Disciplined Rebels: The Revolution of 1880 in Buenos Aires." *Journal of Latin American Studies* 40 (Aug. 2008): 483–511.

Young, Elliott. *Catarino Garza's Revolution on the Texas-Mexico Border.* Durham, NC: Duke University Press, 2004.

———. "Red Men, Princess Pocahontas, and George Washington: Harmonizing Race Relations in Laredo at the Turn of the Century." *Western Historical Quarterly* 29 (Spring 1998): 45–85.

Zimmerman, Andrew. *Alabama in Africa: Booker T. Washington, the German Empire, and the Globalization of the New South.* Princeton, NJ: Princeton University Press, 2010.

———. "Reconstruction: Transnational History." In *Interpreting American History: Reconstruction,* edited by John David Smith, 171–96. Kent, OH: Kent State University Press, 2016.

Zuczek, Richard. *State of Rebellion: Reconstruction in South Carolina.* Columbia: University of South Carolina Press, 1996.

INDEX

abolitionists, 18, 103, 109–12, 114–15
Acapulco, Mexico, 68, 70–72, 78, 181, 210
African Americans: Black Codes, 150; Black refugees, 110–11; Black soldiers, 40, 69, 109–10, 221n8; Black suffrage, 148–52; and Democrats, 166; education, 109–13; emancipation, 1, 6, 17–18, 52, 75, 83, 109–12, 221n8; framing enemies as savage, 142; Mississippi elections, 200; race and racism during Reconstruction, 148–51; teachers, 114–15; violence against, 148–51, 166–74, 185–87, 195–200, 211
Akerman, Amos T., 173
Alabama, 150, 170, 206
Alamos, Mexico, 183, 192, 208
Alatorre, Ignacio, 210
Alden, Farrelly, 94–95
Alexandria (VA) Gazette (newspaper), 199
Allen, William, 60–61
Alsina, Adolfo, 203, 212
Álvarez, Diego, 64, 181–82, 184, 210–11
Alvez, Luis, 85
Alya, Thomas, 150
American Legion of Honor, 61
Ames, Adelbert, 192–93, 201, 266n75
amnesty: in Argentina, 146, 149–50, 160, 205, 212; in Mexico, 190–92, 211; as solution to rebellions, 149–50, 188–89, 199; in the United States, 149–50, 173
Anchorena, Tómas de, 106
Annual Message to Congress, 1862, 47–48
anti-Catholicism, 116–18
Antietam, 1

anti-Latin Americanism, 8, 123
Antillón, Florencio, 209
anti-US sentiment, 8, 93–97, 243n74
Arce, F. O., 182, 184, 209–10
Argentina: amnesty, 146, 149–50, 160, 205, 212; Argentine Confederation, 4, 7, 20, 35, 37, 48, 100, 105; Argentine Congress, 25–29; citizenship, 25–29; compared with 1865–1867 in the US, 148–53; conquered provinces, 1861–1867, 141–48; educational reform and efforts, 102–7; education and citizenship, 107–8; education and cooperation, 113–15; education and internal improvement, 115–22; election of 1868, 164–65; election of 1874, 137; election of 1880, 201, 212–13, 267n87; electoral violence, 137; emancipation in, 6; Fourth of July, 76–77, 80, 84–86, 99; historical background, 19–21; Italian immigration to, 229n62; Italians in Wars of Unification, 35–38; and Lincoln, 3–4; linked nature of conflicts, 5–12, 213–16; and Mayer, 40; nativism and xenophobia, 92, 95, 98, 243n74; order and stability, 138, 140, 211; Pan-American cooperation, 92–98, 218–20; Plumb's vision, 123–24; provinces, 252n22; punishing revolutionists, 164; response to violence, 172–79, 187–89, 191, 197–98; Revolution of 1874, 137, 191, 201–5; transition from war to peace, 159–62; transnational nature of the world, 100–101; transnational warriors, 25–31, 68; vanquished in, 123. *See also* Sarmiento, Domingo F.

1874, 202–3; and Sarmiento, 100, 105–8
Bureau of Refugees, Freedmen, and Abandoned Lands, 150
Burnside, Ambrose, 2
Bush, George W., 217, 270n2
Butler, Andrew, 18
Butler, Benjamin F., 110, 147

Caesarism, 173, 204, 206
Calhoun, John C., 18
Camilla, Georgia, 170
Campo, José María del, 144
Canada, 121
Canales, Servando, 155–57, 160, 179–80, 192, 196, 198, 208
Carvajal, José María de Jesús, 59–60, 61, 68–69, 235n49, 236nn54–55
Caseros, 177
Castillo, Don Ramon, 157
Catholic Church, 108, 116–18
caudillos (Argentine), 10; amnesty, 150, 152–53, 160; compared with pronunciamientos, 163, 183; conditions of political parties, 161; disorder, instability, and chaos, 140; Entre Ríos rebellion, 179; and Federales, 101–3; internal improvements, 119, 174. *See also* Peñaloza, Ángel Vicente; Rosas, Juan Manuel de; Urquiza, Justo José de
Cavada, Adolfo Fernández, 41
Cavada, Federico Fernández, 41
Census, US (1850), 108
Centennial of the United States, 85, 90–91
Central Argentine Railroad, 119–20
Cepeda, Victoriano, 192, 193, 196
Chamberlain, Daniel Henry, 207–8
Chambers, David, 38
Charras, Martiniano, 205
Chase, Franklin: and Canales, 156; Fourth of July, 77–78, 86; and Garza, 240n8; Maximilian's execution, 159, 257n114; revolutionary disturbances in Tamaulipas, 179–80; transnational warriors, 68–69
Chase, Salmon P., 256n99
Chicago Tribune (newspaper), 137

Chihuahua, Mexico, 87–88, 93–95, 98, 154, 159
Chile, 19, 102, 104–5
Church question, 117
Cincinnati Daily Enquirer (newspaper), 167, 198–99
citizenship, 25–27, 29, 107–9
civilization, 37, 103–4
Civil War (United States): African Americans, 148–49; conclusion of, 49; education and, 109–12; Fourth of July, 78–79; French Intervention, 46–47; and Lincoln, 1–4, 19, 48; linked nature of conflicts, 4–12; Pan-American cooperation, 74; sister republics, 50, 55, 63–64; transnational warriors, 25–29, 32, 34, 38, 41–42
Clay, Henry, 17
clemency. *See* amnesty
Cleveland (OH) Daily Plain Dealer (newspaper), 64
Clingman, Thomas L., 152, 256n90
Coahuila, Mexico, 192–93, 196
Cole, Gilbert, 70–72
Colfax, Schuyler, 53
Colfax Massacre, 195–96
Colorados, 29–30
Comonfort, Ignacio, 16–17, 116, 153
Compromise of 1850, 18
Compromise of 1877, 207–8
Conesa, Emilio, 178
Confederacy (United States), 1–2, 11, 42, 43–48, 148–49, 256n100
Confederation (Argentine), 4, 7, 20, 35, 37, 48, 100, 105, 177
Congress of Tucumán, 19–20
Conner, Edward, 51, 72–73
Conquista del Desierto, 114, 122
Conservatives (Mexican): in body politic, 152; education system, 117; French Intervention, 49, 52; Maximilian's execution, 257n114; occupation, 144; order and stability, 11; Pan-American cooperation, 52; post-1867 period, 158; realignments, 161–62; and rebels, 46; resentment, 123; War of the Reform, 17, 21

Pan-American cooperation, 8–10, 13; after
1880, 215–16; educational reform and efforts, 99, 101, 112–15; histories of, 217–20;
and nationalism, 92–98; US and Mexico,
52, 62, 74, 78, 80, 83, 87, 89, 91, 157, 219–20.
See also Fourth of July
Panic of 1873, 199–200, 204
Paraguayan War, 175
paramilitary organizations: and Democrats,
168–69, 173, 185–87; Mississippi elections,
200; violence of, 6, 169–74, 183, 185–87,
195–200; voter suppression, 166; White
League, 195–99. *See also* Ku Klux Klan
(KKK)
Paraná (gunboat), 203
paranoia, 28
pardons, 150, 160
patria, 36–37
Paunero, Wenceslao, 26, 142–47, 253n33
Pavón, Desiderio, 86, 157
Paz, José María, 36–37, 84
Peace Democrats (Copperheads), 1
Peñaloza, Ángel Vicente, 144–47, 150–53,
160–61, 175, 188
Peninsula Campaign in 1862, 1
Personal Memoirs (Sheridan), 67
Pesqueira, Igancio, 72–73, 183, 192
petitions, 150, 206. *See also* pronunciamientos
Philadelphia Times (newspaper), 201
Pickett, John T., 31–35, 42, 227n48
Pierce, Edward L., 111
Pierce, Franklin, 50
Pigna, Felipe, 176
Pinchback, P. B. S., 194
piracy, 70
Plan de Ayutla, 16, 116–17
Plan de Iguala, 16, 181
Plan de la Noria, 174, 183, 184, 190–91
Plan de Tuxtepec, 91, 141, 208
Plumb, Edward Lee, 54–55, 62–63, 66, 74–75,
123–24
Polk, James K., 8–9, 50, 90
Porteños/porteño armies, 20, 35–37, 145, 175,
212, 230n73, 253n28

port strategies, 210
Powell, Thomas, 152
prejudices, racial, 110–11, 113–15, 248n71
Preliminary Emancipation Proclamation, 38
presidential elections. *See* elections
Price, Dan, 170
Proclamation of Amnesty and Reconstruction, 149. *See also* amnesty
pronunciados (Mexico), 141, 160–61, 188, 190,
192–93
pronunciamientos: Canales, 156–57; of Díaz,
183–85, 208, 214; election of 1871, 182–83;
election of 1876, 208; Guerrero, 181; internal state affairs, 192; Negrete, 163; overview, 140–41
Protestant denominations, 116–18, 250n119
Puebla, Mexico, 3, 69, 163, 237n1
Puritans, 118

Querétaro, Mexico, 157–58, 181, 257n105
Quiroga, Juan Facundo, 101–3, 183–84

race and racism, 142, 148–51, 172
radicalism, 211
radical papers, 167
Radical Republicans, 13, 67, 151–52
railroads, 119–21
Ransom, Matthew W., 200
rapprochement. *See* Pan-American
cooperation
Rawson, Guillermo, 84, 147, 152, 255n62
rebellions: 1872–1876, 191–205; amnesty, 149–
50, 188–89, 199; in Argentina, 201–5; Battle
of Liberty Place, 137, 198–99; body politic,
152; Díaz's pronunciamientos, 183–85; dis-
couragement of in Mexico, 157; El Chacho,
145–47; Entre Ríos, 175; in Guerrero, 182;
incorporation of, 152–53; internal state affairs, 192; Johnson's response to, 171; López
Jordán's, 177–79; in Mexico, 159; Negrete's,
163–64; pan-American cooperation, 157;
Plan de la Noria, 185; in San Luis Potosí,
88; in Tamaulipas, 179–80; Tejedor's, 212–
13; violence, 151